Toivonen

Pauli, Henri & Harri

Finnlands schnellste Familie
Finland's fastest family

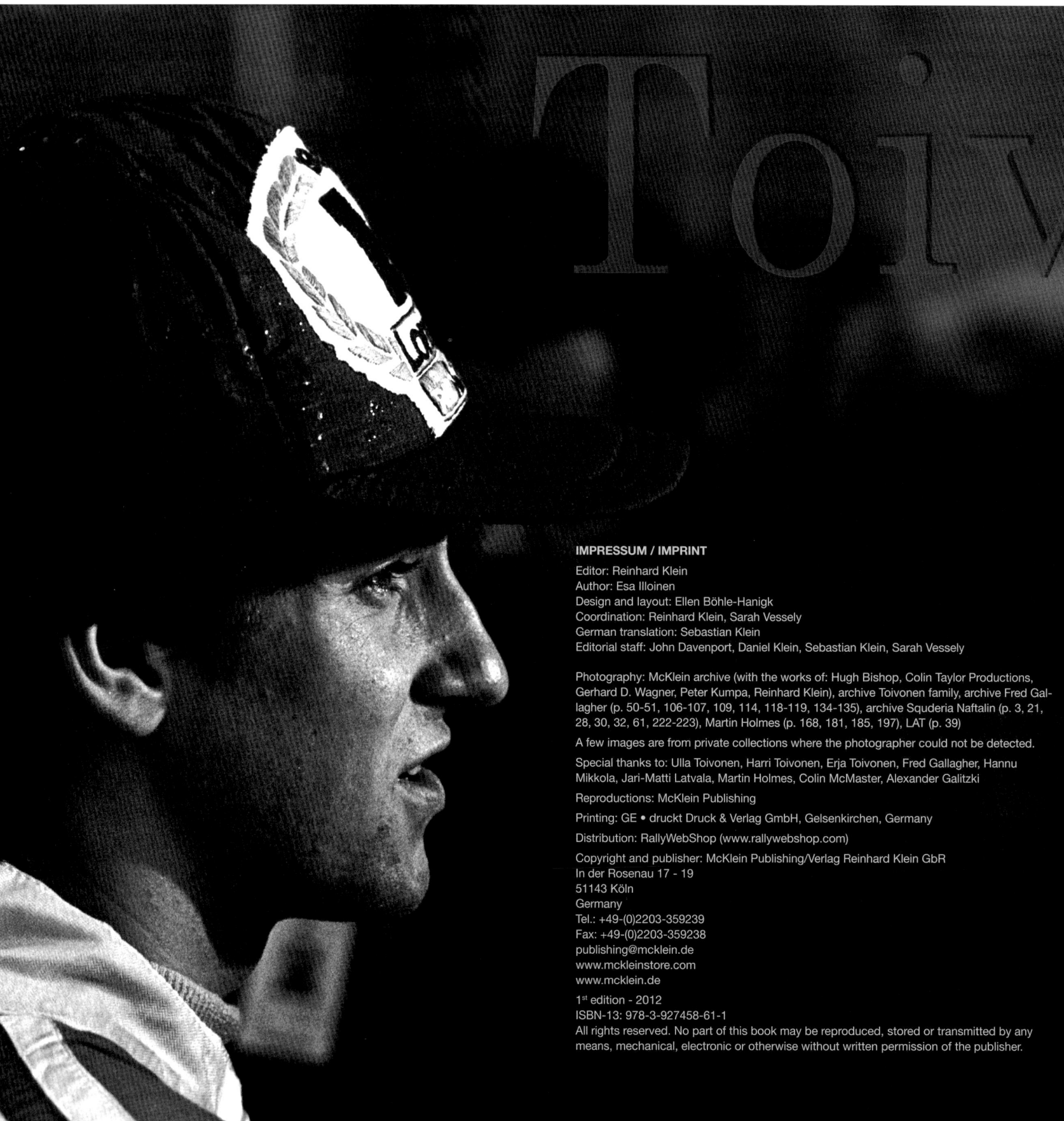

IMPRESSUM / IMPRINT

Editor: Reinhard Klein
Author: Esa Illoinen
Design and layout: Ellen Böhle-Hanigk
Coordination: Reinhard Klein, Sarah Vessely
German translation: Sebastian Klein
Editorial staff: John Davenport, Daniel Klein, Sebastian Klein, Sarah Vessely

Photography: McKlein archive (with the works of: Hugh Bishop, Colin Taylor Productions, Gerhard D. Wagner, Peter Kumpa, Reinhard Klein), archive Toivonen family, archive Fred Gallagher (p. 50-51, 106-107, 109, 114, 118-119, 134-135), archive Squderia Naftalin (p. 3, 21, 28, 30, 32, 61, 222-223), Martin Holmes (p. 168, 181, 185, 197), LAT (p. 39)

A few images are from private collections where the photographer could not be detected.

Special thanks to: Ulla Toivonen, Harri Toivonen, Erja Toivonen, Fred Gallagher, Hannu Mikkola, Jari-Matti Latvala, Martin Holmes, Colin McMaster, Alexander Galitzki

Reproductions: McKlein Publishing

Printing: GE • druckt Druck & Verlag GmbH, Gelsenkirchen, Germany

Distribution: RallyWebShop (www.rallywebshop.com)

Copyright and publisher: McKlein Publishing/Verlag Reinhard Klein GbR
In der Rosenau 17 - 19
51143 Köln
Germany
Tel.: +49-(0)2203-359239
Fax: +49-(0)2203-359238
publishing@mcklein.de
www.mckleinstore.com
www.mcklein.de

1st edition - 2012
ISBN-13: 978-3-927458-61-1

All rights reserved. No part of this book may be reproduced, stored or transmitted by any means, mechanical, electronic or otherwise without written permission of the publisher.

Inhalt / Contents

	Vorwort	Foreword	4-7
	Einleitung	Introduction	8-9
• Pauli	Der Charmeur	Slick operator	10-21
	Die Geburt des „Tigers"	Emergence of Tiger	22-35
	Gipfelstürmer	Mountain king	36-51
	Der Champion	Champion!	52-63
• Henri	Generationswechsel	Next generation	64-71
	Auf in den Kampf	Into battle	72-89
	Ruhm und Ehre	Fame and fortune!	90-101
	Der jüngste WM-Sieger	Youngest ever WRC winner	102-107
	Mit Talbot zum WM-Titel	Helping make Talbot champion	108-119
	Die nächste Station: Opel	Rallying with Opel	120-135
	Eine frustrierende Zeit	Frustration	136-167
	Großes Finale, tragisches Ende	Crescendo	168-199
• Harri	Der Unvollendete	Unfulfilled promise	200-223

Vorwort / Foreword
Hannu Mikkola

1983 World Rally Champion
WRC wins: 18

Im Herbst 1963 sprang ich als Beifahrer von Pauli Toivonen ein, der gerade die Motorsportabteilung von VW Finnland gegründet hatte. Bei der Rallye in Finnland wurden wir knapp hinter Simo Lampinen im Saab Zweite und da wir nah beieinander lebten, bin ich danach auf ein Bier zu ihm nach Hause. Es war schon spät und Pauli sagte, wir sollen ruhig sein, weil seine Söhne oben schliefen. Damals hatte ich noch keine Ahnung, dass diese beiden später meine Gegner bei internationalen Rallyes sein würden.

Wenige Monate später half mir Pauli, einen Platz in einem VW bei der 1000 Seen Rallye zu bekommen. Letztlich entwickelte sich daraus eine lange Freundschaft, die bis ins neue Jahrtausend andauerte. Wenn ich beispielsweise von Jyväskylä nach Hause fuhr, rief ich ihn an. Wenn ich dann in seinem Büro ankam, wartete bereits ein Kaffee auf mich.

Pauli hat mir viel übers Rallyefahren beigebracht. Besonders interessant war, dass sich Pauli nicht die WP-Strecken als solche merkte, stattdessen speicherte er in seinem Kopf, wie man diese Strecken zu fahren hat. Pauli verwendete einzigartige Wörter, um Kurven zu beschreiben. Das war eine völlig neue Herangehensweise für mich.

Vielleicht konnte ich durch mein Training mit Henri ein bisschen was von dem zurückgeben, was ich bei Pauli gelernt hatte. Henri und ich sind die Strecken der 1000 Seen mindestens ein- oder zweimal zusammen abgefahren. Man merkte schon ganz früh, dass Henri bereit war, an Grenzen zu gehen, in die ich selbst nicht vordringen wollte.

Als Harri 1986 in den Gruppe-B-Metro stieg, war auch er ein direkter Gegner von mir in der britischen Meisterschaft. Trauigerweise war ich an jenem düsteren Tag im Mai in Cardiff, als Harri und Pauli die Nachricht von Henris Unfall erfuhren.

Dieses Buch bringt allerdings hauptsächlich freudige Erinnerungen zurück. Es war für mich keine Überraschung, dass Pauli ein buntes Leben geführt hat, bevor ich ihn kennengelernt habe. Aber ich habe trotzdem spannende Dinge erfahren wie seinen Hintergrund als Musiker. Wer sich schon immer gefragt hat, warum Henri eine so extravagante Persönlichkeit war, der wird das nach diesem Buch besser verstehen.

Hannu Mikkola

Back in the autumn of 1963 I ended up co-driving in a Finnish rally with Pauli Toivonen, who had just started up Volkswagen's Finnish competition department. We finished a close second to Simo Lampinen's Saab and, living close to each other, went to Pauli's house for a beer afterwards. It was very late at night and Pauli said we should be very quiet, because he had two young sons sleeping. Little did I know that one day both of them would be my competitors in international rallies.

A few months later Pauli helped me out with a VW drive for the 1000 Lakes Rally and from all that a friendship developed, which lasted over four decades. We still kept in touch this side of the Millennium and if I was returning home from Jyväskylä, for example, I'd give him a call. By the time I got to his office there would always be coffee waiting.

He had taught me a lot about rallying. Particularly significant was my realisation that Pauli did not memorise the roads of the special stages, as such, but rather absorbed in his mind the way to drive them. He could use unique phrases to describe a bend, which made you understand the way to approach it in an entirely new light.

Maybe I managed to pay back a little bit of what I picked up from him, when I later did some recces with Henri. We spent a lot of time together practicing the 1000 Lakes Rally stages on at least one or two occasions. From very early on, it was obvious Henri was prepared to push the limits back to areas I did not wish to contemplate myself.

Then, when Harri stepped up to the Group B MG Metro in 1986, he too became a direct competitor of mine in the British series. Sadly, I was there on that grim day in Cardiff, when the news of Henri's accident came through to Harri and Pauli.

This book mainly brings back bright memories, however. And while it comes as no surprise that Pauli had a colourful life before I ever knew him, it has still been interesting to learn things like his background as a musician. If you ever wondered where Henri's flamboyant personality came from, this will give you a better understanding.

Hannu Mikkola

Vorwort / Foreword
Jari-Matti Latvala

WRC wins: 7

Im Jahr 1991 – ich war gerade sechs Jahre alt – geschah etwas Entscheidendes in meinem Leben. Damals sah ich ein Video, das mich nachhaltig beeindruckte. Das Video handelte von Henri Toivonen und von diesem Moment an war ich ein Fan von ihm. Ich wollte mehr wissen über diesen charismatischen Rallyefahrer. Also begann ich, allerhand Souvenirs von ihm zu sammeln. Schon bald hatte ich die ersten Fotos, später folgten Overalls, ein Helm, seine Rallyelizenz, eine Rothmans-Jacke und so weiter. Heute bewahre ich all das in einem Trophäenschrank auf.

Ich war noch viel zu jung, um einen Führerschein zu haben, als mir mein Vater einen alten Sunbeam Avenger gab. Das war angeblich Henris altes Rallyeauto. Dies stellte sich zwar als falsch heraus, dennoch bauten wir den Avenger als exakte Kopie von Henris Gruppe-1-Auto auf, so wie er ihn zu Beginn seiner Karriere gefahren war.

Henri war immer mein Vorbild gewesen. Dass ich bei der Schweden Rallye 2008 als jüngster Sieger eines WM-Laufs in seine Fußstapfen trat, war für mich von ganz großer Bedeutung. Ganz ehrlich: Dieses Gefühl kann man nicht in Worte fassen, da ich mich so eng mit Henri verbunden fühlte. Wir haben ja beide diese Alles-oder-Nichts-Mentalität und in schwierigen Zeiten hat mir dieser Gedanke sehr viel Mut gegeben.

Der König des Rallyesports ist im Moment der mehrfache Weltmeister Sébastien Loeb. Er ist ohne Zweifel der versierteste Fahrer in der Geschichte unseres Sports. Aber in der Gruppe-B-Ära war Henri der mutigste Fahrer und der Mann, der diese Autos am besten beherrschte. Egal wie viele neue Champions es geben mag, diese Tatsache bleibt bestehen.

Natürlich habe ich Henri nie kennengelernt. Das Bild, was ich von ihm habe, basiert auf den Geschichten anderer Leute. Daher ist dieses Buch für mich die erste Gelegenheit, einen genauen Einblick in das Leben meines Idols zu bekommen. Sein Weg in den Rallyesport wurde wie bei mir durch seinen Vater geebnet, deswegen freue ich mich auch, viel über Pauli und den Rest der Familie zu erfahren.

Jari-Matti Latvala

PS: Als ich dieses Vorwort schrieb, hatte ich das Manuskript noch nicht gelesen. Aber glaubt mir: Bevor ihr das Buch zu lesen bekommt, werde ich die Texte schon verschlungen haben!

Something important in my life occurred back in 1991 when I was only six years old. I happened to see a video that made a huge impression on me. It was about the late Henri Toivonen and from that moment I became a fan, immediately wanting to know more about this charismatic rally driver. I started to collect all kinds of memorabilia related to him and soon managed to get some photos, but eventually I also acquired a pair of overalls Henri had worn, a helmet, his competition license, a Rothmans rally jacket, etc. Today these are all kept in my trophy cabinet at home.

I was still way too young to drive on the road when my father gave me an old Sunbeam Avenger that was rumoured to have once been Henri's rally car. That turned out not to be the case, but nevertheless we went on to prepare it as an exact copy of the Group 1 Avenger he used early in his career.

Having always looked up to Henri Toivonen, it meant the world to me, when I managed to succeed him as the youngest ever winner of a World Championship rally in the Swedish Rally of 2008. Honestly, words cannot express the way it made me feel as I had so closely associated myself with him. Indeed, we seemed to have a similar all-or-nothing approach to the sport and, at times of trials and tribulations in my career, that thought has given me encouragement.

The current king of rallying is multiple World Champion, Sébastien Loeb. He ranks as indisputably the savviest driver in the history of our sport, but in the Group B era it was Henri who mastered those cars best, as well as being the bravest of them all. No matter how many new champions emerge, that fact will stay with us.

Of course, I never met Henri, so the image I have of him is mostly built on random stories told by older people. Therefore, this book about Henri will offer a first opportunity to gain a proper insight into the life of my idol. His way into rally driving was, like mine, paved by his father, so I'm also looking forward to learning about Pauli and the rest of the family.

Jari-Matti Latvala

PS: At the time of writing, I have yet to read the manuscript but, believe me, before you read this I will have devoured the story!

Einleitung / Introduction
Esa Illoinen
Autor / Author

„Jetzt wird es also kein Buch geben", lauteten Harri Toivonens Worte, als wir uns bei Henris Beerdigung begegneten. Das ist das einzige Gespräch von diesem traurigen Tag im Mai 1986, an das ich mich erinnere. Harri war einen Monat vorher bei seinem Bruder zu Besuch, als wir entschieden, mit einer Henri-Toivonen-Biografie zu beginnen.

Es sollte keine schnelle Nummer werden, um am Jahresende bei einem möglichen WM-Titel viel Geld zu verdienen. „Lass es uns richtig machen", sagte Henri. „Es soll meine ganze Karriere umfassen." Die Stimmung war überschwänglich. Wir waren entschlossen, etwas Bedeutsames zu erschaffen. Henri fuhr mich nach Hause und wir vereinbarten, die ersten Interviews nach Korsika zu führen. Doch wie das Schicksal so wollte, war das meine letzte Begegnung mit Henri.

Vor diesem Hintergrund gab es kein Zögern, als mich Reinhard Klein fragte, ob ich die Lebensgeschichte von Henri, seinem Vater Pauli und Bruder Harri zu Papier bringen könnte. Ich hatte lange darüber nachgedacht, wie man den Charakterkopf Pauli Toivonen international bekannter machen könnte. Anscheinend hatte sich sein großartiges Charisma kaum auf die Motorsportfans außerhalb Finnlands übertragen, hauptsächlich wegen der Sprachbarriere. Aber um Henri wirklich zu verstehen, war es wichtig, sich auch mit Pauli und Harri zu befassen.

Große Priorität hatte für mich die Zusammenarbeit mit Henris Mutter Ulla. Sie hatte alles hautnah miterlebt – von Paulis frühen Heldentaten bis hin zur Versorgung von Finnlands bekanntester Motorsportfamilie. Ich war nicht sicher, ob sie bereit wäre, die traumatischen Erinnerungen vom Verlust ihres Sohnes noch einmal durchzugehen. Umso dankbarer bin ich, dass sie es getan hat. Ich hoffe, dieses Werk bringt einige Geschichten hervor, die ihr auch ein Lächeln ins Gesicht zaubern werden.

Ebenso wichtig war die Unterstützung von Erja, die schon lange mit Henri zusammen gewesen war, ehe sie 1982 heirateten. Sie war einverstanden und leistete einen ungeheuren Beitrag. Leider konnte ich nicht alles in diesem Buch unterbringen. Dabei war Erja so verblüffend ehrlich, dass sie meine Wahrnehmung von den Hauptpersonen sicherlich beeinflusst hat.

Da ich diese beiden Damen vorrangig genannt habe, könnte man meinen, als hätte ich Harris Unterstützung für selbstverständlich gehalten – vielleicht habe ich das sogar ein wenig. Wir hatten über die Jahre nicht regelmäßig Kontakt, aber wenn wir uns trafen, hatte ich den Eindruck, dass zwischen uns ein Vertrauensverhältnis besteht. Während des Schreibens war es wegen seiner vielen anderen Verpflichtungen nicht immer leicht, an Harri heranzukommen, aber wenn ich ihn traf, war seine Erinnerung scharf, seine Ansichten knackig und bestimmt.

Zudem bin ich vielen anderen Leuten sehr dankbar für die Zeit und Mühe, die sie auf sich nahmen, um zu diesem Buch beizutragen. Einige der Zitate kommen von Gesprächen aus der Vergangenheit, während manche Interviewpartner lieber anonym bleiben wollten. Ich hoffe, dass ich niemandem zu nahe trete, wenn ich keine Namen aus Henris engem Freundeskreis nenne.

Von denen, die die Motorsportkarriere von Pauli, Henri und/oder Harri unmittelbar verfolgt haben, möchte ich folgenden Personen besonders danken: Erik Carlsson, Osmo Kalpala, Jaakko Kallio, Rauno Aaltonen, Anssi Järvi, Cesare Fiorio, Antti Aarnio-Wihuri, Hannu Mikkola, Vic Elford, Martti Tiukkanen, Hannu Kahi, Keke Rosberg, Antero Lindqvist, Matti Alamäki, Max Johansson, Juha Paajanen, Malcolm Wilson, Paul White, Fred Gallagher, Walter Röhrl, Eddie Jordan, David Richards, Ari Vatanen, Juha Piironen, Jürgen Barth, Charles Reynolds, David Lapworth, Markku Alén, Neil Wilson, Michèle Mouton, John Davenport und Ian Dawson.

Rupert Saunders und Peter Foubister haben in „Autosport" über Henris Auftritte in Europa berichtet. Da Henri für sie auf Englisch ins Mikrofon gesprochen hat, sind ihre Zitate eine wertvolle Bereicherung. Für die technische Unterstützung danke ich außerdem Ralf Pettersson und dem „Mobilisti"-Magazin.

Mit diesem Buch wollte ich die Geschichte einer Rallyefamilie zu Papier bringen. Am besten urteilen Sie selbst!

Esa Illoinen
Tapiola, Finnland
Oktober 2012

"There will be no book, then." Those were the words of Harri Toivonen as we came face to face at Henri's funeral, the only conversation I can recall from that sombre day in May 1986. Harri had been present at his brother's house about a month earlier, when a decision had been made to start work on a Henri Toivonen biography.

It was not going to be any rushed job just to cash in on a possible world title at the end of the year. "Let's do it properly", said Henri, "so it will cover my whole career." The mood was ebullient as we were all determined that this would result in something meaningful. Henri drove me home and our plan was to sit down for a first session of interviews after Corsica. As fate would have it, that was the last time I saw Henri.

Against that background, there could never be any hesitation in accepting a proposal from Reinhard Klein to attempt to tell the story of not just Henri, but also his father Pauli and brother Harri. I had long been thinking of ways to raise international awareness of the character that was Pauli Toivonen. It seemed unfortunate that his great charisma had apparently not fully translated to motor sport fans outside Finland, primarily due to linguistic limitations. To really understand where Henri came from, it was essential to deal with Pauli and Harri as well.

An immediate priority was the co-operation of Henri's mother Ulla. She was, after all, the person who had lived through it all, from Pauli's earliest tentative exploits to looking after Finland's best known motor sport family. I was not sure she would be prepared to go through the traumatic memories of losing her son, but I am eternally grateful that she did. I also hope the process uncovered some stories that will bring a smile to her face.

Of equal importance was the support of Erja, already Henri's long-time companion before becoming his wife in 1982. She readily agreed and contributed much more than could ever be fitted into just one book. Almost startlingly honest at times, she certainly influenced my perception of the key figures in this story.

If prioritising the two ladies makes it look like I took Harri for granted, then ... well, yes, I did a bit. Contact between us has not been regular over the years, but whenever we came together, it left me with an impression that there existed a kind of mutual trust. During the writing process Harri was not always easy to access, but when cornered his memory was sharp, his views crisp and firm.

I am also very grateful to numerous other people for the time and trouble they took to contribute to this book. Some of the quotes come from discussions back in the past, while a few people interviewed more recently preferred to stay anonymous. I hope not to offend anyone if I therefore do not mention any names from the circle of Henri's close friends in Finland.

Of those who followed the driving careers of Pauli, Henri and/or Harri from close at hand, particular thanks are due to Erik Carlsson, Osmo Kalpala, Jaakko Kallio, Rauno Aaltonen, Anssi Järvi, Cesare Fiorio, Antti Aarnio-Wihuri, Hannu Mikkola, Vic Elford, Martti Tiukkanen, Hannu Kahi, Keke Rosberg, Antero Lindqvist, Matti Alamäki, Max Johansson, Juha Paajanen, Malcolm Wilson, Paul White, Fred Gallagher, Walter Röhrl, Eddie Jordan, David Richards, Ari Vatanen, Juha Piironen, Jürgen Barth, Charles Reynolds, David Lapworth, Markku Alén, Neil Wilson, Michèle Mouton, John Davenport and Ian Dawson.

Rupert Saunders and Peter Foubister covered many of Henri's European outings for "Autosport" magazine and quotes from Henri recorded by them proved a valuable addition, as these had been uttered in English first hand. Thanks for technical support must go to Ralf Pettersson and "Mobilisti" magazine.

My target has been to outline the legacy of a rally family. You judge!

Esa Illoinen
Tapiola, Finnland
October 2012

Pauli Toivonen

* 22. August 1929 in Hämeenlinna, Finnland;
† 14. Februar 2005 in Kerava, Finnland

*August 22, 1929 in Hämeenlinna, Finland;
† Februar 14, 2005 in Kerava, Finland*

Pauli Toivonen

Der Charmeur
Slick operator

Die meisten Besucher des finnischen WM-Laufs werden die Kauppakatu kennen, die große Shoppingstraße in Jyväskylä. Zur Rallyezeit sind die Bars und Cafés dort immer rappelvoll. Heute ist Kauppakatu eine Fußgängerzone, aber das war nicht immer so. In den 50er-Jahren gab es in der Universitätsstadt in Mittelfinnland zwar noch nicht so viele Autos, aber die durften auch durch die Kauppakatu fahren. Für junge Leute war es der Ort, um zu sehen und gesehen zu werden.

Eines Abends im Jahr 1953 spazierten die 18-jährige Ulla Enlund und ihre Schwester durch diese Straße. Sie waren an der Südküste Finnlands aufgewachsen, in Helsinki zur Schule gegangen und gehörten der schwedisch-sprechenden Minderheit an. Als ihre Familie nach Jyväskylä gezogen war, hatte sich Ulla zunächst fremd gefühlt in der Provinz. Aber mittlerweile hatte sie sich in der Studentenstadt eingelebt und kannte dort viele Leute. Daher ist es schon etwas überraschend, dass Ulla den Fahrer nicht sofort erkannte, als ein VW Käfer neben ihnen stoppte. Am Steuer saß nämlich der Bassist der bekanntesten Tanzband aus der Gegend. „Möchtest du mit mir mitfahren?", fragte der Kerl selbstbewusst. Die Mädels hatten nichts dagegen, zumal sie ein ganzes Stück außerhalb des Stadtzentrums wohnten. „Ich meinte nur dich", sagte der Fahrer und zeigte dabei auf Ulla. „Pauli war ganz schön mutig", erinnert sich Ulla. „Um ehrlich zu sein, habe ich mich mehr für den anderen Kerl interessiert, der bei ihm im Auto saß", gibt die Dame zu, die im Laufe der Jahre die Mutter der bekanntesten finnischen Rallyefamilie werden würde.

1953 war es in Finnland schwer, an einen VW Käfer heranzukommen. Kein Wunder also, dass Pauli Ulla mit der Knutschkugel beeindruckte.

Love Bug. For Finns VW Beetles were hard to come by in 1953. No wonder Pauli made an impression on Ulla.

Das LL-Quintet war eine beliebte Band in der Region um Jyväskylä. Pauli, dem großgewachsenen Bassisten, fehlte es jedenfalls nicht an Charisma.

The LL-Quintet was a very popular dance band in the Jyväskylä area. As its bass player, the tall Pauli was certainly not lacking charisma.

Most visitors to Finland's World Championship rally are familiar with Jyväskylä's Kauppakatu. This town centre pedestrian street lined with sidewalk bars and cafes is bustling with life during a rally weekend. It was not always closed for traffic, of course. Back in the early 1950s cars may have been sparse in the streets of Central Finland's university town, but they were allowed to cruise on Kauppakatu where young people were keen to mingle. If you wanted to see others, or be seen, this was the place.

One evening in 1953, 18-year-old Ulla Enlund was there on a stroll with her sister. Hailing from the southern coast and being from the Swedish-speaking minority, she had started school in Helsinki and at first felt quite alien in the provincial atmosphere of Jyväskylä, when the family had moved there a few years earlier. By now, though, she was fully integrated to the scene, and pretty much aware of who was who in town. It is therefore slightly surprising that when a blue VW Beetle pulled up she did not immediately recognize the driver. It was the bass player of the most popular dance band in the area. "Would you like a ride", uttered the fellow with confidence. The girls certainly would not mind a ride as they lived some way out of the town centre and would be very glad of a lift. "I meant you only", said the driver, pointing to Ulla. "Pauli was nothing if not bold", she admits. "I was actually more interested in the other guy, who was in the car with him", recalls the lady who was to become the mother of Finland's most prominent rally family. Yet, one thing led to another and she started going out with Pauli. Six months later the pair got engaged and one year on they were married.

Damals führte eines zum anderen. Ulla ging mit Pauli aus. Sechs Monate später verlobten sie sich, ein Jahr danach waren die beiden bereits verheiratet.

Zu dieser Zeit tanzte Pauli Toivonen sprichwörtlich auf vielen Hochzeiten. Das „LL-Quintet" – Paulis Band – war erfolgreich, brachte aber nicht genug Geld ein, um ein Auto zu finanzieren und Pauli war verrückt nach Autos. Sein Cousin, Pentti Barck (Gründervater der 1000 Seen Rallye), überzeugte Pauli, 1953 an der Rallye teilzunehmen. Er wollte wissen, wer von beiden der Schnellere war. Während Pentti in einem Peugeot 20. wurde, erreichte Pauli die 43. Position in jenem VW, mit dem er Ullas Aufmerksamkeit gewonnen hatte.

Pentti leitete damals die beiden Hotels seiner Eltern: das Jyväshovi, lange Zeit Hauptquartier der 1000 Seen Rallye, und das Asemahovi direkt neben dem Bahnhof. Pauli Toivonen arbeitete in beiden Hotels an der Rezeption, und in beiden trat auch das LL-Quintet regelmäßig auf. Aber Pauli war ein Unternehmertyp und so machte er mit Bandleader Leo Lehtinen (dessen Initialen der Band ihren Namen gaben) bald einen Plattenladen auf. Pauli fuhr zwischendurch sogar einen Lieferwagen für eine Brauerei, um Geld zu verdienen. Ulla begleitete ihn manchmal und setzte sich gar ans Steuer des klobigen Citroën HY, obwohl sie noch gar keinen Führerschein hatte. „Einmal, als ich gefahren bin, fing Pauli plötzlich an zu lachen", erinnert sich Ulla. „Ich fragte mich, was gerade so lustig war und er sagte: ‚Wo hast du dir denn angewöhnt, bei Gangwechseln Zwischengas zu geben?' Ich konnte seine Verwunderung nicht verstehen; für mich war das ganz normal beim Autofahren!"

Der Rallyesport wurde für Pauli bald eine sehr zeitraubende Spielerei. Pentti Barck hatte schon ein paar Mal an der Rallye Monte Carlo teilgenommen. Bei seinem letzten Anlauf nahm er seinen Cousin als dritten Mann im Peugeot 203 mit. „Ich weiß noch genau, wie ich sie in Jyväskylä verabschiedet habe", sagt Ulla. Pauli musste sich damit begnügen, die Aufgaben des Beifahrers zu teilen, weil der

At this stage, Pauli Toivonen was a Jack-of-many-trades. The LL-Quintet was a successful band, but it did not bring in sufficient income to buy a car and Pauli was crazy about cars. His cousin, Pentti Barck, the man generally acknowledged as the founding father of the "Rally of the 1000 Lakes", had challenged Pauli to take him on in the 1953 event to see which of the two was faster. Pentti finished 20th in a Peugeot, while Pauli was 43rd in the same VW Beetle that was to help him to get Ulla's attention on Kauppakatu.

Pentti Barck was the manager of two hotels owned by his parents: the Jyväshovi, which became a long-time headquarters for the 1000 Lakes Rally, and the Asemahovi, right next to the railway station. Pauli Toivonen worked at the reception in both, with the LL-Quintet frequently performing in these establishments. But he was enterprising, and before long set up a record and music store with bandleader Leo Lehtinen, whose initials had been used to give the quintet its name. At one stage Pauli even drove a delivery van for a brewery. Sometimes Ulla would go along and occasionally the couple would swap seats, with Ulla taking the wheel of a clumsy Citroën HY, even though she still did not possess a driving licence. "Once, when I was at the wheel, Pauli burst out laughing", she recalls. "I asked what was so funny and he said 'where did you pick up that habit of blipping the throttle on gear-changes?' I could not understand his amusement; it felt like a totally natural way of driving!"

Rallying soon became an increasingly time-consuming pastime for Pauli. Pentti Barck had been taking part in the Monte Carlo Rally for some years and, on his last outing in 1954, his cousin joined in as the third crewmember in a Peugeot 203. "I remember waving them off from Jyväskylä", says Ulla Toivonen. Pauli had to be content with sharing co-driving duties, as the supremely fit Pentti Barck drove singlehandedly all the way down to Monte Carlo. They had been delayed along the way, though, and were classified down in 236th.

Bei seinem 1000-Seen-Debüt 1953 verlor Pauli das Familienduell gegen seinen Cousin Pentti Barck, der als Gründer dieser legendären Veranstaltung gilt.
On his 1000 Lakes debut, Pauli could not beat his cousin Pentti Barck who was the man credited with creating the legendary event.

Pauli Toivonen Der Charmeur / Slick operator

Bei der 1000 Seen Rallye 1955 wurde Pauli von Martti Kolari navigiert, mit dem Toivonen 1968 noch große Erfolge feiern sollte.
Pauli's 1000 Lakes co-driver in 1955 was Martti Kolari, with whom he was to later achieve great success during the 1968 season.

Der Peugeot 203 war damals ein beliebtes Rallyeauto in Finnland. Toivonen/Kolari sahen 1955 jedoch nicht das Ziel bei ihrer Heimrallye.
A Peugeot 203 was a very popular rally car in Finland. However Toivonen and Kolari did not make it to the finish of their home event in 1955.

Pauli Toivonen Der Charmeur / Slick operator

erstaunlich fitte Pentti Barck den ganzen Weg nach Monte Carlo selbst gefahren ist. Die Finnen hatten einige Probleme bei der Rallye und wurden als 236. gewertet.

An der 1000 Seen Rallye nahm Pauli natürlich jedes Jahr teil. Manchmal sogar mit dem Auto eines Freundes, bis er 1956 eine längere Bindung zu Saab einging. Gemeinsam mit einem älteren Geschäftspartner begann Pauli, die schwedischen Autos in Jyväskylä zu verkaufen. Bei der Hanki Rallye (zu Deutsch: Schneerallye) hatte Pauli Erik Carlsson kennengelernt und eine Einladung in die Saab-Fabrik nach Trollhättan bekommen. Im kommenden Sommer nahm er diese Einladung wahr, die bei seiner damals schwangeren Frau bleibenden Eindruck hinterließ. „In Schweden nahm uns Erik auf eine Testfahrt in einem rallyefertigen Saab mit. Ich saß hinten, habe mich am blanken Metall festgehalten und um mein Leben gekämpft. Erik hat das Auto richtig hart rangenommen. Das muss im Juli gewesen sein und wir hatten Glück, dass Henri nicht in dem Augenblick zur Welt gekommen ist", schaudert es Ulla. Ihr Nachwuchs kam am 25. August 1956 zur Welt – eine Woche nach Paulis 15. Gesamtrang (und dem zweiten Platz in der Klasse) in einem Saab bei der 1000 Seen. Vater und Sohn feierten ihre Geburtstage oft während der Rallye. Pauli war am 22. August 1929 geboren worden.

Der Fokus von Pauli Toivonen verlagerte sich immer weiter weg von der Musik in Richtung Autos und Familie. Das LL-Quintet war mit Jazz-Klassikern wie „How High the Moon" erfolgreich und Pauli war berüchtigt für seinen Umgang mit dem Kontrabass, den er im Stile von Bill Haley & The Comets durch die Gegend wirbelte. „Pauli hatte lange Arme, das machte es ihm leichter", erklärt Urpo Vihervaara, Paulis Beifahrer in den späten 60ern. Er war selbst auch ein ausgezeichneter Tänzer. „In den Fünfzigern war Pauli ein richtiger Anti-Alkoholiker, weil er als Musiker nie Zeit für einen Drink hatte", sagt Pentti Barck. Auch in den Folgejahren war Pauli nie ein Freund des Alkoholkonsums, der unter seinen Fahrerkollegen in den 60er- und 70er-Jahren weit verbreitet war. Die seltenen Auftritte mit dem Bass

Of course, the 1000 Lakes was tackled every year, sometimes in a car belonging to a friend, until a more lasting liaison with Saab began from 1956. Pauli started a business in Jyväskylä with an older partner to sell the Swedish cars in that area. Competing in the Hankiralli (aka the Snow Rally) in the winter, he had met Erik Carlsson and got an invitation to visit the Saab factory in Trollhättan, Sweden. Come summer, Pauli set off with his now pregnant wife for a trip, which left Ulla Toivonen with at least one memorable moment. "In Sweden, Erik gave us a ride in a Saab stripped out and prepared to rally specification. I sat in the back and hung on for dear life to the bare metal, as he gave that car a real pounding. It must have been July and it was lucky Henri was not born there and then", she shudders. As it happened, the pair's offspring saw the light of day on August 25th, 1956, less than a week after his dad had taken a Saab to fifteenth — and second in class — in the 1000 Lakes Rally. Father and son were to often celebrate their birthdays at rally time in Jyväskylä, as Pauli had been born on August 22nd in 1929.

The focus in Pauli Toivonen's life was now shifting away from music towards cars and family. While the LL-Quintet had thrived on jazz classics such as "How High the Moon", in some faster numbers, Pauli had also become notorious for his handling of the upright bass, smartly swirling it around in the style of Bill Haley & The Comets. "Pauli had long arms, which made it easy for him", says Urpo Vihervaara, himself an ace dance contestant and Pauli's co-driver in the late 1960s. "In the fifties he was a virtual teetotaller, because as a musician he did not have time for a drink", says Pentti Barck. Even in years to come Pauli could never really tolerate the liberal use of alcohol so common among many colleagues in the 1960s and 1970s. Not playing the bass regularly had its price for him when picking up the instrument again. "After the first night of playing his fingers would become raw and bloodied, until the skin grew thicker again", recalls Ulla. And so, music faded away from the daily life of the Toivonen family.

Die 1000 Seen Rallye 1956 bestritt Pauli mit Beifahrer Lauri Hurme, der sechs Jahre später zusammen mit Carl-Otto Bremer bei einem Flugzeugabsturz ums Leben kam.
In 1956 Pauli Toivonen was joined by Lauri Hurme for the 1000 Lakes, who six years later perished in the same airplane crash that took the life of Carl-Otto Bremer.

Bei seiner ersten Monte war Toivonen nur Passagier. Sein Cousin Pentti Barck (rechts) hatte die Rallye schon vorher bestritten und saß auch diesmal am Steuer.
On his first trip to Monte Carlo Toivonen was just a passenger. His cousin, Pentti Barck (on the right), had done the rally before.

Pauli Toivonen Der Charmeur / Slick operator

Ulla Toivonen wird häufig als „First Lady" des finnischen Motorsports bezeichnet, dabei stand sie nur ungern im Rampenlicht.

Ulla Toivonen deserves to be regarded as the first lady of Finnish motor sport, but she usually shied away from the limelight.

hatten für Pauli ihren Preis: „Nach der ersten Konzertnacht waren seine Finger ganz wund und blutig, bis die Hornhaut wieder dicker wurde", erinnert sich Ulla. Und so verabschiedete sich die Musik langsam aber sicher aus dem Leben der Toivonen-Familie.

Pauli wurde Saab-Händler in Jyväskylä und war daher abhängig von der Importeursfirma, geleitet vom aufstrebenden Rallye- und Rennfahrer Carl-Otto Bremer. Die Beziehung war nicht gerade einfach, was auch daran lag, dass Ulla einige Male mit Carl-Otto ausgegangen war, bevor sie Pauli kennenlernte. „Er hat das zwischen uns mit aller Deutlichkeit beendet", sinniert Ulla. „Er war sehr eifersüchtig."

Der Verkauf der Autos brachte eigene Schwierigkeiten mit sich: „Die Saab wurden meist nachts von Helsinki nach Jyväskylä gefahren. Wir lebten in einem großen Mehrfamilienhaus. Unsere Nachbarn waren nicht immer glücklich, wenn Pauli früh am Morgen unter ihren Schlafzimmerfenstern einen lauten Zweitakter für einen seiner Kunden aufwärmte", erinnert sich Ulla. Doch es gab auch gute Neuigkeiten: Trotz des Zwists war Carl-Otto Bremer bereit, Pauli für Veranstaltungen wie die Hanki Rallye 1957 in das offizielle Saab-Team aufzunehmen. Damit wurde Pauli bevorzugt behandelt, zum Beispiel mit neuen Motorsportteilen. Ein Jahr später erwies sich dieser Vorteil aber als zweischneidige Klinge. Als Bremer der Sieg bei der Hanki Rallye 1958 weggenommen wurde, weil sein Werksmotor einen verbesserten Zylinderkopf hatte, war Pauli einer von nur zwei Kunden mit identischem, „illegalem" Material. Mitgehangen, mitgefangen.

Dies war die Zeit, als Saab sehr stark wurde im Rallyesport. Erik Carlsson beispielsweise gewann die 1000 Seen 1957 in einem Saab 93. Der Schwede erinnert sich gern an damals. „In Finnland wurde mein Auto in Paulis Werkstatt in Jyväskylä betreut. Wir sind gute Freunde geworden, obwohl ich kein Finnisch sprach und er kein Schwedisch. Unsere gemeinsame Sprache war ‚Rallye'!"

Eriks Triumph 1957 wurde jedoch von einem bösen Unfall seines finnischen Freundes überschattet, der auf Platz Sieben gelegen

Pauli became Saab's agent in Jyväskylä and in that capacity he was dependent on the Finnish importer, a company run by up-and-coming race and rally driver Carl-Otto Bremer. This was to become an uneasy relationship, not at all helped by the fact that Ulla had been occasionally going out with Carl-Otto at the time she first met Pauli. "He did put a stop to that in no uncertain terms", muses Ulla. "He was very jealous."

Selling cars presented problems of its own as Ulla Toivonen recalls. "Those Saabs were often driven from Helsinki to Jyväskylä at night time. We lived in a big apartment house and our neighbours were not too happy in the winter when Pauli was warming up a noisy two-stroke for a client, in the early hours of the morning underneath their bedroom windows." But on the bright side, despite a growing agenda between the two, Carl-Otto Bremer agreed to include Pauli in the team representing Saab in events like the 1957 Hankiralli. Eventually this would bring preferential treatment with new performance parts and suchlike. Mind you, that turned out to be a double-edged sword one year further on, when Bremer was disqualified from winning the Hankiralli, because his car was equipped with a works-supplied engine, which had a tweaked cylinder head. Pauli Toivonen was one of only two customers to be given similar equipment.

This was the time Saab was beginning to become strong in rallies and Erik Carlsson won the 1957 1000 Lakes in a Saab 93. He recalls the period fondly: "When I went to Finland, my car used to be fixed in Pauli's Jyväskylä garage. We became quite close friends even though I did not speak Finnish and he did not speak Swedish. The common language for both of us was 'rally'!"

Erik's 1957 triumph was slightly overshadowed by a nasty accident that befell his Finnish friend, who had been lying seventh in the rally. Late on the Saturday night, he came across a group of youngsters returning home from a dance pavilion in a lumbering GAZ-M20 Pobeda, quite a common car in post-war Finland. The

hatte. Samstagnachts kam Pauli eine Gruppe Jugendlicher in einem schwerfälligen GAZ-M20 Pobeda entgegen, ein beliebtes Auto im Nachkriegsfinnland. Die Autos kollidierten frontal und Paulis Stirn schoss dabei durch die Windschutzscheibe. „Das sah sehr übel aus, seine Kopfhaut war nach hinten geschoben worden und überall war Blut", erinnert sich Eino Kalpala, dreifacher 1000-Seen-Sieger und später ein wichtiger Wegbegleiter in Paulis Karriere. Die Wunden verheilten zum Glück schnell und Pauli trug keine Folgeschäden davon.

Pauli hatte bei seinen Auftritten im Saab viel Pech. Zusammen mit Bremer und Rauno Aaltonen hätte er der schwedischen Marke bei der Hanki Rallye 1958 zum Teampreis verholfen, wäre da nicht die besagte Disqualifikation wegen der Zylinderköpfe gewesen. Bei der 1000 Seen 1958 wurde Pauli Zweiter in der Klasse zwischen Erik Carlsson und Carl-Otto Bremer, aber die Route und die Bedingungen lagen den kleinen Autos nicht und so sprang für Toivonen nur Gesamtrang 15 heraus. Dann ging das gesamte Saab-Kapitel zu Ende. Pauli lagen Bestellungen für drei Autos vor, die er vorab bezahlte. Aus unbekannten Gründen lieferte der Importeur diese Autos aber nie. Für ein kleines Unternehmen ohne große finanzielle Rücklagen war das eine Katastrophe. Paulis Geschäft war bankrott, und die Beziehung zu Carl-Otto Bremer erlebte ihren absoluten Tiefpunkt.

Doch Pauli Toivonen ist niemand, der solchen Dingen nachtrauert. Er bezahlte schließlich all seine Schulden aus diesem Geschäft. Bevor das jedoch geschehen konnte, zog die junge Familie nach Helsinki, um dort ihr Glück zu versuchen. Als gesprächiger Typ hatte Pauli bei seinen Rallyeaktivitäten viele Kontakte geknüpft. Diese waren jetzt sehr hilfreich und eröffneten ihm Türen für Geschäfte, die in irgendeiner Weise auch mit seinem Sport zu tun hatten.

1959 wurde in Finnland erstmals eine offizielle Rallyemeisterschaft ausgetragen. Pauli Toivonen schaffte es irgendwie, am Auftaktlauf, der Hanki Rallye, in einem Peugeot 403 teilzunehmen und den vierten Platz zu belegen. Pauli nahm unterdessen einen Job beim Simca-Importeur an und lieh sich deren Autos für ein Wochenende aus – um sie im Wettbewerb einzusetzen. Das waren natürlich reine Straßenautos, aber irgendwie erzielte Pauli beim nächsten Lauf den dritten Platz und führte das Championat vor der 1000 Seen Rallye an, die jetzt der Europameisterschaft angehörte. Diesmal war eine

two cars collided head-on and Pauli's forehead went through the windscreen. "It looked bad, his scalp had been pushed back and there was blood all over", recalls Eino Kalpala, three-time winner of the rally with his brother and later an important influence in Pauli's career. The wounds healed quickly, though, and there were no lasting effects.

Pauli was perhaps just a bit unlucky in his outings with Saab. Together with Bremer and Rauno Aaltonen he looked as if he had won the marque team prize of the 1958 Hankiralli until the cylinder-head disqualification mentioned earlier. In the 1000 Lakes that same year, he finished second in class between Erik Carlsson and Carl-Otto Bremer, but the route and prevailing conditions did not favour small cars and in the overall classification Toivonen was classified 15th. Then the whole Saab episode came to an unfortunate end. Pauli had orders for three cars, which he had paid for up-front. For unknown reasons, the importer never delivered them to him. For a small company without any significant capital that was a catastrophe. The Jyväskylä dealership went bankrupt, and relations with Carl-Otto Bremer hit an all-time low…

But Pauli Toivonen was not a man to dwell on failure. He would eventually pay off all outstanding debts from the enterprise. Before that could happen, the young family moved to Helsinki in search of a living. Always a forthcoming character, Pauli had made lots of contacts through his rally activities. They now came in handy and soon doors opened to businesses involved with the sport one way or another.

An official rally championship was run in Finland for the first time in 1959 and Pauli Toivonen somehow managed to do its opening round, the Hankiralli, in a Peugeot 403 and bring it home in a most respectable fourth place. However, having found employment with the Simca importer, he soon got to borrow their cars for a weekend – and use them in competition! These were strictly standard vehicles, of course, but after finishing third in the next Finnish rally round Pauli found himself leading the series before the 1000 Lakes, which was now a round of the European championship. Thorough preparation was in order and this time Toivonen managed to persuade his employer to provide a set of

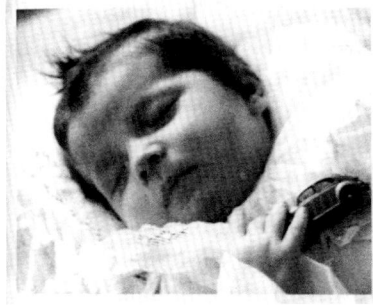

Henri konnte weder laufen noch sprechen und war trotzdem schon ein Autonarr, und das Jyväskylä der 50er-Jahre war für ihn eine fruchtbare Umgebung.

Henri took to cars before he could even speak. Late 1950s Jyväskylä was an environment that hardly discouraged that.

ordentliche Vorbereitung möglich und Toivonen überzeugte sogar seinen Arbeitgeber, ihm einen Satz neuer Michelin-X-Reifen zu geben. „Das geschah unter der Bedingung, dass ich die Reifen direkt nach der Veranstaltung zurückgebe", berichtete Pauli. Dem Simca Aronde in der Ausstattungsvariante Montlhéry wurde generell eine schwache Vorderradaufhängung nachgesagt, die schnell nachgeben konnte. Nicht gerade ideal für die Landungen nach den vielen Sprüngen der 1000 Seen Rallye, die schon damals mit viel Einsatz gefahren wurde. Trotzdem lag Pauli in der letzten Nacht auf Platz Fünf, bevor er auf Rang Neun zurückfiel. In einem Jahr geprägt von der Dominanz der Schweden waren nur zwei einheimische Teams besser. „Und ich konnte das Auto am Montag in tadellosem Zustand wieder auf den Hof stellen", sagte Pauli stolz.

Der vierte und letzte Lauf der finnischen Meisterschaft wurde im Herbst ausgetragen. Die Helsinki Rallye führte über eine Route von 500 Kilometern, von denen Pauli Toivonen 150 ohne Windschutzscheibe zurücklegen musste. Dennoch wurde er Zweiter, nur zehn Sekunden hinter dem großen Citroën von Osmo und Eino Kalpala. Zum Titelgewinn reichte es dennoch nicht. Pauli wurde mit denkbar knappem Abstand Zweiter hinter Peugeot-Pilot Esko Keinänen.

Interessanterweise waren die Kalpala-Brüder in der Saison 1959 Paulis große Gegner auf den Sonderprüfungen. Sie waren erfolgreiche Geschäftsleute, die einen Großhandel für Radios und andere Elektronikgeräte besaßen. Autoradios kamen in Finnland gerade in Mode, das Geschäft der Kalpalas boomte also kräftig. In der Zwischenzeit war Pauli bei den konservativen Simca-Importeuren in Ungnade gefallen. Seine aggressiven Verkaufstaktiken bekamen einige Leute in den falschen Hals. Nach einigen Monaten wurde die Zusammenarbeit beendet, Toivonen vor die Tür gesetzt. In diesem Moment eilten die Kalpala-Brüder zur Hilfe. „Ich bin Pauli in den Straßen von Helsinki über den Weg gelaufen. Ich wusste von seiner Notlage und fragte, was er so macht. Er sagte: ‚Nicht viel.' Ich meinte zu ihm: ‚Es gibt gerade viel zu tun in unserem Lager. Warum hilfst du uns nicht?' Er half und wurde kurz darauf zum Autoradio-Verkäufer", erklärt Osmo Kalpala. „Er war ein unglaublicher Verkäufer", ergänzt Bruder Eino. „Sehr erfolgreich!"

Zu Hause zeigte der kleine Henri die ersten Anzeichen von Benzin im Blut. „Er wachte mitten in der Nacht auf und es gab nur ein Mittel, ihn zu beruhigen: mit kleinen Spielzeugautos spielen, eine Stunde oder so. Dann schlief er friedlich bis zum nächsten Morgen", berichtete Pauli Toivonen Jahrzehnte danach.

new Michelin X tyres for the rally. "This was on the condition that they must be immediately returned after the event", he recounted. The Simca Montlhéry – a mid-range version of the Aronde model – was generally felt to have weak front suspension, which could easily give way on landing from jumps in the 1000 Lakes stages that many competitors were already attacking with vigour. Still, in a year dominated by Swedish drivers, Pauli was holding fifth place during the last night, until dropping to ninth at the finish. Only two domestic crews fared better. "And the car was returned pristine to the company forecourt on Monday morning", he pointed out.

The fourth and decisive round of the Finnish championship took place in the autumn. The Helsinki Rally had a route of 500 kilometres, and as it happened Pauli Toivonen was forced to cover 150 of them without a windscreen! He still finished second, only ten seconds behind the big Citroën of winners Osmo and Eino Kalpala. That was not quite enough to claim the Finnish title, though. Pauli lost out to Peugeot driver Esko Keinänen by the smallest of margins.

Curiously, for most of that 1959 season Toivonen seemed to be battling it out on the stages with the Kalpala brothers. These were successful businessmen running a wholesale company specialized in radios and other electronic appliances. Car radios were just becoming fashionable in Finland, which meant boom times for the business. Pauli, meanwhile, had become the new broom at the decidedly conservative Simca importers. He pushed for aggressive sales methods, which rubbed some people up the wrong way. It led to a split after a matter of months, which again left Toivonen high and dry. At that moment, the Kalpala brothers came to the rescue. "I ran into Pauli in the street in Helsinki and, knowing of his hardships, asked what he was up to. He said: 'Nothing much' and I said: 'Well, there's plenty of packing to be done in our warehouse. Why not join us?' He did and pretty soon moved on to car radio sales", explains Osmo Kalpala. "He was one hell of a salesman", adds brother Eino. "Very effective!"

At home young Henri was showing signs of growing up as a petrol head. "He would wake up in the middle of the night and the only way to appease him was to play with little toy cars for about one hour or so. After that he would sleep peacefully until the morning", explained Pauli Toivonen decades later.

Der finnische Peugeot-Importeur glaubte nicht an Pauli Toivonen. Bei der Hanki Rallye 1959 fuhr er dennoch einen 403 und wurde Vierter.

Peugeot's Finnish importer did not really believe in Pauli Toivonen, but nevertheless Pauli managed to bring this 403 to fourth in the 1959 Hankiralli.

Bei der Tulpen-Rallye bekam Pauli Toivonen diese silberne Tulpe überreicht, die er Ulla und seinen Jungs Henri (links) und Harri stolz präsentierte.

Pauli did a rally in Holland and was rewarded with a silver tulip that he showed to Ulla and his boys Henri (left) and Harri.

Ein paar Mal vertrat Pauli die Marke Saab in Teamwettbewerben. Bei seinen Auftritten für den schwedischen Hersteller hatte er aber selten Glück.
Pauli occasionally represented Saab in team competition, but his seasons with the Swedish marque were mainly unlucky.

Pauli Toivonen
Die Geburt des „Tigers"
Emergence of Tiger

Einer von Pauli Toivonens Gegnern im Jahr 1959 war Timo Korpivaara, Geschäftsführer der finnischen Citroën-Importeursfirma. Korpivaara war von Paulis Fahrkünsten so beeindruckt, dass er ihm für 1960 einen Vertrag anbot. Für Paulis „ja" musste er nicht viel Überzeugungsarbeit leisten, alles passte gut zusammen: Toivonen konnte weiter für die Kalpala-Brüder arbeiten und den Schriftzug ihrer Top-Marke Blaupunkt auf seinem Citroën ID19 spazieren fahren. Zudem gab es einen neuen Copiloten. Bis dato hatte Toivonen, der später für den harschen Umgang mit dem Mann neben ihm bekannt werden sollte, keinen Stammbeifahrer gehabt. Der neue Co hieß Jaakko Kallio, ein freundlich gestimmter und lebensfroher Kollege aus der Firma der Kalpalas. Kallio hatte Osmo Kalpala bei der Hanki Rallye 1958 zum Sieg gelesen, als dessen Bruder Eino sein Land bei den alpinen Ski-Weltmeisterschaften vertreten hatte.

Pauli schätzte den gelernten Bauingenieur Jaakko Kallio sehr. Die beiden wurden im Laufe der Jahre gute Freunde, auch abseits von Arbeit und Rallyes. Im großen Citroën waren sie auf Anhieb konkurrenzfähig. Bei der Hanki Rallye lieferten sie sich ein packendes Duell mit Paulis altem Erzrivalen Carl-Otto Bremer. Die Rallye führte von Helsinki aus in Richtung Norden und als die Teams Jyväskylä erreichten, hatte Pauli fast eine Minute Vorsprung. Diesen baute er sogar aus, bis er nachts auf einer Verbindungsetappe einem entgegenkommenden Bus ausweichen musste und in eine Schneewand raste. Toivonen und Kallio verloren viel Zeit und wurden am Ende nur Fünfte.

Eisrennen wurden damals immer beliebter in Finnland, und natürlich mischte Pauli auch hier mit. Bei den Rennen kam es oft vor, dass die Fahrerfrauen in die eisigen Fußstapfen – oder besser gesagt: Fahrspuren – ihrer Männer traten und mit den Autos ihrer Gatten Wettbewerbe austrugen. Ulla Toivonen wollte sich das natürlich nicht entgehen lassen. Bei ihrem ersten und letzten Rennen legte Ulla, die in den ersten Wochen ihrer zweiten Schwangerschaft war, den Citroën aufs Dach. „Das war mein erster Überschlag", scherzt Harri Toivonen heute darüber.

Im Sommer bei der 1000 Seen Rallye wiederholte sich das Duell von der Hanki Rallye. Wieder kämpften Bremer und Toivonen um die Spitze der Zeitenlisten, doch diesmal gesellte sich Erik Carlsson dazu. Von Jyväskylä aus ging es nach Süden in Richtung Helsinki, wo Toivonen knapp führte. Bremer setzte sich danach ein Stück ab, während Carlsson noch mit Strafpunkten zurücklag, gegen die er aber später erfolgreich protestierte. Doch bei Toivonens Citroën stellten sich Bremsprobleme ein, die so schlimm wurden, dass er deswegen aufgeben musste.

1960 brachte Pauli Toivonen keine großen Erfolge, aber es war nun offensichtlich, dass er es mit jedem Fahrer aufnehmen konnte. „Er musste sich endlich keine Gedanken mehr um die Finanzen machen und konnte sich ganz aufs Fahren konzentrieren", beschreibt Rauno Aaltonen. Zudem erhielt Pauli die Chance, in einem DS21 an der Rallye Monte Carlo 1961 teilzunehmen. Jaakko Kallio konnte ihn bei diesem Abenteuer nicht begleiten, also setzte sich Kauko Ruutsalo nebendran. Bei der Monte zeigte Pauli eine Performance, die für seine Zukunft von großer Bedeutung sein würde. Nach WP-Zeiten hätte Toivonen den vierten Platz belegt. Doch die 61er-Monte ging wegen ihrer kontroversen Handicap-Regelung, die Autos mit kleinen Motoren stark bevorzugte, in die Geschichte ein. Drei Panhard mit

Among Pauli Toivonen's competitors on many events during 1959 was Timo Korpivaara, managing director of Citroën's importer firm in Finland. Korpivaara was sufficiently impressed to suggest a full-time co-operation for 1960. Pauli did not need much persuasion. Everything clicked into place nicely since he would continue to work for the Kalpala brothers and carry the publicity of their top brand, Blaupunkt radios, on his Citroën ID19. Along with the ride came a new co-driver. So far there had not really been a regular partner for Toivonen, who would later become notorious for his abrasive treatment of the men sitting next to him. Now he was paired with Jaakko Kallio, a mild-mannered but fun-loving colleague from the Kalpala Company, who had navigated Osmo Kalpala to victory in the 1958 Hankiralli when Jaakko's brother Eino was representing his country as a downhill skier in the World Championship.

Pauli had a high esteem for Jaakko Kallio, who was a construction engineer by education, and the two became friends even outside work and competition. In the big Citroën they were immediately competitive. On the Hankiralli they engaged in a classic battle with Pauli's old nemesis, Carl-Otto Bremer. The route wound its way from Helsinki way up north and by the time the crews reached Jyväskylä, Pauli held a lead of nearly a full minute. He stretched that advantage until a swerve to avoid an on-coming bus on a night-time road section threw him deep into a snow bank. It took a long time to get going again, which dropped Toivonen and Kallio down to fifth in the final classification.

Ice races were becoming increasingly popular in Finland and Pauli was naturally part of that scene. It was becoming quite trendy for the drivers' wives to follow their husbands on the ice racing trail and they often took part in a class for ladies using the same cars that their husbands had driven. Ulla Toivonen, too, tried her hand at this, but promptly rolled the Citroën in the only race she ever started. She was in the first weeks of expecting her second son at the time. "That was the first time that I was upside down in a car", quips Harri Toivonen.

In the summer, the 1000 Lakes Rally produced a partial repetition of the Hankiralli. Again, it was Bremer and Toivonen fighting at the top of the leader board, but Erik Carlsson was now in the mix too. Heading south from Jyväskylä, by the time that the competition had reached Helsinki, Toivonen led by a narrow margin. Bremer soon edged slightly ahead, while Carlsson was carrying penalties that would later be dropped on appeal. But the Citroën started to lose its brakes and this problem got so serious that the crew had to throw in the towel.

1960 did not bring big results for Pauli Toivonen, but it was now plainly obvious to all that he could offer serious competition to any other driver. "He was at last free of financial worries and could fully focus on driving", offers Rauno Aaltonen. Subsequently Pauli was given a chance to take part in the 1961 Monte Carlo Rally in a DS21. Jaakko Kallio could not join him on this adventure and was substituted by Kauko Ruutsalo. Pauli went and produced a drive that by all accounts became very important for his future. He reached the finish as the fourth fastest driver on scratch times, but this was the year when great controversy was raised by the applied handicaps, which gave an outrageous advantage to cars

Pauli liebte seine Zigarre. Er bestand darauf, dass seine Trainingsautos einen Zigarettenanzünder hatten.
Pauli liked his cigar. He always insisted on having a cigarette lighter in his recce cars.

850-Kubik-Motörchen landeten auf dem Podest, während Toivonen auf der 41. Position geführt wurde. Dennoch zog Paulis Leistung die Aufmerksamkeit von René Cotton auf sich, dem Teamchef der Citroën-Werksmannschaft.

Während Cotton grübelte, kehrte Pauli mit Jaakko Kallio in den nordischen Alltag zurück – mit Platz Fünf bei der Hanki Rallye und Platz Vier bei der Winter Rallye in Norwegen. Von dort kehrte der Sieger Carl-Otto Bremer mit einem blauen Auge in sein Saab-Autohaus in Helsinki zurück. „Wo hast du dir das eingefangen?", wurde er gefragt. „Pauli hat mir auf der Tanzfläche eins verpasst", antwortete er knapp. Bremers Cousin, ein Motorjournalist, hat die Szene live miterlebt. „Pauli tanzte gerade mit der Ehefrau des Fahrtleiters, als Otto ankam und ihm die Dame aus dem Arm riss, so wie er es immer tat. Pauli hat keine Sekunde gezögert und ihm augenblicklich einen Faustschlag verpasst."

Solche Vorfälle wurden jedoch schnell vergessen. Im Frühjahr erhielt Rauno Aaltonen einen Anruf von Pauli. „Ich habe die Möglichkeit, für Citroën internationale Rallyes zu fahren. Aber ich kann das Angebot vielleicht nicht annehmen, weil ich einen Beifahrer brauche, der die richtigen Sprachen spricht, und ich finde einfach keinen", erklärte Pauli. „Könntest du das machen?" Da Pauli nur Finnisch sprach, war es zwingend notwendig, dass sein Nebenmann etwas mehr Sprachwissen aufbrachte. Rauno war dafür die beste Wahl und wurde für drei Rallyes Beifahrer: die Tulpen-Rallye, die Akropolis und die Mille Miglia. „Pauli und ich sind gute Freunde geworden. Er war bei der Hanki Rallye einmal ohne Licht gefahren und ich hatte ihm den Weg gezeigt. Er war meinen Rücklichtern gefolgt", erklärt Rauno. „Es machte nur Sinn, mit ihm zu fahren."

René Cotton hatte beschlossen, das Citroën-Aufgebot durch ausländische Fahrer zu verstärken, und so verpflichtete er den Belgier Lucien Bianchi und eben Toivonen. Cotton leitete das Werksteam aus seiner eigenen Werkstatt heraus und nannte sein Team „Ecurie Paris-Île de France". Trotz der Sprachbarriere besuchte Toivonen Cottons Mannschaft. „Als er aus Paris zurückkehrte, sagte er, dass alles erstaunlich gut verlaufen war", erinnert sich Ulla. „Er hatte nur seine Probleme, aus der Stadt herauszukommen mit all den Kreisverkehren."

Die Tulpen-Rallye war nicht gerade ein Triumph für Toivonen/Aaltonen. Die Strecke führte bis nach Monte Carlo und beinhaltete einige Abschnitte, die Pauli schon von der Monte her kannte, diesmal jedoch ohne Eis und Schnee. Laut Rauno war Pauli noch ein Anfänger auf dem Gebiet des Asphaltglühens. „Die ganze Geschichte war wie eine Aneinanderreihung von Bergrennen", berichtete Pauli damals. Außerdem spielten ihm die Regularien übel mit. Die Dominanz innerhalb der eigenen Klasse war ein wichtiges Kriterium für den Sieg. Das führte bei Standard Triumph zu einer merkwürdigen Taktik: Die Briten nahmen einen Werkswagen aus der Wertung, um Triumph-Privatier Geoff Mabbs zum Gesamtsieg zu verhelfen. Die Citroën konnten in ihrer Klasse nicht mit den Mercedes mithalten und landeten im Nirgendwo. Toivonen/Aaltonen wurden mit einem serienmäßigen Auto Fünfter in einer Klasse, in der auch getunte Autos erlaubt waren.

Die Reise zur Akropolis allein war Abenteuer genug. Pauli flog von Helsinki nach Genf, holte sein Auto ab und fuhr auf Achse durch Jugoslawien nach Athen, um ein Gefühl für seinen DS zu bekommen. Die unbarmherzige Anfahrt beinhaltete große Teile der Liège-Sofia-Liège. Der Citroën war danach so mitgenommen, dass das Team ihn in Athen eigentlich noch einmal für die Rallye hätte vorbereiten müssen. Pauli konnte die Mechaniker davon aber nicht überzeugen.

with small engines. While 850cc Panhards swept into the first three places, Toivonen's name could be found down in forty-first position. Still, his performance had been noted by René Cotton, team manager of the official Citroën works team.

With Cotton left musing, Pauli returned to his Nordic routines with Jaakko Kallio, finishing fifth on the Hankiralli and fourth in the Norwegian Winter Rally. The latter event was won by Carl-Otto Bremer, who returned to his Saab showroom in Helsinki with a black eye. "Where did you get that", he was asked. "Pauli punched me on the dance floor", came the terse reply. Bremer's motoring writer cousin had seen it all and picks up the story: "Pauli had taken the Clerk-of-the-Course's wife to dance, when Otto strode forth and, as was his custom, just wrested the lady from the other guy's arms. Pauli did not hesitate and in the blink of an eye he delivered a straight jab!"

Such things were quickly forgotten, however. As the snows melted Rauno Aaltonen got a phone call from Pauli. "Look, I have been offered this opportunity to drive for Citroën in international rallies, but I may not be able to take it, because I need a co-driver who speaks the right languages and cannot find anyone to join me", he rued. "Could you come?" As Pauli could only speak Finnish himself, it was essential to get someone fluent in a non-Scandinavian language. Rauno fitted the bill perfectly and agreed to do three rallies as his co-driver: the Tulip, Acropolis and Mille Miglia. "I had become firm friend with Pauli. He'd lost his lights in Hankiralli and I showed him the way through the night. He was following my taillights in the dark", explains Aaltonen. "It made good sense to go with him."

René Cotton had decided he needed to strengthen Citroën's hand by employing foreign drivers, and so set his sights on the Belgian Lucien Bianchi and the Finn Toivonen. Cotton ran the factory's works operation from his own premises under the name of "Ecurie Paris-Ile de France". Typically, Pauli did not shy away from visiting the team, despite his linguistic restrictions. "Returning from Paris, he said it had all gone surprisingly well", recalls Ulla Toivonen. "The only problem had been finding his way out of the city, with so many confusing roundabouts!"

The Tulip Rally was not exactly a triumph for the Toivonen-Aaltonen pair. The route went all the way down to Monte Carlo and featured some stretches that Pauli may have known from his southern trip in the winter, but these were now clear of any snow or ice and he was still, as Rauno points out, a novice in driving on asphalt. "The whole affair was more or less a series of hill climbs", reported Pauli at the time. He was clearly put off by the regulations, too, which laid emphasis on the degree of domination by a competitor within his class. This led to Standard Triumph applying strange tactics, where withdrawing a works car from its pursuit of Triumph privateer Geoff Mabbs helped the latter to take overall victory for the manufacturer! The Citroëns were no match for the Mercedes in their class and consequently finished nowhere. Toivonen and Aaltonen in their standard untuned car ended up fifth in a class that included tuned versions.

The trip to the Acropolis Rally was an adventure in itself. Pauli flew from Helsinki to Geneva to collect his car and then drove through Yugoslavia to Athens so that he could get a good feel for it. That meant driving much of the arduous Liège-Sofia-Liège route, where the Citroën got such a hammering that, once arrived in Athens, it really needed to be freshly prepared for the rally. However, Pauli could not convince the mechanics that this was necessary.

Werbeauftritte waren ein wichtiges Element von Toivonens Job für Citroën, und sie machten auch Pauli selbst zu einem bekannten Mann in Finnland.
Promotion became an important part of Toivonen's role with Citroën. And it helped to raise his public profile in Finland.

Pauli Toivonen Die Geburt des „Tigers" / Emergence of Tiger

Bei der Midnight Sun Rallye in Schweden hatte Toivonen nie Glück, dafür siegte er in diesem Citroën wenige Wochen später bei der 1000 Seen Rallye 1962.
Toivonen never had much luck in Sweden's Midnight Sun Rally, but he did win the Rally of the 1000 Lakes 1962 a few weeks later with this same car.

Wenig überraschend schied er kurz vor dem Ziel aus, als die Crew nach ihren eigenen Berechnungen auf Platz Zwei gelegen hatte.

Die Mille Miglia wurde seit dem tödlichen Unfall von De Portago 1957 als Rallye ausgetragen. Citroën ging die Sache etwas halbherzig an. „Mein Auto wurde eigentlich als Servicewagen genutzt und nicht wirklich für den Wettbewerb vorbereitet. Es hatte unter anderem einen maladen zweiten Gang", erklärte Pauli. „Die Straßen hingegen waren sehr schön. Ein Rennen auf dem Autodrom von Monza fiel stark ins Gewicht und es gab einige sehr böse Unfälle", sagte er mit einem Hauch von Sorge. Die Finnen erreichten das Ziel als Sechste in ihrer Klasse. Nach dieser Europatournee hatte Pauli Toivonen ein besseres Verständnis von der internationalen Rallyeszene: „Ich denke, Eugen Böhringer ist der beeindruckendste Gegner von allen."

Dem nächsten Auslandsauftritt fieberte Pauli besonders entgegen, denn er durfte zur Abwechslung ein getuntes Auto fahren. Einen Citroën, der vor Ort für die schwedische Midnight Sun Rallye vorbereitet worden war. Jaakko Kallio kehrte auf den Beifahrerplatz zurück und erinnert sich an Paulis Begeisterung für das Motorgeräusch. „Musik!" nannte es der ehemalige Bassist. Leider fiel Toivonen früh aus.

Mit der für ihn charakteristischen Sorgfalt wählte Rauno Aaltonen sein Auto für die 1000 Seen Rallye 1961 aus und entschied sich für einen privaten Mercedes 220 SE. Der „Professor" war in dem großen Auto unschlagbar, aber Pauli war sein härtester Rivale. Erik Carlsson zog einmal mit Pauli gleich, musste aber aufgeben, weil er mit zu hoher Geschwindigkeit auf einer Verbindungsetappe erwischt wurde. Bei einer unglaublich nassen Rallye fuhr Toivonen das beste Ergebnis seiner bisherigen Karriere ein: Platz Zwei in der Gesamtwertung.

1961 hatte viele Erfahrungen und ein paar Erfolge mit sich gebracht. 1962 konzentrierte sich Pauli wieder mehr auf die finnische und skandinavische Meisterschaft. Der Auftakt zum heimischen Championat glückte. Pauli fuhr erstmals einen Citroën mit Automatikkupplung und gewann vor Rauno Aaltonen, obwohl er sich erst auf das neue Bauteil einschießen musste. Kurz danach war wieder Monte-Carlo-Zeit. Die Konkurrenz hatte den langen Finnen jetzt auf der Rechnung. „Nachdem wir sein Tempo auf den ersten Prüfungen des Vorjahres gesehen haben, haben einige von uns Schweden auf Toivonen gesetzt", sagte Erik Carlsson zu finnischen Reportern. Der Start war vielversprechend. Pauli war Zweiter auf dem Col du Granier und Dritter auf dem Col de Bleine, bevor ihm in Saint Auban die Straße ausging. Game over.

In der Heimat bekam Toivonen einen schlechten Startplatz für die Hanki Rallye zugewiesen, dennoch erkämpfte er Rang Drei. Eine Woche später umging Pauli alle Hindernisse und gewann die norwegische Winter Rallye. Das waren die ersten Läufe zur skandinavischen Meisterschaft und zweifelsohne auch die am härtesten umkämpften Schneerallyes jener Zeit. Paulis Chancen auf den Titel standen jetzt sehr gut. Es gab einen weiteren Sieg in der finnischen Meisterschaft und Platz Zwölf bei der Midnight Sun Rallye in Schweden. Bei der 1000 Seen konnte Pauli mit einem Sieg beide Titel unter Dach und Fach bringen. Doch zwei Wochen vor dem Start waren alle Gedanken an den Titel plötzlich nebensächlich. Carl-Otto Bremer verunfallte mit seinem Privatflugzeug. Bremer sowie zwei weitere bekannte Motorsportler, beide ehemalige Beifahrer von Pauli, kamen dabei ums Leben. Bremer war erst 29 Jahre alt, hatte aber seinen Rücktritt aus dem Rallyesport erklärt, um sich auf seine Geschäfte zu konzentrieren. „Das war ein riesiger Schock. Alle Feindseligkeiten sind in so einem Moment vergessen. Man mag es ihm nicht angesehen haben, aber Pauli hatte auch eine sehr sensible Seite", sagt Ulla Toivonen.

Unsurprisingly he was forced to retire close to the finish when, according to the crew's own calculations, they were lying second.

The Mille Miglia had been run as a rally ever since the fatal accident of De Portago in 1957, but for Citroën this was just a toe in the water effort. "I was given a car normally used for service and it hadn't really been prepared for competitive use. It had a malfunctioning second gear among other things", Pauli explained. "The roads were nice, though. A race around the Monza circuit carried a lot of weight in the results and there were some crashes that looked really nasty", he said with a tinge of concern. The Finns did make it to the finish, sixth in class. After these Continental outings, Pauli Toivonen had a better understanding of the international rally scene. "I think Eugen Böhringer could just be the most formidable opponent of all", he opined.

Pauli Toivonen approached the next foreign event with particular enthusiasm, because for once he got his hands on a tuned car. This was a Citroën locally prepared for Sweden's Midnight Sun Rally. Jaakko Kallio, now back in the co-driver's seat, remembers Pauli's excitement on hearing the engine noise: "Music!" was the description used by the old bass player. Unfortunately the pair was sidelined early.

Using characteristic savvy, Rauno Aaltonen realized a big car was needed to win the 1961 1000 Lakes Rally and he opted to start in a private Mercedes-Benz 220 SE. The combination proved unbeatable, but Pauli Toivonen was his closest pursuer throughout. Erik Carlsson did draw level with Pauli at one point, but was then forced to withdraw after being caught for speeding on a road section. On a horrendously wet event, Toivonen took the best result yet of his career in second place overall.

All good experience and some success in 1961 then, but the next season saw a clearer focus on the domestic and Scandinavian championships. It began well in the first round of the Finnish series, where Pauli was using a Citroën equipped with an automatic clutch for the first time. Despite needing to play himself in with the device, he won from Rauno Aaltonen. Soon after that, it was time for Monte Carlo again. The other competitors now knew to look out for the tall Finn. "Some of us Swedes have placed our bets on Toivonen after witnessing his speed on the opening stages last year", said Erik Carlsson to Finnish reporters. The start was promising enough as Pauli was second fastest over the Col du Granier and third at the Col de Bleine before surging off the road in Saint Auban. End of play.

Back home, Toivonen got a low seeding for the Hankiralli, but despite that came through to finish third overall. Just one week later he overcame all sorts of odds to win the Norwegian Winter Rally. These were the first rounds in the Scandinavian championship and they were undoubtedly the most competitive full-winter events of the period. Pauli's chances in the series now looked extremely good. There was a further victory in the Finnish championship and twelfth overall in Sweden's Midnight Sun Rally, which meant that the 1000 Lakes would settle both series, if Pauli could win it. Less than two weeks before the event all thoughts of success were momentarily swept aside, however. Carl-Otto Bremer crashed in his private plane and was killed with two other prominent motorsport figures, both of whom had been Pauli Toivonen's co-drivers at some stage. Bremer was only twenty-nine years old, but had announced his retirement from the sport to concentrate on business. "It was an immense shock. Any animosities are forgotten in such a moment and despite outward appearance there was always a very sensitive side to Pauli, too", says Ulla Toivonen.

Pauli Toivonen Die Geburt des „Tigers" / Emergence of Tiger

Die finnische Rallyegemeinde hielt inne, bevor sie sich in Jyväskylä versammelte. Pauli fuhr denselben Citroën DS19 wie beim Saisonauftakt mit Semi-Automatik-Getriebe. „Das war ein gutes Auto, aber es hatte seine Macken", beschrieb er später. „Der Citroën war recht schwer. Wenn du einmal Tempo aufgenommen hattest, durftest du nicht mehr das Bremspedal berühren. In Finnland musstest du Kurven zu Geraden machen. Du musstest die Kurven schneiden und hoffen, dass sich kein Stein im Unterholz versteckt. Durch das viele Gewicht vorn untersteuerte das Auto fürchterlich, wenn du am Limit gefahren bist. Seine hydropneumatische Federung hatten wir so entwickelt, dass sie mit den Sprüngen keine Probleme hatte, obwohl das System bei Schotterrallyes recht anfällig war."

Bei seinem zehnten Versuch hatte Pauli endlich alle Zutaten beisammen, um die größte Rallye in seinem Heimatland zu gewinnen. Er übernahm sofort die Kontrolle über die Rallye und kehrte 39 Stunden nach dem Start als Sieger vor das Rathaus von Jyväskylä zurück. Gleichzeitig war Pauli finnischer und skandinavischer Meister. Richtig entspannen konnte er bei der Siegerehrung im Hotel Jyväshovi, in dem er früher Rezeptionist war, aber noch nicht. „Auf dem Weg zurück nach Jyväskylä hatte uns die Polizei wegen Geschwindigkeitsüberschreitung gestoppt", gibt Jaakko Kallio zu. „Das war in einer Tempo-60-Zone und wir waren nicht viel schneller, aber wenn sie den Vorfall den Rallyeorganisatoren gemeldet hätten, hätten wir eine heftige Strafzeit kassiert. Also sagten wir dem Polizisten: ‚Wenn die Sportkommissare das erfahren, wird ein Schwede skandinavischer Meister!' Pauli bezahlte das Knöllchen, danach hörten wir nie wieder etwas von dieser Sache."

Kallio leistete auch seinen Beitrag zum Erfolg. „Wir hatten damals keinen Aufschrieb. Mein Beitrag auf den Prüfungen bestand darin, mein Gesicht so nah wie möglich an die rechte A-Säule zu drücken, um den Kurvenausgang ein bisschen früher zu sehen und dann Pauli zuzurufen: ‚Gas!'. Einige der Straßen kannte Pauli ohnehin ganz gut."

Finnish rally people drew a deep breath and gathered in Jyväskylä for the rally. Pauli had the same Citroën DS19 he'd used to win the championship opener, with the semi-automatic transmission. "It was a good car, but it had its quirks", he explained later. "It was quite heavy and when you had built up speed you had to avoid touching the brake pedal to keep up the momentum. This meant straight-lining bends in Finland. It forced you to be greedy in cutting corners, hoping not to find a rock hidden in the undergrowth. With so much of the weight in the front, the car would understeer fearsomely when taken to the limit. Its hydropneumatic suspension had been developed to handle the jumps without any problem, although the system could be pretty vulnerable on gravel."

On his tenth attempt, Pauli finally had all the pieces in place to conquer the biggest rally in his homeland. He was in control from the outset and thirty-nine hours after setting off from Jyväskylä was greeted in front of the Town Hall as the winner. And Finnish champion. And Scandinavian champion. Yet, even when prize giving was about to start in the Hotel Jyväshovi where he had once worked as receptionist, Pauli could not feel totally at ease. "Driving back towards Jyväskylä we'd been caught for speeding by the police", reveals Jaakko Kallio. "It was in a 60 kph zone and we had not been going too much faster than that, but if the incident was reported to rally organizers, there would surely be a heavy penalty. So we said to the policemen: 'Look, if the Rally Stewards get to know about this, a Swede will be Scandinavian champion!' Pauli paid his fine, but nothing more was ever heard of the whole thing."

Kallio had played his role in the success. "We did not have written pace-notes at the time. My contribution in the stages would come from pushing my face as close as possible to the right-hand windscreen pillar, so I could see a bend opening up slightly earlier than Pauli and then yell 'Gas'! Some of the roads Pauli would know quite well anyway."

1962 wurde Pauli Toivonen zu Finnlands „Fahrer des Jahres" gewählt. Bei der Preisverleihung waren auch sein Mentor und Arbeitgeber Osmo Kalpala (links) und Beifahrer Jaakko Kallio (rechts) anwesend.

At the end of 1962, Pauli Toivonen was presented with Finland's Driver of the Year trophy. He was joined for the occasion by employer and mentor Osmo Kalpala (left) and co-driver Jaakko Kallio (right).

Nach dem Titelgewinn reiste das Duo zum Finale der skandinavischen Meisterschaft. Die Viking Rallye in Norwegen wurde fast zu einem weiteren Triumph, doch wenige Prüfungen vor dem Ziel endete sie beinahe im Desaster. „Das Auto hatte immer wieder aufgesetzt und irgendwann drückte es den Unterbodenschutz gegen eine Bremsscheibe. Auf den Unterbodenschutz war ein bisschen Öl getropft, das durch die Hitze entzündet wurde. Am Ende einer Prüfung stand das Auto in Flammen, die Leute sind alle in den Wald geflüchtet. Zum Glück konnten wir das Feuer löschen, indem wir Sand in den Motorraum geworfen haben."

1962 wurde die Unterstützung von Citroën gekürzt, aber zur Rallye Monte Carlo 1963 stieg Toivonen wieder in einen richtigen Werkswagen ein, begleitet von seinem neuen Co Anssi Järvi. Trotz ungewöhnlich winterlicher Bedingungen absolvierten sie die Sternfahrt von Oslo aus ohne Strafzeit. Dann ging es los von Chambéry aus Richtung Monaco über den langen Col du Granier. Die Bestzeit verbuchte Bo Ljungfeldt im Ford Falcon, der jedoch schon jetzt alle Chancen auf den Gesamtsieg durch einen Kupplungswechsel verspielt hatte. Pauli war mit zwölf Sekunden Rückstand Zweiter und somit der einzige andere Fahrer, der weniger als 41 Minuten brauchte. Sogar Erik Carlsson im wendigen Saab benötigte 41.27 Minuten. Das war ein gutes Omen. Toivonen war auf allen Prüfungen auf dem Weg nach Monaco Zweiter hinter Ljungfeldt, einzige Ausnahme war die kurze Bergrennstrecke Levens, wo Pauli auch Timo Mäkinens Austin Healey 3000 und Carlsson den Vortritt ließ. Dennoch lag er bei der Ankunft in Monte Carlo nicht in Führung. „Wir hatten sch… Informationen über die Bedingungen auf dem Col de Turini", erklärt Anssi Järvi. „Wir wählten Reifen mit ganz wenigen Nägeln und hatten Schwierigkeiten, die steilen Stellen hochzukommen. Der Turini war die letzte WP in den Bergen, da ist uns Carlsson davongefahren." Nach Anwendung der Handicap-Regelung hatte Carlsson vor der letzten Prüfung – drei Runden auf dem Grand-Prix-Kurs in Monaco – zehn Sekunden Vorsprung auf Pauli. „Wir wussten, dass der Saab dort einen Vorteil haben würde", gibt Järvi zu. „Es war klar, dass uns Erik davonfahren und gewinnen würde."

Toivonen hatte mit seiner Leistung viele beeindruckt. Der 23-jährige Cesare Fiorio war gerade dabei, die HF Squadra Corse zu gründen, das spätere Lancia-Werksteam. Fiorio fragte Pauli, ob er interessiert sei, für ihn zu fahren. Der Finne testete einen Flavia auf den Straßen um Monte Carlo, fand das Auto aber ein bisschen schwerfällig. „Cotton hatte uns zwischenzeitlich große Sachen versprochen bei Citroën", eröffnet Anssi Järvi. „Er offenbarte uns ein großes Geheimnis: Citroën würde bald ein Auto mit Maserati-Motor haben. Das klang vielversprechend." Tatsächlich dauerte es noch sieben Jahre, bis es so einen Citroën – den SM – geben sollte.

Gut drei Wochen später reiste René Cotton nach Finnland, um seinen Fahrer bei der Hanki Rallye zu beobachten. Toivonen hatte auf dem Rückweg aus dem Süden als Training an der Bore Rallye in Schweden teilgenommen, seine Fahrt endete aber vorzeitig. „Es gab nur eine Spur im Schnee, und auf diese Spur hatte jemand einen großen Stein gelegt, um uns zu stoppen. Das war Sabotage!", flucht Anssi Järvi. Bei der Hanki Rallye leisteten sie Wiedergutmachung und siegten vor den Augen ihres Chefs, diesen Erfolg wiederholten sie kurz darauf bei der Winter Rallye in Norwegen. Nach den jüngsten Triumphen war Pauli Toivonen in seinem Heimatland ein gefragter Mann. Sein Gesicht tauchte in Werbeanzeigen auf und es war offensichtlich, dass Pauli sogar eine Art Sexsymbol war.

Ulla Toivonen wusste, dass ihr Mann von vielen Frauen begehrt wurde. Doch sie war selbstbewusst genug, um solche Gedanken abzuhaken. „Ich habe mir immer gedacht: Was du nicht weißt, macht dich nicht heiß", sagt sie. „Außerdem war Pauli so ein Fa-

Having clinched their titles, the pair still travelled to the last round of the Scandinavian series. Norway's Viking Rally very nearly became another triumph, but a couple of stages before the finish disaster struck, as Kallio explains. "The car had been bottoming repeatedly and eventually the sump guard got pushed up against a brake disc. There was some oil that had leaked onto the tray and the heat ignited it. We reached the end of a stage on fire and everyone there just ran away into the woods! Luckily we managed to put out the fire ourselves by throwing sand in the engine compartment."

Citroën's support during 1962 had been more subdued, but in 1963 Toivonen stepped into a full works car again for the Monte Carlo Rally, now accompanied by new co-driver, Anssi Järvi. Having cleared the concentration run from Oslo without penalties in unusually wintry conditions, they set off from Chambéry towards Monaco over the long Col du Granier special stage. Fastest on scratch times was Bo Ljungfeldt in a Ford Falcon, but he had lost any chance of outright success with an earlier delay caused by clutch repairs. Pauli was second, just twelve seconds slower and he was the only other driver to break forty-one minutes on the stage. Even Erik Carlsson in his nimble Saab only managed 41min 27s. That set a pattern. Toivonen was second to Ljungfeldt on all the stages down to Monaco with the exception of the short Levens hill climb, where he was also beaten by Timo Mäkinen's Austin Healey 3000 and Carlsson. But on reaching Monte Carlo, he was not in the lead. "We'd had crap information about the prevailing conditions over the Col de Turini", explains Anssi Järvi. "We took tyres that were extremely lightly studded and had great difficulty climbing some of the steepest sections. Turini was the last stage in the mountains and that's where Carlsson edged ahead on the handicap." The corrected gap between the leaders was just ten seconds, but it was still quite a lot to overcome in the final three-lap race around the Principality's GP-circuit. "We knew the Saab would have an advantage there", admits Järvi, "and sure enough Erik pulled further ahead to take the win."

Toivonen's performance had definitely impressed many. Twenty-three year old Cesare Fiorio was just setting up his HF Squadra Corse operation, which would soon become the works team for Lancia, and asked Pauli whether he would be interested in driving. Pauli briefly tried a Flavia in the roads around Monte Carlo, but found the car a bit cumbersome. "Meanwhile, Cotton was also promising great things with Citroën", reveals Anssi Järvi. "As a big secret he told us they would soon have a car with Maserati engine, which sounded promising enough." It would actually take seven years before such a Citroën – the SM – was introduced.

Some three weeks later, René Cotton turned up in Finland to watch his driver in the Hankiralli. Toivonen had got in some practice on his way back from the south by taking part in the Bore Rally, but his drive in Sweden ended prematurely. "There was just a single pair of tracks to follow in the snow and someone had placed a rock in there to catch us out. Sabotage", curses Anssi Järvi. The pair made amends by winning the Hankiralli in front of their boss's eyes and then followed it up by a repeat performance in the Norwegian Winter Rally. These successes made Pauli Toivonen's dashing figure a very visible one in his home country. He was widely used in advertisements and it was quite obvious he was even seen as a bit of – dare one say it – sex symbol.

Ulla Toivonen was fully aware of the fact that many women found her husband very attractive, but confidently shrugged off any thoughts of frivolity on his part. "My mindset was pretty much: what you don't know, you cannot worry about", she says. "And

Pauli Toivonen Die Geburt des „Tigers" / Emergence of Tiger

Anssi Järvi (im Auto) und Pauli Toivonen erzielten gemeinsam viele große Erfolge, darunter den Sieg bei der Hanki Rallye 1963.
Anssi Järvi (behind the wheel) shared many of Pauli Toivonen's most notable successes, including victory in the Hankiralli of 1963.

milienmensch, dass es nie einen Zweifel an seiner Hingabe für uns gab." Anssi Järvi unterstützt diesen Standpunkt: „Er vermisste sein Zuhause so sehr, dass wir das Training unterbrochen haben und nur für ein paar Tage nach Norden gefahren sind, damit er bei seiner Frau und seinen Kindern sein konnte." Mit zwei kleinen Söhnen gab es daheim auf jeden Fall genug zu tun. Die Erinnerung an die alten Zeiten zaubert Ulla ein Lächeln auf die Lippen: „Henri war so ein lebhaftes Kind, er machte immer wieder neue Stunts. Als er vier Jahre alt war, haben wir die Stützräder von seinem kleinen Fahrrad abgemacht. Als nächstes ist er den Berg hinuntergefahren, auf viel befahrene Straßen zu. Ich brüllte ‚Stopp!' und er hat das Ding quergestellt, um es zum Halten zu bringen!"

Im Frühjahr 1963 blieben die Söhne bei ihrer Großmutter. Ulla nahm die seltene Chance wahr, Pauli zur Akropolis Rallye zu begleiten. Gemeinsam mit Aushilfsbeifahrer Väino Nurmimaa, der später die Saab-Fabrik im finnischen Uusikaupunki leiten sollte, und seiner Frau sind sie in einem Auto gefahren. „Es war eine wundervolle Reise, obwohl wir wie verrückt gefahren sind. Auf dem langen Weg nach Süden haben wir nur eine Nacht im Hotel verbracht. Wir haben die Adria von Brindisi aus durchquert und uns dann in Astir Beach bei Athen niedergelassen. Dort habe ich auch das Boot von Onassis gesehen, ‚Christina'. Zum Glück hatten wir in der Stadt ein paar Tage Zeit", erinnert sich Ulla. Die Jungs erledigten ihre Aufgabe gut. Sie kamen als Siebte ins Ziel – als bestes Citroën-Team und mit einer Bestzeit auf den 15 Prüfungen.

Zu Hause bekam Pauli ein Angebot von einem überschwänglichen jungen Mann namens Antti Aarnio-Wihuri, auch AAW genannt. Ein Mann aus gutem Hause. Seine Familie besaß ein Konsortium, dem die finnischen VW- und Porsche-Importeure angehörten. AAW wollte die Verkäufe des neuen VW 1500 ankurbeln und sah im Motorsport die geeignete Plattform. Er wollte eine Motorsportabteilung gründen und hoffte, Toivonen würde diese Operation anführen. Pauli testete einen VW 1500, der von AAW höchstpersönlich getunt worden war, bei zwei Läufen auf einer Pferderennbahn, er gewann beide. Sein Vertrag mit Citroën lief noch bis Ende August, aber zum September heuerte er beim VW-Importeur als Werksfahrer und Marketingleiter an.

Die letzten Monate mit Citroën brachten nicht viel Freude. Pauli schied bei der Midnight Sun Rallye und der 1000 Seen aus. Er tauchte auch in der Nennliste zur Liège-Sofia-Liège auf, da die Rallye aber noch am 1. September lief, ging er dort nicht an den Start. Trotzdem veranstaltete der Citroën-Importeur einen kleinen Empfang für Toivonen und dankte ihm für seine Dienste. In seiner Rede würdigte er auch Ulla Toivonen „für ihre Geduld" und seinem ehemaligen Arbeitgeber Osmo Kalpala, dass er Pauli die Freiheit gewährte, professionell Rallye zu fahren. Wie vorher erwähnt war Osmo Kalpala in der Anfangsphase von Paulis Karriere so etwas wie sein Mentor. „Pauli fragte mich einmal, warum er Kurven nicht so schnell fahren konnte wie ich. ‚Egal, wie schnell ich fahre, ich komme nicht an deine Zeiten heran', sagte er. Ich habe ihm dann erklärt: Es geht nicht um die Geschwindigkeit am Eingang, sondern um die am Ausgang", verrät der Altmeister – der vielleicht erste Rallye-Theoretiker Finnlands.

Paulis nächster wichtiger Wegbegleiter war Antti Aarnio-Wihuri. Bei VW begann Pauli mit der Entwicklung und dem Einsatz des 1500 S. Kleine Erfolge stellten sich schnell ein, so wie Platz Zwei bei der nationalen Helsinki Rallye, zwei Sekunden hinter Simo Lampinens Saab. Beifahrer war diesmal ein junger Kerl namens Hannu Mikkola. „Auf einer WP haben wir vielleicht eine etwas optimistische Zeit bekommen, aber egal, unser Ergebnis war gut", erinnert sich Hannu.

anyway, Pauli was always such a home person that there could never be any doubt about his commitment to us." Anssi Järvi backs up this view. "He was missing home so much that we'd break up the recce and drive back up north just for a few days, so he could be with his wife and kids." With two sons, domestic affairs certainly got the parents' attention. Looking back to those days brings a smile to Ulla's face: "Henri was such a lively kid and he was picking up all kinds of stunts. He was only four when the support wheels were shed from his little bicycle. Next thing I knew he was pedalling down the hill towards a busy high street. I yelled at him to stop and he just whisked the thing sideways to bring it to a halt!"

In the spring of 1963, the boys were left with their grandma, as Ulla got a rare chance to accompany Pauli to the Acropolis Rally. They went by car together with the co-driver and his wife. Väinö Nurmimaa, later to become managing director of Saab's Finnish factory in Uusikaupunki, filled that role on this occasion. "It was a wonderful trip, even though we drove like crazy and only spent one night in a hotel on the long way south. We crossed the Adriatic from Brindisi and settled in Astir Beach, just outside Athens. I remember seeing Onassis' boat 'Christina' there. Luckily we also had time to stroll in the city for a couple of days", Ulla remembers. The guys did a good enough job to bring their Citroën to the finish of the Acropolis Rally in seventh place as the team's best placed crew and having been fastest overall on one of the fifteen stages.

Back home Pauli was getting overtures from an exuberant young man called Antti Aarnio-Wihuri. From a privileged background – his family were owners of a consortium, which included Finland's VW and Porsche importers – AAW, as he would be known, had decided that VW's new 1500 model needed a sales boost and motor sport success would give it just that. He wanted to set up a competition department and hoped that Toivonen would spearhead the operation. Pauli got to try a VW 1500, tuned by AAW in person, in a couple of dirt track races early in the summer, winning both times. He was still contracted to drive for Citroën until the end of August, but agreed to join the VW importer from September, as full-time driver and marketing manager.

The last months with Citroën did not bring much joy, with Pauli retiring from both the Midnight Sun and 1000 Lakes rallies. He had also been entered in the Liège-Sofia-Liège, but as that event would have still been running on September 1st, he never took the start. Still, Citroën's importer called a small reception to formally thank Toivonen for his services to the marque. In his speech, Timo Korpivaara also acknowledged Ulla Toivonen "for her patience" and former employer Osmo Kalpala "for allowing Pauli the freedom to compete professionally". As explained earlier, Osmo Kalpala had been something of a guiding hand in Pauli Toivonen's early career. "He once came to me wondering why he could not drive through corners at the speed I did. 'No matter how fast I attack them, I cannot do the times you do', he said. I told him it's not about how fast you go into them, it's about exit speed", reveals the old master, perhaps the first theorist of the sport in Finland.

The next big influence, however, would be Antti Aarnio-Wihuri. Pauli duly started work at VW, first developing, rallying and racing the 1500 S model. Minor success came quickly, including second place in the national Helsinki Rally, two seconds behind Simo Lampinen's Saab. Co-driver on that occasion was a young man named Hannu Mikkola. "We may have been given an optimistic time on one stage, but never mind, the result was good," recalls Hannu.

Pauli Toivonen Die Geburt des „Tigers" / Emergence of Tiger

Nach der großartigen Leistung von Monte Carlo wollte Pauli logischerweise eine internationale Karriere verfolgen. Im Herbst 1963 ließ er verlauten: „Lancia hat mir ein Auto angeboten. Ich sollte mich bald entscheiden, aber ich will es erst einmal testen." Damit bezog er sich wahrscheinlich auf das Gespräch mit Fiorio im vergangenen Januar. Das war Paulis Art, AAW unter Druck zu setzen, ihm ein Auto für Europa zu besorgen. Letztlich kam Aarnio-Wihuri mit einem Programm auf, das Toivonen 1964 die Teilnahme an einigen europäischen Rallyes ermöglichte. Sein VW wurde dabei vom schwedischen Importeur Scania-Vabis eingesetzt. „Die ganze Geschichte ging sogar mit den Plänen von Wolfsburg einher", erklärt AAW.

Diese Pläne beinhalteten die Teilnahme an der Rallye Monte Carlo in einem Auto, das unter Paulis Leitung aufgebaut wurde. AAWs Motorenmann Keijo Ikäheimo baute ein 1500-S-Aggregat nach Gruppe-1-Reglement. Obwohl das Auto in der Gruppe 2 starten musste, hielten sie in dieser frühen Entwicklungsstufe ein seriennahes Triebwerk für zuverlässiger. Pauli absolvierte ein gründliches Training und zeigte eine Leistung, die er als eine seiner besten einstufte. „Du musstest bergab Zeit gewinnen, weil das Auto bergauf nicht so schnell war", erklärte er. Leichter gesagt als getan, wenn man die schwache Bremsleistung des VW bedenkt. Auf einer fast schneefreien Monte besiegte der Finne die schwedischen VW, gewann seine Klasse und wurde Zehnter im Gesamt. Zudem ließ er alle Citroën hinter sich. Diese Performance brachte Pat Moss-Carlsson dazu, Pauli „Tiger" zu nennen. Ein Spitzname, der blieb.

Öffentlich distanzierte sich das Volkswagen-Werk von diesem Einsatz, aber Toivonen und der Schwede Berndt Jansson wurden zu einer Nachbesprechung nach Wolfsburg eingeladen. „Außer dem VW-Chef waren alle hohen Tiere da", verrät Anssi Järvi. „Alles, was Pauli und Berndt sagten, wurde auf Tonband aufgenommen. Sie erklärten den Leuten von VW, dass die größte Schwachstelle die Trommelbremsen waren."

Im heimischen Winter bestand Paulis größte Errungenschaft darin, Kari O. Sohlberg – der später Vorsitzender des finnischen Motorsportverbands werden sollte – zum Titel in der 1600-ccm-Klasse der finnischen Eisrennserie zu verhelfen. Pauli gewann einen der Läufe

After that great performance in Monte Carlo, Pauli naturally wanted to pursue an international career, too. In the autumn of 1963 he went on record saying: "Lancia has offered me a car to drive. I should decide soon, but will want to test first." This was most likely a reference to the talks with Fiorio back in January and may have been just Pauli's way of putting pressure on Aarnio-Wihuri to find him a drive on the Continent. Whatever the case, AAW did sort out an arrangement where Toivonen got to participate in some 1964 European events with a Volkswagen run by the Swedish importer, Scania-Vabis. "The whole affair actually went along the wishes of the Wolfsburg factory", says Aarnio-Wihuri.

Those wishes apparently included first tackling the Monte Carlo Rally in a car built under Pauli's own watchful eyes. AAW's resident engine wizard, Keijo Ikäheimo, took great care in putting together a 1500 S in what was effectively Group 1 trim, although the car had to run in Group 2 that year. The decision was based on seeking reliability from a design that still lacked development. Pauli put in an exhaustive recce and produced a drive that he was to rank among his very best. "You had to make up time going downhill, because obviously the car was not that fast going up", he pointed out. Easier said than done, considering the VW's less than convincing braking power! On a largely snowless Monte, the Finn outpaced the Swedish VWs to win his class and finish tenth overall. He also left all the Citroëns behind. It was a performance that prompted Pat Moss-Carlsson to call him "Tiger", a moniker that stuck.

Volkswagen publicly wanted to distance itself from the effort, but Toivonen and Swede, Berndt Jansson, were summoned to Wolfsburg for a thorough debrief, reveals Anssi Järvi. "All the top brass except for the Director General were there. Everything Pauli and Berndt said about the cars was recorded on tape. They told VW that the single most important shortcoming was the drum brakes."

At home Pauli's most satisfying achievement of that winter was probably supporting Kari O. Sohlberg – long-time future chairman of the Finnish Automobile Sport Federation – to a Finnish ice racing title in the under 1600 cc class. Pauli personally won one of the

1964

Einer von Paulis unzähligen Beifahrern war ein Bubi namens Hannu Mikkola.

One of Pauli's countless co-drivers was a fresh-faced Hannu Mikkola in 1964.

Die Vorbereitung des VW für die Monte erfolgte unter Pauli Toivonens eigener Leitung in der neuen Wettbewerbsabteilung des finnischen Importeurs.
Pauli Toivonen had personally overseen the preparation of his Monte Carlo VW in the new competition department of the marque's Finnish importer.

Pauli Toivonen Die Geburt des „Tigers" / Emergence of Tiger

Die internationalen Rallyes im Jahr 1964 bestritt Pauli Toivonen größtenteils in einem VW, der in Schweden aufgebaut wurde.
For most of 1964 Pauli Toivonen was driving in international rallies with VW's prepared in Sweden.

selbst und wurde bei anderen Rennen beschuldigt, die Cortina GT absichtlich aufgehalten zu haben. Das waren die größten Gegner von Sohlbergs VW.

Pauli nahm auch an der Rallye dei Fiori in Italien teil, der späteren Rallye Sanremo. Dort hatte er aber kein Glück. Beim Training stieß er mit einem Straßenauto zusammen, dabei brach er sich mehrere Rippen und verletzte sich am Knie. Mit diesem Handicap war er nicht in Bestform. Nach einer langen und entspannten Fahrt von Bologna nach Lucca, wo die Sternfahrt endete, bemerkte er nicht, dass man für zu frühes Ankommen noch mehr Strafzeiten kassiert als für Verspätungen. Pauli sammelte reichlich Strafen und wurde letztlich 51. Alles in allem also eine Rallye zum Vergessen.

Tatsächlich erzielte er bei keiner der internationalen Rallyes, die er in einem schwedischen VW bestritt (erst in einem 1500 S, dann in einem 1300-Kubik-Käfer), ein gutes Ergebnis. Bei der Akropolis, der Liège-Sofia-Liège und der RAC schied er jeweils aus. Das gleiche Schicksal ereilte ihn bei der 1000 Seen, wo sein finnischer Motor auf Platz Vier liegend streikte. Doch Keijo Ikäheimo erkannte das Problem. Der Unterbodenschutz behinderte den kühlenden Luftstrom unterhalb des Motors. Also experimentierte er mit kürzeren Unterbodenplatten herum.

Einer der VW-Fahrer bei der 1000 Seen Rallye 1964 war Hannu Mikkola, dem Pauli gerne half. „Er brachte mir sogar bei, wie man für eine Rallye richtig trainiert", lobt Hannu. „Von ihm habe ich gelernt, wie gut man die Prüfungen kennen muss. Viel später habe ich mich dafür revanchiert, indem ich Henri geholfen habe."

qualifying rounds, but was accused on other occasions of deliberately holding up the Cortina GTs that were the main challengers to Sohlberg's VW.

Pauli had also managed to take part in the Rally dei Fiori, aka San Remo, in Italy. He didn't have much luck there, cracking a couple of ribs and injuring his knee during practice in a collision with a civilian car. Thus handicapped, he was not in best form. After a long and pretty relaxed drive north from Bologna to the concentration city of Lucca, he failed to realise that there was even more penalty for arriving early on the special tests than there was for arriving late. Consequently he amassed heavy penalties and eventually finished fifty-first. All in all, a truly forgettable outing.

In fact, none of the international rallies tackled in a Swedish VW – first 1500 S, then 1300 cc Beetle – brought much joy for Toivonen, as he failed to see the finish in either the Acropolis Rally, the Liège-Sofia-Liège or the RAC Rally. This was also true of the 1000 Lakes, where the Finnish-built engine gave up when Pauli was lying fourth. However, Keijo Ikäheimo recognized the problem. It was that the sump guard impeded the cooling airflow beneath the engine. He would thus continue experimenting with shorter sump guards.

One of the VW drivers in that 1964 1000 Lakes had been Hannu Mikkola, whom Pauli was eager to help. "He actually taught me how to properly recce for a rally", commends Hannu. "I got to understand how well one needs to know the stages. Much later I returned the favour by helping Henri in a similar way."

Die Rallye Monte Carlo 1964 wertete Pauli als eine seiner besten Leistungen. Mit einem fast serienmäßigen VW 1500 S schaffte er den Sprung in die Top Ten.
Pauli ranked the 1964 Monte Carlo Rally as one of his best drives. He took a near-standard VW 1500 S into the top ten overall.

Pauli Toivonen

Mountain king

While he pushed ahead with further development of the Finnish Volkswagens, Toivonen got his hands on something totally different during 1965. AAW persuaded Porsche's team manager, Huschke von Hanstein, to put Pauli in a mighty mid-engined 904 GTS for the Monte Carlo Rally.

This was a world apart from the cars that Pauli had been rallying before, but he was not lacking in confidence. "We did the first part of our recce in a 911 and when it was returned to Zuffenhausen, Pauli quipped: 'Now let's swap this moped for a proper car.' People at the factory were not amused with that!" says Anssi Järvi. The pair did several runs over all the special stages during their recce. "Pauli was extremely conscientious in practicing the stages. He took it all very seriously and we worked long days. There was no partying like with some other drivers", Järvi points out. They started the Monte Carlo Rally from Bad Homburg (near Frankfurt) as one of the hottest favourites to win. The various concentration routes converged at Chambéry and, by the time the Frankfurt starters got there, the weather was rapidly deteriorating with snow falling ever more heavily in the area. Roads around Chambéry became blocked with cars getting stuck. "We tried to look for alternative routes, but some of the minor roads had completely disappeared under the white stuff", Anssi Järvi explains. They eventually made it, but with such penalties that any hopes of success could be forgotten. "Von Hanstein suggested we carry on in the hope of being able to impress with our times on the stages. It was hopeless, though, and after the second stage we packed it in." A huge disappointment for all concerned, but this would not be Pauli Toivonen's last chance in a Porsche 904. He loved the car, as expressed later: "It certainly had a right kind of power-to-weight ratio."

On Finnish events, Pauli still mainly campaigned the VW 1500 S. His most frequent co-driver for the past year or so had been a bright young man called Lars Lindholm, but the poor chap got the boot after 1965 Hankiralli. The pair had been close to VW's biggest Finnish victory yet, but lost out by 29 seconds after being docked 30 seconds of road penalties thanks to a navigational error.

AAW soon bought himself a Porsche 904 to be used as an attraction in Finnish races and Pauli Toivonen got the honour of debuting it in Turku in the presence of Ferry Porsche himself. The track was laid out in an airfield with only parts of the course paved. Toivonen lost ground after the start as an old Jaguar D-type exploited its Hakkapeliitta winter tyres (!) on the loose, but he quickly found his way to the front and eased away from the opposition. Finnish race meetings at the time normally hosted a race for all-comers, called X-class. As AAW subsequently took the wheel of his new Porsche, Pauli was often left with another car tailor-made for that class. Called VW MAC1, it was a stripped Beetle with a 1,720 cc engine developing outstanding power. This Keijo Ikäheimo built projectile became a firm favourite with the fans and reaped successes in Pauli's hands. All that paled into insignificance, however, when he got back in a works Porsche 904 for the Coupe des Alpes in July.

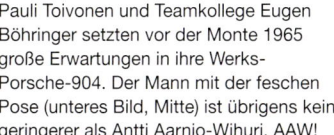

Pauli Toivonen und Teamkollege Eugen Böhringer setzten vor der Monte 1965 große Erwartungen in ihre Werks-Porsche-904. Der Mann mit der feschen Pose (unteres Bild, Mitte) ist übrigens kein geringerer als Antti Aarnio-Wihuri, AAW!

Pauli Toivonen and Eugen Böhringer had great expectations for the 1965 Monte Carlo Rally with their works Porsche 904s. The ebullient figure in the middle is none other than Antti Aarnio-Wihuri – Mr. AAW himself!

Das Auto bot einige neue Kniffe wie eine Gegensprechanlage, um den Aufschrieb im Glasfaser-Cockpit besser hören zu können. „Zudem hatten wir sonderbare Gurte oberhalb unserer Knie, damit unsere Beine nicht hin und her schwankten", erinnert sich Anssi Järvi. Das Training fiel deutlich kürzer aus als bei der Monte. „Wir hatten unser Zusammenspiel so weit entwickelt, dass wir eine Fahrt über die Prüfungen als ausreichend empfanden, wir mussten keine Kontrollfahrten mehr machen." Toivonens Teamkollegen bei dieser Rallye waren Robert Buchet und Eugen Böhringer. Letzterer startete in einem 904 mit Sechszylindermotor in der Prototypenklasse, während die Vierzylinder bei den GTs antraten.

Auf der ersten WP drehte sich Pauli und verpasste die Bestzeit um 28 Sekunden. Was folgte, war eine der beeindruckendsten Fahrten in der Geschichte der Coupe des Alpes. Toivonen verbuchte auf allen verbliebenen zwölf Prüfungen die schnellste Zeit, sein Abstand auf den zweitbesten Fahrer betrug manchmal über eine halbe Minute. Im Ziel wurde zusammengerechnet. Die Summe aller WP-Zeiten betrug bei Toivonen 2:05:54.2 Stunden, die Morley-Brüder im Austin Healey 3000 hatten als zweitbestes Team 2:12.14.4 Stunden gebraucht. Dennoch war Pauli nicht der Gesamtsieger.

Mit der begehrten Trophäe, dem „Coupe des Alpes", wurden nämlich jene Teams ausgezeichnet, die die Rallye ohne Verspätungen bei Zeitkontrollen absolviert hatten. 1965 gelang dieses Kunststück acht Teams, während sich Toivonen und Järvi 660 Strafpunkte eingehandelt hatten. Anssi Järvi erzählt die Geschichte: „Am Anfang gab es eine Kontrolle, wo die Streckenposten in eine Scheune geflüchtet waren, als es angefangen hatte zu regnen. Sie wollten, dass die Beifahrer ihre Bordkarten selbst stempeln. Ich sah aber nur einen leeren Tisch mit Zuschauern drumherum, denn die Streckenposten hatten ihre Longines-Uhr mitgenommen. Und die Zuschauer haben uns überhaupt keine Hilfe angeboten. Sie wollten sehen, wie lange ich brauche, um die Streckenposten zu finden."

Später gab es weitere Probleme: „Ein paar Prüfungen danach war die Lenkung hinüber. Pauli schaute sich das an und sagte, das ganze System sei zusammengebrochen und es sei lebensgefährlich so weiterzufahren. Wir kamen überein: ,Wenn es nun an der Zeit wäre, diese Welt zu verlassen, dann soll es so sein.' ... Pauli war schweißgebadet, als wir den Service erreichten." Trotzdem war es harte Arbeit, das Auto rechtzeitig zusammenzuschweißen. Järvi konnte nur mit einer List vermeiden, wegen maximaler Verspätung disqualifiziert zu werden. „Wir waren gut 300 Meter von der Kontrolle entfernt. Ich bin zu Von Hanstein gegangen und fragte, ob ich mir seinen 911 ausleihen darf. Mit dem bin ich zur Kontrolle und habe mir den Stempel geholt. Als ich dann einen U-Turn gemacht habe und zum Porsche-Service zurück bin, war die Hölle los. Die Streckenposten warfen uns Betrug vor. Aber Von Hanstein wollte davon nichts wissen und so kamen wir ungeschoren davon." Als Nächstes steuerten sie den Mont Ventoux an und erklommen den Berg mit weniger als einer Minute Rückstand auf den Rekord, aufgestellt von Hans Herrmann in einem Abarth-Prototypen – und das mit zwei großen Männern an Bord!

Pauli Toivonen lief nun zu Höchstform auf. Im altbewährten VW 1500 S holte er Platz Drei bei der 1000 Seen Rallye, nur geschlagen von den beiden Werks-Mini-Cooper von Timo Mäkinen und Rauno Aaltonen. Pauli erzählte später von seiner Fahrt über eine neblige Nachtprüfung. Für die brauchte er nur viereinhalb Minuten, und war damit 26 Sekunden schneller als Mäkinen. „Die Prüfung lief in der Nähe von Hämeenlinna, wo ich aufgewachsen bin. Ich bin sie aus dem Gedächtnis gefahren, ohne viel zu sehen", gab Pauli zu.

Zwei Jahre lang hatte Pauli gute Arbeit geleistet und die VW-Verkäufe in Finnland angekurbelt. Aber jetzt war er als Rallyefahrer daheim

The car had some new tweaks, like an intercom system for reading pace-notes in the noisy fibreglass cabin. "And we had peculiar belts just above the knees to keep our feet from wobbling about", Anssi Järvi remembers. The recce this time was much shorter than for Monte Carlo. "Our co-operation had now developed to a level, where we felt only one passage over a stage was enough, without need to make checks." Toivonen's team-mates on this event were Robert Buchet and Eugen Böhringer, the latter having been trusted with a 6-cylinder 904, which ran in the prototype class, while the 4-cylinder ones competed as GTs.

On the very first stage Pauli spun and trailed the fastest time by 28 seconds. What followed after that was one of the most impressive drives ever seen in the Coupe des Alpes. Toivonen was fastest on every single one of the remaining twelve special stages. Sometimes his margin to the next man was well over half a minute. At the finish his total time spent on the stages was 2hr 5min and 54.2sec. The next best total was 2hr 12min 14.4sec set by the Morley brothers in their works Austin Healey 3000! Yet, he did not get to collect the silverware for overall victory.

The Coupe des Alpes was, of course, primarily a competition for an Alpine Cup or Coupe, and these were awarded for a clean run through the route without any lateness at time controls. While eight crews managed that in 1965, Toivonen and Järvi were classified with no less than 660 points from delays at time controls. Anssi Järvi picks up the story. "At quite an early stage there was this one control, where the marshals had escaped inside a barn after it started to rain. The idea was for the co-driver to self-stamp the time card. I could see an empty table with spectators standing around, as the marshals had taken the Longines printing clock inside with them. The spectators were just curious to see how long it took me to find the marshals and did not offer any help at all."

More trouble was to follow: "A few stages further on the steering went limp. Pauli went to look and said the whole system had collapsed and the car was now in a lethal state to carry on. But we shook hands and decided that, if it's our time to leave this world today, then so be it... Pauli was all covered in sweat when we finally made it to service." It was still hard work to get the necessary welding done in time. For the pair to stay within maximum lateness and avoid exclusion, Järvi had to use some guile. "We were maybe 300 metres from the control and I went to Von Hanstein and asked to borrow his private 911. I then drove to the control, passed our time card and got it stamped within the allowed lateness. But when I next made a U-turn and drove back to the Porsche service, all hell broke loose and the marshals accused us of fraudulent conduct. But Von Hanstein would have none of that and we got away with it." They next headed to the Mont Ventoux test and managed to climb the hill in a time less than a minute slower than the record set by Hans Herrmann in an Abarth prototype one month before – and this was done with two big men on board!

Pauli Toivonen was now in truly great form. Back in the trusty VW 1500 S he finished third in the 1000 Lakes Rally, only beaten by the two works Mini Coopers of Timo Mäkinen and Rauno Aaltonen. Pauli later told the story of his drive over a foggy night stage that took a mere four and a half minutes to complete, but where he beat Mäkinen by no less than twenty-six seconds. "That stage was close to Hämeenlinna, where I grew up. I drove it from memory, without seeing much at all", Pauli admitted.

In two years he had done a great job to boost Volkswagen's sales in Finland and was now in demand, both domestically and abroad.

„Er hat gerade so das richtige Leistungsgewicht", mit diesen Worten beschrieb Pauli den Porsche 904, mit dem er den Sieg bei der Coupe des Alpes 1965 wahrlich verdient gehabt hätte.
"It had the power-to-weight ratio just about right!" That's how Pauli summed up his Porsche 904. He would richly have deserved victory in the 1965 Coupe des Alpes.

Pauli Toivonen Gipfelstürmer / Mountain king

und international gefordert. Das führte zur Trennung von AAW, wenn auch nur auf Zeit. Pauli teilte Antti Aarnio-Wihuri im Herbst 1965 mit, dass er zu einem französischen Autohersteller wechseln würde. „AAW gab mir fünf Minuten, um meinen Schreibtisch zu räumen", sagte er damals zu Ulla. AAW mag temperamentvoll gewesen sein, räumte Meinungsverschiedenheiten aber schnell wieder beiseite. Damals hieß es, Huschke von Hanstein hätte sich bemüht, Toivonen bei Porsche zu behalten. Jahre später sprach Pauli von einem Telegramm, in dem ihm ein Auto angeboten wurde, das von AAW aber zurückgehalten worden war. Aarnio-Wihuri weist das zurück und leugnet, Toivonen jemals im Weg gestanden zu haben.

Das Ergebnis von alledem war, dass Pauli Toivonen für die Rallye Monte Carlo 1966 zu Citroën zurückkehrte. Die Veranstalter hatten die Regeln so geändert, dass sie die serienmäßigen Gruppe-1-Autos stark bevorzugten, und das erhöhte die Chancen von Citroën. Auf dem Beifahrerplatz saß nun Ensio Mikander, ein alter Verbündeter aus der VW-Zeit.

Es gibt keinen Zweifel, dass die 1966er-Monte für Pauli Toivonen keine gute Veranstaltung war – abgesehen vom Endergebnis. Das Verhältnis zwischen ihm und Teamchef René Cotton bröckelte schon während der Vorbereitung, als Paulis Trainingsauto schlappmachte und er von der Spitze des Col de Turini bei Citroën anrief. Offensichtlich bat ihn Cotton, sich in Paris ein neues Fahrzeug abzuholen. „Ich bin Rennfahrer, kein Fernfahrer", brüllte Pauli ins Telefon. Die Rallye an sich schien er kein bisschen mehr zu genießen. Pauli war ungewöhnlich niedergeschlagen und beschwerte sich, dass sein Gruppe-1-DS21 langsamer war als sein Trainingsauto. In Monaco erklärte Cotton den finnischen Journalisten sogar, dass er glaubte, Pauli sei ausgefallen. Als Pauli dann aus den Bergen auftauchte, musste Cotton zugeben, dass der „Tiger" noch immer der schnellste Citroën-Pilot war. Auf der letzten Schleife in den Bergen machten Außenstehende eine interessante Beobachtung: Sie sahen, wie bei allen Werks-Citroën die Jod-Nebellichter gegen die in Frankreich üblichen gelben Leuchten ausgetauscht wurden. Als Toivonen an

That led to parting of the ways – albeit temporarily – with AAW. In the autumn of 1965 Pauli went to Antti Aarnio-Wihuri to break the news that he was going to switch his allegiance to a French car manufacturer. "AAW gave me five minutes to clear my desk", he reported to Ulla. AAW had a short temper, but he was also quick to brush differences aside. It was said at the time that Huschke von Hanstein was keen to keep Toivonen in Porsche's camp. Much later Pauli himself talked of a telegram, which offered him a drive, but had been kept back by AAW. This is refuted by Aarnio-Wihuri who denies that he would have stood in Toivonen's way.

The outcome of all this was that Pauli Toivonen returned to Citroën for the 1966 Monte Carlo Rally. The organizers had changed the regulations to heavily favour standard Group 1 cars and this was expected to boost Citroën's chances. Occupying the co-driver's seat was now Ensio Mikander, an old ally from VW days and no mean driver himself.

There is no escaping the fact that the 1966 Monte Carlo was not a happy event for Pauli Toivonen – despite the outcome. The relationship between him and team manager René Cotton was already crumbling during preparation for the rally. Pauli's recce car broke down and he made a phone call to Paris from the top of the Col de Turini. Apparently Cotton asked him to come and get a new car from Paris. Pauli was heard to shout down the phone: "I am racing driver, not transport driver!" He did not seem to enjoy the actual competition much either. Unusually subdued, he complained of the Group 1 DS21 being slower than the one he had used during the recce. Down in Monaco, Cotton told Finnish journalists that he believed Toivonen had dropped out. When Pauli did emerge from the mountains, however, Cotton had to acknowledge the fact that "Tiger" was still the fastest Citroën driver. In the final mountain loop, outsiders witnessed Citroën changing iodine fog lights for regular, yellow French units in all their remaining cars. Toivonen arrived at that service point and made a characteristically sarcastic remark: "All right, boys, start banging your

1966

Der „Scheinwerferskandal" bei der Rallye Monte Carlo 1966 brachte Pauli Toivonen in eine unangenehme Situation. Er hatte zwar wegen der Disqualifikationen gewonnen, wollte sich von den politischen Entscheidungen aber klar distanzieren.

The "lighting scandal" put Pauli Toivonen in an awkward situation after the 1966 Monte Carlo Rally. Winner after the disqualifications, he sought to distance himself from the politics.

Trotz des Sieges bei der 1966er-Monte war das Verhältnis zwischen Toivonen und Citroën nach der Rallye sehr getrübt.
Despite victory in the 1966 Monte Carlo Rally the relationship between Toivonen and Citroën had turned sour.

Pauli Toivonen Gipfelstürmer / Mountain king

Nach der Trennung von Citroën ging Toivonen eine neue „French Connection" ein. Pauli fuhr für Renault nicht nur Rennen und Rallyes, er vermarktete auch deren Autos in Finnland.
Toivonen's French connection remained after he quit Citroën. Before too long Pauli was not only racing and rallying Renaults, but also marketing the brand in Finland.

diesem Servicepunkt ankam, machte er eine sarkastische Bemerkung: „Okay, Jungs, jetzt schlagt euch mal die Köpfe zusammen!" Er war sauer, weil er dachte, er würde stärker abgenutzte Reifen bekommen als die anderen Fahrer. Aber Pauli beruhigte sich wieder, als er merkte, dass die Beschleunigung dank des schmaleren Durchmessers besser war. Im Ziel schien Pauli Fünfter zu sein, was den Umständen entsprechend gar nicht mal schlecht war. Dann kam der vielleicht größte Skandal im Rallyesport, als die vier britischen Autos an der Spitze des Feldes – drei Mini Cooper, ein Lotus Cortina – disqualifiziert wurden, weil sie nicht abblendende Jod-Scheinwerfer hatten. Also hieß der Sieger Pauli Toivonen, wenn auch widerwillig. Bei der Siegerehrung weigerte er sich, den Pokal anzunehmen. Pauli sah sich zweifellos als würdigen Monte-Carlo-Sieger, aber nicht in diesem Auto, nicht in diesem Jahr und nicht auf diese Art und Weise.

Eine Zukunft mit Citroën stand offensichtlich außer Frage, aber dann eilte Renault zu Hilfe. Dort entwickelte sich alles so wie damals bei VW. Zu Beginn bekam Pauli einen Vertrag für ein paar Rallyes bei der Motorsportabteilung von Renault Schweden. In einem Renault R8 Gordini legte er bei der Schweden Rallye und der Rallye dei Fiori gute Starts hin, schied aber früh aus. Bei beiden Rallyes lag er zum Zeitpunkt seines Ausfalls vor dem späteren Sieger. Unglücklicherweise war das Budget von Renault Schweden danach aufgebraucht, also erkundete der neue Teamchef Gunnar Häggbom mögliche Lösungen. Schließlich wurde in Finnland eine Schwesterorganisation gegründet, von der Pauli Toivonen bald der Chef wurde. Er übernahm dort eine ähnliche Rolle wie vorher bei VW und wurde letztlich auch Marketingleiter des finnischen Renault-Importeurs. Pauli mochte es, zu Hause seine Brötchen bei dem Hersteller zu verdienen, für den er auch international antrat.

Bei Renault lag das Problem zunächst beim kleinen 1.135-ccm-Motor, mit dem Pauli in der 1,3-Liter-Klasse gegen stärkere Konkurrenz antreten musste. Beim Prototypenrennen der X-Klasse in Kuopio durfte Pauli den bis dato noch nicht homologierten 1.300-Kubik-Motor fahren und wurde Zweiter hinter Leo Kinnunens VW MAC1 – aber vor dem Porsche 904 von AAW. Eine weitere Parallele mit der VW-Zeit war, dass Pauli bei internationalen Rallyes wieder Teamkollege von Berndt Jansson war, der auch das Lager gewechselt hatte. Bei der Targa Florio teilten sich beide sogar einen Alpine A110. Das legendäre Straßenrennen war eine neue Umgebung für den Finnen, aber er gewöhnte sich schnell ein. Nach wochenlangem Training schied er jedoch mit Getriebeschaden aus und fühlte sich verraten.

Es folgten weitere Rennen mit Jansson. Für Le Mans bekamen sie von Alpine einen erstklassigen A210. Toivonen überraschte Teamchef Jacques Cheinisse mit der besten Qualifying-Zeit aller Alpine-Fahrer. Für Pauli war Le Mans eine interessante Erfahrung: „Wenn du die Dunlop-Kurve voll fährst, fühlt es sich an, als würde das Auto Meter für Meter nach links springen. Das hört erst auf, wenn dir unter der Brücke gerade die Straße ausgeht", erklärte Pauli beim Dinner am Freitagabend. „Und jetzt haben sie entschieden, dass [Mauro] Bianchi und [Guy] Verrier das Rennen schneller angehen sollen als wir." Toivonen und Jansson fuhren auf den 16. Platz nach vorn, ehe sie nach 17 Stunden eine gebrochene Ölleitung stoppte.

Der 1,3-Liter-Motor war zur 1000 Seen noch immer nicht homologiert für den R8 Gordini, also musste das kleinere Triebwerk herhalten. Toivonen machte das Beste daraus und lag nach WP Fünf auf dem vierten Platz – bis er den heftigsten Unfall seines Lebens hatte, bei dem sogar sein Helm zu Bruch ging. Zum Glück blieb die Crew unverletzt, und Pauli blickte schon der nächsten Herausforderung entgegen: der Coupe des Alpes.

heads together!" He was momentarily upset for seemingly getting more worn tyres than the other Citroëns, but calmed down upon realizing that their smaller diameter would give him better acceleration. Back in Monte Carlo, Pauli appeared to have finished fifth, which was not bad in the circumstances. Then, of course, came perhaps the biggest scandal in the sport's history, when all four British cars – three Mini Coopers and a Lotus Cortina – at the top of the leader board were disqualified for having non-dipping iodine headlights. Pauli Toivonen was a reluctant winner for Citroën. He did not accept his trophy at the prize giving. There is no doubt that he considered himself worthy of a Monte Carlo win, just not in that car, in that year and in that way.

A future with Citroën was pretty obviously out of the question, so Renault came to the rescue. In time, it all turned out much as things had been with VW. At first Pauli got a deal to do some events with the competition department of Renault Sweden. Driving a Renault R8 Gordini, the Swedish Rally and Rally dei Fiori both began quite well, but ended in early retirement. On each event he was ahead of the eventual winner at the time that he dropped out. Unfortunately Renault Sweden's whole budget had been consumed after these outings and solutions to carry on were explored by its new team manager, Gunnar Häggbom. These expanded to the idea of setting up a sister operation in Finland. Pretty soon Pauli Toivonen was in charge of that unit. He assumed a role similar to the one he had possessed with VW, eventually also becoming marketing manager for Renault's Finnish importer. Pauli always liked to earn a living from working domestically for the same manufacturer that he represented on continental rallies.

With Renault the problem initially was having to do battle using a 1,135 cc engine, which normally put him up against more powerful opposition in the 1300 class. In a so far un-homologated 1,300 cc version, he did manage to finish second to Leo Kinnunen's VW MAC1 in the X-class of a race meeting in Kuopio – and beat AAW's Porsche 904 into the bargain! One of the parallels with earlier VW life was the fact that Pauli again found himself as teammate to Berndt Jansson in foreign events, the Swede also having changed camps. On the Targa Florio, the two even shared the same Alpine A110. The classic road race was a new environment for the Finn, but he acquitted himself well, although he was soon forced out with gearbox failure. He had practiced for weeks and felt betrayed.

More racing with Jansson followed, when the pair was included in Alpine's Le Mans team, this time sharing a pukka A210 model. Toivonen surprised team boss, Jacques Cheinisse, by qualifying as the fastest Alpine driver. The experience had been interesting. "When you attack the Dunlop curve flat-out, it feels like the car's jumping to the left, metre by metre, until that stops just when you run out of road under the bridge", described Pauli over dinner on the Friday. "And now they've decided to let [Mauro] Bianchi and [Guy] Verrier set off at a faster pace than us in the race", he rued. Toivonen and Jansson climbed to sixteenth overall before succumbing to a broken oil pipe after seventeen hours.

A 1,300 cc engine still was not homologated for the Renault R8 Gordini by the time of the 1000 Lakes Rally, so the smaller unit had to be used once again. Toivonen found good pace from it and was lying fourth after five stages, but then had the biggest crash of his life, which even cracked his helmet. Still, no harm to the crew and Pauli was ready to take on the challenge of the next event, the Coupe des Alpes.

Pauli Toivonen Gipfelstürmer / Mountain king

Als das Budget des schwedischen Importeurs aufgebraucht war, gründete Renault in Finnland sein eigenes Rallyeteam – unter der Leitung von Pauli Toivonen.
When the funds of the Swedish operation ran dry, this led to the setting up of Renault's Finnish competition department, led by a certain Pauli Toivonen.

Pauli liebte den Alpine A210 und schwärmte von Rallyeeinsätzen mit dem A110. Der Wunsch ging aber nicht in Erfüllung, Toivonen fuhr den A110 nur bei der Targa Florio.
Pauli loved the Alpine A210 and spoke wistfully of a chance to use an A110 in rallies. It did not materialize as he only drove one in the Targa Florio.

Pauli Toivonen Gipfelstürmer / Mountain king

In Frankreich fuhr er einen Prototypen mit der braven Haut des Renault R8. Das unhomologierte Auto war mit reichlich Aluminium an der Karosserie, einem 1.440-ccm-Motor und einem Fünfganggetriebe ausgestattet. Der Prototyp war schnell. Toivonen fuhr auf dem Col d'Allos und dem Col de la Cayolle Bestzeit, wenn er auch sonst nicht ganz so schnell war wie der Alfa Romeo GTA von Jean Rolland und der Ford Lotus Cortina von Vic Elford. Doch auch diesmal gab es keine Trophäe für Toivonen, der nach einem Frontalunfall mit einem Straßenauto aufgeben musste, weil sein ganzes Benzin ausgelaufen war.

Den Saisonabschluss bildete die RAC Rallye, wo Pauli mit Co Anssi Järvi und der alten Version des R8 antrat. Der 1,3-Liter-Motor war weiterhin nur in der Gruppe 3 zugelassen. Die RAC war für Toivonen wie eine Zusammenfassung der gesamten Saison. Er zeigte ein gutes Tempo und lag im untermotorisierten Renault auf Platz Fünf, hatte aber schon die Heckscheibe verloren – wie die meisten R8. Pauli musste weitere Rückschläge hinnehmen: Auf einer WP hatte er zwei Reifenschäden an der Hinterachse, später verpasste er eine Kreuzung und fuhr anderthalb Kilometer Umweg. Trotzdem lagen Toivonen und Järvi zur Halbzeit in den schottischen Highlands auf Rang Acht, nur 20 Sekunden hinter dem Viertplatzierten. Wenn man die Ausfälle in Betracht zieht, wäre dieser vierte Platz durchaus möglich gewesen, wenn sie nicht wegen eines Lenkungsschadens selbst ausgeschieden wären. Pauli weigerte sich, mit dem Auto weiterzufahren. Also fuhr Anssi den R8 selbst nach London und gab zu Protokoll: „Die dreispurige Autobahn war gerade breit genug."

Renault blieb auch 1967 Toivonens Arbeitgeber in Finnland. Für internationale Rallyes wechselte er aber zu Lancia, etwa vier Jahre nach dem ersten Angebot von Cesare Fiorio. Die Italiener waren ebenfalls Underdogs mit ihrem 1,2-Liter-Fulvia-HF. Beim Training zur Monte saß Anssi Järvi noch neben Pauli, doch auf dem Rückflug nach Finnland kam die erfolgreiche Partnerschaft zu einem Ende. „Es war eine kleine, dumme Auseinandersetzung, aber mir ging es ums Prinzip und Pauli gab natürlich nicht nach", schmunzelt Järvi heute. Jyrki Ahava, der international schon Erfahrung mit Simo Lampinen gesammelt hatte, diente kurzfristig als Ersatz. Dem Duo gelang zweimal die fünftbeste WP-Zeit, bevor sie auf dem Col du Granier wegen eines Kupplungsschadens aufgeben mussten. In Schweden erreichten sie dafür die sechste Position, was Fiorio zu gefallen schien.

Der Renault R8 Gordini mit dem größeren Motor wurde jetzt endlich in die Gruppe 2 homologiert, und Pauli gewann damit den finnischen Eisrenntitel in der stark besetzten 1,3-Liter-Klasse. Für Rallyesiege reichte es aber noch nicht. Für Toivonens Fahrstil war der ewige Wechsel zwischen Lancia Fulvia mit Frontmotor und Frontantrieb und R8 Gordini, wo sich Motor und Antrieb hinten befanden, sicher nicht hilfreich.

Mit seinem Leben war Pauli zufrieden. Er hatte sich in der schicken Gartenstadt Tapiola vor den Toren Helsinkis ein Haus gekauft. „Als ich 1959 begann, den Sport ernsthaft zu betreiben, beschloss ich: Wenn das Rallyefahren Arbeit wird, muss es mir einen guten Lebensstandard bringen. Das habe ich erreicht, jetzt könnte ich über einen Rücktritt nachdenken", sagte er damals in einem Interview.

„Mein Hauptgrund für die vielen Teamwechsel war, dass ich immer die lukrativsten Angebote angenommen habe. Wenn ich Junggeselle gewesen wäre, hätte ich mein Leben definitiv in Zentraleuropa verbracht", gab er zu und unterstrich damit die Bedeutung seiner Familie. Seine Jungs aufwachsen zu sehen, machte Pauli große Freude. „Die haben so viel Energie! Besonders der Jüngere, der springt vom Dach, wenn ich es ihm erlaube. Und das mache ich natürlich!"

In France, he was back to driving a prototype, although it came in a normal Renault R8 shape. Running as an un-homologated car allowed liberal use of aluminium in the bodywork, as well as the fitting of a 1,440 cc engine and a five-speed gearbox. The car was fast and Toivonen made good use of it, setting top times on Col d'Allos and Col de la Cayolle, if not quite on the pace of Jean Rolland's Alfa Romeo GTA and Vic Elford's Ford Lotus Cortina. Yet, there was to be no Coupe this time either, as the car went no further after losing all its fuel in a crash caused by an oncoming private car.

The season was capped by an entry in the RAC Rally, once again partnered by Anssi Järvi and yet again in the old spec R8, as that 1,300 cc engine was still only eligible for Group 3. The whole thing pretty much summed up 1966 for Pauli Toivonen. He showed adequate speed, soon lying fifth with the underpowered Renault, but already having lost the rear screen like most R8s in the event. More hardships were experienced, with the worst of these being puncturing both rear tyres on one stage and then having to double back about a mile after taking a wrong turn on another. Despite all this, halfway through the rally, up in Aviemore in the Scottish Highlands, Toivonen and Järvi were in eighth place and only some twenty seconds or so away from fourth place. Taking into account later retirements, they might well have got that placing at the finish had they not been sidelined by steering failure. Pauli refused to carry on, but Anssi still drove the car back to London, although "the three-lane motorway was barely wide enough for it".

Renault continued to be Toivonen's paymaster in Finland, but in international rallies he switched to Lancia for 1967, nearly four years after the initial offer from team manager Cesare Fiorio. The Italian team, too, was a bit of an underdog, starting the season with a 1,2 litre engine in its Fulvia HF. Anssi Järvi again did the Monte Carlo recce with Pauli, but their successful partnership came to an end on the flight back to Finland. "It was a silly little argument, but I made it a matter of principle and Pauli typically would not give in", recalls Järvi with a wry smile. Jyrki Ahava had been gaining international experience with Simo Lampinen and was called in to substitute. The pair retired quite early on the Monte Carlo with clutch failure on the Col du Granier after setting the fifth fastest time on two of the stages they did complete, but managed to finish in Sweden and take sixth overall, which seemed to please Fiorio.

Finally getting Group 2 homologation for the Renault R8 Gordini with its bigger engine, Pauli took the Finnish ice racing title in a competitive 1300 class, but still could not quite win rallies with it. It cannot have helped his driving style to be constantly hopping between the front-engined and front-wheel drive Lancia and Renault having both his engine and drive in the rear.

He was content with life, however. Having bought a house in the fashionable Tapiola Garden City just outside Helsinki, he reflected in an interview: "When I took to the sport seriously in 1959, I decided that if it becomes work, it must give me a satisfactory standard of living. I have achieved that goal and could perhaps think of retiring now…"

"My prime reason for quite often changing teams has been to grab the most lucrative offers. But if I'd been a bachelor, I would definitely have based myself in central Europe", he confessed, once again underlining the importance to him of his family. It obviously gave him great joy watching the boys grow up: "There's fantastic energy in them. The younger one, especially, will jump from the roof if I let him. And I do, of course!"

1966 musste Toivonens Renault R8 Gordini wegen fehlender Homologation ohne den größeren 1300-Kubik-Motor auskommen.

Toivonen soldiered on through 1966 without homologation of the bigger 1300cc engine for the Renault R8 Gordini.

Lancia rechnete in Schweden keineswegs mit einem Sieg, sie werteten Platz Sechs durch Toivonen/Ahava als Erfolg.

Lancia did not expect to win in Sweden, so sixth place for Toivonen/Ahava was deemed a success.

Pauli Toivonen Gipfelstürmer / Mountain king

1967 wurde Pauli für seine Rallyeeinsätze ordentlich entlohnt. Er sagte selbst, der Lancia-Vertrag sei lukrativ. Auch sein alter Freund Huschke von Hanstein (oben rechts) hatte weiterhin ein Auge auf Toivonen.

By 1967 Pauli Toivonen felt he had been well rewarded by his sport, insinuating that the Lancia contract had been lucrative. His old friend Huschke von Hanstein (top right) still had an eye on him, too.

Bei den kleineren Rennen in Finnland, die er im Renault bestritt, wurde Toivonen oft als Held gefeiert. Dabei waren Topresultate im Lancia selten. Ein aussichtsloser Auftritt bei der Akropolis endete vorzeitig wegen eines gerissenen Benzintanks, und sogar bei der 1000 Seen war nicht mehr drin als Platz Sieben, womit Teamchef Fiorio anscheinend auch zufrieden war.

Anfang Oktober platzte das Fahrerlager bei den 500 km von Keimola aus allen Nähten. Dort teilte sich Pauli einen Porsche 911 mit Zeitungsmagnat Olli Lyytikäinen. Gerüchten zufolge war der Auftritt in dem deutschen Auto von Paulis Arbeitgeber nicht genehmigt, weswegen Pauli Renault verlassen würde. Pauli selbst bestätigte, dass er mit Porsche im Gespräch war. Und so dauerte es nicht lange, bis Stuttgart einen Werksvertrag mit Toivonen für 1968 verkündete.

Für den Rest des Jahres 1967 gab es zumindest noch den Lancia-Vertrag. Auf Korsika fuhr Pauli sein erstes gutes Ergebnis auf internationaler Bühne seit der Rallye Monte Carlo 1966 ein. Lancia brachte die Prototypen-Variante des Fulvia HF zur Tour de Corse mit einem aufgebohrten 1.440-ccm-Motor, weniger Gewicht und speziellen Lampen von Carello. Bei starkem Nebel und Regen hielt Toivonen den Porsche von Vic Elford hinter sich und wurde Zweiter hinter Teamkollege Sandro Munari. Ein triumphaler Doppelsieg für Lancia. Während der 25 Stunden andauernden Rallye hatte Pauli seinen Lancia nur vier Mal verlassen! Korsika war Toivonens letzter Auftritt für die Italiener. Der geplante Einsatz im Fulvia-Prototyp bei der RAC Rallye kam nicht zustande, weil die Veranstaltung in letzter Minute wegen der Maul-und-Klauen-Seuche abgesagt werden musste.

Toivonen was routinely hailed as a hero in the smaller Finnish races and sprints he entered with the Renault, but top results were still hard to come by with Lancia. An unpromising run in the Acropolis ended prematurely with a fractured fuel tank and even in the 1000 Lakes he could only finish seventh, which still apparently satisfied team boss Fiorio.

In early October the paddock of Keimola circuit was buzzing as Pauli Toivonen turned up to share the Porsche 911 of publishing magnate Olli Lyytikäinen in a 500 km race. Word had it that his Finnish employer did not approve of their man driving the German car and that Pauli would leave Renault. He confirmed that he had been having talks with Porsche for some time and it did not take long before a works deal for 1968 was announced via Stuttgart.

There was still the Lancia contract to honour for the rest of 1967, though, and in Corsica, Pauli finally got his first good international result since the 1966 Monte Carlo Rally. Lancia entered the Tour de Corse with prototype versions of the Fulvia HF. The engines had been bored out to 1,440 cc, considerable weight had been shed off the cars and they also had lighting specially made for the event by Carello. In heavy rain and fog, Toivonen was able to just fend off Vic Elford's Porsche and follow team-mate Sandro Munari home, thus giving Lancia a triumphant 1-2 result. Through the whole 25-hour competition Pauli only managed to step out of his Lancia four times! It would be his last drive for the team, when a second drive in a Fulvia prototype came to nothing as the RAC Rally was cancelled due to foot-and-mouth disease.

Nach der Trennung von Anssi Järvi erwies sich Last-Minute-Verpflichtung Jyrki Ahava (rechts) als guter Ersatz.

Jyrki Ahava proved an able last-minute substitute when Pauli Toivonen split up with Anssi Järvi.

Toivonen
Pauli, Henri & Harri

Monte Carlo 1966

HORS-COURSE

N° Compét.	Point de Départ	CONCURRENT ET CO-ÉQUIPIER	Nationalité	Marque	Groupe	Classe	Cylindrée	Observations
2	LIS	MAKINEN T. - EASTER P.	SF	Cooper	1	2	1,275	s/décision Commissaires Sportifs
75	LON	CLARK R. - MELIA B.	GB	Ford	1	2	1,558	d°
79	LON	SILVERTHORNE S. - GRIFFITH R.	GB	Austin Cooper	2	1	0,999	s/parcours de concentration
87	LON	BAXTER R. - J. SCOTT	GB	Triumph	2	2	1,293	s/décision Commissaires Sportifs
96	LON	POWER H. - PRICE D.	GB	Austin Cooper	2	2	1,275	s/parcours de concentration
102	LON	APPLEBY H. - McGHIE R.	GB	Ford	2	3	2,000	s/parcours de concentration
107	LON	SMITH R. (Miss) - DOMLEO V. (Miss)	EIR	Hillmann	1	1	0,875	s/décision Commissaires Sportifs
112	LON	LANE M. - DOIDGE R.	GB	Simca	1	1	0,944	d°
115	LON	CUFF J. - BAGULEY N.	GB	Jaguar	1	4	3,780	d°
130	BAD	JENSEN B. - ZOBBE E.	DK	Ford	2	3	1,998	s/parcours de concentration
154	REI	"KELLER" - DESBONNET P.	F	N.S.U.	1	1	0,996	s/parcours commun
157	REI	YSCHARD R. - LAROUSSE G.	F	N.S.U.	1	1	0,996	d°
184	REI	GREDER H. - DELALANDE M.	F	Ford	1	4	4,740	s/décision Commissaires Sportifs
194	OSL	VAN DEN BERGH L. - HENDRIKX M.	NL	Porsche	3	2	1,582	s/parcours commun
202	OSL	SKOTVEDT A. - STRANDRUD T.	N	Morris Cooper	1	2	1,275	s/décision Commissaires Sportifs
205	OSL	SODERSTROM B. - PALM G.	S	Ford	1	2	1,558	s/décision Commissaires Sportifs
223	VAR	ELFORD V. - DAVENPORT J.	GB	Ford	1	2	1,558	d°
224	VAR	DUGUET G. - ZUZULA E.	F	Renault	2	2	1,108	d°
230	VAR	HOPKIRK P. - LIDDON H.	GB	Cooper	1	2	1,275	d°
240	ATH	ANAGNOUSTOU L. - MORPHY C.	G	Wartburg	2	1	0,992	d°
242	ATH	AALTONEN R. - AMBROSE T.	SF	Cooper	1	2	1,275	s/décision Commissaires Sportifs

Liste der disqualifizierten Teams
List of disqualified teams

Im vorläufigen Ergebnis der Monte 1966 wurde Timo Mäkinen im Mini Cooper S als Sieger geführt. Auf den weiteren Plätzen folgten seine Teamkollegen Rauno Aaltonen und Paddy Hopkirk sowie Roger Clark im Ford Cortina Lotus. Im offiziellen Endergebnis tauchte dieses Quartett jedoch nicht mehr auf - ihre Disqualifikation wurde eine Stunde später verkündet.

Der Veranstalter hielt die vier britischen Autos für nicht regelkonform, da ihre Scheinwerfer mit Einfaden-Jodlampen ausgestattet waren statt der normalen Abblendlichter. Das Abblenden erfolgte durch das Umschalten auf Nebellichter. Die Proteste der British Motor Corporation wurden zwar abgeschmettert, doch die umstrittene Disqualifikation brachte dem Team vermutlich mehr positive PR ein als es ein Dreifachsieg getan hätte.

XXXV° RALLYE AUTOMOBILE MONTE-CARLO 1966 — CLASSEMENTS

Offizielles Endergebnis
Official final classifications

In 1966, initial results showed Timo Mäkinen in a Mini Cooper S as winner of the Monte Carlo Rally, with team-mates Rauno Aaltonen and Paddy Hopkirk next and Roger Clark fourth in a Ford Cortina Lotus. When the final results were posted, all four were missing from the list. An hour later it was announced they had been disqualified.

It was alleged that these cars did not comply with the technical regulations, because their headlamp bulbs had been replaced by single filament quartz-iodine units and dipping was achieved by switching to fog lamps. Protests followed, but were turned down. Ironically, all this served to give the British Motor Corporation probably more positive publicity than a straight 1-2-3 result would have done.

Toivonen
Pauli, Henri & Harri

Pauli Toivonen

Der Champion
Champion!

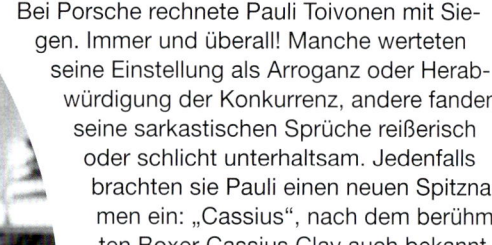

Bei Porsche rechnete Pauli Toivonen mit Siegen. Immer und überall! Manche werteten seine Einstellung als Arroganz oder Herabwürdigung der Konkurrenz, andere fanden seine sarkastischen Sprüche reißerisch oder schlicht unterhaltsam. Jedenfalls brachten sie Pauli einen neuen Spitznamen ein: „Cassius", nach dem berühmten Boxer Cassius Clay auch bekannt als Muhammad Ali. Wie man ihn auch empfand, Toivonen war einzigartig in der Wahl seiner Worte.

„Got beaten!" („Ich wurde geschlagen") – mit diesen Worten stieg Toivonen nach der Rallye Monte Carlo 1968 aus seinem roten Porsche 911. Diesmal war es Sarkasmus. Pauli kann eigentlich nicht bitter enttäuscht gewesen sein, denn er lag im Ziel eine Minute hinter Teamkollege Vic Elford und sicherte Porsche damit den Doppelsieg. Aber er hatte mehr erwartet, und er war nicht der Einzige. Sein alter Freund Erik Carlsson hatte Toivonen als Favorit gesehen: „Ich denke, Pauli wird gewinnen, zumindest wenn Schnee auf den Prüfungen liegt. Nach 1966 möchte er es diesmal richtig machen, das ist eine große Motivation." Die 1968er-Monte war jedoch ungewöhnlich trocken. Die meiste Zeit jagten Elford und Toivonen den führenden Alpine von Gérard Larrousse, bis der Franzose die beiden 911er in der letzten Nacht passieren ließ und dann von der Straße rutschte, weil Zuschauer Schnee auf die Fahrbahn geworfen hatten. Pauli verkürzte die Lücke zu Elford, verlor auf dem Col de la Couillole aber kolossale 40 Sekunden. Damit war die Angelegenheit geklärt, daran änderten auch Bestzeiten bei der zweiten Fahrt über den Turini und Couillole nichts. „Die Erfahrung auf Slicks hat vermutlich den Unterschied ausgemacht", räumte Elford im Ziel ein. Slicks waren im Rallyesport damals noch nicht weit verbreitet, der Sport- und Tourenwagenfahrer Vic Elford fühlte sich auf den Rennreifen hingegen pudelwohl.

With Porsche, Pauli Toivonen fully expected to win. Every time! Some took his attitude as arrogance and belittling towards the opposition, others got to view his trademark sarcastic one-liners as poignant and tremendously amusing. A new nickname was established: "Cassius", named after the famous boxer Cassius Clay aka Muhammad Ali. Whichever way one looked at it, there's no denying that the man had a unique way with words.

"Got beaten!" Those were Pauli's first words, when stepping out of his red Porsche 911 on the Monte Carlo waterfront after the season opener. There it was sarcasm. He could not reasonably be deeply disappointed in trailing team-mate Vic Elford by just over a minute and securing a 1-2 for Porsche. But yes, he had expected better. He was not the only one. Old friend Erik Carlsson had also been backing Toivonen before the rally. "I think Pauli will win, at least if there is any snow on the stages. I believe that after 1966 he wants to do it properly and that will be a huge motivation", Erik predicted. The 1968 Monte Carlo Rally was run in unusually dry conditions. Through most of it, Elford and Toivonen were chasing the Alpine of Gérard Larrousse, until the Frenchman got passed on the last night and was then caught out by some snow thrown on the road by spectators. Pauli momentarily reduced the gap to Elford, but then dropped a whopping forty seconds on the first run over Col de la Couillole. That pretty much settled the issue despite fastest times on the second runs over Couillole and Turini. "More experience of racing tyres might have made a difference", conceded Pauli at the finish. These had not yet been widely used in rallies and Vic Elford must have been more comfortable on them, having been active in both sports and touring car racing.

1968

„Ich wurde geschlagen!" Das Lächeln auf Paulis Gesicht verriet aber, dass er dem zweiten Platz bei der Monte auch etwas Gutes abgewinnen konnte.

"Got beaten!" The smile suggests that Pauli could still see positives in a second-place finish in Monte Carlo.

Es ist angerichtet. 1968 gewann Toivonen im Werks-Porsche sechs EM-Läufe, in Monte Carlo musste er sich aber Vic Elford geschlagen geben.
All set to rule. Toivonen took six wins with a works Porsche in 1968, but had to concede defeat to Vic Elford in Monte Carlo.

Pauli Toivonen Der Champion / Champion

Auf der Rennstrecke verbrachte der Brite auch den Großteil der Saison, während Toivonen Porsches Nummer Eins bei Rallyes war. Pauli fuhr den 911 T von der Monte auch bei der Rallye Sanremo (vorher Rallye dei Fiori). Dort schüttelte er die Alpine-Fahrer Jean-François Piot, Jean Vinatier und Jean-Pierre Nicolas ab und gewann überzeugend. „Wir haben anfangs den Unterbodenschutz verloren, das war unser einziges Problem", berichtete Pauli. „Es hätte schlimmer kommen können …" Hören Sie ein gewisses Selbstvertrauen heraus?

Toivonen hatte zwar schon Rücktrittswünsche angedeutet, aber 1968 war er so beschäftigt wie nie zuvor. Pauli verbrachte gerne Zeit zu Hause mit seiner Familie, aber das war nicht der einzige Grund, warum er das Reisen als nicht besonders attraktiv empfand. Pauli saß nicht gerne im Flugzeug. „Es ist nicht so, dass mich Flugangst plagt. Ich habe einen hochempfindlichen Gleichgewichtssinn, das macht das Fliegen für mich sehr unangenehm", erklärte Pauli.

Trotz dieser Unannehmlichkeiten ging es für Pauli volles Programm weiter. Bei den folgenden EM-Läufen in Deutschland holte er zwei Gesamtsiege, einen diesseits und den anderen jenseits des Eisernen Vorhangs. Bei der DDR-Rallye schieden die Alpine von Piot und Vinatier aus, so blieb Teamkollege Sobieslaw Zasada im 911 L (Gruppe 2) als einziger Konkurrent übrig. Toivonen gewann im 911 T (Gruppe 3) alle zwölf Prüfungen und die Rallye. Bei der Rallye Wiesbaden waren dieselben Hauptdarsteller. Die Rallye wurde zu zwei Dritteln in der Tschechoslowakei ausgetragen, und sie hatte 60 Prozent Schotter- und 40 Prozent Asphaltanteil. Und wieder war Toivonen schneller als Zasada, Piot und Vinatier. Porsche war mit seiner Strategie erfolgreich, die 911er in unterschiedlichen Gruppen einzusetzen. Alpine hingegen verspielte den zweiten Platz dadurch, dass beide Autos in der Gruppe 3 genannt waren und sich somit gegenseitig Strafen einbrachten. Vinatier handelte sich eigentlich keine Strafzeiten ein – außer auf den Prüfungen, wo Piot schneller war als er.

That was where the Briton would be spending most of his season, leaving Toivonen as Porsche's main man in rallies. Pauli took the same 911 T used in Monte Carlo to the Sanremo Rally (previously Rally dei Fiori) and shook off the Alpines of Jean-François Piot, Jean Vinatier and Jean-Pierre Nicolas to take a commanding win. "Losing the sump guard early in the event was our only problem", he reported, well pleased with the result. "It could have been worse…" Can you hear that tinge of confidence?

Toivonen may have dropped hints of a desire to retire from full-time driving, but 1968 was becoming his busiest season ever. As mentioned earlier, Pauli liked to stay at home with his family, but this was not the only reason that often made travelling a less than attractive prospect. He did not like flying. "It's not that I'm afraid in an airplane, but I have supersensitive balance, which makes it very unpleasant for me to sit in one", he explained.

Forgetting such discomforts, Pauli carried on with his hectic campaign. He next took back-to-back victories in the two German rounds of the European Drivers Championship, held on opposite sides of the Iron Curtain. First came the DDR Rally, where the Alpines of Piot and Vinatier dropped out leaving just Porsche teammate Sobieslaw Zasada in a Group 2 911 L to threaten Pauli's Group 3 911 T. Toivonen was fastest on all twelve special stages. The chief protagonists were the same in the Deutschland Rally, also known as Wiesbaden Rally, where two thirds of the competitive mileage lay on Czechoslovakian terrain. There was a split of 60% gravel, 40% asphalt, and again Toivonen outpaced Zasada, Piot and Vinatier. Porsche stuck to its policy of running its cars in different classes (with Pauli using Elford's victorious 911 T from the Monte), while Alpine-Renault missed out on second place by putting both its entries in the same one, which meant Piot's faster stage times made penalties for Vinatier, who otherwise had an unpenalised run on the road.

Seltene Niederlage: Toivonen führte die Akropolis Rallye 1968 an, hatte aber Probleme bei einem Reifenwechsel und so triumphierte Ford.
The one that got away. Toivonen led the Acropolis Rally in 1968, but damage from a puncture allowed Ford to triumph instead.

Martti Tiukkanen war seit Herbst 1967 der neue Copilot von Toivonen. Tiukkanen saß auch beim Gewinn des EM-Titels 1968 meist neben Pauli.

Martti Tiukkanen had joined Toivonen late in 1967 and shared much of his success during the European Championship season of 1968.

Alpine trat nicht bei der Akropolis Rallye an, wo sich die Porsche-Gegnerschaft aus Ford, Lancia und BMC zusammensetzte. Der neue Escort Twin Cam zeigte von Beginn an großes Potenzial, dennoch setzte sich Toivonen wenig überraschend von den Ford ab, bis er bei 165 km/h hinten einen Reifenschaden erlitt. Steinschläge deformierten den Aufnahmepunkt des Wagenhebers so stark, dass der Wagenheber nur mit viel Mühe benutzt werden konnte. Toivonen verlor über vier Minuten und damit auch den Sieg, der an Roger Clark im Escort TC ging, gefolgt von Zasadas Porsche.

Selbst jetzt widmete sich Pauli Toivonen nicht zu 100 Prozent dem Rallyefahren. Zu Beginn des neuen Jahres kehrte er zum Wihuri-Konzern zurück. Diesmal arbeitete Pauli aber nicht für den VW/Porsche-Importeur sondern für das Händlernetz der Rootes-Gruppe, das auch den Wihuris gehörte. Pauli und Antti Aarnio-Wihuri waren wieder dicke Kumpels, sie teilten sich sogar AAWs Porsche Carrera 6 beim 1000-Kilometer-Rennen auf dem Nürburgring, wo sie nach halber Strecke auf Platz 13 liegend ausfielen. Pauli war bekannt wie nie zuvor, und das wollte AAW natürlich nutzen. Also lud er Pauli und Vic Elford für zwei Rennen nach Finnland ein und ließ beide in Gruppe-2-Porsche-911 gegeneinander antreten. Zwischen den Rennen wurden die Autos getauscht. Pauli gewann den Auftakt in Ahvenisto, aber in Keimola drehte Elford den Spieß herum. Trotzdem war Vic nur Zweiter hinter Olli Lyytikäinen in einem älteren 911er. „Ich erinnere mich noch, wie großzügig Antti war. Er lud mich ein und nahm mich danach sogar mit auf eine Tour über die Seenlandschaft in seinem Wasserflugzeug, das er selbst flog", beschreibt Elford seine zwei Wochen im hohen Norden.

The Alpines did not tackle the Acropolis Rally, where works teams from Ford, Lancia and BMC provided the challenge to Porsche. The new Escort Twin Cams had shown great promise immediately, but it was still hardly a surprise that Toivonen began to pull out a lead on them until he suffered a rear puncture at 165 kph. Hitting rocks had damaged the jacking point under the Porsche and made it difficult to operate the jack so that over four minutes were lost changing the wheel. This cost Pauli the win and he ended up third behind Roger Clark's Escort TC and Zasada's Porsche.

Even now, Pauli Toivonen was not 100% committed to rally driving. Early in the New Year he had gone back to work for the Wihuri corporation, albeit not with the VW/Porsche importer this time, but with another of the group's automobile dealerships representing the Rootes marque. So, Pauli and Antti Aarnio-Wihuri were buddies again and even shared the latter's Porsche Carrera 6 in the Nürburgring 1000 km, where they retired just after half-distance while holding thirteenth overall. With Pauli's profile at an all-time high, AAW was keen to exploit it and invited Vic Elford to race for him on Finnish circuits. Each man was given one of AAW's Group 2 Porsche 911s to drive, with the cars swapped between a first race in Ahvenisto and a second one in Keimola. Pauli emerged victorious in the Ahvenisto encounter, but Vic turned the tables on him in Keimola, although he still only finished second as Olli Lyytikäinen beat both of them in an older 911. "I remember Antti's generosity in inviting me, and especially in taking me on a trip around the lakes afterwards in his seaplane that he piloted himself", says Elford of his fortnight spent in the north.

Pauli Toivonen Der Champion / Champion

Bei der Donau-Rallye hatte Toivonen keine richtigen Gegner in Werkswagen, dennoch war die Veranstaltung keine einfache Angelegenheit. „Die Straßen gehörten zu den schlimmsten, auf denen ich je Rallye gefahren bin", berichtete der Sieger. „Der Start war in Regensburg, dann gab es eine WP in Österreich, eine in der Tschechoslowakei und eine in Ungarn. Die letzten acht waren in Rumänien. Wir fuhren auf allen Prüfungen Bestzeit, litten aber unter starken Unterkühlungen!" Pauli fuhr als erstes Auto und raste in eine geschlossene Bahnschranke, die die Frontscheibe des Porsche zerstörte. „Wir mussten uns beeilen und fuhren mit 150 km/h im strömenden Regen einige Stunden ohne Scheibe. Selbst mit einer neuen Scheibe und Heizung an waren wir nach zwölf Stunden noch nass."

Eine Woche später saß Toivonen wieder in einem Rennwagen. Beim Straßenrennen von Mugello holte er mit Erich Bitter im Porsche Carrera 6 Platz Vier und den Klassensieg. In Gedanken war Pauli aber schon bei der 1000 Seen. Zu Hause zählte nichts anderes als ein Sieg. Beim Training gab es sogar Zeit für die Familie – vor allem für Henri. „Anfangs haben wir uns zu viert in den Porsche gequetscht, aber irgendwann wurden meine Mutter und ich abgesetzt, um im Wald Beeren zu pflücken", beschreibt Harri. „Henri wollte uns nicht im Auto haben, er ist geistig komplett in das Training eingetaucht."

Paulis Stammbeifahrer seit der letzten Tour de Corse war Martti Tiukkanen, ein ruhiger und bescheidener junger Mann, den er aus VW-Zeiten kannte. Tiukkanen musste einige Rallyes wegen Rückenbeschwerden auslassen, kehrte zur Donau-Rallye aber zurück. Er erinnert sich an die hohe Erwartungshaltung vor der 1000 Seen Rallye: „Pauli setzte sich selbst stark unter Druck. Er hatte sich offensichtlich mental auf die Saison mit Porsche vorbereitet. Pauli wertete den zweiten Platz bei der Monte eindeutig als Niederlage."

„Und dann hat uns Leo Kinnunen im AAW-Porsche auf der Auftaktprüfung der 1000 Seen geschlagen. Es war weniger als eine Sekunde, aber es hat Pauli richtig geärgert! Auf der nächsten WP sind wir nach 600 Metern fast abgeflogen. Ich sagte, er solle lieber langsam das Tempo erhöhen und er wurde dann auch etwas ruhiger." Toivonen/Tiukkanen gingen kurz darauf in Führung, hatten auf WP Sechs aber einen Reifenschaden bei Highspeed. „Der Bauer muss gedacht haben: ‚Was bekomme ich denn heute für eine Lieferung'", beschrieb Pauli. „Wir haben seinen Briefkasten abgeräumt und sind rückwärts auf sein Haus zugerast. Wir kamen erst kurz vor der Tür zum Stehen." Von da an ging es keinen Meter weiter.

On the Danube Rally, Toivonen did not face any real works opposition, but it was still not plain sailing for him. "Those were some of the worst roads I've ever rallied on", reported the winner on his return from Romania. "The start was from Regensburg, followed by one stage in Austria, one in Czechoslovakia and one in Hungary with the remaining eight in Romania. We were fastest on all of them, but came close to hypothermia!" Running first car on the road, Pauli had crashed into a closed railway level-crossing gate, which broke the Porsche's windscreen. "We had to hurry and carry on for a couple of hours without it at about 150 kph in teeming rain. Even with a new screen and the heater on, that still kept us wet for another twelve hours."

Just one week later, Toivonen was racing again in a Porsche Carrera 6 and, partnered by Erich Bitter, he finished fourth in the Mugello road race, the pair winning their class. But the main focus was already shifting towards the 1000 Lakes Rally. At home nothing short of victory would do for Pauli. This was an opportunity to share some of the recce period with the family – above all with Henri. "We'd all squeeze into the Porsche at first, but soon I'd be dropped off with mum to pick berries in the forest for a day", says Harri. "Henri did not want us in the car, because he just immersed himself in Dad's practicing!"

Pauli's main co-driver since the previous year's Tour de Corse had been Martti Tiukkanen, a quiet, unassuming young man known to him since the VW years. Sidelined for a couple of rallies because of back trouble, Tiukkanen had returned for the Danube Rally and well remembers the weight of expectation before the 1000 Lakes: "Pauli really was putting pressure on himself. He had obviously been mentally building up for that season with Porsche. He clearly viewed second place in Monte Carlo as a defeat."

"Then on the opening 1000 Lakes stage we were beaten by Leo Kinnunen in AAW's Porsche. It was by less than a second, but boy did that upset Pauli! We very nearly had an off after just 600 metres of the next stage. I suggested he could take his time to build up the speed and he did calm down a bit." Toivonen and Tiukkanen soon seized the lead, but after half-a-dozen stages suffered a puncture at high speed. "The farmer must have thought he was getting a special delivery", Pauli reflected. "We took out his mailbox and were fast approaching his house backwards. Stopped just short of his door!" They went no further.

 1968

In den 60er-Jahren rührte Castrol kräftig die Werbetrommel für die Donau-Rallye. Dazu zählten auch PR-Termine mit Starpiloten wie Toivonen.

Castrol did a lot to promote the Danube Rally in the sixties. It meant PR functions for star drivers like Toivonen.

Der größte Gegner von Toivonen/Tiukkanen bei der Donau-Rallye waren die Bedingungen, die durch anhaltenden Regen zusätzlich erschwert wurden.
Prime opposition for Toivonen and Tiukkanen in the Danube Rally came from the weather conditions. Persistent rain did not help.

Der geplante Start im Porsche bei der Coupe des Alpes wurde abgesagt – eine Erleichterung für Pauli, der sich darüber beschwerte, zu wenig Zeit für seine Büroarbeit zu haben. Aber es gab noch ein paar wichtige Läufe in seinem Terminkalender. Der erste war die RACE Rallye im Oktober, die nur der Markeneuropameisterschaft angehörte und nicht der Fahrer-EM. Alpine-Pilot Jean-François Piot und sein Beifahrer Jean Todt rechneten offensichtlich nicht mit Toivonen, sie konnten den Finnen nicht vom Sieg abhalten. In Spanien sprang Urpo Vihervaara, ein Spezialist für Navigationsfahrten, für Stamm-Co Martti Tiukkanen ein: „Ich hatte keine Angst vor dem Fahren, nur vor Paulis Ruf! Aber wir haben uns gut verstanden. Das Training war sehr gründlich, elf bis 16 Stunden am Tag. Pauli trainierte eine Prüfung, die dem Alpine sehr gut lag, besonders hart, und es hat funktioniert. Unsere Zeit auf dieser WP war für die ein psychologischer Schlag ins Gesicht. Ich weiß noch: Im Ziel waren meine Beine taub, weil ich unterbewusst die ganze Zeit mit beiden Füßen gebremst habe!"

Danach musste sich Pauli sputen, um von Spanien zur Rallye de Genève zu kommen. Trotz verkürztem Training behielt Toivonen die Oberhand gegenüber Jean Vinatier. Der Finne führte nach der letzten WP mit 38 Sekunden, als der Alpine wegen einer defekten Antriebswelle ausfiel. Somit gewann Pauli locker vor den Alfa Romeo GTA von Lucien Bianchi und Guy Verrier. Die Finnen waren ein wenig verwirrt von den Organisatoren, die Zeitkontrollen einfach verlegten. „Auf einer Wertungsprüfung haben wir angehalten und Pauli hat sogar seinen Helm abgenommen, bis uns wild gestikulierende Zuschauer zu der Erkenntnis brachten, dass das Ziel 100 Meter weiter war", erklärt Vihervaara.

Pauli hatte nun den Titel in der Fahrer-EM gewonnen, dennoch wurde er von Porsche zur Tour de Corse geschickt, wo Vic Elford ins Team zurückkehrte. Beide Fahrer erhielten den furchteinflößenden Porsche 911 R mit 250 PS, der in der Prototypenklasse startete. Während Elford direkt nach dem Start ausfiel, fuhr Pauli mit gewohntem Elan weiter. Auf der ersten WP hatte er noch das Nachsehen gegenüber den Alpine, aber dann markierte er drei Bestzeiten in Folge und lag zur Halbzeitpause auf Siegkurs. Leider verhinderte eine defekte Kraftübertragung, dass Toivonen seine fantastische Saison mit einem weiteren Sieg krönen konnte.

Porsche's proposed entry to the Coupe des Alpes was cancelled, which came as a relief for Pauli, who was complaining of not having enough time for work in the office. However, important rallies still remained in his calendar. First of them was the Spanish R.A.C.E. Rally in October. This was a qualifying round for the Makes, not the Drivers series, and apparently Jean-François Piot had not expected to face Toivonen in Spain. Co-driven by Jean Todt, the Frenchman did his best, but could not stop the Finn collecting yet another win. Standing in for Martti Tiukkanen in Spain was Urpo Vihervaara, a specialist of navigational events: "The ride did not frighten me, but Pauli's reputation did! We got on fine, though. The recce was very thorough, eleven to sixteen hours a day. Pauli practiced especially hard on one stage that he felt would favour Alpine and it worked. Our time on that one was a psychological blow to them. At the finish my legs were numb, though, because I'd subconsciously been pushing a brake pedal with both!"

There was a rush to get to the Rally de Genève from Spain, which reduced the recce for that event. It did not matter. Toivonen generally had the upper hand over Jean Vinatier and was leading by thirty-eight seconds, when the Alpine was sidelined with a broken driveshaft after the last stage. This left Pauli an easy winner from the Alfa Romeo GTAs of Lucien Bianchi and Guy Verrier. The Finns were a bit bemused by the rally organisation, which kept changing the location of time controls. "On one stage we stopped and Pauli even took off his helmet before gesticulating spectators made him understand the finish was 100 metres further down the road", explained Vihervaara.

Pauli Toivonen had now clinched the European Drivers Championship, but was still sent by Porsche to the Tour de Corse, where Vic Elford was back with the team. Here, the drivers were supplied with fearsome Porsche 911 Rs, running in the prototype class with nearly 250 bhp. Elford was sidelined as soon as the event got underway, but Pauli carried on with his now habitual panache. Having been beaten on the first special stage by the Alpines he then set fastest times on the next three and, at the half-way point, seemed poised to win. Sadly, transmission failure stopped him from crowning a fantastic season with yet another victory.

Pauli Toivonen Der Champion / Champion

Der EM-Titel war nach der Monte-Niederlage eine Wiedergutmachung für Pauli, aber er wagte noch einen Versuch bei der „Mutter aller Rallyes" – in einem von drei Porsche-Werkswagen. Dank seiner Erfahrung standen die Chancen auf den Sieg auch 1969 recht gut, aber Toivonen hatte vom Start an Probleme. Auf Spikes war er auf der Auftakt-WP Saint Auban der schnellste Porsche-Pilot, aber die Nägel funktionierten auf dem nassen Eis der folgenden Prüfungen nicht. Toivonen rutschte in die Botanik und die Reifen zeigten danach in alle Himmelsrichtungen. Das Handling war katastrophal, was zu weiteren Ausrutschern und letztlich auch zum Aus führte.

In Finnland herrschte große Begeisterung über die Nachricht, dass Toivonen nach einigen Jahren wieder an der Hanki Rallye teilnehmen würde. Pauli bekam einen Gruppe-2-Porsche von AAW und war damit natürlich Favorit. Pauli selbst klopfte einen seiner markanten Sprüche: „Ich erwarte nicht viel von der Hanki Rallye. Mit einem Sieg wäre ich schon zufrieden!" Dass er am Ende nur Dritter wurde hinter einem Saab und einem Renault, war ein kleiner Schock. Fairerweise muss man aber sagen, dass die Bedingungen mit tiefem Schnee auf schmalen Straßen nicht gerade ideal waren für einen Porsche.

Bei der Targa Florio erhielt Pauli seine zweite Chance, den Porsche 911 R zu bewegen. Toivonen teilte sich das Auto mit Dieter Spoerry und beeindruckte im Anfangsstint mit einem guten zwölften Platz, bis ihn in der dritten Runde ein Feuer im Motorraum zur Aufgabe zwang. So musste Pauli den langen Weg in die Box zu Fuß vollenden.

Im Mai war Pauli viel unterwegs, schließlich musste er auch noch das Training zur Akropolis im Kalender unterbringen. Pauli und Beifahrer Martti Kolari arbeiteten 16 bis 18 Stunden am Tag und spulten 5.000 Kilometer auf schlechten Schotterstraßen ab. Bei der Rallye fuhren sie einen 911 S, den Porsche nach Paulis Meinung besser bei einer sanften Asphaltrallye eingesetzt hätte. Das Fahrwerk lag bedenklich tief und der Motor war zu stark getunt. Den drei Porsche standen ebenso viele Ford gegenüber, man musste also von Beginn an attackieren. Toivonen übernahm früh die Führung und fuhr dem aufstrebenden Porsche-Star Björn Waldegård ohne Probleme davon. Als Paulis Motor an Leistung verlor, musste er jedoch dem Escort von Ove Andersson den Vortritt lassen. In der zweiten Rallyehälfte überschlug sich Andersson und war draußen, wodurch Pauli uneinholbar an der Spitze lag. Der zweitplatzierte Roger Clark im Ford lag nach einem Ausrutscher meilenweit zurück. Dieses Polster erwies sich am Ende als enorm wichtig, weil Toivonens Motor aus dem letzten Loch pfiff und nur noch bis 5.000 Touren drehte. Auf der

The European title was certainly a vindication for Pauli, but he still wanted to have one final go in Monte Carlo. With his experience, chances of victory as a member of a three-car Porsche team seemed at least reasonably good, but in 1969 Toivonen was in trouble nearly from the start. Lightly studded tyres were good for the opening Saint Auban stage and enabled him to be fastest of the Porsches, but they did not work later on wet ice. Toivonen visited the scenery, which left the car's wheels pointing in different directions. The handling went awry, leading to more offs and eventually retirement.

In Finland great excitement was caused by the news that Toivonen would be driving in the Hankiralli after an absence of a couple of years. His mount would be a Group 2 Porsche from AAW's stable, which automatically made him pre-event favourite. The man himself came up with a classic quote: "I'm not expecting much at all from Hankiralli, I'll be happy just to win!" It was a bit of a shock that he could only come third behind a Saab and a Renault, but in fairness, the conditions were hardly ideal for the German car, with deep snow on many narrow stages.

A second chance to experience Porsche's 911 R was given to Pauli at the Targa Florio. Sharing with Dieter Spoerry, Pauli took the opening stint and was impressing onlookers in a good twelfth overall, when a fire in the car's engine compartment put him out on lap three, leaving the driver with a long trek back to the pits.

May was a busy month, since a recce for the Acropolis Rally had to be fitted in as well. Working as much as sixteen to eighteen hours a day, Pauli and co-driver Martti Kolari covered 5,000 kilometres on an exceptionally rough route. In fact, the 911 S models Porsche used for this event would, in Pauli's opinion, have been better prepared for a smooth tarmac rally. Their ground clearance was precariously low and the engines were perhaps too highly tuned. Three Porsches were challenged by as many cars from Ford, which meant it was hard to keep anything in reserve. Toivonen seized an early lead and notably left emergent Porsche star Björn Waldegård behind with apparent ease. His engine soon started to lose power, however, and Ove Andersson took command in a Ford. But as the rally entered its latter half, the Swede rolled into retirement and Pauli found himself with an unassailable lead. Towards the end he was miles ahead of Ford's Roger Clark, who had lost a chunk of time with an off. The buffer was useful indeed, as Toivonen's engine was on its last legs and could only

Björn Waldegård war das aufstrebende Talent bei Porsche. Bei der Akropolis 1969 hatte aber Altstar Toivonen die Nase vorn und beendete seine Werksfahrerkarriere mit einem schönen Sieg.

Björn Waldegård was the coming man of Porsche's rally team, but Toivonen managed to contain him in Greece in 1969 to cap his works career with a fine win.

Pauli fuhr einen Porsche 911 R bei der Targa Florio, gegenüberliegende Seite, und der Tour de Corse. Beide Male war er unglaublich schnell, schied aber jeweils aus.

Pauli got to drive a Porsche 911 R in both Targa Florio, opposite page, and Tour de Corse. Both times he was spectacularly fast, but failed to finish.

1969

Pauli Toivonen Der Champion / Champion

Nach dem verpassten Sieg im Vorjahr leistete Pauli Toivonen bei der Akropolis 1969 Wiedergutmachung und beendete seine Karriere mit einem weiteren Höhepunkt.

After the disappointment of 1968, it was fitting that Pauli Toivonen should win the 1969 Acropolis Rally and walk away from works level participation on a high.

letzten WP auf dem Flugplatz von Tatoi stotterte der Boxermotor mit 2.000 Touren vor sich hin. Aber Pauli hatte es geschafft: Er hatte die Akropolis Rallye gewonnen, und das bei seinem letzten Einsatz in einem Werkswagen.

Im Sommer übergab das Porsche-Werk einen 908 Spyder an das Racing Team AAW. Der erste Auftritt war das Straßenrennen von Mugello, wo sich Toivonen das Cockpit mit Gérard Larrousse teilen sollte. Vor dem Rennen hatte das Team Probleme mit der Kupplung, weswegen Larrousse im Training keine einzige Runde fahren konnte. Damit durfte er nicht am Rennen teilnehmen und Pauli stand nun als Einzelfahrer da. „Pauli war ganz der Macho und sagte, er würde die Distanz locker meistern", erinnert sich Teamchef Hannu Kahi. Im Qualifying erreichte er Platz Fünf, aber nach dem ersten Stint war Toivonen vollkommen erschöpft. „Er musste aus dem Auto herausgehoben werden. Er ist den 908 quer gefahren wie ein Rallyeauto, das hat ihn ausgelaugt. Das Rennen gewann Arturo Merzario als Einzelfahrer. Als Pauli gesehen hat, wie der kleine Arturo quicklebendig aus seinem Abarth gehüpft ist, hat er sich richtig geschämt", schmunzelt Kahi. Mugello war eines der wenigen Male, dass die Toivonen-Familie Pauli ins Ausland begleitete, um ihn fahren zu sehen. Pauli war sehr um das Wohl seiner Liebsten bemüht. „Wir standen in einer Sperrzone und die Carabinieri kamen, um uns da wegzujagen. Pauli wurde richtig sauer, ging mit seinem Gesicht ganz nah an das des Polizisten heran und brüllte: ‚Das ist meine Frau! Fass' sie bloß nicht an!'", erinnert sich Ulla mit einem Lächeln.

Kurz darauf wagte Toivonen einen weiteren Versuch im 908. In Hockenheim wurde er Siebter hinter diversen Lola, Porsche und Alfa Romeo. Danach gab es einen privaten Test in Keimola, bei dem Leo Kinnunen eindeutig schneller war als Pauli. In diesem Moment beschloss er, das Rennfahren in Prototypen bleiben zu lassen.

Zumindest fast. 1970 machte sich das Racing Team AAW in der Sportwagen-Weltmeisterschaft einen Namen, wo es das Erfolgsduo Hans „Hasse" Laine und Gijs van Lennep einsetzte. Nach einigen

be revved to 5,000 rpm. In the last test on Tatoi airfield, it came close to expiring and was reduced to a trickle at just 2,000 rpm. But Pauli had done it; he had conquered the Acropolis Rally in what was to be his last event in a works car.

Later in the summer one of the Porsche 908 Spyders was released from the factory to AAW Racing Team. Their first outing with it was the classic Mugello road race, where Gérard Larrousse was recruited to share it with Toivonen. The team had worries with the 908's clutch, which prevented Larrousse from completing a single lap in practice. It meant he did not qualify for the race and Pauli was left without a co-driver. "Pauli was very macho about it and said he could easily do the whole distance", recalls team manager Hannu Kahi. He qualified well in fifth, but was totally spent after the first stint. "He had to be lifted from the car. He'd driven the 908 sideways, like a rally car, which simply wore him out. The race was won by Arturo Merzario, driving solo, and when Pauli saw little Art bounce out from his Abarth fresh as a daisy, he was so embarrassed", chuckles Kahi. Mugello had been a rare opportunity for the whole Toivonen family to watch the father race abroad and Pauli made sure of their wellbeing. The memory brings a smile to Ulla Toivonen's face: "I remember we'd been standing in a prohibited area and the Carabinieri came to chase us out. Pauli got upset and, putting his face inches from the policeman's, shouted: 'This is my woman! Do not touch her!'"

There was one more try in the 908 shortly afterwards in Hockenheim, where Toivonen finished seventh behind assorted Lolas, Porsches and Alfa Romeos. But when Leo Kinnunen proved conclusively faster in a private test session in Keimola, Pauli realized it was time to forget about racing prototypes.

Well, almost. In 1970, Racing Team AAW was making a name for itself in the International Championship for Makes, where it ran the very rapid pair of Hans "Hasse" Laine and Gijs van Lennep. After several impressive finishes the team decided to field no less than

beeindruckenden Resultaten beschloss das Team, beim 1000-Kilometer-Rennen auf dem Nürburgring nicht weniger als drei Autos einzusetzen. Pauli Toivonen wurde ins Boot geholt und saß beim Training in einem Porsche 917.

Das Samstagstraining war fast vorbei, als Pauli völlig niedergeschlagen in die Box kam. „Da draußen brennt ein Auto. Ich glaube, es ist Hasse", sagte er zu Teamchef Kahi. Der Porsche 908 ist auf einer der Kuppen nach der langen Geraden im Streckenabschnitt Tiergarten abgehoben, ist auf dem Dach gelandet und dabei sofort in Flammen aufgegangen. Für den 26-jährigen Finnen gab es keine Chance zu überleben. Es war ein gewaltiger Schock für die kleine AAW-Mannschaft. Zwei Nennungen wurden gestrichen, aber der 911 S nahm am Rennen teil. Toivonen und Dieter Fröhlich gewannen darin die GT-Klasse auf Platz 14 der Gesamtwertung. „Mein Vater rief an dem Samstag an und sagte, dass alles in Ordnung sei", erinnert sich Harri Toivonen. „Er sollte eigentlich den 908 fahren und war besorgt, dass falsche Meldungen über den Unfall zu Hause für Verwirrung und Angst sorgten."

Paulis ernsthafte Motorsportkarriere war damit endgültig vorbei. In seiner Rolle als Marketingleiter des finnischen Rootes-Importeurs trieb er die Entwicklung des Sunbeam Imp für den Motorsport voran und versuchte, so die Verkäufe anzukurbeln. Zu diesem Zweck gab er dem jungen Markku Alén 1970 ein Auto für die finnische Eisrennmeisterschaft. Markku gewann zwei Läufe und den Titel in der Klasse bis ein Liter Hubraum, Pauli holte sich den anderen Sieg und den Vizetitel.

In der Firma ließ Pauli wieder einmal seine Muskeln spielen, manchmal kratzte er sogar an der Autorität von AAW. Seit 1969 gab es immer wieder Gerüchte, dass ein AMC Javelin importiert werden sollte, damit ihn Pauli in der stärksten Klasse der finnischen Rennmeisterschaft fahren konnte. Hannu Kahi bekam die Story hautnah mit. „Pauli gab eine Bestellung für das Auto in den USA auf. Aber als AAW die Dokumente sah, riss er sie in Stücke!"

three cars in the Nürburgring 1000 km classic. Pauli Toivonen was drafted back into the fold and ended up practicing a Porsche 917!

With Saturday practice nearly over Pauli arrived back in the pits, glum-faced. "There's a car on fire, I think it is Hasse", he said to team manager Kahi. The Porsche 908 had got airborne from one of the crests on the long straight after Tiergarten, flipped and landed upside down, immediately catching fire. The 26-year-old Finn perished in the inferno. It was an immense shock to the small AAW outfit. They scratched two entries, but ran a Porsche 911 S in Sunday's race, Toivonen steeling himself to win the GT-class with Dieter Fröhlich in fourteenth place overall. "Dad had phoned us on the Saturday to say he was all right", Harri Toivonen remembers. "He was originally down to drive that 908 and worried that initial reports of the accident might be confused and cause anxiety back home."

The serious competition career of Pauli Toivonen was effectively over. In his role as the marketing manager for the Rootes importer in Finland, he had been typically active in developing Sunbeam Imps for the sport and promoting their sales. That led to him offering young Markku Alén a car to drive in the 1970 Finnish ice-racing series. Markku won twice and became champion in the under 1-litre class, while Pauli took the other win to end up second.

Pauli was obviously flexing his muscles in the company, maybe even to the extent of sometimes challenging AAW's authority. From 1969 there had been an enduring rumour about an AMC Javelin that was going to be imported for him to race in the big class of the Finnish Championship. Hannu Kahi witnessed the story unfold: "Pauli was placing an order for a car from the States, but when AAW saw the papers, he just tore them up!"

Der tragische Tod von Hans Laine (Mitte) war ein großer Schock für AAW (links) und Pauli Toivonen (rechts).

The tragic fate of Hans Laine (centre) was an immense shock to both AAW (left) and Pauli Toivonen (right).

Henri (rechts) und Harri zeigten ein immer größeres Interesse am Beruf ihres Vaters.

Henri (right) and Harri took an ever increasing interest in Pauli's competition activities.

Pauli Toivonen Der Champion / Champion

Pauli fuhr diesen furchteinflößenden Porsche 917 beim Training zu den 1000 Kilometern Nürburgring. Das Auto wurde wegen Laines Unfall vor dem Rennen zurückgezogen.
Pauli Toivonen drove the fearsome Porsche 917 during practice of the Nürburgring 1000 kms. But the entry was withdrawn before the race due to Laine's accident.

Henri Toivonen

* 25. August 1956 in Jyväskylä, Finnland;
† 2. Mai 1986 in Corte, Korsika

*August 25, 1956 in Jyväskylä, Finland;
† May 2, 1986 in Corte, Corsica*

Henri Toivonen

Generationswechsel
Next generation

1971 gab es plötzlich zwei finnische Meister im Hause Toivonen. Während Pauli im Sunbeam Imp weiterhin die Ein-Liter-Klasse auf der Rennstrecke beherrschte, rückte Henri als aufstrebendes Talent ins Rampenlicht. Henri sicherte sich im Kart den A-Junioren-Titel. Im selben Jahr gewann übrigens ein gewisser Keijo „Keke" Rosberg die „große" finnische Kart-Meisterschaft. Keke nahm von dem Newcomer natürlich Notiz: „Jeder hat auf ihn geschaut. Schließlich war es der Sohn von Pauli Toivonen, der jetzt Rennen fuhr." Keke war damals 22 Jahre alt und auf dem Sprung in die Formel V. Sein größter Herausforderer hieß Antero Lindqvist, von dem wir später noch hören werden.

„Im Alter von neun Jahren fuhr Henri erstmals Auto", verbreitete Pauli mit Stolz. „Daran erinnere ich mich nicht mehr, aber es hätte mich auch nicht weiter gekümmert", sagt Ulla. „Das Autofahren war in unserem Haushalt so eine normale Sache. Die Jungs saßen immer auf etwas mit Rädern: Bobbycars, Kettcars oder eben richtige Karts." Zudem war es in Finnland nicht ungewöhnlich, dass Kinder die Autos ihrer Eltern noch vor ihrem zehnten Lebensjahr auf zugefrorenen Eisseen bewegten.

Mit dem Kart-Virus hatte sich Henri 1969 richtig infiziert. AAW hatte die Rennstrecke von Keimola übernommen und Pauli einmal gefragt, ob er bei einem Kartrennen dabei sein könnte, um die Pokale zu überreichen. Pauli nahm seine Jungs mit, und die Erfahrung war für sie eine Offenbarung. Harri war noch zu jung zum Kartfahren, aber es dauerte nicht lange, bis Henri den Sport ernsthaft betrieb. Dass er ein außerordentliches Talent besaß, war sofort offensichtlich. Für sein erstes Rennen lieh sich Henri das Go-Kart eines Freundes, der einige Jahre älter war. „Pauli bat mich, ein paar Runden vor Henri zu fahren, um ihm die Linie zu zeigen", erzählt der Jugendfreund. „Dann sollte ich ihn vorbei lassen und von hinten zuschauen. Aber da gab es nicht viel, was ich ihm beibringen konnte. Er war ein Naturtalent."

Zweiradfan! Mit diesem Moped fuhr Henri ab seinem 15. Lebensjahr zur Schule.

Moped menace! From the age of fifteen this was Henri's transport to school.

Antero Lindqvist wurde verpflichtet, um die Kart-Karriere der Toivonen-Brüder voranzutreiben.
Antero Lindqvist was the first person recruited to nurture the brothers' karting careers.

In 1971, there were suddenly two Finnish champions in the Toivonen family. Pauli was still busy with his Sunbeam Imps and ruled the 1-litre class on the circuits, but much attention was now focused on the talent of Henri, who won his first title in karting's A-junior class. In that same year, the national champion in the premier A-class was one Keijo "Keke" Rosberg. He did not fail to take notice of the newcomer. "Everybody was paying attention! It was after all the son of Pauli Toivonen now racing", quips Keke. On the verge of stepping up to Formula Vee, Keke was twenty-two years old, the same age as his nearest challenger Antero Lindqvist; more of him shortly.

"Henri first drove a car at the age of nine", Pauli used to proclaim with apparent pride. "I don't remember that, but I would not have paid much attention anyway", says Ulla. "It just seemed such a natural thing in our household. The boys were always driving something: pedal cars, pedal karts or real ones." It was not uncommon in Finland for kids not yet in their teens to tentatively try their parents' cars on ice, as all lakes get frozen over in the winter.

The karting bug really bit Henri hard at the turn of the decade. AAW had taken over the Keimola circuit in 1969 and on one occasion asked Pauli Toivonen to attend a karting event there to present the prizes. He took the boys along and the experience turned out to be a revelation for them. Harri was still too young to race karts, but it did not take long for Henri to get seriously into the sport. To all concerned it was immediately obvious that he was an exceptional talent. For his very first race, a kart was borrowed from a friend who was a couple of years older: "Pauli asked me to lead Henri for a couple of laps to show him the lines and then let him overtake and to watch from behind. There was nothing much to teach him, he was just a natural."

1971, in seiner ersten Meisterschaftssaison dominierte Henri Toivonen die Juniorenklasse nach Belieben, sein Punktevorsprung war gewaltig. 1972 wurde der 15-Jährige sogar offizielles Mitglied des Racing Team AAW. Die Mannschaft ließ Leo Kinnunen im Porsche 917/10 Turbo in der Interserie starten, Lasse Sirviö in der Formel Super V, Marcus Grönholms Vater Ulf bei Rallyes in einem Käfer, Pauli Toivonen bei finnischen Rennen – und eben Henri im Kartsport. „Henkka", unter diesem Spitznamen war Henri überall bekannt, bekam ein Kart und einen Mechaniker zur Verfügung gestellt. Der Mechaniker arbeitete eigentlich für den VW-Zweig der Wihuris. Pauli ließ einmal mehr seine Muskeln spielen und überzeugte AAW sogar davon, in Keimola eine eigene Kartbahn zu bauen. Dort verbrachte Henri natürlich sehr viel Zeit. Er schaffte es sogar, an der Rennstrecke seinen Konfirmandenunterricht zu verbringen. Diese Erfahrung teilte er übrigens mit Matti Alamäki, der in den 1980er-Jahren mehrfacher Rallyecross-Europameister wurde. „Henris Anfänge im Kart wurden mit großem Aufwand betrieben, dagegen fühlte ich mich provinziell", verrät Alamäki. „Damit möchte ich ihm aber nichts unterstellen. Er war unglaublich schnell." Ein weiterer Beweis: 1972 gewann Henri seinen zweiten Juniorentitel in Finnland, den Titel in Skandinavien und den Lapland Cup in Schweden. Die letzteren Triumphe sind erwähnenswert, weil die Kart-Kultur in Schweden deutlich weiter entwickelt war als in Finnland.

Der Lapland Cup bestand aus drei Läufen im dünn besiedelten Norden. Ein Freund von Henri erinnert sich an die Rivalität zwischen ihren Vätern, als Erster an der nächsten Strecke anzukommen. „Pauli besaß einen großen AMC Javelin als Zugfahrzeug für sein Wohnmobil. Ich habe nicht verstanden, warum wir so sehr in Eile waren, aber offensichtlich wollte er meinen Vater schlagen. Es endete damit, dass wir irgendwo falsch abgebogen und mitten in der Wildnis ohne Sprit gestrandet sind …"

In that first championship season of 1971, Henri Toivonen was a standout winner of the junior class with a points total way ahead of the opposition. For 1972 this 15-year-old became an official member of Racing Team AAW! The team ran Leo Kinnunen in the Interserie in a Porsche 917/10 Turbo, Lasse Sirviö in Formula SuperVee, Marcus Grönholm's father Ulf in rallies with a VW Beetle, Pauli in Finnish races … and Henri in karting. Henri – or "Henkka", as he was known by all and sundry in his home country – had a kart and mechanic supplied by the team. The mechanic had been commissioned into the sporting operation from Wihuri's VW business. Pauli had been flexing his muscles within the corporation and he even persuaded AAW that a purpose-built karting track was needed in Keimola. Henri subsequently spent a lot of time there. He even managed to arrange to go to confirmation classes at the circuit, actually sharing this experience with the young Matti Alamäki who was to become a multiple European rallycross champion in the 1980s. "Henri did his karting in style, which made me feel a bit provincial", admits Alamäki. "But I don't mean to take anything away from him. He was awesomely fast." To prove the point, in 1972 Henri secured another Finnish junior title as well as a Scandinavian one and won the Lapland Cup in Sweden. These last achievements were notable simply because karting culture in Sweden was way more advanced than in Finland.

The Lapland Cup consisted of three qualifying rounds in the sparsely populated north. A friend of Henri remembers how a rivalry developed between the contestants' fathers to be the first to arrive at the next venue. Alamäki picks up the story: "Pauli had a big AMC Javelin to tow the caravan. I could not understand why there had to be such a rush, but he obviously wanted to beat my dad. Somewhere along the way he ended up taking a wrong turn, however, and ran out of fuel in the wilderness …"

Pauli war für seine sorgfältige Kleiderwahl bekannt. Im Kart-Fahrerlager konnte es aber auch mal locker zugehen. Der Anzug von Henri (Zweiter von links) hingegen passt wie angegossen.

Pauli was known to be pin-sharp with his dress code, but this could apparently be relaxed in a karting paddock. Henri (second from left) certainly seems properly attired.

Henri Toivonen Generationswechsel / Next generation

Henri war Nachwuchspilot des berühmten Racing Team AAW, das der finnische VW-Importeur leitete.
Henri was a junior member of the famous Racing Team AAW, set up by Finland's VW importer.

„In der Anfangszeit gab es keine speziellen Schuhe zum Kartfahren. Also haben wir ein Paar Ringerschuhe für Henri zurechtgeschnitten", erinnert sich Erja.

"In the early days they didn't make special boots for karting, so a pair was tailored for Henri from wrestling boots", Erja recalls.

Die Väter von Kartfahrern sind eine sehr eigene Spezies, die besonders berüchtigt sind, wenn sie sich dem Hobby ihrer Sprösslinge zu intensiv widmen. Pauli war in dieser Hinsicht sicherlich keine Ausnahme, sein Temperament brachte ihn manchmal in Schwierigkeiten. „Die Menschen reden immer über ‚Muttertiere' und wie sie ihre Kleinen beschützen. Ich sag' euch eins: Wenn diese Beschreibung jemals zu einer Person gepasst hat, dann zu Pauli. Trotz seines Geschlechts", sagt Ulla mit Nachdruck.

Es gab aber nicht nur den Pauli, der wollte, dass seine Söhne gut sind. Es gab auch jenen Pauli, dem die Gefahren des Motorsports durchaus bewusst waren. Zu Beginn von Henris Karriere offenbarte er seine Bedenken über ihre Zukunft als Rennfahrer: „Die Formel V ist wahrscheinlich noch sicher genug – nicht zu schnell –, aber ich würde die Jungs nicht gerne in der Formel 1 oder 2 sehen, von einem Prototypen ganz zu schweigen." Pauli hielt Henri und Harri an der kurzen Leine. 1973 durfte sein jüngerer Sohn auch offizielle Rennen bestreiten und so kam es, dass der Toivonen-Nachwuchs zusammen an einem Langstreckenrennen in Keimola teilnahm. „Das Training war samstags und Pauli setzte ihnen eine Frist: Sie mussten vor 9 Uhr abends zu Hause sein, sonst …", erinnert sich ein Freund. „Aus irgendeinem Grund waren die Jungs abends zu spät, und am Sonntag tauchten sie nicht auf. Pauli hatte sie einfach unter Hausarrest gestellt." In einem Punkt gab es auf jeden Fall keine Bedenken bei Henri: Er trainierte sehr gewissenhaft. Diese Eigenschaft hatte er vielleicht von seinem Vater gelernt, aber die Leute merkten ihm auch eine große Motivation an. „Er trainierte sogar spät abends. Wenn wir beispielsweise Eislaufen waren, dann trainierte Henri das Autofahren einfach danach", erzählt ein Freund. „Und er war ein harter Gegner. Er hat dir keine Lücke gelassen. Einmal starteten wir beide aus der ersten Reihe, ich stand auf Pole. Henri kam vor dem Start zu mir und sagte, dass ich ihm in der ersten Kurve besser Platz mache, sonst würde er mich abschießen. Das war keine Feindseligkeit, wir waren schließlich gute Freunde, es war nur Henris Art, seine Einsatzbereitschaft zu zeigen."

"Karting fathers" are notoriously a breed of their own and they are often viewed as an infamous one if they get too involved with their offspring's hobby. Pauli was certainly no exception and his temperament sometimes got him in trouble. "People always talk about 'tiger mothers' and how they're protective towards their cubs. Well I'll tell you, if ever there was a person fitting this description, that was Pauli, gender notwithstanding", says Ulla emphatically.

It was not just that Pauli wanted his sons to do well; there was another side to this, too. He was deeply conscious of the dangers involved in the sport. Quite early in Henri's karting career he admitted his concern about a future in racing. "A Formula Vee is probably still safe enough – not too fast – but I would not like to see the boys in Formula One or Two, or even in a prototype," he professed. He kept Henri and Harri in tight rein. By 1973 his younger son could also race in official competitions and one weekend both Toivonen lads were going to take part in an endurance kart race in Keimola. "Practice was on Saturday and Pauli had set the boys a curfew: they had to be back home by 9 pm or else", recalls a friend. "For some reason they were late and guess what – they failed to turn up at all on Sunday. Pauli had imposed house arrest on them!" On one account at least there should have been no worries about Henri. He practised conscientiously. This may have been a trait picked up from his father, but people also recognized an immense motivation in him. "He'd even do it late at night. If we went skating, for example, Henri would still go and practice driving afterwards", a friend reveals. "And he was a fierce competitor. He just did not leave any margins at all. One time we started a race from the front row with me on pole. Henri came to me before the start to say that I should leave room for him in the first corner, or he'd take me out. There was no animosity, we were quite close, but it was simply an expression of his commitment and ambition."

Antero Lindqvist (links) wurde vom Kart-Mechaniker zu Henris erstem Rallyebeifahrer.
Antero Lindqvist (left) moved up from karting mechanic to rally co-driver.

Henri Toivonen Generationswechsel / Next generation

Henris Karriere beim Racing Team AAW dauerte nur ein Jahr, dann musste das Team Geld sparen und konzentrierte sich ganz auf die Interserie. Die Toivonen-Familie betrieb den Motorsport fortan selbst mit Unterstützung von außen, beispielsweise durch Keke Rosberg. „Ich habe ihnen geholfen, spezielle Motoren aus dem Ausland und ein, zwei Chassis zu bekommen. Auf der anderen Seite unterstützte mich Pauli, indem er mir das Sponsoring von Colt vermittelte. Er empfahl mich dort und sein Wort hatte Gewicht. Ohne diesen Deal hätte ich keine Rennen fahren können, die weiter weg waren als Schweden", räumt Keke ein.

Nach dem Ende der Juniorenzeit fuhr Henri gegen erfahrenere Gegner, trotzdem war er unglaublich schnell und fuhr viele Siege ein. Ein weiterer Titel war ihm im Kart aber nie vergönnt. 1974 nahm er an der Kart-Weltmeisterschaft in Estoril teil, wo er als einziger Finne ins Finale vordrang. Während Riccardo Patrese vor Eddie Cheever Weltmeister wurde, musste sich Henri mit Platz 18 begnügen – „nach einer Kollision mit Alain Prost", betonte Pauli. Henris Mechaniker war seit 1973 Antero Lindqvist, jener Kerl, der früher einmal Keke Rosbergs größter Gegner im Kart gewesen war. Lindqvist hatte aber eine noch wichtigere Aufgabe als die Vorbereitung des Go-Karts. Pauli hatte ihn auch als Vermittler zwischen Vater und Sohn eingestellt. „Pauli hatte seine eigenen Vorstellungen von der korrekten Linie, aber die waren für Karts nicht immer richtig. Ich habe ihm gesagt, dass man nicht zwangsläufig so fahren muss wie die anderen. Man muss auch nach Möglichkeiten suchen, die anderen zu überholen. Wenn du einfach deinem Vordermann folgst, schaffst du das nie. Henri hatte dafür ein sehr gutes Auge", erklärt Lindqvist.

Ungefähr zu dieser Zeit betrat eine sehr wichtige Person Henris Leben. Die Toivonen-Familie war in ein größeres Haus ein paar Kilometer weiter stadtauswärts gezogen. In diesem Vorort von Helsinki gab es ein Shoppingcenter, wo eine Gruppe von Teenagern oft rumhing. Eine von ihnen war ein hübsches, dunkelhaariges Mädchen mit sportlicher Veranlagung. Erja Minkkinen war kein typisches finnisches Mädchen. Während die meisten Finnen Lutheraner sind, war sie römisch-katholisch. Ihre Mutter stammte ursprünglich aus Polen und ihr Vater war ein finnischer Diplomat, der eine Weile in Bangkok stationiert war. Dort ging Erja anfangs zur Schule. Bei der Rückkehr nach Finnland in den später 60ern schrieben die Eltern ihre Tochter in die englischsprachige Schule von Helsinki ein, weswegen sie bilingual aufwuchs. Die Familie war kulturell sehr aufgeschlossen. Erjas Freunde scherzten darüber, dass sie die „italienischste Familie" in der Nachbarschaft waren. Bei den Minkkinens stand die Tür sprichwörtlich immer offen.

Erja und Henri waren zunächst nur gute Freunde. Es dauerte eine Weile, bis sie ein Paar wurden. „Ich war damals etwas schüchtern, vielleicht weil mein Finnisch noch nicht perfekt war. Henri war mir gegenüber sehr nett und fürsorglich. Nach einiger Zeit entwickelte sich zwischen uns eine starke Bindung. Als Paar sahen wir sehr lustig aus, weil ich deutlich größer war als er. Es dauerte lange, bis er seine 1,75 m erreichte. Und selbst dann sagte er noch, er wäre 1,78", lacht Erja. „Was bei uns besonders toll war: Jeder hat dem anderen seinen eigenen Raum gelassen. Es gab immer diese unausgesprochene Freiheit. Ich war ein starker Familienmensch, ausgehen und Party machen hat mich nicht interessiert. Aber es machte mir nichts aus, wenn Henri mit seinen Kumpels unterwegs war, so lange wir genug Zeit für uns hatten, wenn wir zusammen waren."

Zwei Dinge bemerkte Erja schnell, und das waren Henris Zielstrebigkeit und sein Konkurrenzdenken. Erjas ganze Familie begeisterte sich für Squash, was im Finnland der 70er-Jahre eine neue Sportart war. Erja spielte sehr gut Squash und so war es wenig überraschend, dass sie anfangs besser war als Henri. „Das konnte er nicht

Henri's career as a Racing Team AAW driver only lasted for one season before the team had to rationalize and concentrate its resources solely on the Interserie. The Toivonen family now ran the show for themselves, but got assistance from others, including Keke Rosberg. "I helped them get some special engines from abroad and even a chassis or two. On the other hand, Pauli offered huge support for me in getting Colt sponsorship. He recommended me to the company and his influence weighed a lot. Without that sponsorship I would never have raced cars further afield than Sweden", concedes Keke.

After progressing from the junior ranks Henri was still impressively quick against more experienced opposition, but never won another national title despite taking numerous victories. In 1974 he took part in the Karting World Championships in Estoril and was the only Finn to make it to the finals. While Riccardo Patrese was crowned champion and Eddie Cheever finished second, Henri was classified eighteenth – "after colliding with Alain Prost" according to Pauli. His mechanic from 1973 had been Antero Lindqvist – the guy who used to be Keke Rosberg's main challenger in Finnish karting. Lindqvist actually assumed a bigger role than attending to the kart. He had been recruited by Pauli and would often act as an intermediary between father and son. "Pauli had his ideas about the correct racing lines, but they did not always hold true in karting. I tried to make the point that you don't necessarily have to drive like the others, but rather make sure you get an opportunity to pass. If you just follow the guy ahead, you're never going to make it. Henri had a very good eye for that", argues Lindqvist.

At about this time another important – very important – influence entered the life of Henri Toivonen. The family had moved to a bigger house a couple of kilometres further out from Helsinki, but still in the suburbs. There was always a group of teenagers hanging out around the local shopping centre and amongst them was a pretty, dark-haired girl with a sporting disposition. It is fair to say Erja Minkkinen was not a very typical Finnish girl. First of all, she was a practising Roman-Catholic, while the vast majority of Finns are Lutherans. Her mother's family had its roots in Poland, while her father was a diplomat stationed in Thailand where Erja started school in Bangkok. On her return to Finland in the late sixties, it was therefore natural to enlist in Helsinki's English school, which made her bilingual. The whole family had a cultural mindset and friends used to joke that theirs was the most Italian household in the neighbourhood. Open doors were the order of the day for the Minkkinen family.

Erja got friendly with Henri, but it took a while before they actually became a couple. "I was a bit timid at the time, maybe because my Finnish was still not perfect. Henri was very nice and caring towards me. After a while a bond developed between us. We were a funny-looking pair, though, because I was noticeably taller than him. It took a long time for him to grow up to his eventual height of 175 cm or so. Even then he'd tell people he was 178", Erja chuckles. "The one thing that really clicked between us was that we both readily gave room for each other. There was always an unsaid degree of freedom. I was so much a family girl and did not care for going out or partying. But I didn't mind Henri going with his mates, as long as we still had that own thing of ours, when we were together."

One of the things that she soon came to realize was the huge determination and competitiveness that existed in Henri. Erja's whole family had immediately fallen for squash, which was a new sport for Finland in the 1970s. She quickly became very good at it and it therefore came as no surprise that at first she had the upper hand

ertragen. Er trainierte und trainierte, bis er mich geschlagen hat. Henri war in den meisten Sportarten sehr gut, sogar im Basketball, obwohl er so klein war. Für Mannschaftssportarten hatte er ein sehr gutes Auge, was vermutlich an seinem räumlichen Vorstellungsvermögen lag." Erja begleitete Henri nicht oft zu Rennen. Bei einigen Auslandsreisen war sie aber dabei und fungierte oft als Übersetzer. „Wir sind zu einem Kartrennen in Norwegen oder Schweden gefahren. Dort wurde beschlossen, dass Henris Lauf noch einmal gefahren werden musste. ‚Das mache ich auf gar keinen Fall, ich hab' doch schon gewonnen', argumentierte er. Ich musste seinen Fall sogar den Sportkommissaren vortragen, aber ich bezweifle, dass wir erfolgreich waren."

Der 25. August 1974 war für Henri Toivonen ein Feiertag: Er bekam seinen Führerschein. Dazu gab es einen grünen Simca Rallye 2 von Pauli, der nach der Übernahme der Rootes-Gruppe durch Chrysler nun die französische Marke in Finnland vermarktete. Die örtlichen Taxifahrer kannten den Simca schnell. Ihr Taxistand befand sich nämlich auf der Innenseite einer Kurve, die Henri als „schnelle Links bergab" beschrieben hätte. Mehrmals am Tag flog Henri im ausgedrehten dritten Gang und in bedenklicher Schräglage vorbei. Henri fuhr selbst kürzeste Distanzen mit dem Auto. Auch die 500 Meter zu Erjas Haus – keine Chance, dass Henri dorthin gelaufen wäre. Der eine Kilometer zur Schule: die gleiche Geschichte. Seine Rektorin war eine sanftmütige und bei den Schülern beliebte Dame, gut 60 Jahre alt: Frau Annikki Rimminen. „Bei Henri weiß ich noch, dass er immer zu spät zum Unterricht kam. Wir hörten ein Motorengeräusch, eine Rieseln im Schotter, eine zufallende Autotür, und dann kam Henri ins Zimmer, ein oder zwei Minuten zu spät. Ich habe ihm vorgeschlagen, doch mal ein bis zwei Minuten früher loszufahren, aber es war immer dasselbe", beschreibt die heute 95-Jährige, die früher Henris Englischlehrerin war. „Er schien eine besondere Motivation zu haben, Fremdsprachen zu erlernen. Er fuhr schon damals Rennen im Ausland und merkte vermutlich, dass es das Leben leichter machte." Die bilinguale Erja fand Henris Englisch dagegen fürchterlich: „Es war nicht nur die Aussprache. Einmal waren wir in einem Restaurant irgendwo in Europa. Henri wollte ein Dessert bestellen und sagte zum Kellner: ‚May I have a disaster'."

when playing against Henri. "He could not stand it! He practised and practised until he could beat me. Henri was very good at most sports, even basketball despite his small stature. He had an excellent eye for team games, which probably came from spatial awareness." Erja did not often follow Henri to races, but she did go along to some trips abroad, often ending up as an interpreter with her command of English. "We went to a kart race in Norway or Sweden, where for some reason it was decided to rerun Henri's heat. 'I bloody well won't, I already won it', he argued. I had to present his case to the stewards, but I doubt we were successful."

August 25th, 1974 was red letter day for Henri Toivonen – he got his driving licence. With it came a green Simca Rallye 2 from Pauli, who was now actively marketing the French make in Finland after the takeover of Rootes by Chrysler. This Simca became a familiar sight to the taxi drivers of the Toivonen suburb. Their stand was located on the inside of a bend, which to Henri would have been a "fast downhill left". Several times a day he would fly past, flat in third, the car leaning heavily on its offside suspension… He used the car for even the shortest of distances. Erja lived only some five hundred metres away, but no way would Henri walk to get there. School was just over a kilometre away and of course it was the same story. The headmistress was Mrs. Annikki Rimminen, a gentle lady approaching sixty years of age and well-liked by her pupils. "The thing I remember about Henri Toivonen is that he was always late for class. We would hear the buzz of an engine, a shower of gravel, the slam of a car door and then Henri would enter the classroom, one or two minutes late. I tried to suggest to him that perhaps it would be wise to get going a minute or two earlier, but it was always the same," recalls the sprightly 95-year-old. Mrs. Rimminen taught Henri English. "He did seem to have a motivation to learn foreign languages," she says. "He'd already been racing abroad and probably realized it would make life easier." The bilingual Erja still found her boyfriend's English appalling: "It wasn't just the pronunciation. Once in a restaurant somewhere in Europe Henri wanted to have a dessert. 'May I have a disaster' is what he said to the waiter!"

Trotz Erjas (links) steigendem Einfluss versuchte Pauli, Henri an der kurzen Leine zu halten.
Even with Erja's increasing influence, Pauli still wanted to keep Henri in leash.

Beim Foto von Henri und Erja durfte der kleine Harri natürlich nicht fehlen.
When the kids got up to mischief, Harri did not want to be left out either.

Henri Toivonen
Auf in den Kampf
Into battle

Im Finnland der 70er-Jahre war der Führerschein nicht automatisch eine Lizenz zum Rallyefahren. Fahranfänger mussten in ihrem ersten Jahr einen Aufkleber auf der Heckscheibe haben, der besagte, dass sie nicht mehr als 80 km/h fahren durften. Wem dieser Kleber anhaftete, durfte natürlich nicht an Rallyes und eigentlich auch nicht an Rennen teilnehmen. Durch seine Kart-Erfolge wurde Henri aber davon befreit, er durfte ab Januar 1975 Rennen fahren.

Henri schien jahrelang auf diesen Moment gewartet zu haben. Seine Familie hatte die Wochen nach Weihnachten meist am Päijänne-See verbracht, der sich von Jyväskylä aus über 100 Kilometer Richtung Süden erstreckt. Auf dem gefrorenen See pflügten die Toivonens eine Strecke frei, auf der die Jungs – besonders Henri – stundenlang fuhren. Sie bewegten meist kleine Autos wie einen Sunbeam Imp oder Simca. In 14 Tagen legte Henri zwischen 5.000 und 7.000 Kilometer zurück. Sein mit Spannung erwartetes Wettbewerbsdebüt fand beim Eisrennen in Kokkola statt. An Finnlands Westküste startete er im Lauf für Gruppe-1-Autos unter 1.600 ccm. Mit einem Simca Rallye 2 mit 1,3-Liter-Motor stand er 15 Gegnern gegenüber, von denen etwa die Hälfte potenzielle Sieger waren. Dennoch gelang Henri die Sensation: Er gewann. Und wer wurde Zweiter? Sein Vater Pauli am Steuer eines Sunbeam Avenger mit 1.600 Kubik.

Doch natürlich war der Weg zum Ruhm nicht so einfach, wie dieses Rennen vermuten ließ. In den nächsten sechs Monaten startete Toivonen jr. bei mehr als 20 Rennen auf Eis, Schotter und Asphalt, dabei gelangen ihm nur zwei Siege. Einer davon bei einem Lauf zur finnischen Eisrennserie in einem Sunbeam Avenger. Pauli nahm meist an denselben Rennen teil und konnte Henris Fortschritt so ganz genau verfolgen, manchmal sogar im eigenen Rückspiegel. „Pauli führte ein Eisrennen an und sah, dass Henri hinter ihm um den zweiten Platz kämpfte", erklärt Harri. „Der andere Fahrer trickste ihn aus. Er tauchte in die Innenseite ein und tippte Henri an, sodass er sich über die Schneewand hinweg überschlug. Als das Rennen vorbei war, lief Pauli zu diesem Kerl, noch bevor dieser aus dem Auto steigen konnte. Am Helmband zog Pauli den Kopf durch das Seitenfenster und brüllte: ‚Du Idiot! Stell' dir vor, was dabei alles passieren kann! Wenn jemand verletzt worden wäre …' Ich zog an Paulis Ärmel und quietschte: ‚Papa, bitte bring ihn nicht um!'"

Obwohl er nicht dafür bezahlt wurde, für das Team seines Vaters zu fahren, war Henri schon so etwas wie ein Profi-Rennfahrer. Vater und Sohn hatten sich geeinigt, dass Henri die Schule noch vor seinem Abschluss beenden durfte. Er konnte sich also komplett auf seine Fähigkeiten hinter dem Lenkrad konzentrieren. Trotz des anstrengenden Trainingsplans lebte Henri nicht enthaltsam. Er hatte genug Zeit, den normalen Hobbies eines Teenagers nachzugehen. Der Sohn eines Bassisten, beispielsweise, war sehr musikalisch. Henri hörte gerne Tamla Motown, hatte aber auch nichts gegen härtere Musik. Die „Hurriganes" (das g im Namen war volle Absicht) waren 1975 die angesagteste Band Finnlands. Ein lautes, hartes Trio, das puren Rock 'n' Roll spielte. Durch die Radiosendung „European Pop Jury" wurde die Band mit ihrem Hit „Get on" sogar international bekannt. Und der Gitarrist der „Hurriganes" war Ile Kallio, der Sohn von Paulis früherem Beifahrer Jaakko. Als die „Hurriganes" im örtlichen Club ein Konzert spielten, gingen Henri und Harri natürlich hin. „Unsere Kumpels waren sehr beeindruckt, dass wir Ile kannten", sagt Harri. Auch der Gitarrist erinnert sich noch an dieses Ereignis: „Ja, sie haben mir damals hallo gesagt. Es war schön, weil wir als Kinder viel

In 1970s Finland, a driving licence was not an immediate passport into motorsport. First-year drivers were obliged to carry a sticker in the rear window of their cars signifying the fact that they were not allowed to exceed 80 kph. This excluded the possibility of participation in rallies and normally in races, too. With his karting pedigree however, Henri managed to get dispensation to race from January of 1975.

He seemed to have prepared for ages for this moment. The family had made a tradition of spending a couple of weeks after Christmas in a holiday resort by the huge Päijänne lake, which stretches over a hundred kilometres south from Jyväskylä. They would have a track ploughed out on the ice, where the boys – Henri in particular – could drive for hours on end in a small car, usually a Sunbeam Imp or a Simca. Henri reported that he often covered between 5,000 and 7,000 kilometres in a fortnight. His much-anticipated debut took place in an ice race meeting in Kokkola on Finland's western coast. Henri was entered in the race for Group 1 cars of under 1,600 cc. He took the start in a 1,300 cc Simca Rallye 2 with fifteen other competitors, at least half a dozen of whom were potential winners. Sensationally, Henri won the race. Guess who was second: Pauli! Oh, and he was driving a full 1,600 cc Sunbeam Avenger …

Of course the road to stardom was not going to be quite as easy as this might have suggested. In the next six months Toivonen Jr made over twenty starts in events on ice, tarmac and gravel, but only notched up two more victories, one of them being in a Finnish ice-racing championship round for a change driving a Sunbeam Avenger. Driving in the same races much of the time, Pauli could keep a close eye on Henri's progress, sometimes through his own rear-view mirror, as Harri explains. "Dad was leading an ice race and saw Henri battling for second place behind. The other guy was much more experienced and he pulled a trick, diving to the inside and tipping Henri into a huge roll over the snow bank. When the race was over Dad went to this guy before he managed to get out of the car, pulled his head through the side window from the strap of his helmet and shouted: 'You idiot, can you imagine the consequences, if someone had been hurt!' I was hanging to his sleeve and remember squealing: 'Dad, please, don't kill him!'"

Although Henri was not paid to drive in his father's team, in effect he was now a professional racing driver. Father and son had held talks over the fundamental issue of school and came to an agreement whereby Henri was allowed to quit before graduation. This meant he could fully concentrate on things that would hone his skills at the wheel. Still, despite the arduous practising schemes, life was not all ascetic. Henri found plenty of time to do what was normal for teenagers. The bass player's son was quite musical, for instance. He liked Tamla Motown kind of stuff, but was not averse to more brutal tones either. In 1975, the hottest group in Finland was "Hurriganes" (deliberately spelled with a g) – a loud, hard-driving trio that played rock 'n' roll as pure as it comes. They even achieved international fame in a well-known radio show called "European Pop Jury", when they won the vote with their trademark number, "Get On". Guitar man of the combo was Ile Kallio, son of Pauli Toivonen's former co-driver Jaakko. When "Hurriganes" played a gig in the local youth club, Henri and Harri went to check them out. "Our mates were hugely impressed to discover

Zeit miteinander verbracht, uns aber eine Weile nicht gesehen hatten. Von Henris Rennerfolgen wusste ich und es dauerte nicht lange, bis er berühmter war als ich."

Zwei Tage nach seinem 19. Geburtstag hatte Henri seinen 80-km/h-Sticker entfernt und fuhr seine erste Rallye, und das war keine geringere als die 1000 Seen. Mit Beifahrer Antero Lindqvist hatte er sorgfältig trainiert, doch mit dem kleinen Simca fuhr er im Niemandsland. Vergleiche mit etablierten Fahrern fallen da schwer. Lindqvist bestätigt, dass die Rallye gut lief, bis die überhitzten Dämpfer nachgaben und der Unterbodenschutz bei einer Landung zu hart auf den Boden aufschlug. Die Ölwanne riss, das Öl lief aus. Motorschaden.

Henri hatte zwar die Schule abgebrochen, machte sich aber Gedanken über die Zukunft nach dem Rallyefahren. Er wollte in einem Wirtschaftsinstitut studieren, doch seine Zulassung wurde abgelehnt. Davon unbeirrt setzte er sich am ersten Tag in den Vorlesungssaal. Der Namensaufruf entlarvte Henri als blinden Passagier, wobei er darauf bestand, rechtmäßig dort zu studieren. Am folgenden Tag stellte das Institut fest, dass die Bewerbung des Herrn Toivonen nicht akzeptiert worden war. Es folgte ein offenes Gespräch mit dem Direktor, in dem der Bewerber auf sein „Recht zu studieren" beharrte. Das Ergebnis war ein Wunder: Henri überzeugte den Direktor und durfte bleiben.

Henri wäre 1976 vermutlich für Größeres bereit gewesen, doch wegen der kommerziellen Interessen seines Vaters fuhr er den Großteil der Saison einen Simca. Pauli war mittlerweile Geschäftsführer jener Firma, die alle Chrysler-Marken importierte, und das beeinflusste natürlich die Fahrzeugwahl seines Sohnes. Für Henri begann das Jahr im Gruppe-2-Simca mit einem Gesamtsieg bei einer kurzen Rallye, deren Prüfungen ausschließlich auf Eis stattfanden. In der finnischen Eisrennserie wurde er Dritter in der 1,3-Liter-Klasse. Und da gab es ja noch die Verlockung der Formelautos.

that we knew Ile", says Harri. The axeman still remembers the occasion: "Yeah, they came to say hello. It was nice because we'd spent a lot of time together as kids but had not now seen one another for a while. I was aware of Henri's racing exploits and it didn't take long before he was more famous than I was."

Two days after his nineteenth birthday Henri got rid of his 'new driver' 80 kph sticker and was allowed to start his first rally, the 1000 Lakes, no less. Paired with Antero Lindqvist he had done a thorough recce, but with a little Simca he was in no-man's land, where meaningful comparison to established names was difficult. Lindqvist attests that their rally was going well until overheated suspension dampers allowed the sump guard to hit the ground hard after a jump. The blow cracked the sump and the subsequent oil loss damaged the engine beyond repair.

Despite dropping out of school, Henri did give some thought to a career after driving. He decided he wanted to study in a business institute, but his application failed. Undeterred, he walked in on the first day of autumn term and sat in a class. The roll call exposed him as the odd man out, but Henri insisted he was a legitimate student. The matter was sorted out the following day, when it was finally discovered that Mr. Toivonen had never been accepted to the institute. A frank exchange with the principal followed, with the aspirant pleading to "a citizen's right to study" or some other vague concept like that. Miraculously, he persuaded the principal to let him stay!

Henri might have been ready to move on to more potent equipment in 1976, if his father's commercial interests had not kept him in a Simca for most of the season. Pauli was by now managing director of the company importing all Chrysler brands and this naturally affected his choices for his son. Henri began the year in a Group 2 Simca by winning outright a fairly short rally with special

Henri fuhr anfangs einen Simca Rallye 2 in Gruppe-2-Ausführung. Seine Fahrzeugwahl beschränkte sich auf Chrysler-Produkte, da Pauli als Geschäftsführer der Importeursfirma fungierte. Bei einigen Rennen traten Vater und Sohn zudem gegeneinander an.

Henri Toivonen first drove a Simca Rallye 2 in Group 2 tune. His choice was limited to Chrysler products because father Pauli was managing director of the importer and was also often competing against Henri on racing circuits.

Henri Toivonen Auf in den Kampf / Into battle

In den 70er-Jahren leitete Pauli Toivonen sein familieneigenes Team. Antero Lindqvist (links) spielte im „Team Toivonen" eine zentrale Rolle als Beifahrer und Mentor von Henri.

Through the 1970s, Pauli Toivonen ran a family team where Antero Lindqvist, on the left, played a key role both as a co-driver and as a tutor to Henri.

Henris Rallyedebüt fand bei der 1000 Seen Rallye 1975 statt, und natürlich war Lindqvist sein erster Beifahrer.

For Henri's rally debut in the 1975 1000 Lakes Rally, Antero Lindqvist was a natural choice in the co-driver's seat.

Henris erste Fahrt in einem Formel-V-Rennwagen hinterließ bei Max Johansson, Konstrukteur der Marke Veemax, bleibenden Eindruck. „Ich war dabei, als Henri die Chance erhielt, eines meiner Autos auszuprobieren. Der Stammpilot war viel größer, deswegen mussten wir den Sitz mit Jacken und Mänteln ausstopfen, damit Henri sich darin irgendwie wohlfühlen konnte. Er fuhr los und in der zweiten Runde war er zwei Sekunden schneller als die Rekordzeit dieses Fahrzeugs. Er war außergewöhnlich. Das größte finnische Talent, das ich bis dahin gesehen hatte, obwohl direkte Vergleiche mit Keke Rosberg schwierig sind." Pauli beschloss, in Schweden einen gebrauchten Veemax für seinen Sohn zu holen. Eigentlich sollte er damit nur trainieren. Doch als ein Mechaniker das Auto abholte, wurde er auf der Fähre wegen eines Telefonats in das Büro des Chefstewards gebeten. Am Telefon war Pauli: „Henri hat seine Rennlizenz erhalten, bring das Auto direkt zum Rennen in Seinäjoki!" Auf dem Straßenkurs gab es kaum Zeit für einen Shakedown. Nichtsdestotrotz sprang Henri in das Auto und wurde Dritter.

Der Kurs von Mo I Rana am Polarkreis ist die nördlichste permanente Rennstrecke der Welt und hier machte sich Henri einen Namen in der Formel V. Auf dieser Strecke wurde ein Lauf zur skandinavischen Formel-V-Meisterschaft ausgetragen und der Newcomer eroberte die Spitze im Sturm. Im Training stellte er seinen Veemax auf Pole und im Rennen fuhr er dem amtierenden Meister Calle Jonsson auf und davon. Jonsson hatte zuvor Fahrer wie Arie Luyendijk und Marc Surer im European Silver Cup geschlagen. „Nach den ersten vier Runden bin ich nicht mal mehr voll gefahren", gab der Sieger damals zu. Für den Rest des Sommers verließ Henri das Glück. Bei Jonssons Heimrennen in Knutstorp kollidierte er mit dem Lokalmatador, danach litt er an technischen Problemen. Die einzigen weiteren Siege fuhr er im Spätsommer beim Meeting in Keimola ein, weswegen Henris Position in der Meisterschaft wenig berauschend war.

Im Herbst waren wieder Rallyes angesagt und Henri fuhr einen Sunbeam Avenger in der Gruppe 1. Bis ins Jahr 1977 hinein bestritt er ein halbes Dutzend Rallyes, sein Beifahrer war Paulis alter Co Martti Tiukkanen. „Ich denke, Pauli wollte einen Vergleich zwischen Henri und ihm", glaubt Tiukkanen. „Er löcherte mich oft mit Fragen über die Fahrkünste des Jungen. Ich sagte ihm, dass Henri ein Künstler ist. Er könnte selbst mit einem Lenkrad aus Glas fahren, so sanft behandelt er es."

Gegen Ende des Winters erschien ein neues Gesicht auf dem Beifahrersitz. Juha Paajanen, Henris bester Schulfreund, hatte ihn schon bei unzähligen Trainingsfahrten nachts im Wald begleitet, eine Rallye hatte er aber noch nicht bestritten. „Ich weiß nicht, wie diese Idee aufkam", erklärt Paajanen. „Vielleicht dachte ‚Henkka', dass es cool wäre, wenn wir auch zusammen im Rallyeauto sitzen würden. Den Großteil unserer Freizeit verbrachten wir sowieso gemeinsam." Henri, Erja und Juha waren lange Zeit unzertrennlich. „Für Henri und Erja war ein Date oft mit einem Fahrtraining gleichzusetzen", berichtet Paajanen. Im Winter fuhren sie oft zu einem Eissee, manchmal brachte Erja sogar das Auto ihres Vaters mit. „Mein Vater hatte einen neuen Saab", erzählt Erja. „Ich habe mich bei Henri beschwert, dass ich den nicht zum Driften bringe. Er sagte nur: ‚Du musst die Bremse benutzen ... Ich zeig dir, wie es geht!'"

„Von 1977 an bin ich mit meinem Auto jeden Donnerstag um neun Uhr abends in den Wald, um ein paar hundert Kilometer zu fahren, ich wollte alles lernen", erklärte Henri einmal. Juha Paajanen ergänzt: „Pauli gab uns eine Karte und zeigte uns die Straßen, die wir trainieren sollten." Erja war bei den Ausflügen oft dabei. „Die Schrammen am Kopf habe ich heute noch", verrät sie. „Ich habe versucht, auf dem Rücksitz zu schlafen, und bin mit dem Kopf immer gegen den Käfig geknallt."

stages exclusively on ice, and then finished third in the 1,300 cc class of the Finnish ice racing championship. However, the allure of single-seaters was now playing on his mind.

Henri's first encounter with a Formula Vee left a lasting impression on Max Johansson, designer and builder of the successful Veemax marque. "I witnessed the occasion, when Henri was given a chance to try one of my cars. The regular driver was a lot taller, so all sorts of coats and anoraks had to be thrust in the seat to make Henri even remotely comfortable. Off he went and on the second lap he was two seconds faster than the best time the car had ever recorded before. He was quite supreme, the best talent I'd yet seen come from Finland, although it's difficult to make a direct comparison with Keke Rosberg." Pauli agreed to buy a second-hand Veemax from Sweden for his son, but the idea initially was to use it for practice only. A mechanic was sent to fetch the car and on the return trip he received a phone call in the purser's office of the ferry. It was Pauli: "Henri has been granted a licence to race it, bring it straight to the meeting in Seinäjoki!" The event was held on a street circuit and there was hardly any time for a shakedown or suchlike. Nevertheless, Henri hopped in the car and drove it to third place.

Mo I Rana on the Polar Circle has been labelled as the northernmost permanent racing circuit in the world and that was where Henri Toivonen really stamped his authority on Formula Vee. The track was hosting a round of the Scandinavian FVee championship and the newcomer took the scene by storm. He planted the Veemax on pole and then simply drove away from people like Calle Jonsson, the reigning champion, who previously had beaten names such as Arie Luyendijk and Marc Surer in the European Silver Cup. "And after the first four laps I wasn't even going flat out", quipped the winner. Unfortunately, he didn't have much luck for the rest of the summer, colliding with Jonsson in the latter's home race at Knutstorp and also suffering technical failures. A couple of victories in a late summer meeting at Keimola were the only other triumphs, so his championship positions were rather less than brilliant.

Come autumn the focus shifted towards rallying again, with Henri now in a Group 1 Sunbeam Avenger. Pauli's old co-driver Martti Tiukkanen was drafted to sit with him for a programme of half a dozen events, which took the pair well into 1977. "I think Pauli wanted a comparison between Henri and himself", believes Tiukkanen. "He certainly quite often grilled me about the boy's driving. I said Henri was an artist: He could have had a steering wheel made of glass, he was so gentle with it."

Towards the end of the winter season a fresh face debuted in the co-driver's seat. Juha Paajanen was Henri's best mate from school, who had accompanied him on numerous night-time practice drives in the forest, but never participated in competition before. "I'm not sure what the idea was all about", muses Paajanen. "Maybe 'Henkka' just thought it would be cool to see, if we could join forces for rallies, because we spent most of our spare time together anyway." In fact, for several years Henri, Erja and Juha formed a virtually inseparable threesome. "A date for Henri and Erja often meant a driving session", Paajanen remarks. In the winter they'd all go to a nearby ice track and sometimes Erja would bring her father's car. "I remember when he'd just got a new Saab", she relates. "I complained to Henri I couldn't make it slide. He said 'You must use the brakes – I'll show you how!'"

"From 1977 every Thursday at 9 pm I'd take my car to the forest and drive a few hundred kilometres. Learning about all the panics and things", Henri once explained. "Pauli would give us a map and

Für sein Rallyedebüt wandte sich Paajanen an seinen Namensvetter Juha Piironen: „Ich bat ihn, mir zu erklären, worum es bei dieser Beifahrersache ging, und wir legten gleich los!" Das Debüt verlief wenig aufregend: Toivonen/Paajanen schieden aus und Antero Lindqvist kehrte auf den Beifahrersitz zurück. Dies ist aber nicht das letzte Mal, dass wir von Paajanen hören sollten. „Es gab eine Zeit, da war er wie ein dritter Sohn für mich", erinnert sich Ulla Toivonen.

Im Frühjahr kaufte das Team Toivonen seinen zweiten Veemax. Das Auto kam vom amtierenden finnischen Meister und damit dominierte Henri die heimische Formel V. Er gewann den Titel mit der Maximalpunktzahl. Den letzten Saisonsieg holte er beim Rennen in Keimola, wo Henri eine noch viel beeindruckendere Kostprobe seines Talents ablieferte. Pauli Toivonen hatte seit seinem Sieg bei den 500 Kilometern von Keimola Anfang der 70er nicht mehr in einem GT-Rennwagen gesessen. Jetzt wollte er einen letzten Versuch wagen. Pauli kaufte einen 911 RSR, der schon einige Langstreckenrennen auf dem Buckel hatte und mit „Holzreifen" angeliefert wurde. Nach einiger Quengelei erlaubte Pauli seinem Sohn, den Porsche in Keimola zu testen. Da der Vater seine guten Reifen vor dem Rennen nicht hergeben wollte, bekam Henri die harten „Holzreifen". Ein zweiter Sitz wurde eingebaut, damit Pauli seinem Sohn zunächst die richtige Linie zeigen konnte. Als Henri dann losgelassen wurde, ging Pauli zur Strecke. Nach zehn Runden kehrte Pauli zurück. Er war aufgebracht, weil Henri nicht die vorgegebene Linie fuhr.

point out the roads he wanted him to practice", adds his friend Juha Paajanen. Erja often joined the boys on those nightly escapades. "And I still bear the scars on my scalp for that", she snaps. "I tried to sleep in the rear seat, but kept banging my head against the roll cage!"

For his rally debut, Paajanen turned to namesake Juha Piironen: "I asked him to explain to me what this co-driving thing was all about, and off we went!" It was to be an innocuous start: Toivonen/Paajanen failed to make the finish and Antero Lindqvist soon returned to navigate for Henri, but this was not the last we would hear of Paajanen. "There was a time when he was like a third son to me", recalls Ulla Toivonen fondly.

In the spring a second Veemax was added to the Toivonen stable. It was bought from the reigning Finnish champion and with it Henri totally dominated Finnish Formula Vee. He took the title with maximum points. The last of his wins was achieved in Keimola in a meeting that became the scene for an even more impressive show of his talent. Pauli Toivonen had not raced GTs since the early 1970s, when he'd accompanied Antti Aarnio-Wihuri in a Porsche 911 to victory in the Keimola 500 endurance race. Now he suddenly felt the desire to have a last fling with that kind of car and acquired a 911 RSR. With a history of racing in long-distance events, it came with what the mechanics dubbed "wooden tyres".

In der Formel V fühlte sich Henri wie ein Fisch im Wasser. Harri und Erja, links im Bild, begleiteten ihn stets zu den Rennen.
Henri took to Formula Vee like a duck to water. Harri and Erja, in the photo on the left, were his constant companions at the circuits.

Henri Toivonen Auf in den Kampf / Into battle

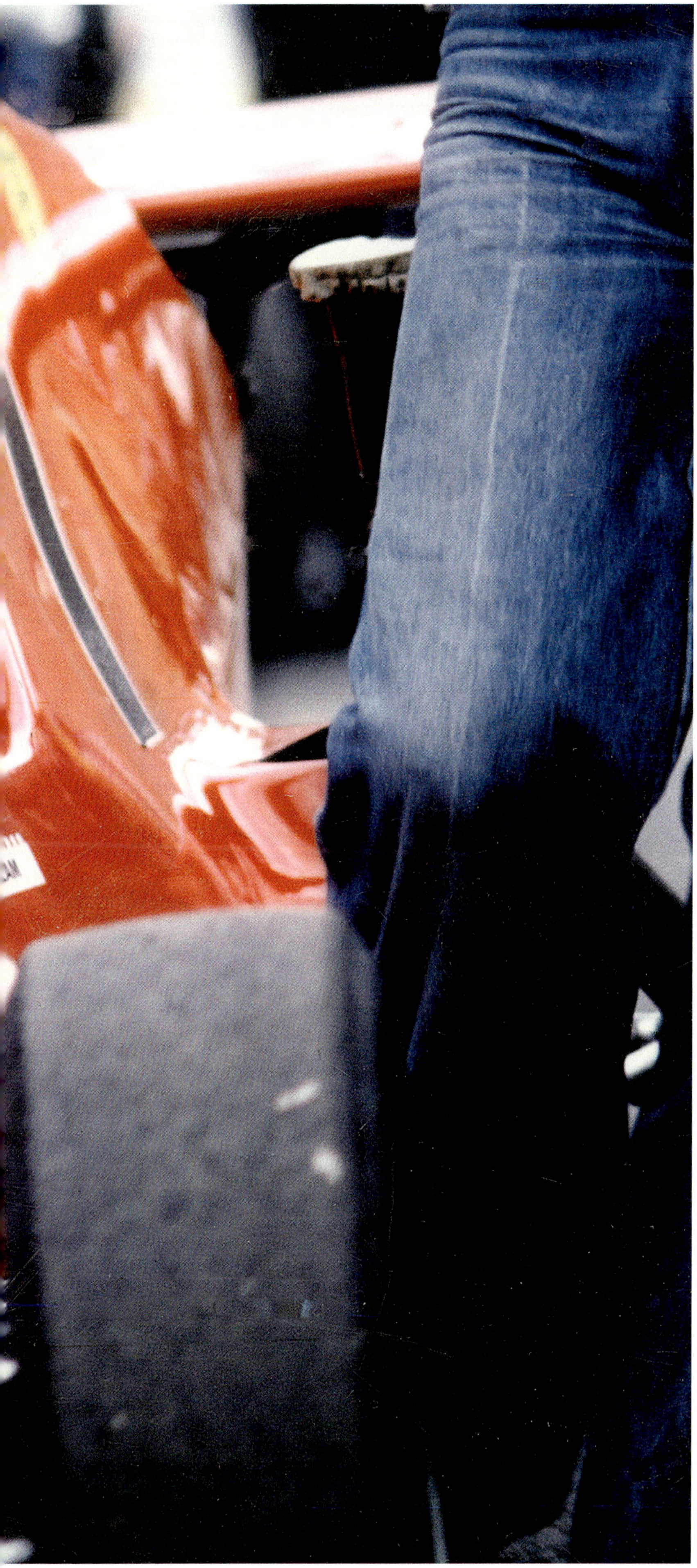

„Henkka" – so wurde Henri von seinen Freunden genannt – feierte seinen größten Formel-V-Erfolg im Schatten der norwegischen Berge auf der Rennstrecke Mo i Rana. Von Pole gestartet, dominierte er das Rennen.

To all his friends Henri Toivonen was "Henkka". His most notable success in Formula Vee came in the shadow of Norwegian mountains, in Mo I Rana, where, from pole position, he simply ran away with the race.

Doch dann sah er die Rundenzeiten. In Runde Vier war Henri genauso schnell wie sein Vater, danach unterbot er die Zeit deutlich. Pauli stellte auch fest, dass die „Holzreifen", die er selbst nie auf Temperatur gebracht hatte, jetzt glühten. Das überzeugte ihn, dass Henri seinen Platz fürs Rennen einnehmen sollte. Und der Junge beeindruckte. Henri jagte den großen 911-Meister Leo Kinnunen, der ein ähnliches Auto fuhr, das ganze Rennen und quetschte sich vor der Zielflagge an ihm vorbei. Für viele Beobachter war dies der bis dato beste Auftritt von Toivonen jr. Danach mögen Gedanken an eine Zukunft im Rennsport aufgekommen sein – doch nur bis zur nächsten Rallye.

Drei Wochen später gewannen Toivonen und Lindqvist die Gruppe-1-Wertung bei der 1000 Seen Rallye als Gesamtfünfte. Zugegeben: Der Schwund unter den Topteams war groß, dennoch machte das Ergebnis Schlagzeilen. „Wir haben nicht gezaubert, wir haben nur eine saubere, konstante Leistung gezeigt", beschreibt Lindqvist. „Das war das grüne Licht für den Rallyesport", gab Henri zu. „Bis dahin hatte ich Rennen bevorzugt und auch danach war ich mir nicht immer sicher, ob Rallyes oder Rennen besser waren. Wenn ich an einem sonnigen Tag ein paar Runden auf der Rennstrecke fuhr, spürte ich wieder den Nervenkitzel." Vielleicht war es der reifere Antero Lindqvist, der mehr Beständigkeit in Henris Herangehensweise an den Rallyesport brachte. Lindqvist begleitete Henri auch beim Training und gab ihm Tipps. „Ich habe ihm gesagt, dass er das Fernlicht beim Training auslassen soll. Durch die schlechtere Sicht brauchte er in brenzligen Situationen immer noch dieselben Reflexe, aber sein Tempo war geringer und falls etwas schiefging, war auch der Schaden weniger schlimm. Im Wettbewerb bemerkte er etwas anderes: Wenn wir im Avenger den dritten Gang verloren, passte sich Henri daran an. Er fuhr sanfter und unsere Zeiten waren immer noch genauso gut, wenn nicht sogar besser."

Durch gute Ergebnisse zum Saisonende belegte Henri Platz Zwei in der finnischen Gruppe-1-Meisterschaft, die von Kyösti Hämäläinen dominiert wurde. Also von jenem Fahrer, der die 1000 Seen Rallye auf einem Gruppe-4-Ford-Escort-RS1800 sensationell gewonnen hatte. Die Partnerschaft zwischen Toivonen und Lindqvist war in jeder Hinsicht ein Erfolg, dennoch ging das Stühlerücken weiter. 1978 nahm Juha Paajanen die Rolle von Henris Stammbeifahrer ein. Nur für die beiden langen Winterrallyes, die Arctic und die Hanki, wurde Martti Tiukkanen verpflichtet. „Ich schätze, dass sie immer noch dachten, ich wäre zu grün hinter den Ohren", räumt Paajanen amüsiert ein. Gleichzeitig stieg Henri in die Gruppe 2 um. Wobei viele Beteiligte sagen, dass der Avenger in dieser Ausführung nicht zwangsläufig schneller war als in der Gruppe 1. Wie auch immer. Platz Zwei bei der Arctic Rallye war auf jeden Fall ein gute Leistung von Henri. Ari Vatanen gewann in einem Werks-Ford, Markku Alén fiel mit dem Fiat 131 Abarth des Autonovo Teams durch technische Probleme hinter Toivonen zurück. Durch die geheime Route und noch höhere Schneewände als üblich hatten alle Top-Leute früher oder später in der weißen Pracht festgesteckt. „Ich weiß noch, wie meine Seite im Schnee vergraben war und die Tür nicht mehr aufging", erinnert sich Tiukkanen. „Henri hat sich prächtig amüsiert. Er meinte, er hat noch nie jemanden gesehen, der so schnell durch ein Seitenfenster geflüchtet ist." Die Chance auf eine ähnlich gute Position bei der Hanki Rallye vergaben sie durch einen Ausritt, der acht Minuten kostete und sie auf Platz Acht zurückwarf.

Für eine kleine Winterrallye in Jyväskylä kehrte Paajanen ins Cockpit zurück. Danach begann für die unerschrockenen Jungspunde das große Abenteuer. Das Citroën-Werksteam hatte sie für den portugiesischen WM-Lauf verpflichtet. Seit René Cottons frühem Tod wegen einer Krebserkrankung 1971 war seine Frau Marlene für die Geschicke von Citroën im Rallyesport verantwortlich. 1978 hatte sie eine

After some pestering, Pauli decided to let Henri try the Porsche in Keimola, just before that August meeting. He wanted to save the good tyres for the weekend, so Henri was given the hard compound "wooden" ones. A spare seat was installed so Pauli could first drive the son around to show the right lines. When Henri was let loose, Pauli wandered off to watch a series of corners just after the pits. After a stint of some ten laps Pauli came back very upset that Henri had not used the lines shown by him. But then he saw the lap times. On the fourth lap Henri had equalled the best time set by him and then dived well below it. Pauli also noticed that the "wooden tyres" he'd never managed to light up were now steaming hot. That convinced him and Henri would take his place for the race. And the boy sure delivered. Up against Leo Kinnunen in a similar car he hustled the renowned 911 master until pushing his nose just in front at the flag. To many observers this had been Henri Toivonen's most convincing drive yet. It may have swayed thoughts towards a future in racing – until the next rally, that is.

Three weeks later Toivonen and Lindqvist had won Group 1 in the 1977 1000 Lakes Rally and taken a stunning fifth overall! Admittedly this had been a rally of attrition amongst top crews, but the result still made headlines. "We managed to put together a clean, consistent performance for once. There was no magic to it", says Lindqvist. "That was the green light for rallying", Henri admitted. "So far I'd preferred to go racing and even later, if it was a sunny day at a race track and I did a few laps, I felt the thrill again and didn't know what to do." Perhaps it was the more mature Antero Lindqvist who managed to put some consistency into Henri's approach to rallies. He went along to practice drives, too, and gave some advice: "I told him not to use the lights on high beam, while training. With reduced visibility he'd still need just the same reactions to panic situations, but the speed would be slower, so if he got it wrong the damage would not be quite so severe. Another thing I noticed in actual competition was that if we lost, say third gear in the Avenger, Henri would adapt to it, drive more smoothly, and we'd still do similar times, if not even better!"

Good late season results gave Henri second in the Finnish Group 1 championship, which had been dominated by Kyösti Hämäläinen. It says something of Hämäläinen's level that when he was rewarded with a full Group 4 Ford Escort RS1800 for the 1000 Lakes Rally, he sensationally took outright victory. To all intents and purposes the partnership of Henri Toivonen and Antero Lindqvist had been a success, but still the game of musical chairs went on. Juha Paajanen now assumed the role of Henri's regular co-driver for 1978, although for the two long winter events, Arctic Rally and Hankiralli, Martti Tiukkanen took his place. "I guess I was still considered to be wet behind the ears", concedes Paajanen cheerfully. This all coincided with a move to Group 2, although those concerned say an Avenger in this higher specification was not necessarily much quicker than in Group 1. Be that as it may, second overall in Arctic Rally was in any case a fine performance from Henri. Ari Vatanen won the rally in a works Ford Escort, but Markku Alén had suffered myriad mechanical problems in his Autonovo Team Fiat 131 Abarth and dropped behind Toivonen. With a secret route and amid snow banks even higher than usual, virtually all the front-runners spent time stuck in the white stuff. "My lasting memory from that event is how we got buried in the snow on my side and the door would not open", recalls Martti Tiukkanen. "Henri was highly amused, saying he'd never seen anyone escape through the side window as quickly as I did!" Chance of an equally strong result in Hankiralli was lost with an off that cost the pair eight minutes and reduced them to eighth.

Paajanen returned to win a small winter rally with Henri in Jyväskylä, but after that the intrepid youngsters faced a true adven-

Schlüsselmoment in Henris Karriere: Nach dem Gruppe-1-Sieg bei der 1000 Seen 1977 konzentrierte er sich komplett auf den Rallyesport.

Career defining moment. Henri's Group 1 win in the 1977 1000 Lakes persuaded him to focus on rallies.

Paulis letztes Rennen in einem starken Auto war mit diesem Porsche 911 (Nr. 15) in Ahvenisto. Später in Keimola besiegte Henri mit dem Elfer überraschend den großen Leo Kinnunen.

Pauli's last fling in a powerful car was with this Porsche 911 n°15 in Ahvenisto. Henri later used it to sensationally beat Leo Kinnunen in Keimola.

originelle Idee: „Sie wollte die Söhne von zwei früheren Citroën-Stars fahren lassen als Erinnerung an die großen Zeiten", erklärt Paajanen. Das führte zur Verpflichtung der Sprösslinge von Pauli Toivonen und René Trautmann, die beide auf den Namen Henri hörten. „Madame Cotton rief an und fragte, ob ich interessiert wäre, für sie zu fahren. Mein Vater wollte sowieso nach Frankreich in den Urlaub, also ist er bei ihr vorbei und hat den Vertrag unterschrieben", erklärte der junge Toivonen. Henri und Juha reisten einige Wochen im Voraus nach Portugal, um sich so gut wie möglich vorzubereiten. Dabei dachten sie nicht immer nur an ihre Arbeit, wie Paajanen verrät. „Wir waren schon verantwortungsbewusst, nahmen das aber nicht immer zu 100 Prozent ernst. Für das Training hatten wir einen Citroën GS, und den machten wir schnell platt. Sie gaben uns einen neuen, aber auch der überstand nur zwei Tage. Das Training haben wir dann in einem Leihwagen beendet …"

Bei der Rallye fuhren sie einen Citroën CX 2400 GTi im Gruppe-1-Trimm, der wog 1.400 Kilogramm und hatte nur 128 PS. „Das ist kein richtiges Rallyeauto", sagte Henri später. „Er war schwer und auch schwer zu fahren. Du musstest das Tempo kontrollieren, niedrig halten." Trotzdem fuhr Henri energisch und führte die Gruppe 1 nach WP Drei an. Vier Prüfungen später war er nach einem Dreifachsalto draußen. Die Familien der beiden erzählten später, dass ihre Jungs in Portugal fast verhungert wären. „Nach dem Unfall mussten wir zwölf Stunden warten, bis wir aus der Prüfung kamen", berichtet Paajanen. „Aber glaubt mir: Essen war nicht das Erste, woran zwei junge Nordlichter in Portugal denken."

In Griechenland bekamen sie ihre zweite Chance, diesmal in der robusteren Gruppe-2-Version, die aber noch denselben Motor hatte. Doch auch in dieser Ausführung war das Auto nicht stark genug, um dem jugendlichen Überschwang standzuhalten: ein gebrochener Auspuff, ein undichter Tank, ein gebrochener Unterbodenschutz und eine abgerissene Benzinleitung sind der Beweis dafür. Der Speed hingegen war gut. Nach zwei von fünf Etappen lagen Toivonen/Paajanen auf Platz Zehn. Wenn man die weitere Entwicklung betrachtet, wäre Rang Sechs oder sogar Fünf möglich gewesen. Henri Traut-

ture. They had been recruited to drive Portugal's WRC event in the Citroën works team! After René Cotton's untimely death with cancer in 1971, his wife Marlène had carried the torch for Citroën in rallies and in 1978 she got a novel idea. "They decided they wanted to have the sons of two former Citroën stars driving as a reminder of the great days", explains Juha Paajanen. This led to the recruitment to the team of René Trautmann's son, also called Henri, and Pauli Toivonen's offspring. "Madame Cotton phoned me and asked if I was interested in some drives. Father was going to France for a holiday so he went to see her and signed the contract for me," recounted Toivonen Jr. The two young Finns arrived in Portugal weeks in advance to prepare as thoroughly as possible. Paajanen admits they did not view it as all work, however. "Of course we were going to be responsible about it, but not 100% serious! We had a Citroën GS for recce and promptly drove it to the ground. They gave us a new one and it only lasted two days. We eventually concluded the recce in a rental car…"

For the rally they had a Group 1 Citroën CX 2400 GTi, which weighed about 1,400 kilos and only produced 128 bhp. "It's not really a rally car", Henri later reflected. "It's heavy and difficult to drive. You have to control the speed, bring it down." He still attacked the stages with vigour and was leading Group 1 after three stages. After another four he was out, having overturned three times. The families later spread stories of their boys nearly starving in Portugal. "We had to wait for twelve hours before getting out from that stage after the accident", says Juha Paajanen. "But I promise you, food was not the first thing in the minds of two young northerners in Portugal!"

They got another chance in Greece, now in a more strongly built Group 2 version of the CX 2400 GTi, but still with the same engine. Even in that configuration the car was not strong enough to withstand such youthful exuberance: a broken exhaust, a leaking fuel tank, a broken sump guard and finally a ruptured fuel line after driving over a rock tell their own story. The speed had been good. After two of the event's five legs Toivonen/Paajanen were

Die Überraschungen der 1000 Seen 1977: Gesamtsieger Kyösti Hämäläinen (links) und Gruppe-1-Gewinner Henri Toivonen. Seinen ersten Werkseinsatz im folgenden Frühjahr ging Henri sehr entspannt an.

The surprise winners of the 1977 1000 Lakes Rally: Kyösti Hämäläinen (overall, left) and Henri Toivonen (Group 1). Henri's works debut some months later was treated in a more relaxed manner.

Der Citroën CX2400 GTI war, besonders in der Gruppe-1-Variante, nicht gerade das beste Rallyeauto. Aber immerhin fuhr Henri für ein Werksteam und seine erste Rallye in Südeuropa.

A Citroën CX2400 GTI was not among the quickest of rally cars, especially in Group 1 tune, but this was a works team and it gave Henri his first taste of rallying in southern Europe.

mann hatte Portugal ausgelassen. Er stieß in Griechenland dazu, kam aber auch nicht ins Ziel. Trotz des Doppelausfalls hat Henri Toivonen gute Erinnerungen an diese Zeit: „Madame Cotton war sehr nett zu uns, wie eine zweite Mutter."

Zu Beginn des Sommers flirtete Henri erneut mit dem Rennsport und nahm am Lauf der europäischen Formel-Super-V-Serie in Keimola teil. Sein Veemax war mehr als ein Jahr alt und wurde von einem luftgekühlten Motor angetrieben, die Konkurrenz hatte größtenteils schon das neue wassergekühlte Triebwerk aus dem VW Golf. Henri schien das wenig zu interessieren, er fuhr auf Pole. Beim Start wurde Henri von March-Pilot Helmut Hentzler überlistet, danach lieferte er sich ein packendes Duell um Platz Zwei mit Veemax-Werksfahrer Jac Nelleman. Erst in der letzten Runde setzte sich der Däne durch und verwies den Lokalmatador mit 0,4 Sekunden Rückstand auf Rang Drei.

Bei Rallyes war Henri gefrustet, weil er im untermotorisierten Sunbeam Avenger nicht um Siege kämpfen konnte. Daher beschloss Pauli, seinem Sohn für die 1000 Seen ein richtig heißes Gerät zu geben. Bei Walter Röhrl lieh er sich einen Porsche 911 Carrera, mit dem der Bayer die Hunsrück-Rallye bis zu seinem Ausfall angeführt hatte. Der Dreilitermotor hatte angeblich eine Leistung von 273 PS. Leider gab es zwei grundlegende Probleme: Einerseits gab es keine Möglichkeit, das Auto in Finnland richtig zu testen, andererseits absolvierten Henri und Juha ihr Training in einem VW Käfer. Die Realität holte sie schnell ein. „Unser Aufschrieb funktionierte überhaupt nicht", offenbart Paajanen. „Wir hatten ständig brenzlige Situationen, weil wir uns in dem Käfer überhaupt nicht ausrechnen konnten, wie die Prüfungen im Porsche sein würden. Aber das Auto war echt cool, es hatte ein spezielles Auspuffsystem. Wenn eine Klappe geschlossen war, war die Lautstärke straßentauglich. Aber wenn du sie für die WP geöffnet hast, war die Hölle los!" Henris Rallye endete auf WP Zehn, als sich eine Zündkerze löste. Da der Zylinder wegen des Unterbodenschutzes schwer zugänglich war, konnten sie das Problem an Ort und Stelle nicht beheben. Bis dahin hatte Henri ohnehin außerhalb der Top Ten gelegen, der ganze Einsatz hatte also nichts gebracht.

lying tenth, and looking at how things eventually panned out for the other competitors, a sixth or even fifth place result might have been possible. Henri Trautmann had missed Portugal, but was in the ranks for Greece, although he did not make the finish either. The experience left the Finns with good memories though. "Madame Cotton was very kind to me and like a second mother," said Henri Toivonen.

Early in the summer Henri again flirted with racing. He got to drive a Veemax Formula Super Vee in Keimola's round of the European series. The car was over a year old and powered by an air-cooled engine, whereas many of the regulars had already switched to the newer water-cooled unit used in the VW Golf. None of that seemed to matter as Henri stuck the thing on pole. March driver Helmut Hentzler outfoxed him at the start, leaving the interloper to engage in an enthusiastic tussle over second place with Jac Nelleman in the works Veemax. On the last lap the Dane prevailed, dropping the home hero to third, just 0.4 second behind.

In rallies, Henri had been frustrated by his perpetual inability to fight for outright wins with the underpowered Avenger. Pauli thought that he would give his son an opportunity to experience some real grunt and hired him a Porsche 911 for the 1000 Lakes. The car came from Walter Röhrl, who had impressively led the previous year's Hunsrück Rally with it. Its 3-litre engine was said to produce 273 bhp. Unfortunately, two essential problems surfaced. There was no proper opportunity to test the car in Finland, plus Henri and Juha had to do their recce in a VW Beetle. Once the rally started they immediately faced reality. "Our pace-notes did not work at all", agonizes Paajanen. "We were getting into panic situations all the time, because in that Beetle we just hadn't been able to figure out what the stages would be like in the Porsche. It was a cool car, though. It had a system in the exhausts, where shutting a gate kept the noise level within road norm, but when you opened it for the special stage all hell broke loose!" Henri's rally ended when a spark plug came out on the tenth stage and the cylinder's tricky location behind the sump guard made it impossible to reinstall in the conditions.

Henri Toivonen Auf in den Kampf / Into battle

1978

Selbst in der Gruppe-2-Version war der Citroën nicht robust genug für einen jungen Toivonen auf griechischen Pfaden.
Even in Group 2 spec the Citroën was not strong enough to withstand a young Toivonen attacking the Greek roads.

Im Sommer 1978 brachte ein Rennen zur Formel Super V Henris großes Talent als Rennfahrer zum Vorschein. Gegen die besten Fahrer Europas fuhr er mit dem alten Veemax auf Pole.
In the summer of 1978, a one-off drive in Formula Super Vee came as a reminder of Henri's racing prowess. Against Europe's best, he stuck the old Veemax on pole.

Henri Toivonen Auf in den Kampf / Into battle

Der Citroën CX2400 war vielleicht nicht das beste Auto für die Akropolis, aber der ungetestete Porsche 911 war kaum besser für eine 1000 Seen Rallye.
A Citroën CX2400 may not have been the ideal car for the Acropolis Rally, but then neither was an unsorted Porsche 911 Carrera the best car for the 1000 Lakes.

Die Herangehensweise an das Projekt zeigte, dass Pauli vielleicht nicht mehr ganz auf Höhe der Zeit war, wenn es ums Rallyefahren auf Spitzenniveau ging. Doch schon bald sollte sich für Henri das Blatt wieder zum Guten wenden.

Im September gewann Toivonen jr. endlich einen Lauf zur finnischen Meisterschaft. Bei der Champion Nordic Rallye in Tampere fehlten wegen der Überschneidung mit dem WM-Lauf Critérium du Quebec und der Manx Rallye einige der großen Namen. Die Rallye bestand aus 29 Prüfung und Henri übernahm früh die Führung. Bei Nebel schüttelte er Antero Laines Saab ab, obwohl sich Henri einmal überschlug und sein Avenger dabei alle Zusatzlampen verlor. Für den nächsten Lauf bekam Henri ein neues Auto. Pauli hatte einen neuen Talbot Sunbeam in eine Rallyewaffe verwandelt, in der sich Henri sofort wohl fühlte. „Durch den kürzeren Radstand ist er viel aggressiver zu fahren als der Avenger", so Henri. „Das Fehlen des Kofferraums ist auch schön: Man hat kein überhängendes Heck, mit dem man Dinge treffen kann." Der Vollständigkeit halber sollte noch erwähnt werden, dass der Sunbeam anfangs als Chrysler verkauft wurde, erst Mitte 1979 erhielt der Kompaktwagen den Namen Talbot, unter den ihn die Leute heutzutage kennen. Deswegen wird der Sunbeam in diesem Buch fortan als Talbot bezeichnet.

Bei der Tott Rallye mussten zwei der schnellsten Fahrer vorzeitig aufgeben. Timo Salonens Fiat 131 Abarth überlebte nicht einmal die erste WP und bei Antero Laine ging zur Halbzeit in Führung liegend der Motor hoch. Damit staubte Henri Toivonen die Lorbeeren ab: ein vielversprechendes Debüt des neuentwickelten Sunbeam. In den kommenden Wochen wurde der 1,8-Liter-Motor durch ein Zweiliter-Aggregat ausgetauscht, allerdings weiterhin mit Stößelstangen. Danach wurde der Sunbeam zur RAC Rallye gebracht. Das Werksteam hatte seine Unterstützung versprochen und so wurde das Auto zur Untersuchung direkt zum Werk nach Coventry gebracht. „Sie führten ein paar Vergleichstests durch", verrät Antero Lindqvist, der die Expedition als Mechaniker begleitete. „Tony Pond fuhr den Werkswagen mit Lotus-Motor, aber unser Auto war bei einigen Tests schneller. Danach bekamen wir die überlebenswichtige Unterstützung des Werks."

Im Vorfeld der RAC hatte Henri eigene Vorbereitungen für die Rallye getroffen. „Mikkola, Airikkala und all die Top-Fahrer haben mir gesagt, das schwierigste in Großbritannien sind die blinden Kuppen. In einer Landkarte habe ich ein paar Straßen in Finnland herausgesucht, die ich nicht kannte, und bin da hingefahren, um dort die brenzligen Stellen zu finden", erklärte Toivonen.

Henri hatte den klaren Auftrag, sein Auto bei dieser harten Rallye ins Ziel zu bringen. Er erfüllte sein Soll und lieferte zudem eine Leistung ab, die seinen internationalen Durchbruch bedeutete. Besonders das späte Bremsen beeindruckte die britischen Kenner. „Das ist teils auf seine Wurzeln im Kart zurückzuführen, aber Henri hatte auch ein außergewöhnliches dreidimensionales Sehvermögen für Distanzen", sagte Antero Lindqvist. Der Sunbeam war alles andere als ein Panzer, er verschliss ein Getriebe nach dem anderen. Kurz vor dem Ziel brauchte der Sunbeam sein fünftes Getriebe. Glücklicherweise eilte das Werk zur Hilfe, nachdem der Vorrat des Privatteams aufgebraucht war. Henri war zwar durch einen Reifenschaden zurückgeworfen worden und ein halbes Dutzend Prüfungen ohne zweiten Gang gefahren, trotzdem brachte er das Auto auf Platz Neun ins Ziel. Talbots legendärer Motorsportchef Des O'Dell war überglücklich, denn er erkannte, welchen kommerziellen Nutzen ihm dieses Ergebnis einbrachte. „Das ist nur ein Zweiliter-Stößelstangenmotor. Das ist der gleiche Motor, den wir auch in den Servicewagen haben. Wir könnten solche Autos ohne Probleme am Fließband herstellen", schwärmte er.

He had remained just outside the top ten and the whole effort proved futile. The very approach just may have been a sign of Pauli perhaps losing a bit of his grip with the realities of top level rallying. But better things lay just around the corner for Henri.

In September he finally succeeded in winning a round of the Finnish rally championship. The Champion Nordic Rally, based in Tampere, also hosted a Scandinavian team competition, yet some of the biggest regular names were missing due to date clashes with the WRC Critérium du Québec and the British series Manx Rally. Champion Nordic was quite a long event with twenty-nine special stages and Henri soon found himself leading. In foggy weather he beat off Antero Laine's Saab despite once barrel rolling the Avenger and losing its auxiliary lights. For the next round of the series he had a new car. Pauli Toivonen's team had been building a new Chrysler Sunbeam – also known by its code number "424" – into a rally weapon. This car was marketed under the Chrysler brand before it was sold as a Talbot from mid-1979 onwards [as most people remember the Sunbeam as a Talbot, it has been used this way henceforth]. The Sunbeam immediately pleased Henri. "With the shorter wheelbase it's a lot more aggressive to drive than the Avenger. The lack of a boot is also nice: less rear overhang to hit things with", he said.

The Tott Rally, another round of the Finnish series, possibly lost its two fastest competitors, when Timo Salonen's Fiat 131 Abarth never emerged from the first test and leader Antero Laine blew his engine just after half-distance. That left Henri Toivonen collecting the spoils; a promising debut for the team's newly developed Talbot. In the next weeks its 1.8-litre engine was swapped for a full 2-litre – albeit still a push-rod one – and the car was shipped to the RAC Rally for Henri's first outing in Britain. Factory assistance had been promised and once in the UK, the car was instantly delivered to Talbot's Coventry competition department for assessment. "They carried out some back to back testing with Tony Pond driving the works Lotus-engined car and ours proved quicker in some tests", reveals Antero Lindqvist, who joined the entourage as a mechanic. "We subsequently got some absolutely vital support from the factory."

In the build-up to the RAC Henri had been carrying out his own preparations in Finland. "Mikkola, Airikkala and all these top people said the most difficult thing in Britain was the blind brows. I found from the map some roads in Finland that I didn't know and went out to find the panic places," he reported.

Without doubt Henri had been briefed to bring the car to the finish of this arduous event. He truly delivered and gave a display, which was to be his real breakthrough to international acclaim. The lad's habitual late braking particularly impressed the British cognoscenti. "It came partly from his karting background, but Henri also had exceptionally precise three-dimensional eyesight for distances", says Antero Lindqvist. The Sunbeam was by no means bulletproof as it kept eating gearboxes with an alarming appetite, but once the private team had used up its own boxes, more were handed to them from the factory. Before the finish, it had needed a fifth gearbox to be installed! Despite delays like a puncture and running at least half-a-dozen stages without second gear, Henri still brought the car home in ninth overall. Des O'Dell, Talbot's competitions manager, was overjoyed. He saw the potential commercial benefits behind the achievement. "That's only a 2-litre pushrod; it's the same engine we fit to the service barges. We could churn out those cars down a production line with no trouble at all", he enthused. "I really tried to treat the rally as one where I gain experience, so I didn't drive 100% quickly, maybe 85%", said Henri.

Henri Toivonen Auf in den Kampf / Into battle

„Ich habe wirklich versucht, die Rallye zu nutzen, um Erfahrungen zu sammeln. Ich bin nicht 100 Prozent gefahren, vielleicht 85 Prozent", sagte Henri. Nach der RAC gab Henri dem Autosport-Redakteur Rupert Saunders sein erstes langes Interview auf Englisch. „In Finnland musst du gewinnen", so Henri. „Entweder du gewinnst oder du bist nichts. Ich denke, das war 1977 mein Problem. Ich bin fast immer in der zweiten Prüfung abgeflogen." Gleichzeitig blickte Henri in die Zukunft: „O'Dell hat mir versprochen, dass er mir sein drittes Auto [einen Talbot Sunbeam Lotus] gibt, wenn er eines einsetzt. Das ist aber noch nicht fix. Vielleicht passiert das zum Ende des Jahres. In der Zwischenzeit muss ich weiter Rallyes fahren."

Im Alter von 22 Jahren hatte Henri Toivonen schon mehr als 100 Starts bei Rallyes oder Rennen hinter sich. Damals konnte es noch niemand ahnen, aber zu diesem Zeitpunkt hatte er schon die Halbzeit seiner Karriere erreicht. Ein erschreckender Gedanke.

Post-event he gave his first long interview in English to Rupert Saunders of "Autosport". "In Finland you must win. Either you win or you're nothing", Henri said. "I think it was a problem for me in 1977. Almost always on the second stage I would go off", he confessed. He was now looking to the future: "O'Dell has promised that the third car (a Talbot Sunbeam Lotus) that he gets running might be for me. It's not definite; maybe it will be at the end of the year. Meanwhile I must still rally."

At the age of twenty-two, Henri Toivonen now had over a hundred race or rally starts to his name. No one could have known it at the time, but it is chilling to think that in this respect he was approximately halfway through his post-karting career …

Henri bestritt die RAC Rallye 1978 eigentlich als Privatfahrer, doch Talbot-Motorsportchef Des O'Dell bot schnell seine Hilfe an. Ohne ihn hätte der Sunbeam nie das Ziel erreicht.

Henri's entry in the 1978 RAC Rally was a private one, but Talbot's competitions manager Des O'Dell was immediately prepared to offer assistance. Without it the car would never have seen the finish.

Henri fuhr die RAC, wie er selbst sagte, mit 85 Prozent. Seine beständige Fahrt brachte ihm Platz Neun ein. Viel wichtiger war jedoch: Sie öffnete vielen Leuten die Augen und ihm die Tür zum Talbot-Werksteam.

Henri at 85%, or so he said. A tenacious drive was rewarded with ninth overall in the 1978 RAC Rally. It opened people's eyes as well as the door to Talbot's factory team, although that had to wait for another year.

Henri Toivonen
Ruhm und Ehre
Fame and fortune!

Nicht nur die Leute bei Talbot waren begeistert von Henri Toivonens Fahrt bei der RAC 1978. Es war diese Leistung, die die internationale Phase seiner Karriere endgültig einläuten sollte. Im Februar 1979 verkündete der Ölkonzern Total sein Programm mit zwei Ford Escort RS1800 in der britischen Meisterschaft. Einen davon sollte Henri Toivonen fahren, den anderen Malcolm Wilson. „Die beiden sind derzeit sicherlich zwei der schnellsten 22-Jährigen im Rallyesport", schwärmte ein Sprecher von Total. Henris Auto wurde von der Firma Peter Clarke Autos vorbereitet, Wilsons Escort von Thomas Motors.

In der Heimat hatte die Saison da schon begonnen. Toivonen fuhr weiterhin den familieneigenen Chrysler/Talbot Sunbeam. Die finnische Meisterschaft war damals in drei Kategorien unterteilt: Gruppe 1, 2 und 4. Henri holte zwar nicht den Gesamtsieg, aber er sammelte wichtige Punkte in der Gruppe 2, bis er bei der Arctic Rallye mit defekter Zylinderkopfdichtung stehen blieb. Es war eine zermürbende Rallye, bei der Henri sogar in Führung gelegen hat, nachdem Fahrer wie Hannu Mikkola und Markku Alén ausgefallen waren.

Juha Paajanen begleitete Henri nicht nach England. Die Rallyes wurden „blind" gefahren, also ohne Aufschrieb, daher war die Streckenkenntnis des Beifahrers ein wichtiges Kapital. Beim Saisonauftakt, der Mintex Rallye, saß Bryan Harris neben Toivonen. Die Veranstaltung wurde wegen starken Schneefalls fast abgesagt, konnte am Ende aber mit veränderter Route durchgeführt werden. Henri war vom Speed seines Escort begeistert, hatte aber die klare Anweisung, es ruhig angehen zu lassen. Mit Eis und Schnee auf fast allen Prüfungen war die Mintex eine einzige Rutschpartie. Stig Blomqvist und sein frontgetriebener Saab 99 waren in ihrem Element, während Toivonen durch einen Abflug anderthalb Minuten verlor. Henri kämpfte sich zurück und schob sich an Per Eklunds Triumph TR7 V8 vorbei auf Platz Zwei. Kurz danach traf Henri einen Baum und verlor drei Minuten. Auf der längsten WP namens Dalby Forest teilten sich Toivonen und Blomqvist die Bestzeit. Im Ziel lag Henri auf Platz Drei, weniger als eine Minute hinter Eklund – insgesamt ein sehr vielversprechender Start in die Saison.

Am folgenden Wochenende stand die Hanki Rallye auf dem Programm. Nach Aléns Abflug behauptete Henri im Talbot Platz Zwei hinter Antero Laine. Der Spitzenreiter überschlug sich, doch kurz darauf wurde Henri mit 82 km/h von der Polizei geblitzt und disqualifiziert. Laut Roadbook lag das erlaubte Tempo bei 80 km/h, wegen einer Baustelle war diese jedoch auf 60 reduziert. „Es ist die Aufgabe des Beifahrers, solche Dinge zu bemerken, und das habe ich versäumt", gibt Juha Paajanen zu.

It was not just the people from Talbot who had been impressed by Henri's drive in the 1978 RAC Rally. It was this performance that led to an opportunity, which meant the truly international phase of his career was just beginning. In February 1979 came an announcement from Total Oil that they would be running two Ford Escort RS1800s in Britain's Sedan Products Open Championship, one of them for Henri Toivonen. The other driver under Total's umbrella would be Malcolm Wilson. "They must surely be two of the fastest twenty-two year olds in the sport today", enthused a representative of the oil company. Henri's car was going to be prepared by Peter Clarke Autos while Thomas Motors would maintain Wilson's Escort.

The new season had already started back home where Toivonen carried on with the family-owned Chrysler/Talbot Sunbeam. The Finnish championship was run for three categories – Groups 1, 2 and 4 – and, while Henri did not win outright, he scored good points in Group 2 until retiring from the Arctic Rally with a blown head gasket. It had been a race of attrition and after drivers like Hannu Mikkola and Markku Alén were sidelined Henri had even led for a while.

Juha Paajanen did not follow Henri to Britain, where pacenotes were not normally allowed and the local knowledge of a co-driver was reckoned to be a definite asset. On the season-opening Mintex Rally, Bryan Harris partnered the newcomer. The Yorkshire event was nearly snowed off, but eventually went ahead with adjustments to its route. Henri was impressed by the speed of his Escort, but was under strict orders to take things gently. With snow and ice on virtually all of the stages it was an endeavour of slipping and sliding. Stig Blomqvist in the front-wheel drive Saab 99 Turbo was in his element, while Toivonen went off losing a minute and a half. He then climbed back up the order to pass Per Eklund's Triumph TR7 V8 for second, but promptly slid wide and hit a tree losing another three minutes. The route was made up of mostly short stages but, on the longest one in Dalby Forest, Henri shared fastest time with Blomqvist. He ended up third, less than a minute behind Eklund, all of which was a most encouraging start to the campaign.

The following weekend it was time for the Hankiralli back in Finland. In the familiar Talbot, Henri held second behind Antero Laine after Alén had gone off, but then, just when the leader rolled, Henri was caught in a police speed trap at 82 kph and got excluded. The limit according to the roadbook had been 80 kph, but in reality this had been lowered to 60 kph because of road works. Juha Paajanen puts his hand up: "It's the co-driver's job to spot such things and I didn't."

The Circuit of Ireland presented an interesting new challenge but, from the start, Henri was struggling with pulling brakes. He managed one second, one third and one fourth fastest time, before a broken input shaft to the Escort gearbox spelled early retirement. This was a shame, because three fastest times by Malcolm Wilson

Nach einigen zeitraubenden Ausrutschern wurde Henri bei der Mintex Rallye Dritter. In Anbetracht seiner guten Leistungen überrascht es jedoch, dass dieser Podestplatz sein bestes Ergebnis in der britischen Meisterschaft 1979 bleiben sollte.

Several time-consuming off-road excursions reduced Henri to third place in the Mintex Rally. Considering the promise shown by him, it was surprising that this was to be the best result of his British programme in 1979.

Die Mintex Rallye fiel fast dem starken Schneefall zum Opfer. Die Bedingungen waren alles andere als ideal, um ein neues Auto kennenzulernen. Trotzdem war Henri von seinem Escort begeistert.

The 1979 Mintex Rally was nearly snowed off and the conditions were hardly ideal for learning a new car, but Henri was impressed by the speed of the Peter Clarke Autos Escort.

Henri Toivonen Ruhm und Ehre / Fame and fortune!

Der Circuit of Ireland war für Henri eine interessante neue Herausforderung, doch leider zog seine Bremse vom Start weg. Er fuhr eine zweitbeste, eine drittbeste und eine viertbeste Zeit, dann sorgte eine gebrochene Getriebeeingangswelle für das frühe Aus. Das war eine Schande, zumal drei Bestzeiten von Malcolm Wilson andeuteten, dass der Escort auf dem irischen Asphalt konkurrenzfähig gewesen wäre. Henris Teamkollege war trotz allem von dessen Asphalt-Fahrkünsten begeistert. „Ich bin auf losem Untergrund groß geworden und zuvor noch nie auf Asphalt gefahren, während Henri zwei Jahre auf der Rundstrecke verbracht hat", lobte Malcolm damals. „Ihm zuzuschauen ist fantastisch, er fährt so sanft."

Durch die Auftritte in Großbritannien war Henri jetzt viel öfter unterwegs. Die Beziehung zwischen Henri und Erja hatte sich über die Jahre weiter gefestigt. Im Herbst 1977 hatten sie sich verlobt, und die Bindung war stärker als je zuvor. „Von seinen Reisen schickte er mir immer liebevolle Postkarten. Er schrieb darauf Gedichte und unterzeichnete sie mit „MRS" (Minä Rakastan Sinua, Finnisch für „Ich liebe Dich"). Er konnte so süß sein", schwärmt Erja.

Vor der Wales Rallye lag Henri mit Magenbeschwerden im Bett, doch rechtzeitig zum Start war er wieder fit und lieferte sich einen lebhaften Zweikampf mit Teamkollege Wilson um Platz Zwei. Die Führung hatte Hannu Mikkola im Werks-Escort inne. Bryan Harris nutzte die spezielle Fähigkeit der britischen Beifahrer, eine Art Aufschrieb aus Landkarten zu lesen. Auf der WP Dyfnant erkannte er eine „schnelle" Kurve, die in Realität aber alles andere als schnell war. Der Escort krachte seitlich in einen Baum. Sie konnten zwar weiterfahren, verloren später aber noch mehr Zeit durch ein Bremsproblem und eine Offroad-Einlage. So blieb nicht mehr als Platz Sechs.

Die Schottland Rallye war eine ereignisreiche Veranstaltung. Der erste Teil war eine Wiederholung von Wales. Mikkola führte und Toivonen kämpfte mit Wilson um Platz Zwei, bis der Brite durch Reifenschäden zurückfiel. Wobei auch Henri acht Kilometer mit einem Plattfuß zurücklegte. Danach hatte Hannu seinerseits einen Reifenschaden, ehe er auf der ersten WP nach dem Nachtstopp abflog. Jetzt lag Toivonen in Führung und musste sich gegen Tony Ponds Triumph und Pentti Airikkalas Vauxhall zur Wehr setzen, als seine Bremsbalance verrücktspielte und die komplette Bremskraft an die Hinterräder gab. Als das Problem behoben war, zog Toivonen davon, bis seine Kupplung zu rutschen begann und er sein Auto an einer Haarnadel abwürgte. Sechs Minuten verstrichen, ehe Wilson an die Stelle kam und seinen Teamkollegen anschob. Kurz vor Ende ließ sich der Ford-Motor am Start einer WP nicht mehr starten, da weder Anlasser noch Kupplung funktionierten. Beifahrer Bryan Harris hatte schon eine Startzeit erhalten, die Uhr tickte also bereits. Dann ließ Henri das Auto bergab rollen – von der Startlinie weg in Richtung Zeitkontrolle. Als der Motor wieder zum Leben erwachte, drehte Henri den Escort herum und sauste mit fliegendem Start in die Prüfung. Dieser Vorfall wurde den Sportkommissaren gemeldet und da er den Start angeblich zweimal passiert hatte, wurde Toivonen disqualifiziert. All das konnte jedoch nicht von der Tatsache ablenken, dass er der zweitschnellste Fahrer der Rallye war. Nur Sieger Hannu Mikkola war zweifellos schneller gewesen.

Während Henri in Großbritannien beschäftigt war, unternahm Bruder Harri seine ersten Gehversuche bei finnischen Rallyesprints in einem VW 1302 S. Im Juli trat das Brüderpaar sogar gemeinsam im familieneigenen Talbot Sunbeam an. Die Salora Rallye wurde „blind" gefahren, Harri hätte sich auf dem Beifahrersitz eigentlich zurücklehnen und die Lenkradakrobatik seines großen Bruders genießen können. Entspannend war das für Harri aber nicht: „Ich habe es gehasst. Ich hatte richtig Angst! Ich fahre ohnehin nicht gerne bei anderen Leuten mit und Henri ist wie ein Idiot gefahren. Ein- oder

In Großbritannien fuhr Henri 1979 zwar einen Ford Escort, dennoch war er sicher, dass seine Zukunft bei Talbot liegen würde.

Despite driving a Ford Escort on the British scene in 1979, Henri was certain that his future would be with Talbot.

indicated that, without its problems, the car could have been competitive on the Irish tarmac lanes. Henri's driving on sealed surfaces had already made an impression on his team-mate. "I have been brought up on loose surface and I've never done any tarmac, whereas Henri has done two years of circuit racing. Just to watch him has been absolutely fabulous, he is so smooth", praised Malcolm.

The British programme meant spending a lot more time away from home. The relationship between Henri and Erja was now well established – they had got engaged in the autumn of 1977 – and the bond was obviously stronger than ever. "He used to send lovely postcards from his travels that were written in the format of a poem and always signed with "MRS" (Minä Rakastan Sinua = I Love You). He could be so sweet", extols Erja.

Before the Welsh Rally, Henri was laid up with a stomach complaint, but he was fit to take the start and engage in a brisk battle for second with team-mate Wilson, as it was Hannu Mikkola that held the lead in his works Escort. Bryan Harris used the British co-drivers' specialist skill of calling notes from Ordnance Survey maps, but in the Dyfnant stage he urged Henri into a "fast" corner that was anything but that and the pair crashed sideways into a tree. They still managed to keep going, but later lost more time with brake problems and another off road excursion finally ending up sixth overall.

The Scottish Rally certainly turned out to be eventful. Its first part was a repeat of what had happened in Wales. Once again Mikkola led, with Toivonen and Wilson fighting over second until the Briton dropped back with punctures. In fact, Henri also drove for some eight kilometres with a flat tyre. Next it was Hannu's turn to suffer a puncture, and when he went off on the morning's first stage after an overnight rest, it left Toivonen in the lead. Henri held off Tony Pond's Triumph and Pentti Airikkala's Vauxhall, but began to have problems with a broken brake balance control, which put all the bias to the rear. Once this was rectified he managed to pull ahead, until a fading clutch caused him to stall after spinning on a hairpin. The cable supplying power to the starter motor had come loose and six minutes were lost before Wilson arrived to give Henri a push. With about one fifth of the rally remaining, the engine would not fire up at a stage start as the starter motor still did not work and neither did the clutch. Co-driver Harris had already accepted a start time and the clock was ticking, so Henri tried rolling the car downhill, back and away from the starting line. The engine then coughed into life, he turned the car round and took a flying

Bei der Hanki Rallye kämpfte Henri um den Sieg, bis er von der Polizei auf der Verbindungsetappe geblitzt und disqualifiziert wurde.
A home win was on the cards at the Hankiralli, but Henri and co-driver Juha Paajanen were caught out by a police speed trap.

Henri Toivonen Ruhm und Ehre / Fame and fortune!

zweimal ist das Auto nach einem Sprung leicht versetzt und ich war sicher: Das war's jetzt für uns." Trotz allem gewannen sie und somit sammelte Harri fleißig Punkte für seine Lizenz, die den Aufstieg von den Junioren bedeutete.

Die 1000 Seen Rallye rückte näher und da Markku Alén von Fiat einen Werkswagen bekam, brauchte der Importeur einen Ersatz für den zweiten Abarth 131 des Autonovo-Teams. Stammpilot Ulf Grönholm fuhr den einen Fiat, das andere blau-weiße Auto wurde Henri Toivonen gegeben. Bei einem Lauf zur finnischen Meisterschaft drei Wochen vorher durfte sich Toivonen auf das Auto einschießen und wurde Dritter hinter Kyösti Hämäläinens Ford Escort und Grönholm, obwohl er es ruhig angehen ließ. „Wir waren begeistert, dass wir das Auto fahren durften", erklärt Juha Paajanen. „Für uns war das ein Vollblut-Rallyeauto."

Bei der 1000 Seen erlitten sie einen frühen Rückschlag. Die Gegensprechanlage fiel aus und im lauten Cockpit war es unmöglich, die Ansagen des Aufschriebs zu hören. „Ich habe es mit Zeichensprache versucht und mit meinen Händen in die jeweilige Richtung gezeigt", beschreibt Paajanen. Trotz dieser Umstände lag Henri nach 130 WP-Kilometern auf Rang Fünf. Als die Rallye nachts zurück in Richtung Norden führte, ging Henri sogar an Ford-Mann Björn Waldegård vorbei auf Platz Vier, doch in den frühen Morgenstunden wurden sie Opfer ihres Kommunikationsproblems. Nach einem Sprung fuhren sie geradeaus, während die Straße einen Rechtsbogen machte. Auf einer Seite riss es die Fiat-Aufhängung heraus. Das war leider auch

start to the stage. He was reported to the stewards for having gone through the start twice and got excluded. Still, none of this could obscure the fact that he had been second fastest driver in the rally, with only the winner, Mikkola, indisputably quicker.

With Henri busy in Britain, brother Harri had been taking his first steps in Finnish rally sprints with a VW 1302 S, but in July the two joined forces in the "family" Talbot Sunbeam. They entered the Salora Rally, often a round of the national championship although run this time outside the series. There were no pacenotes so in theory Harri could just relax and enjoy big brother's acrobatics on the stages. It did not turn out quite like that. "I hated it", barks Harri. "I was frightened! I don't like to ride with other people anyway and Henri drove like an idiot! There was a moment or two, when the car went into a tank-slapper after a jump and I was sure that was it for us." They won, nevertheless, and this meant Harri was quickly accumulating points on his licence for promotion from the junior ranks.

The 1000 Lakes Rally was approaching and, as Markku Alén would be in a full works Fiat, the manufacturer's Finnish importer needed a stand-in for one of its Autonovo team's two Fiat Abarth 131s. While Ulf Grönholm was the regular occupant of one car, the other blue-and-white Fiat was entrusted to Henri Toivonen. He was allowed a dress rehearsal in a Finnish championship rally three weeks before the big one, and still "taking it easy" finished third behind Kyösti Hämäläinen's Ford Escort and Grönholm. "We were

Zwischen den Total-Escort-Teamkollegen Henri Toivonen und Malcolm Wilson herrschte ein gesunder Konkurrenzkampf.
There was a healthy rivalry between the Total-sponsored Escorts of Henri Toivonen and Malcolm Wilson.

Henri fuhr nur ein paar Läufe im Fiat 131 Abarth. Bei der 1000 Seen Rallye hatte sich Toivonen gerade an den Fiat gewöhnt, als die Gegensprechanlage streikte, er abflog und ausfiel.
Henri only had a few drives in a Fiat 131. He just seemed to be getting the hang of it in the 1000 Lakes, when an intercom problem led to an off-road excursion and retirement.

ein schlechtes Omen für den Rest der Saison. Henri fuhr den Fiat bei einem weiteren Lauf zur finnischen Meisterschaft und flog früh ab. Bei der Manx Rallye war das Training erlaubt und daher saß Schulfreund Paajanen neben Henri. Doch die Asphaltrallye war eine Farce: Auf WP Zwei hatten sie einen Reifenschaden und stellten fest, dass sie keinen Wagenheber im Escort hatten. Auf der fünften Prüfung kam dann das Aus durch Zündungsprobleme.

Bei der Castrol 79 Rallye streikte die Zylinderkopfdichtung auf der allerersten Prüfung. Der Motor wurde repariert und so konnte Henri auf den Nachmittagsprüfungen außerhalb des Wettbewerbs testen. Bei der Ulster Rallye kam er nur unwesentlich weiter. Auf der ersten richtigen WP flog Toivonen gegen einen Baum und war draußen.

Eine Woche vor dem Saisonfinale bei der RAC Rallye gewann Henri die Helsinki Rallye im Talbot. Sein Bruder Harri hatte sich gerade von seinem 80-km/h-Sticker für Fahranfänger befreit und feierte seine Rallyepremiere in einem Chrysler Avenger. Trotz des kleinen 1,6-Liter-Motors zeigte Harri eine gute Leistung und wurde Zweiter in der seriennahen Gruppe 1. „Die zweite Prüfung war sehr ermutigend, ich habe nur fünf Sekunden auf Henri verloren", erinnert sich Harri. Doch es gab auch ein Missgeschick: „Mir ist die Straße ausgegangen und ich habe mir danach den Schaden angeschaut. Die Stoßstange war kaputt und ich hatte solche Angst, was Pauli dazu sagen würde." Lag es vielleicht daran, dass sein Vater wegen seines aufbrausenden Gemüts sarkastisch auch „Sunshine" genannt wurde?

Im November verdichteten sich die Gerüchte, dass Henri 1980 für das Talbot-Werksteam fahren würde. Bei der Technischen Abnahme zur RAC Rallye wurde Henri eine generelle Frage zu Talbot gestellt, die nichts direkt mit seinem Engagement für das Team zu tun hatte.

thrilled to be given a go in that car", says Juha Paajanen. "To us it was a proper thoroughbred."

In the 1000 Lakes, the pair suffered an early setback when the intercom system in their helmets failed and it became impossible to hear pacenotes in the noisy cockpit. "I tried to use sign language, pointing the direction of turns with my hands", says Juha Paajanen. Despite this quite major inconvenience, Henri still held fifth place after some 130 km of stages. As the route headed back north in the darkness towards Jyväskylä, he passed Ford's Björn Waldegård into fourth place but, in the early morning hours, Henri and Juha finally fell foul of their communication problem. They went straight on from a jump where the road turned right and tore off the Fiat's suspension on one side. Unfortunately that pretty much set the tone for the rest of the season. Henri had one more run in the Fiat in a Finnish championship rally, but went off early. Paajanen came along to the Manx Rally, which allowed pacenotes, but that outing turned into a farce as, after a puncture on the second stage, they found that the Escort lacked a jack. Retirement followed on stage five with ignition failure.

In the Castrol 79 Rally, the Escort's head gasket went on the very first stage, but the engine was repaired so Henri could rejoin the Welsh event for its afternoon stages, just for the purpose of testing. Then, in the Ulster Rally he was off on the first proper stage when he landed heavily against a tree …

One week before the seasonal climax of the RAC Rally, Henri won the short Helsinki Rally with his Talbot. Harri had just been released from the 80 kph limit of a first year driver and made his rally debut in a Group 1 Chrysler Avenger. It only had the small

Henri Toivonen Ruhm und Ehre / Fame and fortune!

Bevor er seinen Mund öffnen konnte, mischte sich Pauli ein: „Es ist schwer, etwas über ein Team zu sagen, das uns völlig fremd ist!" Henri schaute seinen Vater nur verlegen an, als wollte er sagen: „Was?" Für die RAC bekam Toivonen jr. einen neuen Ford Escort RS1800, der vor der Rallye nicht getestet wurde und allerhand Probleme hatte. „Erst Fehlzündungen, dann Bremse, dann Getriebe und jetzt blockieren die Bremsen", zählte Henri im Service auf. Wie so oft hätte der omnipräsente Pauli jetzt das Handtuch geworfen, aber Interimsbeifahrer Phil Boland wollte weiterfahren und setzte sich durch. So ging die Misere weiter, bis Getriebeöl in die Kupplung eindrang und die Crew im Lake District aufgab. Toivonen/Boland hatten nur ein paar Prüfungen ohne Probleme überstanden und sind eine zweite Zeit im Bramham Park sowie eine dritte auf einer der Kielder-Prüfungen gefahren.

Im Dezember wurde eines der am schlechtesten gehüteten Geheimnisse gelüftet: Talbot verkündete Henri Toivonen als Werksfahrer für die Saison 1980. British Leyland (Triumph) hatte auch Interesse bekundet, aber der Vertrag mit Talbot war immer das wahrscheinlichere Szenario gewesen. Das geplante Programm war nicht sehr umfangreich, es beinhaltete aber einige WM-Läufe, bei denen trainiert werden durfte. Pauli sorgte dafür, dass Antero Lindqvist auf den Beifahrerplatz zurückkehrte. „Ich glaube, er wollte einen älteren Beifahrer haben, der da draußen in der weiten Welt auf sein Kind aufpasst", beschreibt Lindqvist. Die Saison begann zunächst im familieneigenen Talbot Sunbeam, der jetzt mit einem 2,2-Liter-Twincam-Motor von Lotus ausgestattet war, aber sonst nicht im Werkstrimm daherkam. Bei der Arctic Rallye, die 30 Prozent kürzer war als zuvor und nur 17 Prüfungen umfasste, war das nicht weiter schlimm. Toivonen nutzte seine spätere Startposition hinter Airikkala, Hämäläinen und Alén, ging auf WP Drei in Führung und hielt seine Verfolger anschließend locker in Schach. Henri setzte zwölf Bestzeiten und siegte mit großem Abstand, weil die Konkurrenz Federn ließ. „Gut, dass wir früh in Führung waren", strahlte der Sieger. „So kann niemand sagen, dass wir nur Glück hatten. Heute ist definitiv der schönste Tag meiner Karriere."

In Lappland trug der Talbot das Namensschild „Henri P. Toivonen" auf der Fahrertür. Das P stand für Pauli, Henris zweiter Vorname. Auf dem Werkswagen von der Mintex Rallye tauchte diese väterliche Huldigung nicht auf. Henri lag an vierter Stelle, als das Team seinen Ausfall wegen „defekter Ölabsaugpumpe" verkündete. „Die hat er an einem Baum zerstört", verriet dagegen ein anderer Teilnehmer.

Das ernste Leben als Werksfahrer in der WM begann in Portugal. Talbot setzte zwei Autos ein. Während Guy Fréquelin klar die Nummer Eins im Team war, fuhr Henri durch seinen FIA-Prioritätsstatus „B" hinter den großen Namen mit Startnummer 20. Fréquelin hielt sich von Problemen fern und rückte Platz für Platz auf. Henri verlor Zeit durch eine defekte Zündung und einen Ausritt. Dadurch lag er so weit zurück, dass das Team ihm freie Fahrt gewährte, um Boden gut zu machen. Toivonen fuhr wie entfesselt und setzte einige Bestzeiten, ehe er durch Hinterachsschaden ausfiel. Fréquelin kam nie in Reichweite einer Bestzeit, seine konstante Fahrt brachte ihm aber Platz Drei ein – sehr zur Freude des Talbot-Teams.

Das WM-Programm brachte die kleine Talbot-Mannschaft schnell an ihre Grenzen. Die Trainingsautos für die Akropolis Rallye wurden nicht rechtzeitig fertig und so wurde der Einsatz gestrichen. Stattdessen sollte Henri die 1000 Seen Rallye bestreiten, weswegen er das Angebot von Autonovo für einen Fiat-Einsatz ablehnen musste. Den Frühling und Sommer fuhr Henri bei britischen Rallyes im Werkswagen sowie in seiner Heimat im altbewährten Familien-Talbot. Selbst mit dem Gruppe-2-Lotus-Motor fehlte es dem Sunbeam an Leistung gegenüber der Konkurrenz aus der Gruppe 4. Bei den

1,600 cc engine, but he made a very good impression by finishing second in class. "I remember the second stage being encouraging, because I only lost five seconds to Henri", he points out. There had been a mishap, too. "I had an off and went out to check the damage. The bumper was bent and I was so scared of what dad would say about it!" One commonly used nickname for Pauli Toivonen was "Sunshine" …

By November it was taken as granted that Henri would be joining the Talbot factory team for 1980. While lining up for RAC Rally scrutineering in Chester, he was asked something general about Talbot, not specifically about his own involvement with the team. Before he could open his mouth, Pauli interfered with: "It's hard to say anything about a team totally alien to us!" Henri just sheepishly glanced at his father, as if to say: "Oh?" He had a brand new Ford Escort RS1800 for the rally. It was untested and presented all sorts of problems from the off. "First misfiring, then brakes, then gearbox and now the brakes are locked solid," listed Henri ruefully at service. As was so often the case, the omnipresent Pauli was all for calling it a day, but this time co-driver Phil Boland managed to win the argument for carrying on. They struggled on until oil from the gearbox leaked onto the clutch in the Lake District and persuaded the crew to give up the fight. They had only managed a couple of relatively trouble-free stages, being second in Bramham Park and third on one of the Kielder stages.

In December, one of the sport's worst kept secrets was made public when Talbot announced Henri Toivonen would be driving for the Coventry team in 1980. There had also been some interest from British Leyland, but this outcome with Talbot was always the most likely scenario. The planned programme was not very big, but it included WRC rallies with the use of pacenotes, and it was mainly Pauli's decision to reinstate Antero Lindqvist in the co-driver's seat. "I guess he wanted someone slightly older to look after his kid out there in the world", believes the man himself. Henri actually began his season in the family team Talbot Sunbeam, which had now received a 2.2-litre Lotus twin-cam engine, but was not otherwise in works specification. That was not such a handicap in the revamped Arctic Rally, which had been shortened by about 30% to comprise only seventeen special stages and even then there was a lot of double usage. Toivonen enjoyed a favourable position on the road behind Airikkala, Hämäläinen and Alén and seized the lead on the third stage. From then on he confidently kept all pursuers at bay. He was fastest on a dozen stages altogether and, as the main opposition wilted, picked off the win by a huge margin. "Good job we hit the front early, so no one can say we were just lucky. This is definitely the best day of my career yet", reckoned the winner.

In Lapland, the Talbot Sunbeam had been adorned with the name "Henri P. Toivonen" on the driver's door. Pauli was his middle name, but this mark of ancestral respect was absent from the works car Henri used in the Mintex Rally. Maybe it was just as well when the team reported him retired with "oil scavenge pump failure" after lying fourth. "Knocked it off against a tree", revealed a fellow competitor …

The really serious business as a works driver in the WRC began in Portugal. Talbot ran two cars with Guy Fréquelin in the other one and the Frenchman was expected to lead the team as Henri's FIA "Priority B" status put him at number twenty, behind all the other top names. Fréquelin avoided any significant trouble and steadily climbed up the order, while Henri was delayed by ignition pack failure and a small excursion. This left him so far behind that the team decided to let him go flat-out to make up ground. Let off the

Beifahrer Phil Boland musste bei der RAC viel Überzeugungsarbeit leisten, damit Henri weiterfuhr. Nach anfänglichen Problemen hatte Pauli seinem Sohn zur Aufgabe geraten – und man weiß ja, wie schwer es war, Pauli zu überstimmen.

Co-driver Phil Boland had to use all his persuasive powers to keep Henri running in the RAC Rally. After early problems, Pauli Toivonen had urged them to throw in the towel and it was hard to overrule Henri's father.

Zur RAC Rallye erhielt Henri einen neuen Escort RS1800 von Peter Clarke Autos. Der Ford war aber schlecht abgestimmt und so konnte sich das Team kaum in Szene setzen.
The Peter Clarke Autos Ford Escort RS1800 was a new car for the Lombard RAC Rally. However, it was unsorted and thus did not really give the crew a chance to show their best.

Sommerrallyes war das ein Handicap, was sich zumindest teilweise in den Ergebnissen widerspiegelte.

Bei der Circuit of Ireland kam Henri immer besser in Fahrt und hatte gerade seine erste Bestzeit markiert, als er einen Richtungspfeil auf einer Kuppe falsch interpretierte, sich drehte und rückwärts in einen Sumpf schoss. Auf der nächsten WP war er wieder Schnellster, doch danach rutschte er außen in einer Kurve in eine Mauer. Der Schaden war so stark, dass er nicht weiterfahren konnte. In Nordirland hatte Lindqvist neben Henri gesessen. Bei den Rallyes in Wales und Schottland sollten Talbot-Teamkoordinator Paul White beziehungsweise der erfahrene Neil Wilson den heißen Sitz einnehmen. In Wales fuhr Henri nur eine Bestzeit und wurde Vierter. In Schottland entfernte das Team nach anfänglichen Problemen den Bremskraftverstärker, doch auch danach hatte Henri kein Vertrauen in die Bremse. Nach mehreren Remplern brach ein Federbein beim Eingang in eine Kurve und der Talbot kam quer über einem Graben zum Stehen. Toivonen verlor über 30 Minuten und beendete die Rallye im Niemandsland.

Nach wenig überwältigenden Ergebnissen bei kleineren finnischen Rallyes stand die 1000 Seen bevor. Das Sprungfestival begann mit einem Frühstart auf WP Eins, der eine Strafminute zur Folge hatte. Henri biss die Zähne zusammen und kletterte in den Ergebnislisten schnell nach oben: Platz Vier nach zehn Prüfungen. Henri war angriffslustig. Er holte den Triumph TR7 V8 von Altmeister Timo Mäkinen zweimal ein und beschädigte sich dabei die Frontlichter. Dann kam Beifahrer Lindqvist angeblich aus dem Aufschrieb heraus, Henri fuhr die Strecken aus dem Gedächtnis und überschlug sich nach einer Kuppe. „Es war keine falsche und zu späte Ansage, es war ein Fehler im Aufschrieb", verteidigt sich der Navigator. „Entweder war die Beschreibung falsch oder es fehlte einfach eine Information."

leash, he immediately set a couple of fastest times, but soon retired with axle failure. Fréquelin never got close to a fastest stage time, but was consistent enough to end up third, which delighted the team.

The small Talbot operation soon found itself stretched to the limit by the WRC programme, and when recce cars could not be prepared in time for the Acropolis Rally, the entry was withdrawn. Instead, Henri would be sent to the 1000 Lakes, so he turned down an existing Autonovo offer to drive a Fiat there. This meant that the spring and summer were spent driving a works car in British events and the trusty old family Talbot in national rallies at home. Even with its Group 2 Lotus engine, the car suffered from a lack of power at the top end in comparison with the Group 4 opposition. In summer conditions this was bad news, and was at least partially reflected in the results.

In the Circuit of Ireland, Henri was speeding up and had just taken his first fastest time, when misunderstanding the arrows on the top of a crest led to a spin backwards into a bog. He was then fastest again on the next stage, but crashed into a wall on the outside of a corner, which did too much damage to go on. While Lindqvist had been sitting beside Henri in Ireland, Talbot team manager Paul White and the experienced Neil Wilson were on the maps for the Welsh and Scottish rallies respectively. Wales saw just one fastest stage time on the way to fourth. For Scotland the team took the brake servos off Toivonen's car as a reaction to earlier problems, but still he could not find confidence in the anchors. After various hitches Henri found himself with a loose strut when committed to a corner and ended up straddled across a ditch. That cost more than half an hour and he finished nowhere.

Zu Beginn seiner Profikarriere hatte Henri Schwierigkeiten, den richtigen Copiloten zu finden. Dabei war es eigentlich egal, wer neben Henri saß, schnell war er immer.

One of Henri's early challenges as a works driver was finding the right co-driver. However, it did not stop him going fast, when everything else was right.

In Portugal verlor Henri anfangs viel Zeit. Danach gab ihm das Talbot-Team „Feuer frei" für den Rest der Rallye.
An early delay in Portugal meant the Talbot team then gave their young charger permission to go flat out.

Henri Toivonen Ruhm und Ehre / Fame and fortune!

Antero Lindqvist stand jetzt unter Druck, aber es bestand kein Zweifel daran, dass er seinen Anteil an Henri Toivonens Aufstieg in die WM hatte. „Es war oftmals sinnvoll, wenn jemand zwischen Henri und Pauli stand", sagt Lindqvist. „Ich nahm die Rolle als Sündenbock an. Aber ich konnte auch bei kleinen Dingen helfen, die sie sonst abgelenkt hätten. Henri fummelte immer mit seinem Sitz herum. Die Mechaniker schraubten herum, aber Henri war einfach nicht glücklich. Letztlich habe ich ihm gesagt, er solle gehen, während ich den Sitz anpasste. Wir waren etwa gleich groß, damit war das Problem gelöst."

An der Heimatfront standen Veränderungen für die Familie Toivonen bevor. Als Pauli in den frühen 70er-Jahren Geschäftsführer des Chrysler-Importeurs gewesen war, hatte ihm Antti Aarnio-Wihuri ein VW-Autohaus übertragen. Beide Marken wurden damals in Finnland ja von derselben Firma vertrieben. Das Autohaus befand sich im Örtchen Kerava an der Eisenbahntrasse von Helsinki nach Norden. Später hatte Pauli den Chrysler-Job aufgegeben, um sich komplett auf das Autohaus zu konzentrieren. 1980 hatte er das Pendeln von der Küste aber so satt, dass er ein neues Haus in der Nähe der Filiale kaufte. „Anfangs war das schrecklich", seufzt Ulla. „Es dauerte eine Weile, bis wir eine Waschmaschine hatten und ich musste die dicke Unterwäsche, die sie unter den Overalls trugen, per Hand waschen!" Die Jungs lebten noch zu Hause. Henri hatte wenigstens ein bisschen Privatsphäre in seiner eigenen Holzhütte abseits des Hauptgebäudes. „Darin gab es keine Toilette und nicht mal fließendes Wasser", beschreibt Ulla. „Erja arbeitete in Helsinki und musste jeden Morgen in das Haupthaus kommen, um die Zähne zu putzen,

Das richtige Spielzeug für die finnischen Rallyefahrer: Mit dem Schneemobil beeindruckten sie Journalisten und sogar ihre Fahrerkollegen.

For several Finnish rally stars, snowmobiles were a toy they could use to entertain foreign colleagues and journalists.

After indifferent results in a couple of minor Finnish rallies, it was time for the 1000 Lakes Rally. That too began badly, when a jump-start brought a full minute's penalty on the very first stage. Henri gritted his teeth and soared up the leader board to hold fourth after ten stages. Toivonen was in feisty mood and greatly irritated when stones kicked up by the slower Triumph TR7 V8 of old master Timo Mäkinen broke his lights on two long stages. Then Lindqvist reputedly lost his way with the notes, Henri drove from memory and rolled after a crest. "More than a wrong or mistimed call, it was a mistake with the notes themselves", defends the co-driver. "Either the description was wrong or there should have been more information."

Antero Lindqvist was under pressure, but there can be no doubt he had been able to contribute to Henri Toivonen's performance in his progression to world level rallying. "It was often useful to have somebody between Henri and Pauli", he says. "I'd accepted the scapegoat role, but was also occasionally able to help in simple little matters that could become a distraction. Henri was forever fidgeting about his seat, for example. The mechanics changed it, but still he wouldn't be happy. Eventually I told him to go away, while I made his seat fit for me. We were pretty much the same size and that solved the problem."

On the home front, changes were afoot in the Toivonen family. In the first part of the 1970s, when Pauli had been managing director of the company importing Chrysler models, AAW had also surrendered one of the corporation's Volkswagen dealerships to him. This was located in Kerava, a little town by the main railroad heading north from Helsinki. Some years down the line, Pauli decided to resign and fully concentrate on this business of his own. By 1980 he had got fed up with daily commuting from his home on the coast and bought a house close to the dealership. "It was awful at first", cries Ulla Toivonen. "It took some time to get a washing machine to the new place and I had to wash by hand that thick underwear they had under the overalls!" The boys still lived at home and Henri got some privacy by setting up a camp in a little wooden hut outside the main building. "There was no toilet or even running water there. Erja worked in Helsinki and she used come into the main house to brush her teeth in the morning before Henri took her to the railway station," Ulla sighs. Such was the luxurious life of a young international rally pro in 1980.

Italian rally fans immediately took to Henri Toivonen, when he showed his stuff in the Sanremo Rally. To them, here was a driver in the Nuvolari mould: full of spirit, bravery and attack! And total commitment! In a Talbot Sunbeam Lotus with slightly more power and ventilated rear discs Henri was a revelation. First he kept catching Harry Källström's works Datsun on every stage. Then, on the Tuscan gravel he was a pacesetter with Alén and Vatanen, but had an off caused by a wrong pacenote. "I'll take that one on the chin. That was a co-driver's mistake, no two ways about it," admits Antero Lindqvist. The steering and suspension were bent, causing eleven minutes penalty on the road plus one lost in the stage, but Henri was not done yet. On the last night's tarmac stages he was fastest of all on the first two and rapidly caught team-mate Fréquelin who was lying fourth. Then the team apparently told Henri to slow down so as not to overtake the Frenchman who was nursing an ailing engine – this even though the Finn seemed to have a chance to make it past Mikkola to third. Ending up fifth, Henri had actually been second fastest driver in the rally after Fiat's Walter Röhrl, with nine fastest stage times to his name.

bevor Henri sie zur Bahnhaltestelle brachte." So sah also das Leben eines jungen Rallyeprofis im Jahre 1980 aus.

Die italienischen Rallyefans liebten Henri Toivonen sofort, als er bei der Rallye Sanremo sein Können zeigte. Für sie war er ein Fahrer wie Nuvolari: voller Temperament, Mut, Angriffslust und Hingabe! Im Talbot Sunbeam Lotus mit mehr Power und innenbelüfteten Scheibenbremsen war Henri eine Offenbarung. Harry Källströms Werks-Datsun holte er auf jeder Prüfung ein. Auf dem Schotter der Toskana gab er mit Alén und Vatanen das Tempo vor, durch einen Aufschriebfehler büßte er jedoch Zeit ein. „Der ging auf meine Kappe", gibt Antero Lindqvist zu. „Das war ein Fehler des Beifahrers, da gibt es keine zwei Meinungen." Toivonen verlor eine Minute auf der WP und kassierte elf Strafminuten durch den anschließenden Service, wo Lenkung und Aufhängung gerichtet wurden. Damit war Henri aber noch nicht geschlagen. Auf den ersten beiden Asphaltprüfungen der letzten Nacht fuhr er allen davon. Der Finne war drauf und dran, seinen Teamkollegen Fréquelin von Platz Vier zu verdrängen, ehe er durch sein Team eingebremst wurde. Toivonen sollte hinter dem Franzosen bleiben, der sich mit einem kränkelnden Motor ins Ziel rettete. Dabei hätte Henri sogar die Chance gehabt, Mikkolas dritten Platz zu erobern. Henri wurde Fünfter, war mit neun Bestzeiten aber der zweitschnellste Fahrer der Rallye hinter Walter Röhrl im Fiat.

Der Disput mit seinem Beifahrer spitzte sich unterdessen weiter zu. Der geplante Start bei der Tour de Corse wurde sogar gestrichen, weil sich kein passender Ersatz für Lindqvist finden ließ. Als eine Art Entschädigung versprach Talbot seine maximale Unterstützung für die RAC Rallye. „Das ganze Team steht hinter ihm", verkündete Des O'Dell. „Wenn Henri neue Federbeine haben möchte, geben wir ihm zwei Sätze. Wenn er neue Bremsbeläge braucht, bekommt er neue Bremsen. Er bekommt alles, was er will." Für die Sanremo hatte das Team ein gutes Schotter-Setup entwickelt und das wollte Henri auch in Großbritannien fahren, wo er von Paul White navigiert wurde. Die Hoffnung vor dem Saisonhöhepunkt war groß.

The problems with his co-driver now came to a head and Toivonen's entry for Tour de Corse was scratched, because no suitable substitute for Lindqvist could be found in time. By way of compensation, Talbot promised maximum support for the RAC Rally with Des O'Dell proclaiming: "The whole team will be behind him. If Henri wants new struts, we'll give him two sets. If Henri wants new brake pads, we'll give him new brakes. Anything he wants, he'll get." A great set-up had been found for the gravel stages of Sanremo and Henri felt confident using them in Britain, too, so there was an air of expectation about the seasonal climax, where he would be paired with Paul White.

Ein gefragter Mann bei Medienvertretern und Kollegen: Henri Toivonen im Gespräch mit dem schwedischen Reporter Thomas Lindberg (oben) und beim Scherzen mit Hannu Mikkola, daneben sitzen Walter Röhrl und Christian Geistdörfer.

It came naturally to Henri Toivonen to mix with members of the media as well as with fellow competitors. Above, he is chatting with Swedish reporter Thomas Lindberg and below, sharing a joke with Hannu Mikkola, Walter Röhrl and Christian Geistdörfer on the left.

Henri Toivonen
Der jüngste WM-Sieger
Youngest ever WRC winner

Drei Wochen vor der RAC Rallye 1980 gab es einen Zwischenfall, der Henri Toivonens Start um ein Haar verhindert hätte. Henri hatte seinem Bruder Harri bei einem finnischen Meisterschaftslauf zugeschaut, als der seit Jahren schwerste Herbststurm in der Region aufzog. Henri war mit Erja und ein paar Freunden im Talbot Sunbeam Lotus auf dem Heimweg. Er fuhr 80 km/h, wo weniger gute Autofahrer vermutlich nur 30 gefahren wären. Zudem hatte Henri seine eigene Sichtweise zum Thema Gurte. Er riet seinen Passagieren nur dazu sich anzuschnallen, wenn sie schlafen wollten. Erja war gerade dabei wegzunicken und schnallte sich daher auf Henris Empfehlung an. Etwa fünf Minuten später kam ein Lada aus einer Seitenstraße. Der Fahrer stoppte, fuhr dann aber erst weiter, bis der Talbot ihm schließlich in die Seite rauschte. Erja wurde ohnmächtig, blieb aber unverletzt, während sich Henri an Knie und Handgelenk verletzte. Der Talbot war ein Totalschaden, ansonsten hatten sie Glück im Unglück, dass nichts Schlimmeres passierte.

Als der Youngster in Talbot-Diensten zur RAC in Bath ankam, waren die Verletzungen ausgestanden. Sein Team war froh, nach Unruhen in der britischen Talbot-Fabrik überhaupt dabei sein zu können. Auf welch dünnem Eis der Optimismus des Teams gebaut war, zeigte sich beim Funktionstest, bei dem Toivonen Probleme mit dem Motor hatte. Sein Triebwerk hatte größere Ventile, leistete 15 PS mehr und das über ein breiteres Drehzahlband. Bei der Technischen Abnahme schienen die Probleme aussortiert, dennoch spielte Henri seine Chancen auf den Sieg herunter. „Ich glaube nicht, dass ich genug Rallyes in Großbritannien bestritten habe, um bei der RAC 100 Prozent zu geben", sagte er. „Das reicht nicht, um die Rallye durch Fahrkönnen zu gewinnen. Wenn ich gewinne, dann weil ich Glück und andere Probleme haben. Hannu Mikkola kennt die Wälder wie seine Westentasche. Es macht keinen Sinn zu versuchen ihn zu schlagen. Du musst warten, bis er Probleme hat."

Die Zuschauerprüfungen zu Beginn spielten keine große Rolle für das Endergebnis und hier ging Henri auf Nummer sicher. Doch als die Rallye in die Wälder führte, ergab sich ein überraschendes Bild. Der große Favorit Hannu Mikkola im Escort hatte durch einen Ausritt Zeit verloren, er litt jedoch noch mehr unter dem schlechten Grip seiner Dunlop-Reifen bei den nassen und rutschigen Bedingungen. Stattdessen gaben die Michelin- und Pirelli-bereiften Autos das Tempo vor. Anders Kulläng führte im Opel Ascona 400 vor Björn Waldegårds Toyota Celica. Die Talbot – ebenfalls auf Michelin unterwegs – folgten auf den weiteren Plätzen. Toivonen lag als bester Talbot-Fahrer auf Platz Drei, als die Rallye Yorkshire erreichte. In Windermere, am Ende der langen ersten Etappe, war er anderthalb Minuten hinter Kulläng. Den Rückstand hatte er zuvor in nur drei Prüfungen um 30 Sekunden reduziert. Mikkola hatte sich auf die vierte Position hochgekämpft und war jetzt drei Minuten im Rückstand. Den Ford-Piloten durfte man also auch noch nicht abschreiben.

Nur zwei Prüfungen weiter auf dem Rückweg nach Süden zeigte sich ein komplett anderes Bild: Kulläng hatte in Grizedale zwei Reifenschäden hinten, Waldegårds Motor einen Lagerschaden. Und Henri Toivonen führte die RAC Rallye an! Aber noch standen 31 Prüfungen bevor, darunter die anspruchsvollen Sektionen in Wales. Mikkola würde den Druck sicher noch erhöhen, das wusste auch Toivonen. „Ich habe nichts gegessen und Unruhe im Bauch", verriet er im ersten Service des Tages. Mikkola war zunächst durch kleinere Probleme aufgehalten worden, in Wales blies er jedoch zum Angriff.

Three weeks before the 1980 RAC Rally, Henri Toivonen came perilously close to missing the event altogether. He had been out watching brother Harri drive in a Finnish championship rally, when the heaviest autumn blizzard in a decade hit the area as night closed in. Driving back home in his civilian Talbot Sunbeam Lotus with Erja and a couple of friends, he was doing perhaps 80 kph, where less skilled drivers were sticking to maybe 30 kph. Henri had his own ideas about seatbelts, advising passengers to only buckle up if they were going to sleep. Erja, sitting beside Henri, was beginning to nod off and harnessed herself in the seat upon his suggestion. Some five minutes later, a Lada emerged from a side road and with the driver first stopping, then moving again, got collected square by the Talbot. Erja passed out, but was basically all right once she came around while Henri hurt his knee and wrist. The Talbot was a write-off, but it could have been so much worse.

The injuries no longer bothered Talbot's emergent star when he arrived in Bath for the RAC Rally. The team, too, were happy simply to be there after recent industrial unrest at Talbot's British factory. Almost as a reminder of the frailty of their mounting optimism, Henri Toivonen then experienced problems with his new engine in a shakedown test. This was a unit with bigger valves, reckoned to give about 15 bhp more and deliver it over a wider rev range. However, by the time he turned up for scrutineering everything seemed to be in order. Henri wanted to play down speculation that he could be a potential winner. "I don't think I have done enough rallies in Britain to go 100 % on the RAC", he said. "Not enough to win the rally just by driving skill. If I win, it will be because I have a little bit of luck and some of the others have trouble. I mean Hannu Mikkola knows the forests like the back of his hand, so there's no use trying to drive to beat him. You have to wait for him to have trouble."

Sunday's opening spectator stages meant little for the eventual outcome and Henri had pledged to play safe through them, but once the rally entered the forests a surprising picture soon emerged. Pre-event favourite Hannu Mikkola had lost time in his Escort with an off, but was apparently suffering more from the poor grip of his Dunlop tyres in the wet and extremely slippery conditions. Instead, it was the Michelin and Pirelli equipped cars that set the pace with Anders Kulläng in an Opel Ascona 400 leading from Björn Waldegård in a Toyota Celica. The Michelin shod Talbots were hanging on with Toivonen their best hope and Henri was up to third by the time the competition left Yorkshire. At the end of the long first leg in Windermere, he was trailing Kulläng by a minute and a half. Notably, he had reduced the gap by thirty seconds in just the last three stages before the rest halt. Mikkola had steadily climbed back up to fourth, but was nearly three minutes behind, although no one dared to discount him yet.

Only two stages into the southward bound return leg it was all change. Kulläng had punctured both his rear tyres on the long Grizedale stage and the engine in Waldegård's Toyota had run its bearings. Henri Toivonen was leading the RAC Rally! As thirty-one special stages and the entire challenging Welsh route still remained, Mikkola was expected to pile on the pressure. Henri wasn't oblivious to it. "No food, now I have a bird in my stomach", he said at the day's first service. The challenge from Mikkola duly came in Wales, but before that he had been hampered by niggling

Talbots große Stunde schlug bei der RAC Rallye 1980: Toivonen war eigentlich nicht in der Favoritenrolle, doch mit dem ruhigen Paul White an seiner Seite wuchs Henri über sich hinaus und siegte.

Talbot's finest hour. Before the start, Henri Toivonen was not the hot favourite to win the 1980 RAC Rally, but, helped by the calming influence of co-driver Paul White, he rose to the occasion.

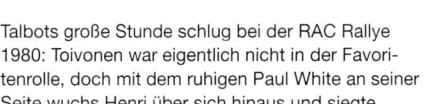

Henri Toivonen Der jüngste WM-Sieger / Youngest ever WRC winner

Aber Henri schlug zurück. Er fuhr sechs Bestzeiten hintereinander und brach Hannu damit das Genick. Mikkola hatte auf den ersten beiden dieser sechs Prüfungen Reifenschäden und gab sich danach geschlagen. In der Great Pulteney Street von Bath konnte Hannu nur anerkennend zuschauen, wie Henri Toivonen und Paul White auf der Zielrampe Champagner versprühten.

Im letzten Service war Des O'Dell außer sich vor Freude: „Das ist unglaublich. Von solchen Dingen habe ich seit Jahren geträumt!" Henri hatte die Rallye nicht nur für Talbot gewonnen und sich zum bis dato jüngsten WM-Sieger gekürt, seine Teamkollegen Guy Fréquelin und Russell Brookes hatten zudem die Plätze Drei und Vier belegt. Es war so, als würde Des O'Dell die Stufen zum Rallyezentrum hochschweben. Er hatte versprochen nicht zu weinen, aber seine Stimme zitterte spürbar vor Freude. Drei Stunden nach der Zieldurchfahrt traf sich das Team mit geladenen Gästen und den Medien in Bath. Es war ein bewegender Moment für alle Beteiligten. Es gab niemanden, der Henri Toivonen diesen Sieg nicht gönnte.

Viele Menschen sagen, dass der Erfolg Henri nicht verändert hat. Es gab zwar einige, die seine Karriere mit Neid verfolgten und ihn als verwöhntes Wunderkind sehen wollten, aber selbst diese Leute behaupteten nicht, dass er sich durch den Ruhm verändert hätte. Dies wurde kurz nach der RAC offensichtlich, als Henri bei einer kleinen Rallye in Finnland von Mikael Sundström geschlagen wurde. Im Parc Fermé nach dem Ziel sagte Henri: „Wow. Auf der letzten WP habe ich im Nebel versucht, deinen Spuren zu folgen, aber mir ist die Luft ausgegangen." Henri hatte es gehasst zu verlieren, aber er war kein schlechter Verlierer. Es gab nur eine Ausnahme, aber dazu später mehr.

little problems. Then Henri showed his hand and hit back. He set a string of six fastest times, which broke the back of Hannu's offensive. Having picked up two punctures on the first of those stages, the older Finn conceded defeat. In Bath's picturesque Great Pulteney Street, Hannu looked on approvingly as Henri and Paul White enthusiastically sprayed the champagne on the finish ramp.

At the last service point Des O'Dell had been beside himself with joy: "It's incredible! Things like this I've been dreaming about for years!" It was not just that Henri had conquered the most important rally for Talbot as the youngest-ever winner of a WRC event but Guy Fréquelin and Russell Brookes had brought their cars home in third and fourth places. Jogging up the steps to Rally HQ, O'Dell's feet barely touched the ground. He had promised he would not cry, but his voice was clearly shaking with emotion. Three hours after the finish, the team gathered with invited guests and media in Bath's Georgian Pump Rooms. It was a happy moment for all concerned. No one wanted to deny Henri Toivonen this success.

It has been said by many that success never really changed Henri. Some viewed him from a very early age with envy and liked to see him as a spoiled prodigy, but even those people would not claim he became a different person with fame and fortune. That much was obvious when, fresh from the RAC Rally, he entered a minor Finnish event and got beaten by Mikael Sundström. Arriving in parc fermé at the finish Henri had this to say: "Wow, I tried to follow your tracks on that last stage in the fog, but just ran out of breath!" He may have hated defeat, but he was never a sore loser. Well, there was one exception and more of that Manx tale later.

Im Ziel gab es viele sehr emotionale Momente. Doch niemanden schien der Erfolg mehr zu ergreifen als Des O'Dell. Im Pump Room, einem bekannten Restaurant in Bath, feierte er gemeinsam mit Guy Fréquelin, Henri, Paul White und Jean Todt.

There were emotional scenes at the finish and no-one seemed more emotionally moved than Des O'Dell, winding down in Bath's Pump Rooms with Guy Fréquelin, Henri, Paul White, Jean Todt plus assorted friends and admirers.

Rechts: Henri war 24 Jahre, 3 Monate und 24 Tage alt, als er die RAC gewann – zu einer Zeit, als sonst nur erfahrene Piloten bei den großen Rallyes siegten.

Right: Henri was 24 years, 3 months and 24 days old when he won the RAC Rally, at a time when the big rallies were mainly won by experienced drivers.

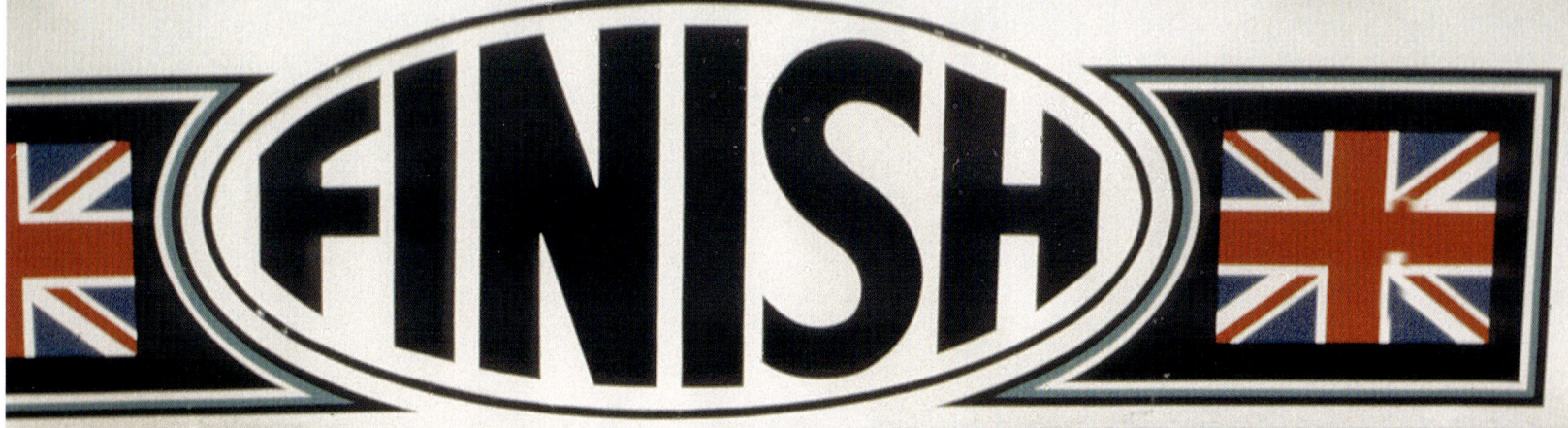

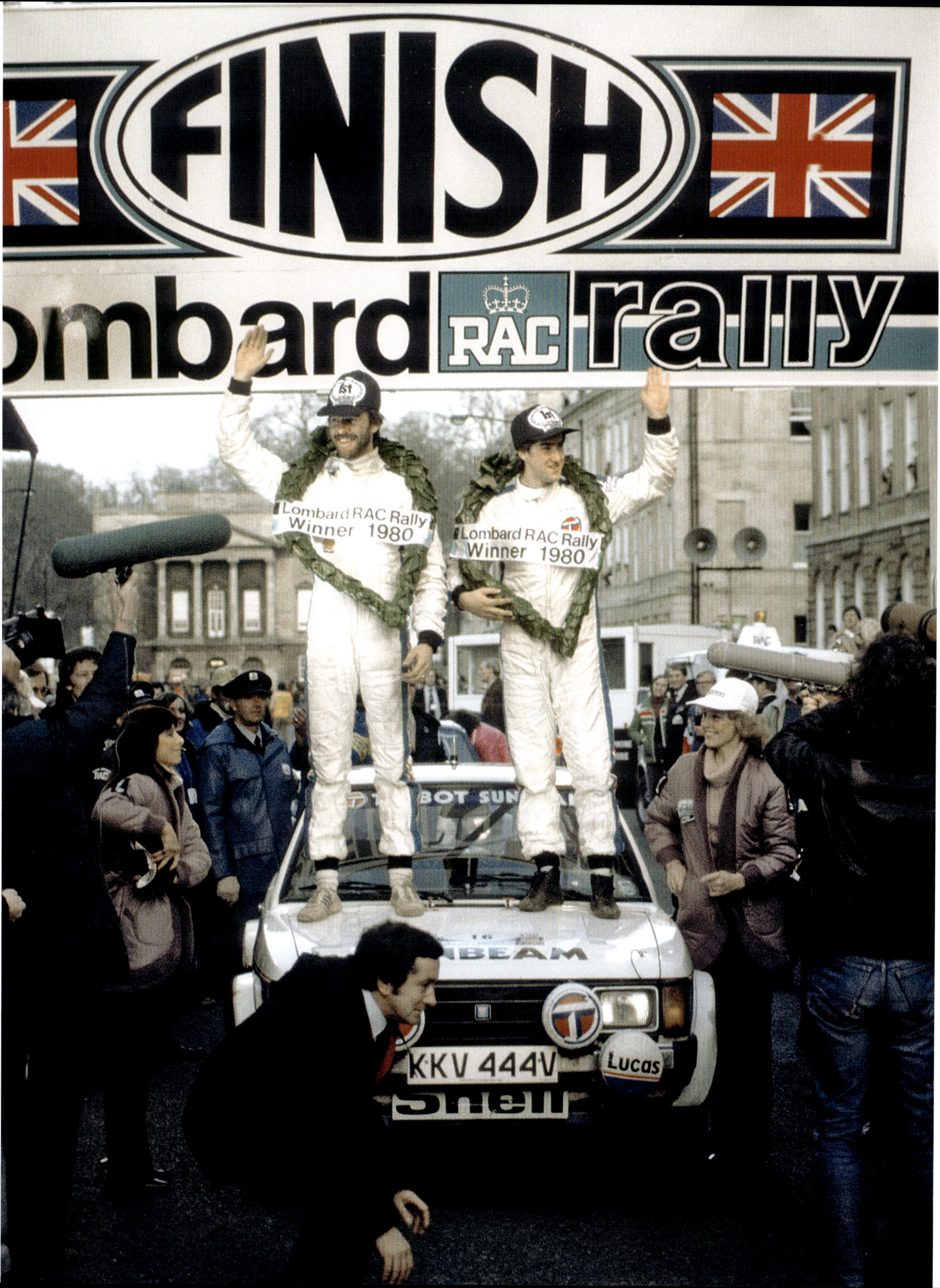
FINISH
ombard RAC rally
Lombard RAC Rally Winner 1980
Lombard RAC Rally Winner 1980
KKV 444V
Lucas
Shell

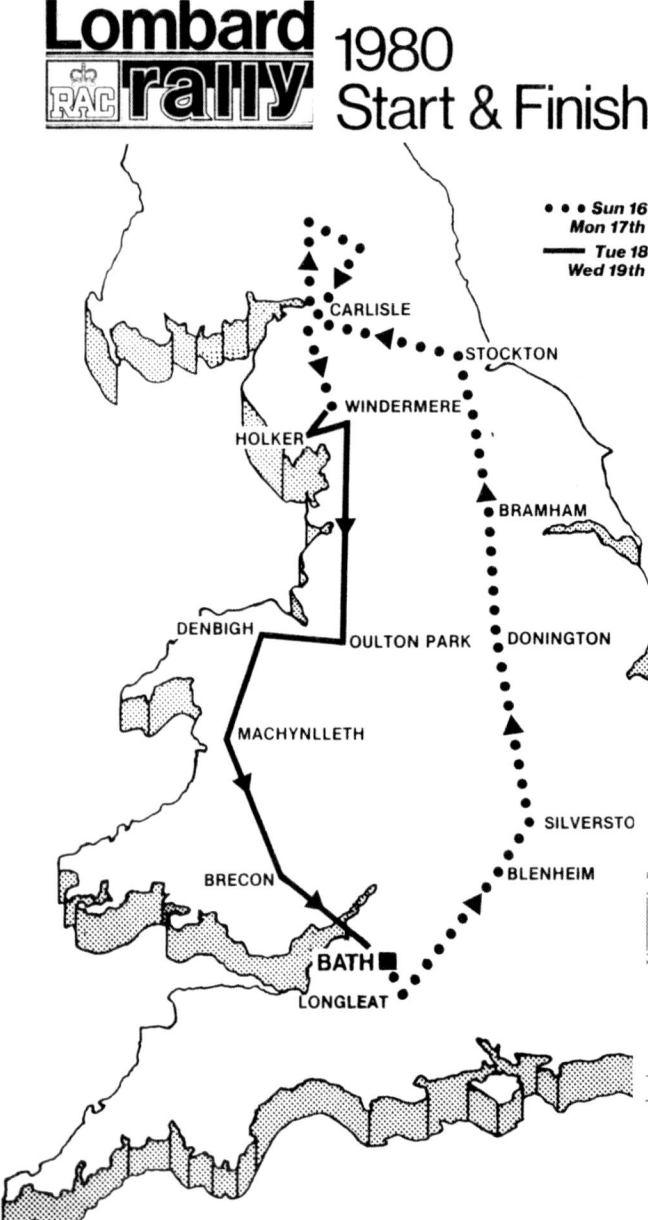

Toivonen
Pauli, Henri & Harri

RAC 1980

Oft hieß es, Henri Toivonen hätte sich mit seinem unbedingten Siegeswillen (sogar mit unterlegenem Material) am Anfang seiner Karriere selbst im Weg gestanden. Bei der RAC 1980 war das definitiv nicht der Fall. Vielleicht lag es an der Gelassenheit von Beifahrer Paul White, der den Übermut des 24-Jährigen erfolgreich bändigte. Nach einem vorsichtigen Start übernahm Henri erst die Initiative, als die Führenden Probleme hatten. Doch der Talbot-Fahrer nutzte seine Chance perfekt. Obwohl ihm der Sieger der letzten beiden RAC Rallyes, Hannu Mikkola, an der Stoßstange klebte, blieb Henri cool und wehrte die Attacke des Finnen mit einer Reihe von Bestzeiten ab.

It has been said that early in his career Henri Toivonen was hindered by a desire to win outright, even when he had inferior equipment. However, his approach to the 1980 RAC Rally was not like that at all. Perhaps it was the calmness exuded by Paul White sitting alongside him that tempered the 24-year-old's exuberance. After a sensible start Henri was handed the initiative when the leaders hit trouble, but from that moment he grabbed the opportunity in a most convincing manner. With the winner of the previous two RAC Rallies breathing down his neck, young Toivonen kept his composure and repelled Hannu Mikkola's attack with a string of fastest stage times in Wales.

Lombard RAC Rally 1980

Henri Toivonen proved them all wrong. They were sure that a Talbot could never beat a Ford, convinced that a group 2 car could never win the RAC, sure that the big-valve Sunbeam Lotus engine was only good for a few hundred miles, certain that the special pressures of leading an RAC Rally could only be contained by a really experienced driver. At twenty-four years old, he became easily the youngest driver to win the RAC Rally, making it quite clear that if he can win by so convincing a margin so soon in his career, he has the possibility of being the greatest rally driver in history.

Martin Holmes

Henri Toivonen
Mit Talbot zum WM-Titel
Helping make Talbot champion

Henris Beifahrerproblem wurde am Tag vor der RAC Rallye 1980 gelöst, als er in Bath auf Fred Gallagher traf. Der Brite war auf der Suche nach einem Cockpit, weil British Leyland sein Projekt mit dem Triumph TR7 beendet hatte. Fred und Henri waren sich schnell einig und legten kurz darauf mit der Arbeit los. Im Dezember begann das Training für die Rallye Monte Carlo auf dem Col de Turini, wo sich Henri erst einmal mit den englischen Ansagen vertraut machen musste. „Wir haben ein einfaches englisches Aufschriebsystem verwendet und einige finnische Wörter eingebaut um Formen zu beschreiben, für die wir keinen feststehenden Begriff haben", erklärt Gallagher. „Wir haben zum Beispiel das Wort ‚sumppu' genutzt für eine Kurve, die außen stärker zu macht als innen." Das System schien gut zu funktionieren, auch wenn Fred heute noch darüber lachen muss, welche Probleme sein Fahrer mit der englischen Sprache hatte: „In einer der ersten Kurven bei der Monte habe ich so etwas gesagt wie ‚very long fast left, tightens, ice on the inside at apex'. Daraufhin fragte mich Henri: ‚Was bedeutet dieses Apex?'" [Apex = Scheitelpunkt]

Für Fahrer und Beifahrer war es die erste Rallye Monte Carlo, dennoch hatten sie einen vielversprechenden Start mit der fünften Zeit auf WP Eins. Sie waren zwar fast eine Minute langsamer als Hannu Mikkola, aber das waren praktisch alle, denn Audi schockte die Rallyewelt mit dem neuen Quattro. Bruno Saby lag als Zweitschnellster im Renault 5 Turbo nur sechs Sekunden vor Toivonen. Dann kam die

A solution to Henri's co-driver problems was found the day before the RAC Rally when he came across Fred Gallagher in Bath. The latter was looking for a new deal, since British Leyland's Triumph programme was coming to an end and he asked whether Henri had anything planned. He did not and agreement was quickly reached. The new partnership started work almost immediately, as in December they began the recce for the 1981 Monte Carlo Rally over the Col de Turini. This involved the adoption of English pacenotes for Henri Toivonen. "We used a basic English system of notes with some Finnish words to describe shapes for which we don't have a single word," explains Fred Gallagher. "For example, we'd use 'sumppu' to describe a corner, where the outside tightens more than the inside." The system seemed to work well enough, even though it still makes Gallagher smile how the driver could at that time struggle with his English: "On one of the early corners in Monte Carlo I had to say something like 'very long fast left, tightens, ice on the inside at apex', and Henri asked 'what does it mean: apex'!"

This was the first time either of them had done the Monte, but they got off to a promising start by being fifth quickest on the first stage. Sure, they were nearly a full minute slower than Hannu Mikkola, but then so was practically everyone else as Audi shocked the rally world with its Quattro. Bruno Saby as second fastest in the Renault 5 Turbo was only six seconds quicker than Toivonen. Next came the long Chartreuse stage over the Col du Granier, where Henri got a puncture. Spectators were on hand to lift the car, but they dropped it every time another competitor passed, so seven minutes were lost with that incident. "With hindsight, we shouldn't have trusted outside help", says Fred Gallagher. "It led to us practising wheel changes during recce. Whenever either of us shouted 'puncture' we'd immediately stop to change a wheel." Toivonen/Gallagher recovered to finish fifth in the rally, but second

Neuer Co, neue Sprache: Durch die Partnerschaft mit Fred Gallagher wechselte Henri auf englische Noten.
Partnership with Fred Gallagher meant swapping to English pace-notes.

Henris erste Monte bedeutete harte Arbeit, aber der fünfte Platz war für zwei Neulinge kein schlechtes Ergebnis.

Henri's first Monte Carlo Rally was hard work, but fifth place for two event debutants was by no means a bad result.

Chartreuse-Prüfung über den Col du Granier, wo Henri einen Platten hatte. Die Zuschauer waren schnell zur Stelle, um das Auto anzuheben. Doch jedes Mal, wenn ein anderer Teilnehmer vorbeikam, ließen sie den Talbot einfach los. So waren sieben Minuten beim Teufel. „Im Nachhinein hätten wir uns besser nicht auf fremde Hilfe verlassen", erklärt Gallagher. „Es führte dazu, dass wir beim Training Reifenwechsel übten. Immer wenn jemand ‚Reifenschaden' brüllte, hielten wir sofort an um zu wechseln." Bei der Monte erreichten Toivonen/Gallagher noch den fünften Platz. Ihre Teamkollegen Guy Fréquelin und Jean Todt wurden Zweite – nur drei Minuten hinter dem Sieger – und zeigten, zu was der Talbot im Stande war. „Jean hatte bei uns im Team damals schon die Fäden in der Hand", verrät Gallagher. Das wurde besonders deutlich, als Henri und Fred von Monte Carlo zur Arctic Rallye aufbrachen. „Wir hatten eine kurze Nachbesprechung in Jeans Badezimmer, dann eilten wir nach Finnland."

Wegen des engen Zeitplans verbrachte die Fahrerpaarung die Nacht im Haus der Toivonens in Kerava, bevor sie einen Flug zum Polarkreis nahmen. „Mir war das so peinlich. Wir mussten Fred im Wohnzimmer unterbringen, wo er auf der Couch geschlafen hat", seufzt Ulla Toivonen. Am Flughafen von Rovaniemi wurden Fred und Henri von Pauli abgeholt, der sie direkt zur Startrampe fuhr. Dort wartete der Talbot Sunbeam Lotus mit Startnummer Eins auf sie. Während der Rallye hatten sie einen Ausrutscher und erreichten das Ziel einer WP mit dem aufgewühlten Ulf Grönholm im Rückspiegel. In der Prüfung war der Fiat dem Talbot mehrmals ins Heck gefahren, im Ziel ging das Spiel mit Beschimpfungen und Schubsern weiter. Grönholm wurde für sein Verhalten verwarnt, dennoch gewann der heißblütige Bauer die Rallye. Henri wurde Dritter.

Vier Wochen später war Ulf Grönholm tot. Er und sein Beifahrer kamen bei einem Unfall beim Training zur Hanki Rallye ums Leben, als ihr Fiat einen Schneepflug frontal rammte und in Flammen aufging. Diese Tragödie überschattete die Hanki Rallye, bei der Henri mit Motorschaden ausfiel.

In Portugal kehrte Toivonen in den Werkswagen zurück. Während Hannu Mikkola dem Feld im Quattro unaufhaltsam davonzog, kämpfte Henri mit Ari Vatanen und Markku Alén um Platz Zwei. Kurz nach der Halbzeit hatte Toivonen einen Reifenschaden und beim Wechsel fiel der Talbot vom Wagenheber. Dieser Vorfall und ein Problem mit dem Schalthebel kosteten drei Minuten. Nachdem Mikkola und Vatanen ausgefallen waren, kam Henri bis auf zwei Sekunden an den führenden Alén heran, der zuvor ebenfalls Zeit verloren hatte. In Arganil hatte Henri seinem Widersacher auf halber Strecke nach eigener Schätzung 30 Sekunden abgenommen, als die hintere Radnabe brach. Das Rad war nicht mehr an der Antriebswelle befestigt und drehte nur noch durch. Henri musste immer querfahren, damit das Rad überhaupt noch Vortrieb entwickelte. Das kostete sechs Minuten in der WP und brachte vier Minuten Strafzeit auf der Verbindungsetappe. Henri wurde Zweiter, neun Minuten hinter Alén. Vom Tempo her war er aber auf Augenhöhe mit dem Sieger gewesen. Sein Team war überglücklich und feierte schon vor der letzten Schleife in Sintra. „Ich habe ihnen gesagt, dass das wohl ein bisschen verfrüht wäre", sagt Gallagher. „Dann sagte Des O'Dell etwas, was ich nie vergessen werde: ‚Wir zahlen dir nicht genug Geld!' Ich habe sein Angebot von 10.000 Britischen Pfund pro Jahr sofort akzeptiert, bei British Leyland hatte ich nur 8.000 bekommen."

Für Henri war die Tour de Corse ein weiterer neuer WM-Lauf, Fred war mit Tony Pond schon zweimal dort gefahren. Von Fréquelin wurde hier natürlich viel erwartet, deswegen bekam er einen neuen Talbot Sunbeam Lotus, der 50 Kilo leichter war und eine härtere Aufhängung hatte. Henri zeigte trotz eines weiteren Reifenschadens eine beachtliche Leistung und lag als bester Ausländer auf Platz Sieben, als ein

place for the team's other car of Guy Fréquelin/Jean Todt – just three minutes behind the winner – showed what was possible with the Talbot. "Jean was very much the man pulling the strings in the team at this time", reveals Gallagher. That much was evident, when Henri and Fred had to rush from Monte Carlo to the north for the Arctic Rally. "We had a quick debrief in Jean's bathroom, then hurried off to Finland", he slips in.

The tight schedule meant the pair spent the night at the Toivonen's house in Kerava before taking another flight to the Polar Circle. "I was so embarrassed as we had to put Fred in the living room, where he slept on the couch", sighs Ulla Toivonen. Up in Rovaniemi, Pauli picked up the pair from the airport to drive them straight to the start ramp, where a Talbot Sunbeam Lotus waited for them with number one on its flanks. Once into the stages they soon had an off and were followed to the end of a stage by an agitated Ulf Grönholm. The Fiat had been bumping them up the rear in frustration and at the finish control much shouting, pushing and shoving followed, which led to the marshals reporting Grönholm to the stewards. The hot-headed farmer still went on to win the rally with Henri back in third.

Four weeks later Ulf Grönholm was dead, perishing with his co-driver in a tragic practice accident the night before the Hankiralli. They hit a snowplough head on and the Fiat erupted into flames. The tragedy rather threw a shadow over that event, where Henri retired with engine trouble.

In Portugal, Toivonen was back in the works car and, while Hannu Mikkola was inexorably pulling clear in the Quattro, Henri fought for second with Ari Vatanen and Markku Alén. Just after halfway, Toivonen got a puncture and while changing the wheel the car fell off the jack. This and a problem with the gearlever cost some three minutes, but once Mikkola and Vatanen had dropped out, he closed within two seconds of new leader Markku Alén, who also had lost a lot of time earlier. In the middle of the long Arganil stage Henri thought he had pulled about thirty seconds on Markku, but then the rear hub broke, leaving the wheel spinning around, no longer connected to driveshaft. He had to throw the car sideways in order to lock the wheel and get some forward motion. This meant a loss of six minutes in the stage and a further four on the subsequent road section leaving him to finish second, nine minutes behind Alén. Toivonen's speed on special stages had been comparable to the winner throughout. The team was very pleased indeed. Before the last group of stages in Sintra they were celebrating. "I remember saying to them this was still a bit premature", says Fred Gallagher. "Des then said something I'll never forget. He said 'We're not paying you enough money'! I'd immediately accepted his offer of £10,000 per annum, because I had only got £8,000 from British Leyland."

Tour de Corse was another new event for Henri, although Fred had been there twice before with Tony Pond. Fréquelin was naturally expected to be stronger here, so he got a new Talbot Sunbeam Lotus for the event, fifty kilos lighter and with harder suspension. Henri still did a most respectable job, despite yet another puncture, to hold seventh as the best non-French driver until a ball-joint on the track control-arm broke. He struggled to the end of the stage with very little directional control, but by the time the problem was fixed he was over his maximum lateness and had to give up.

The Acropolis Rally was fraught with trouble and it started during the recce where, entirely without any fault on his part, Henri was in collision with a VW Bus.

Nach einigen zeitraubenden Reifenschäden begannen Toivonen/Gallagher Reifenwechsel zu üben. Beim Training wurden diese Übungen sogar irgendwann zum Ritual.
After experiencing costly punctures, Toivonen and Gallagher started to practice wheel changes. Their routines were honed by regular drills during the pre-rally period.

Henri Toivonen — Mit Talbot zum WM-Titel / Helping make Talbot Champion

Nach dem Triumph bei der RAC 1980 brachte das Jahr 1981 ein Wechselbad der Gefühle. In Portugal (links) beeindruckte Henri mit Platz Zwei nach einem tollen Kampf mit dem siegreichen Markku Alén, in Griechenland (oben) schied er jedoch aus.

After the triumph on the 1980 RAC Rally, there were mixed fortunes for Henri Toivonen. He was impressive in Portugal (left) where he finished second after battling with winner Markku Alén, but Greece was the scene of another retirement (above).

Henri Toivonen Mit Talbot zum WM-Titel / Helping make Talbot Champion

Kugelgelenk am Querlenker brach. Obwohl der Talbot praktisch unlenkbar war, schaffte er es noch bis zum Ende der Prüfung. Bei der Reparatur wurde aber die Karenzzeit überschritten und Henri musste aufgeben.

Bei der Akropolis hatte Toivonen ein Problem nach dem anderen. Das begann beim Training, als er völlig unverschuldet mit einem VW-Bus kollidierte. „Ich glaube, wir hatten bei fast jeder Rallye einen Trainingsunfall", erinnert sich Gallagher. Während der Rallye waren Staub und Reifenschäden ständige Begleiter. „Ich habe eine Minute Strafzeit auf mich genommen, um an Mehta vorbei zu kommen", sagte Henri damals. „In der nächsten WP habe ich prompt einen Platten und er ist wieder vorn." Auf den langen Prüfungen löste sich die Lauffläche des Reifens häufig von der Karkasse, allein auf der ersten Etappe hatte Henri vier Reifenschäden. Zudem musste ein Getriebe getauscht werden, dessen Wechsel zu einer Zeitstrafe führte. Auf einer 45-Kilometer-WP musste Henri zweimal zum Reifenwechseln stoppen und zu allem Überfluss brachen dann auch noch die Radmuttern ab. „Ich versteh' das nicht, wir sind keine 30 Meter auf dem platten Reifen gefahren", schimpfte Henri. „Zumindest hatten wir Reifenwechsel geübt", ergänzt Fred. Nach 22 von 57 Prüfungen war die Akropolis für sie Geschichte.

Der Talbot Sunbeam Lotus des Toivonen-Teams war im Herbst 1980 durch ein neues Auto ersetzt worden. Im folgenden Frühjahr gab es Gerüchte, dass Harri den Talbot bei einer Rallye außerhalb Finnlands einsetzen würde. Doch am Ende war es Henri, der mit diesem Wagen die Hunsrück-Rallye bestritt – angelockt vom Veranstalter, der ausländische Fahrer in der Hoffnung auf ein WM-Prädikat einlud. Im Hunsrück war Henris alter Kumpel Juha Paajanen Beifahrer. Der Ausflug hätte durchaus zum Sieg führen können, denn auf der ersten WP war Henri nur eine Sekunde langsamer als Walter Röhrl im Porsche 924 Carrera GTS. Doch auf der nächsten WP über 38 Kilometer hatte der Talbot zwei Reifenschäden. Beim anschließenden Hinterachswechsel wurde das Zeitlimit überschritten. Henri nahm die nächste Prüfung als Test in Angriff und fuhr Bestzeit.

Die 1000 Seen Rallye war eine neue Erfahrung für Fred Gallagher. Die Partnerschaft mit Henri hatte sich weiter gefestigt, doch in seinem Heimatland fuhr Henri scheinbar mehr nach dem Gedächtnis als nach den Noten. Henri war phasenweise in einem tranceähnlichen Zustand. Er fuhr nach Instinkt und hörte nicht mehr auf die Ansagen, als wäre er in seiner eigenen Welt. Das führte manchmal zu unglaublichen Leistungen, andere Male zu schweren Unfällen. In der ersten Hälfte der Rallye regnete es, was für Henri ein Prob-

"We seemed to have a recce accident in nearly every event", recalls Gallagher. In the actual rally, dust and punctures were perennial worries. "I take a one minute penalty to get in front of Mehta and then on the next stage I get a puncture, so he is in front again", Henri complained. On long fast sections, the tread of the tyres had a tendency to lift away from their casing and in the first leg alone he suffered four flat tyres. A gearbox change was needed too, but the box would not fit properly and modifying the mountings brought road penalties. Still picking up punctures, he stopped twice on a long 45 km stage and on the next road section the wheel nuts sheared. "I don't understand it, we never drove more than 30 metres on a flat tyre", Henri rued. "At least we'd practiced changing wheels by now", adds Fred. The pair was out after twenty-two of fifty-seven stages.

The "Team Toivonen" Talbot Sunbeam Lotus had been replaced with a new one late in 1980 and by the following spring rumours were circulating of Harri getting a chance to use it on an event outside Finland. However, it was Henri who took this car to the Hunsrück Rally, whose organisers lured foreign entries in hope of promotion to the WRC. He drove down to Germany in a recce car, once again joined by his old chum, Juha Paajanen. The escapade could have brought success as the pair was second on the first stage, only one second behind Walter Röhrl's Porsche 924 Carrera GTS, but two punctures on the next 38 km stage necessitated a change of rear axle, which put them OTL. Henri still drove the next stage just to check the car and was fastest of all!

The 1000 Lakes Rally was a novel experience for Fred Gallagher. The partnership had just started to really gel, but in his home country Henri seemed to drive more from memory than from the pacenotes. There would be occasions, when Henri seemed to go into a trance-like state, where he did not really listen to the notes, but drove instinctively, as if on a different level. Sometimes it would yield outstanding performances, but other times it could lead to costly incidents. For the first part of the 1981 1000 Lakes Rally it was raining and, as Talbot had only brought hard compound, dry-weather tyres, Toivonen was in trouble. "We are always on oversteer, from one ditch to another", he confessed. Then the sun came out and at last he was on the right tyres. Holding third place, he was hunted down by the delayed Mikkola. "I was just about to give up the chase, when he stopped", said Hannu. Distributor failure spelled retirement for the Talbot. Henri had never been fastest on a stage, but ten times second, usually to Mikkola's Quattro.

Fred Gallagher: „Ich glaube, wir hatten bei fast jeder Rallye einen Unfall im Training."
Fred Gallagher: "We seemed to have a recce accident on nearly every event."

Ein Entertainer auf vier Rädern: kein Wunder, dass Henri in Italien viele Freunde hatte.
The great entertainer's dashing style found immediate favour in Italy.

lem war, weil Talbot nur harte Trockenreifen mitgebracht hatte. „Wir hatten immer nur Übersteuern, von einem Graben zum nächsten", gab Henri zu. Dann kam die Sonne heraus und er hatte endlich die richtigen Reifen. Toivonen lag auf Platz Drei und hatte den nach vorne preschenden Hannu Mikkola im Nacken. „Ich wollte den Angriff gerade einstellen, als er stehengeblieben ist", erklärte Hannu. Der Grund für den Ausfall war der Verteiler. Henri war zwar keine einzige Bestzeit gefahren, aber zehnmal Zweiter gewesen, meist hinter Mikkolas Audi Quattro.

In Sanremo setzte Talbot erstmals die neuen TRX-Reifen von Michelin ein. Guy Fréquelin mochte sie nicht, bei Henri war das genaue Gegenteil der Fall. Der sonst so konstante Fréquelin erlebte eine Rallye zum Vergessen: Der Anwärter auf den WM-Titel schied nach einer dürftigen Vorstellung durch Motorschaden aus. In Siena, als der Großteil der Schotterprüfungen schon vorbei war, lag Henri auf Platz Vier, obwohl er seitlich einen Baum getroffen hatte und sein Auto krumm war. Als Ari Vatanen und Walter Röhrl ausfielen, erbte Henri die zweite Position, womit Talbot der Herstellertitel eigentlich nicht mehr zu nehmen war. Des O'Dell war außer sich vor Freude: „Henri war unglaublich in diesem Auto, so krumm wie es nach dem Baum war. Das war schrottreif und trotzdem ist er damit im Expresstempo gefahren. Da wundert man sich über das Gerede über Übersteuern und Untersteuern! Macht das etwas aus?"

Am selben Wochenende lieferte Bruder Harri die bis dato beste Kostprobe seines Könnens ab. Er hatte den Familien-Talbot sowie Beifahrer Juha Paajanen von seinem großen Bruder geerbt und gewann damit fast den Lauf zur finnischen Meisterschaft in Nokia, der Heimat des Mobiltelefonherstellers. Harri war am führenden Kyösti Hämäläinen vorbeigezogen und lag drei Prüfungen vor Schluss elf Sekunden vorn, als er sich an einem Stein, genau wie viele andere Teilnehmer, einen Reifenschaden einfing. Bemerkenswert ist, dass Harri zu diesem Zeitpunkt erst so wenige Wettbewerbe in Autos bestritten hatte wie Henri, als dieser 1975 an der 1000 Seen Rallye teilgenommen hatte. Nach der Rallye gab es Gerüchte, Harri hätte illegal trainiert. „Eine Woche vorher sind wir mit Henri rausgefahren, um die Prüfungen für Harri zu trainieren", gibt ein Freund zu. „Ich habe einen Satz Gebetbücher bekommen, aber ich schwöre, ich habe sie nicht im Auto mitgenommen", widerlegt Paajanen.

Talbot used Michelin's latest TRX tyres for gravel for the first time in Sanremo. Guy Fréquelin disliked them, but for Henri it was quite the opposite. For the normally super-consistent, championship-chasing Frenchman this was an unhappy event and he retired with engine problems after a lame showing. With the bulk of gravel stages done, Henri was lying fourth in Siena, despite hitting a tree sideways that had left the car banana-shaped. As Ari Vatanen and Walter Röhrl dropped out, he ended up a fine second, which practically clinched the Makes title for Talbot. Once more Des O'Dell did not hide his delight: "Henri was magnificent in that car, all bent round a tree it had been ... we'll have to write it off ... yet he went like a train in that. Makes you wonder when they all start talking about oversteer and understeer! Does it matter?"

That same weekend Harri Toivonen gave by far the most impressive demonstration of his talent yet. Now a regular incumbent of the family team Talbot, he had also inherited Juha Paajanen as co-driver and they so nearly won a round of the Finnish rally championship in Nokia, near Tampere. Harri had hauled in leader Kyösti Hämäläinen to have eleven seconds in hand with three stages to go. Unfortunately a stone that caught out several top runners then punctured the Talbot's rear tyre and ruined the day. It is worth noting that Harri had by now only started as many competitive events in cars as Henri had when he drove that little Simca in the 1975 1000 Lakes Rally. Afterwards there were inevitable rumours of Harri having illegally practiced the rally in Nokia. "We once went out with Henri a week in advance to recce the stages for Harri", a friend confesses. "I was once given a set of pacenotes, but swear I never took them in the car with me", refutes Paajanen.

As preparation for the RAC Rally, Henri took part in the Pace National Rally, formerly known under the name of its previous title sponsor Castrol. "It all seemed very strange without Fred reading me the notes", he said of the "blind" event format. Henri and Fred fought with the similar Talbot of Russell Brookes and Jimmy McRae's Opel Ascona 400, but won easily in the end.

Just as Grizedale forest had been a fortuitous place for Henri in the 1980 RAC Rally, in 1981 it spelled the beginning of the end for him. He experienced engine problems in the first Grizedale

Henri Toivonen Mit Talbot zum WM-Titel / Helping make Talbot Champion

Zur Vorbereitung für die RAC nahm Henri an der Pace National Rallye teil, die vorher unter dem Namen Castrol Rallye bekannt war. „Es war sehr merkwürdig, weil Fred mir keine Noten vorgelesen hat", sagte Henri damals über die „blinde" Rallye. Toivonen kämpfte mit Markenkollege Russell Brookes und Jimmy McRae im Opel Ascona 400 und siegte am Ende deutlich.

1980 hatte Henri im Grizedale Forest den Grundstein zum Sieg gelegt, 1981 war eben dieser Wald Schauplatz für den Anfang vom Ende. In der ersten Grizedale-WP hatte Henri Motorprobleme und sah, wie der Öldruck absackte. Der Motor war angeschlagen und hatte nicht mehr die volle Power. Um das Triebwerk zu schonen fuhr Toivonen bei der zweiten Grizedale-Durchfahrt nur mit niedriger Drehzahl. Henri nahm eine enge Kurve zu schnell, überschlug sich und verlor ein paar Minuten. „Die Kurve war eine von der Sorte, wo man die zusätzliche Leistung einfach gebraucht hätte", so Gallagher. „Das Auto ist einfach aufs Dach gerollt." Im Kielder Forest eroberten sie zwar Platz Drei, doch in Schottland quittierte der Lotus-Motor endgültig den Dienst. Henri war gerade drei Bestzeiten gefahren, seine einzigen im Laufe der Rallye.

Einige Wochen zuvor hatten Henri und Erja endlich ihr eigenes Heim bezogen. An der Südküste, etwa 15 Kilometer westlich von Helsinki, wohnten sie in einem großen, neuen Mehrfamilienhaus mit Meerblick. Die Küche hatten sie anfangs aber noch nicht eingerichtet, weswegen sie am Saisonende an der Marcello Rallye teilnahmen. Als Preisgeld für den Sieger stiftete der Hauptsponsor Küchengeräte. Henri wollte eigentlich mit Erja als Copilotin fahren. „Ich hatte nie an Rallyes teilgenommen und wollte das jetzt nicht mehr anfangen", beschreibt Erja. „Ich konnte mich da irgendwie rauswinden und Juha [Paajanen] hat meinen Platz eingenommen. Die Jungs haben gewonnen und wir haben unsere Küche bekommen."

Am Jahresende 1981 waren die Talbot-Fahrer in einer schwierigen Situation. Das Team konnte ihnen kein Programm für 1982 garantieren, doch für gute Deals war es fast schon zu spät. Henri sichert sich letztlich einen Platz im neuen Rothmans-Opel-Team, wo er aber nur eine Nebenrolle spielen sollte. „Wir haben unseren Vertrag bei der RAC Rallye unterschrieben", verrät Fred Gallagher. „Teamchef Tony Fall sagte uns, dass er für uns eigentlich nur ein Programm in Großbritannien vorgesehen hatte, dass er uns aber auch ein paar WM-Starts geben musste. Das zu hören war sehr merkwürdig. Damit waren wir Nummer Zwei hinter Walter Röhrl in der Weltmeisterschaft und praktisch auch Nummer Zwei hinter Jimmy McRae in Großbritannien."

test, mainly seeing a low oil pressure. Trying to save the unit from damage, he drove the second Grizedale keeping the revs low, but tackled a tight corner too quickly and rolled, losing a couple of minutes. The engine had partially seized and lost power. Gallagher explains: "We got to a corner and it was one of those, where you need that extra little bit of power and it just fell onto the roof." Through Kielder the pair climbed up to third, but once in Scotland the Lotus engine seized for good. Henri had just set three fastest times, his only ones in the event.

Earlier that autumn Henri and Erja had finally moved into a place of their own, back down on the southern coast, some fifteen kilometres west of Helsinki. It was in a big new apartment house where they had a nice view overlooking the sea. They still needed to equip and decorate the kitchen, though. That led to the idea of participating in the end of season Marcello Rally where the title sponsor would donate the necessary kitchenware to the winners. Henri thought that Erja could co-drive. "I had never been involved in rally competition and did not want to start now", says Erja. "I somehow managed to wriggle out of it and Juha [Paajanen] took my place instead. The boys duly won and we got our kitchen!"

Towards the end of 1981 Talbot's drivers were left in a difficult situation. The team advised them that there were no guarantees of a programme for 1982, but it was very late in the day to grab new deals. However Henri did manage to secure a place for himself in the new Rothmans-sponsored Opel team, although he would find himself in a supporting role there. "We signed our contract at RAC Rally time in Chester", reveals Fred Gallagher. "It was very strange to hear the Opel team principal, Tony Fall, say that he really only wanted us for a British programme, but was forced to give us a few WRC events, too … It left us number two to Walter Röhrl in the World Championship and in effect also very much number two to Jimmy McRae in Britain."

1981

Zum Abschluss ihrer Talbot-Zeit bei der RAC 1981 verbuchten Toivonen/Gallagher drei Bestzeiten. Talbot konnte dem Duo für 1982 kein Programm garantieren, und so mussten sie sich nach Alternativen umschauen.

Three fastest stage times during the RAC Rally proved to be the Talbot swansong for Toivonen and Gallagher. Talbot could not guarantee them a programme for 1982, so they had to chase a new drive somewhere else.

Bei der RAC 1981 ließ sich Henri von niedrigem Öldruck und einem Überschlag nicht aufhalten, erst ein Motorschaden brachte das Aus.
In the 1981 RAC Rally, Henri battled on despite low oil pressure and then a roll until finally the engine seized.

With love
from Henri ...

Toivonen
Pauli, Henri & Harri

Der Beruf des Rallyefahrers war zu Henris Zeiten kein Nine-to-Five-Job. Während der langen Trainingsphasen konnten die Piloten viel vom Land sehen und teils auch mit ihren Fahrerkollegen entspannen.

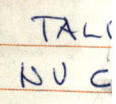

Rallying was not a nine-to-five job in Henri's era. During the long recces, the crews got to see something of the countries that they visited and also took the chance to relax with many of their fellow competitors.

Henri Toivonen
Die nächste Station: Opel
Rallying with Opel

Für Opel absolvierte Henri Toivonen 1982 zwar ein Doppelprogramm, Chancen auf den Titel hatte er aber nur in der britischen Meisterschaft – wenn überhaupt. Denn Audi UK hatte mit dem Quattro durch den Allradantrieb auf Schotter einen klaren Vorteil, auf dem Papier war Henri deutlich unterlegen. Den jungen Toivonen interessierte das erwartungsgemäß herzlich wenig. Erstaunlicherweise glänzte er im Laufe der Saison durch konstantes Punktesammeln – bis dato eigentlich nicht unbedingt die Stärke des Finnen. Diese Konstanz ist umso verwunderlicher, wenn man sich das Hoch und Runter bei den einzelnen Rallyes genauer anschaut. Henri Toivonen sorgte in der britischen Rallyeszene ohne Zweifel für hohen Unterhaltungswert. Bei seinem Debüt im Opel Ascona 400 bei der Mintex Rallye jagte er Mikkola, Airikkala und Vatanen. Dann hatte die Opel-Crew eine Schrecksekunde, als ein Zuschauer dem Opel einen Stein in die Windschutzscheibe warf, der direkt vor Freds Augen landete. Trotzdem setzte Henri auf der Prüfung die Bestzeit! Mikkola fuhr im Quattro allen davon, dann fiel Airikkala aus. Zwei Prüfungen vor Schluss lag Vatanen auf Platz Zwei – zwei Sekunden vor Toivonen. Auf den letzten beiden Asphaltprüfungen fuhr Henri die Bestzeit und ging an Ari vorbei.

Beim fünftägigen Circuit of Ireland rechnete das Team damit, dass Toivonen das Tempo bestimmen würde, und dass er die Mechaniker beschäftigen würde. Der Anfang wurde von den Taktikspielen der Beifahrer bestimmt. Niemand wollte auf der langen Schleife nach Süden vorn liegen. Letztlich einigten sie sich darauf, dass Jimmy McRae die Führungsrolle übernehmen würde. „Damit musste Ian [Grindrod] die Streckenposten aufwecken", verkündete Henris Co Fred Gallagher. „Henri half das. Er konnte an den gefährlichen Stellen die Bremsspuren sehen." Trotzdem gab es Dramatik bei Toivonen. Henri rutschte mit dem Fuß vom Bremspedal und das Auto krachte mit der vorderen Ecke gegen eine Böschung. Beim Aufprall schlitzte das Lenkrad Henris Hand auf. Die Verletzung wurde im Krankenhaus behandelt und sogar geröntgt um sicherzugehen, dass Henri weiterfahren konnte. In Henris Abwesenheit musste Gallagher den Opel aus dem Parc Fermé fahren. „Das hat Hannu wirklich verärgert", schmunzelt Fred. „Wir hatten sonst nie ein Problem mit ihm, aber da hat er sich aufgeregt und meinte, wir würden gegen die Regeln verstoßen." Henri fuhr danach meist mit nur einer Hand, dennoch holte er den zweitplatzierten Russell Brookes im Vauxhall Chevette langsam ein. Doch durch anhaltende Kupplungsprobleme kassierte Henri Zeitstrafen. Im letzten Service war der Opel in einem jämmerlichen Zustand: Der Motor keuchte und das Heck war ramponiert. „Das Heck kam herum und ich konnte das Auto mit einer Hand nicht einfangen …", entschuldigte sich Henri bei seinem Team. Er versprach, den Motor auf der Schluss-WP zu schonen, fuhr dort die zweitbeste Zeit und wurde Dritter.

Ende April schlossen Henri und Erja den Bund fürs Leben. Es war eine römisch-katholische Hochzeit mit ungewöhnlichen Bräuchen. „Henri musste unterschreiben, dass er nicht impotent ist", lacht Erja. „Das wäre ein Grund gewesen, die Ehe für ungültig zu erklären." Für Flitterwochen war leider keine Zeit, der Bräutigam musste schnell weiter zur Wales Rallye.

Da Mikkola für Audi Sport in Korsika war, setzte Audi UK Björn Waldegård ans Steuer des Quattro. Der Schwede war mit seinem Arbeitsgerät nicht vertraut, zudem wurden die Prüfungen je zur Hälfte auf Asphalt und auf Schotter ausgetragen. Henri hatte also gute

So, it was a clearly two-pronged programme for Henri Toivonen in 1982, with only the Rothmans/RAC Open Championship offering any hope of shooting for a title. In reality he was pretty much an underdog in that, too, as the Audi UK-entered Quattro had an obvious advantage on gravel with its four-wheel drive. Henri seemed oblivious to this fact, though, as one should probably have expected … In an almost perverted way, the keyword for his British campaign became consistency. Not really a cachet of the man so far and certainly a strange outcome considering the rough-and-tumble nature of his performances on most rallies in the series. Indisputably, Henri Toivonen in an Opel Ascona 400 became the great entertainer of the British rally scene. His Opel debut in the Mintex Rally began by chasing Mikkola, Airikkala and Vatanen. A rock thrown by a spectator startled the crew as it hit the windscreen just in front of Fred, but they still took a first fastest time on that stage! No one could stay with Mikkola's Quattro, but when Airikkala dropped out, Vatanen led Toivonen by a mere two seconds before the last two tarmac stages at Oliver's Mount. Henri was fastest here both times and beat Ari to finish second.

In the five-day Circuit of Ireland, the team expected Toivonen to set the pace, but also to keep the mechanics busy … At first the co-drivers were playing tactics, because they felt it was better not to lead on the long run south. Eventually Gallagher reported an agreement had been made for Jimmy McRae to lead: "It means that Ian [Grindrod] has to wake up the marshals, and for Henri it will help, as you can see the tyre marks on the road if there is a dangerous place." This could not save them from drama. Henri's foot slipped off the brake pedal and the car went into a bank front corner first, whipping the steering wheel around and gashing his hand. The injury needed hospital treatment and later an X-ray to be sure Henri could carry on. With all this going on, Fred Gallagher had to drive the Opel out of parc fermé while Henri was still on his way from hospital. "That really upset Hannu", smiles Fred. "We never ever otherwise had a problem with him, but this time he was agitated and accused us of breaking the rules. But Henri was in real pain and it came very close to me actually driving some of the stages." Henri had to drive with one hand mostly, but he was still catching Russell Brookes' second-placed Vauxhall Chevette. Repeated clutch trouble brought road penalties, however, and in the last service the Opel was in a sorry state with sick engine and its rear end in a mess. "The car went around and I could not catch it with just one hand …" Henri gave his excuses to the team, promising to look after the engine on the last stage. He still set second fastest time to end the event in third place.

In late April, Henri tied the knot with Erja. It was a Roman-Catholic wedding and involved routines that some might consider unusual. "Henri had to sign a document to say he was not impotent", chuckles Erja. "That would have been a cause for declaring the marriage void." There was no time for a honeymoon, however, as the bridegroom had to rush off to the Welsh Rally.

With Hannu busy in Corsica on WRC duties for Audi Sport, Audi UK now put Björn Waldegård in its Quattro instead. The Swede's unfamiliarity with his mount, plus the fact that the Welsh stages were half gravel, half tarmac, gave Henri a fighting chance. He got a puncture on the edge of the tarmac in Epynt and lost one minute, but surprisingly closed the gap to Waldegård on gravel to

Gegen die Kombination Mikkola/Quattro waren Henri und der Ascona 400 zumindest auf losem Untergrund nur Außenseiter. Dafür bewegte Toivonen den Hecktriebler immer spektakulär um die Ecken. Zum Auftakt der britischen Meisterschaft bei der Mintex Rallye wurde er Zweiter.

Against the Audi Quattro, Henri and his Ascona 400 were always going to be the underdogs, at least on loose surfaces. But there is no doubt that his two-wheel drive technique was more spectacular. His British campaign started with second place in the Mintex Rally.

Henri Toivonen Die nächste Station: Opel / Rallying with Opel

Henri und Erja heirateten im Frühjahr 1982. Am Tag vor der Hochzeit feierte er mit Harri und ein paar Freunden seinen Junggesellenabschied. Mit diesem ungewöhnlichen Gefährt „kurvte" Henri durch Helsinki.

Henri and Erja got married in the spring of 1982. The day before Henri was set up for a riotous stag night by Harri and a few close friends. That involved cruising all kitted up in central Helsinki.

Chancen. Auf dem Asphalt von Epynt fing er sich einen Plattfuß ein und verlor eine Minute, doch auf dem Schotter war er schneller als der Quattro und verkürzte den Rückstand auf 30 Sekunden. Dann fuhr Waldegård drei Bestzeiten und Toivonen begnügte sich mit Platz Zwei, der ihm in der Meisterschaft einen gesunden Vorsprung einbrachte, zumal Vatanen disqualifiziert wurde, weil er auf einer WP den falschen Weg eingeschlagen hatte. Stig Blomqvist war mit sieben Minuten Rückstand Dritter. Stig fuhr einen ähnlichen Sunbeam Lotus wie Henri im Jahr zuvor.

„Die Schottland Rallye war die einzige, bei der wir nicht mit Jimmy mithalten konnten", blickt Fred Gallagher auf McRaes Heimrallye zurück. Henri haderte von Anfang an mit der Leistung seines Ascona 400 und er hatte Mühe das Tempo zu halten. Die Mechaniker hatten zunächst die Elektrik geprüft – vergeblich. Erst ein neuer Verteiler löste das Problem. Henri kämpfte sich von Platz Vier nach vorn. Dann traf er einen Stein und als er die Lenkung gewechselt haben wollte, weil er merkte, dass damit etwas nicht stimmte, gab es Spannungen im Team. Im Nachhinein entschuldigte sich Henri, anscheinend hatte sich nur ein Stein in der Lenkung verfangen und sich später von alleine wieder gelöst. Durch die Ausfälle von Vatanen und Blomqvist rückte Henri auf die dritte Position vor, hinter Mikkola und McRae. Damit führte Toivonen die Meisterschaft noch knapp an. Als einziger der Top-Fahrer hatte er bei jedem Lauf gepunktet – eine konstante Leistung.

Die britische Meisterschaft erreichte ihren Höhepunkt bei der Manx Rallye mit einem Dreikampf zwischen Vatanen, Toivonen und McRae. Opel gab seinen Fahrern Leichtbauautos, außerdem bekam Henri einen hoch drehenden Phase-3-Motor mit 268 PS. Trotzdem hatten Toivonen und Gallagher früh den Eindruck, dass ihr Team nicht wollte, dass sie diese Rallye gewinnen. „Vor dem Start wurde uns gesagt, dass es eine Stallorder geben könnte, wenn wir auf den Plätzen Eins und Zwei liegen", erklärt Fred. „Aber als wir vorn

get within thirty seconds of the Quattro. The leader then set three fastest times, which persuaded the pursuer to settle for points. Second place gave Toivonen a healthy lead in the series, when Vatanen was excluded from third for taking a wrong route on a stage. Stig Blomqvist in third was seven minutes behind, driving a new Talbot Sunbeam Lotus similar to the one Henri had used the year before.

"The Scottish was the only time we couldn't live with Jimmy", says Fred Gallagher about McRae's home event in June. From the outset Henri was complaining of lack of power and struggling to keep pace. Mechanics had checked the electrics in vain until a change of distributor cured the problem, allowing him to challenge from fourth place. After hitting a rock, there was tension in the team when Henri felt something wrong with the steering and demanded that it be changed. But later he backed off to apologize as it was assumed that a stone had got wedged in the mechanism and then was dislodged. When Vatanen and Blomqvist dropped out, Henri ended up third behind Mikkola and McRae, which still left him narrowly leading the series. Alone among the top drivers he had scored in every round so far – consistency …

The British series came to its climax with a furious battle between Vatanen, Toivonen and McRae on the Manx Rally. Opel supplied its drivers with lightweight Asconas and Henri also had a high-revving Phase 3 engine giving a reputed 268 bhp. Yet, Toivonen and Gallagher soon got a distinct impression their team did not want them to win. "Before the start we were told there could be team orders, if we were running 1-2", Fred relates. "But while we were ahead, they never came." Henri had been leading after the first day, but the next morning he got a puncture although the crew could not remember hitting anything. This dropped them to third, but when Vatanen rolled his Escort the battle for victory was then exclusively between the Opel drivers. Henri set an absolutely

Jimmy McRae war Henris Teamkollege, aber auch sein größter Gegner auf der Insel.
Jimmy McRae was Henri's team-mate, but also his fiercest rival in British events.

lagen, kam sie nicht." Henri hatte nach Tag Eins in Führung gelegen, fing sich am nächsten Morgen aber einen Reifenschaden ein, dabei konnte sich die Crew nicht daran erinnern, etwas getroffen zu haben. Sie fielen auf Platz Drei zurück und als sich Vatanens Escort überschlug, machten die Opelaner den Sieg unter sich aus. Henri legte ein atemberaubendes Tempo vor und fuhr Bestzeiten nach Belieben. Vor der zweiten Pause eroberte er die Führung zurück, doch noch immer blieb das Team ruhig: keine Stallregie. Am Start zur ersten WP am nächsten Morgen stotterte das Auto und kam kurz danach zum Halt. Die Besatzung öffnete die Motorhaube und entdeckte, dass das Verteilerkabel lose war. Als McRae gerade vorbeigezogen war, setzte Toivonen die Fahrt fort. Doch nur 400 Meter später rutschte er von der Strecke. Beleidigt verließen Henri und Fred die Insel und flogen direkt zum Trainieren nach Sanremo. Das Team feierte derweil Jimmy McRaes Meistertitel, war vom Verhalten seiner anderen Crew aber alles andere als begeistert. „Wir mussten uns in Sanremo bei allen Mechanikern entschuldigen", wendet Gallagher ein. „Aber Jahre später habe ich von einem führenden Techniker erfahren, dass das Team tatsächlich an der Verteilerkappe herumgepfuscht hat."

Zwischen seinen Auftritten auf der Insel hatte Toivonen einige sehr beeindruckende Vorstellungen in der WM abgeliefert. Die erste war im März in Portugal. Die Rallye begann mit drei Asphaltprüfungen in den Hügeln von Sintra, die je dreimal gefahren wurden. In den ersten beiden Durchgängen fuhr Henri alle Bestzeiten. Die letzte Schleife begann ähnlich, bis Henri einen Reifenschaden hatte und hinter Mikkola zurückfiel. „Ehrlich gesagt gab es schon einen Grund für diese Zeiten", gibt Fred zu. „Auf den Videos von Sintra sieht man, dass die Leute bei Röhrl, der mit Nummer Eins fuhr, noch viel näher standen. Wir hatten Nummer Sechs, da waren die Leute schon zurückgeschreckt." Nach dem Übergang auf Schotter hatte Toivonen viel Pech mit Reifenschäden und Probleme mit der Bremse, den Achsen und der Kardanwelle. Der Finne fiel zurück und musste den Staub der langsameren Autos schlucken. Wenn das Auto lief, fuhr Henri

cracking pace, seemingly rolling off fastest times at will. He retook the lead before the second overnight halt, but from the team there was silence: no team orders. Starting the first stage on the last morning the car stuttered from the line and ground to a halt. The crew opened the bonnet and after some frantic scanning found the distributor cap loose. McRae had just passed when they got going again, but then they went off terminally 400 metres down the road … Henri and Fred left the island in a huff, flying straight to Sanremo for recce. That left the team celebrating a championship title for Jimmy McRae, but somewhat unamused by their other crew's behaviour. "We had to apologize to all the mechanics in Sanremo", Fred Gallagher admits. "But years later I heard from a leading technician of the team that the distributor cap had definitely been tampered with …"

In between the British outings, Henri Toivonen had been putting in a couple of very impressive drives in the World Rally Championship. The first of these was in Portugal in March. The rally began with three asphalt stages in the Sintra area, each run three times. On the first two loops Henri was fastest on all of them. The last round looked to be going the same way until he punctured, dropping behind Mikkola. "In honesty, there was a reason for those times", says Fred Gallagher. "If you look at footage from Sintra, the crowds were standing a lot closer when Walter Röhrl went through at number 1. We were number 6 and they had already been scared off a bit." Once the rally moved to gravel, a long string of adversity commenced including punctures and issues with the brakes, axle and propshaft. This all dropped the number 6 Opel down the order, where it had to endure the dust kicked up by slower cars. Fastest times were still clocked when everything was in order, but the end came as the clutch exploded with just five stages remaining. A quick glance at the stage times reveals that only the winner, Michèle Mouton in an Audi Quattro, had bettered Toivonen in Portugal.

Henri Toivonen Die nächste Station: Opel / Rallying with Opel

In Portugal begeisterte Henri zunächst mit tollen Asphalt-Zeiten, doch auf Schotter verließ ihn das Glück. Nach vielen Problemen brachte eine defekte Kupplung das Aus.
Henri stunned everyone with his times on the first Portuguese stages in 1982, but after all sorts of problems later in the event, his run came to an end with clutch failure.

weiter Bestzeiten, bis fünf Prüfungen vor Schluss die Kupplung explodierte. Ein Blick auf die Statistik zeigt: Nur die Siegerin Michèle Mouton im Audi Quattro hatte in Portugal mehr Bestzeiten verbucht.

Bei der Akropolis war Henri erneut der größte Gegner der Audi. Nachdem Favorit Mikkola an der ersten Hürde gestolpert war, jagten Toivonen und die anderen Opel-Fahrer den Quattro von Mouton. Nach WP Sechs hatte Henri sogar geführt, doch gegen Michèle war er chancenlos. Als das erste Drittel vorbei war, lag Toivonen auf Platz Zwei, nur 24 Sekunden hinter der Französin. Doch an seinen Händen bildeten sich die ersten Blasen. „Er sollte nicht so verdammt schnell fahren, oder etwa doch?", kommentierte sein Teamchef Tony Fall. Henri beteuerte zwar, dass er auf das Auto aufpassen würde, allerdings machte der Ascona Grund zur Sorge. Am Ende der 45 Kilometer langen Meteora-Prüfung brauchte der Opel seine dritte Hinterachse. Toivonen verlor auf der WP und beim Service Zeit, damit war Mouton ungefährdet an der Spitze. Toivonen fiel auf Platz Vier zurück und fuhr wieder im Staub von langsameren Gegnern. Opel beschloss, dass McRae den dritten Rang halten soll, um den FIA-A-Prioritätsstatus zu bekommen. Auf der letzten WP fiel der Schotte aber durch einen Elektrikdefekt aus und Henri erbte Platz Drei.

Der frühere Beifahrer David Richards koordinierte damals die Sponsoring-Aktivitäten von Rothmans. Da die Zigarettenmarke auch das Formel-1-Team von March unterstützte, organisierte er für Henri im Sommer eine Testfahrt im March 821. Der Test in Silverstone war ein

The Acropolis Rally was another event where Henri found himself as the main challenger to Audi. When pre-event favourite Mikkola fell at the first hurdle, Toivonen was left to chase Michèle Mouton's Quattro with the other Opels. Henri had actually led after six stages, but was powerless to fend off Mouton. With about one third of the event over he was second, still just twenty-four seconds behind, but his hands were sore with blisters. "He shouldn't drive so bloody fast, should he?", was the comment from team manager Tony Fall. Although Henri swore he was thinking of the car, it was soon giving cause for concern. At the end of the 45 km Meteora Monastery stage his Opel needed its third rear axle. The problems delayed him in the stage and, with road penalties from the service time added, it left Mouton unchallenged at the top. Toivonen dropped to fourth and again had to follow slower cars on the dusty stages. It was decided he should not challenge McRae in third, so the Scot would gain an A-seeding, but when an electrical problem stopped Jimmy on the last stage it handed the place to the Finn.

Former co-driver David Richards was at this time pulling strings for Rothmans which also sponsored the March team in Formula 1, and in the summer he arranged an opportunity for Henri to have a go in a pukka March 821 in Silverstone. This was a pure publicity stunt – a speedway champion also tried the car at the same time – but Henri was understandably eager to grab it. Regular driver Raul Boesel first warmed up the car on a damp track, but when it

Von der harten Rivalität der britischen Meisterschaft war bei den WM-Läufen nichts zu spüren. Hier jagten die Opel-Teams Toivonen/Gallgher und McRae/Grindrod ja auch nicht ein und demselben Titel hinterher.

Despite fierce rivalry on British events Opel's team spirit gelled in the more relaxed atmosphere of foreign events, where Toivonen/Gallagher and McRae/Grindrod were not both chasing the same title.

reiner PR-Gag, dennoch war Henri sehr ehrgeizig. Stammpilot Raul Boesel wärmte das Auto auf feuchter Strecke auf und als Henri das Steuer übernahm, begann es stark zu regnen. Die Zeiten war nicht aussagekräftig, aber der Vollständigkeit halber möchten wir sie doch anführen: Für seine erste Runde benötigte Henri 1.50 Minuten, im Laufe der Zeit verbesserte er sich auf 1.39,8 Minuten. Der Rundenrekord lag damals übrigens bei 1.14,4 Minuten.

Als er bei Opel unterschrieb, war Henri davon ausgegangen, schon früh in der Saison den neuen Manta 400 zu fahren. Doch Probleme mit der Homologation verzögerten das Debüt. Im Juli erschien das Auto endlich bei der Rallye des Mille Pistes, allerdings als Prototyp. Die Veranstaltung wurde auf dem Militärgelände von Canjuers in Südfrankreich ausgetragen und bestand aus fünf Mal fünf Schotterprüfungen. Der erste Durchgang wurde jedoch nur zur Erstellung des Aufschriebs genutzt. Das Starterfeld war beeindruckend: Jean Ragnotti, Jean-Luc Thérier und Bruno Saby fuhren Renault 5 Turbo, Jean-Pierre Nicolas startete für Toyota. Am schnellsten von allen war aber Toivonen mit drei Minuten Vorsprung. Obwohl er außerhalb der Wertung fuhr, bekam er ein ähnlich hohes Preisgeld wie der siegreiche Thérier. Dieses Preisgeld sorgte daheim in Finnland für Verwirrung. „Es gab damals diese weichen Rothmans-Taschen", erinnert sich Erja Toivonen. „Henri nahm sie mit auf seine Reisen, und einmal fand ich beim Auspacken bündelweise Dollarscheine zwischen seinen Overalls und der dreckigen Unterwäsche. Es war keine unbedeutende Summe. Vielleicht 5.000 Dollar. Ich habe das Geld in einem Küchenfach verstaut und Henri ein paar Tage später gefragt: ‚Vermisst du irgendetwas?' Er war verwundert. Er wusste nicht, wovon ich spreche."

Im Spätsommer war die 1000 Seen erneut ein wichtiger Termin für die Toivonen-Familie – neben den Geburtstagen. Pauli hatte für Harri einen von David Sutton vorbereiteten Ford Escort RS besorgt. Damit sollte der jüngere Sohn sein Können einem internationalen Publikum zeigen. Henri kehrte in den Ascona 400 zurück, um gegen die Audi zu kämpfen. Beide konzentrierten sich beim Training vor allem auf die Nachtprüfungen, von denen Harri manche bis zu 25 Mal fuhr.

Auf den nassen und rutschigen Straßen war die Zweiradfraktion im Nachteil. Dennoch blieb Henri an den Audi dran und als Stig Blomqvist einen Reifenschaden hatte, übernahm er Platz Zwei hinter Hannu Mikkola mit nur 19 Sekunden Rückstand. Erstaunlicherweise fuhr Toivonen sogar Bestzeiten und reduzierte den Abstand auf 14 Sekunden. Dieses Tempo konnte er aber nicht halten, sodass Blomqvist bald an ihm vorbeizog. In der WP Ruuhimäki am Ende der zweiten Etappe hatte Henri vorn einen Reifenschaden. Er fuhr weiter und kam auf eine breitere und schnellere Straße. „Das war ein Moment, wo ich ihn vielleicht besser angebrüllt hätte", beschreibt Fred Gallagher. In einer langen, schnellen Linkskurve wollte das Auto nicht einlenken. Mit der Front traf der Ascona eine mit Sand gefüllte Holzbox, mit dem Sand wurden im Winter die Straßen bestreut. Der Opel war stark ramponiert, Henri hatte sich den Daumen ausgekugelt und Fred einige Rippen geprellt. Doch Henri bestand darauf weiterzufahren. Er schleppte den Ascona zum Service nach Jyväskylä, wo das Team Probleme hatte, irgendwo Lampen anzubringen. Wie durch ein Wunder konnte das Auto wieder straßentauglich gemacht werden und Henri die Stadt-WP Harju in Angriff nehmen. Er fuhr die zweitbeste Zeit. Doch durch den Wasserverlust nach dem Unfall war die Zylinderkopfdichtung hinüber. Der Ausfall war für Fred Gallagher eine Erleichterung: „Ich hatte fürchterliche Schmerzen!" Harri Toivonen hatte nach einem Frühstart und der resultierenden Zeitstrafe gerade den richtigen Rhythmus gefunden und lag knapp außerhalb der Top Ten, als er sich heftig überschlug. So endete die 1000 Seen Rallye damit, dass beide Brüder mit bandagierter Hand herumliefen.

was Henri's turn to take the wheel rain began to fall heavily. In the conditions times were meaningless, but for the record, his first lap of 1min 50sec was consequently improved every time around to end up at 1min 39.8sec. Silverstone's contemporary lap record was 1min 14.4sec.

At the time of signing for Opel, Henri had expected to be driving a new Manta 400 early in the new season, but problems with homologation kept delaying it. In July the car finally made its debut in his hands at the Mille Pistes Rally, albeit still as a prototype. The French event was run on the military grounds of Canjuers and comprised five laps of five gravel stages, though the first passage through these was only used for making pacenotes. The entry was good with people like Jean Ragnotti, Jean-Luc Thérier and Bruno Saby in Renault 5 Turbos and Jean-Pierre Nicolas representing Toyota. Toivonen proved quickest of the lot by some three minutes and, although he was running outside the official classification, was awarded similar prize money to the winner Thérier. The money won apparently caused some confusion back home. "Remember those soft Rothmans bags?", queries Erja Toivonen. "Henri used them on his travels and one time unpacking them I found bundles of dollar notes tucked in among the overalls and dirty underwear. It was not an insignificant sum, something like $5,000 maybe. I put it all on a shelf in the kitchen and after a few days asked Henri: 'Are you missing anything?' He was bewildered by that. He didn't understand what I was talking about."

Late summer, the 1000 Lakes Rally was once again a focal date for the Toivonen family. Birthdays aside, Harri too was now in the spotlight as Pauli had acquired a David Sutton-prepared Ford Escort RS for the younger son to show his worth to an international audience. As for Henri, back in the Ascona 400 to fight the Audis, Harri was very much focusing on the night-time stages during the recce, driving some of them as many as twenty-five times! Wet and slippery roads immediately put two-wheel drive cars at a disadvantage, but Henri still managed to stay quite close to the Audis and when Stig Blomqvist punctured he found himself trailing Hannu Mikkola by only nineteen seconds. Amazingly in the circumstances he was able to set fastest times and reduce the gap to just fourteen seconds. It could not go on forever, of course, and the recovering Blomqvist soon powered ahead. At the end of the second leg Henri suffered a front puncture in the Ruuhimäki stage, but managed to continue onto a section of much wider and faster road. "That was a time when perhaps I should have shouted a bit", says Fred Gallagher with foreboding. On a long fast left-hander the car would not turn in and hit a wooden box full of sand, used for gritting the road in wintry conditions. The front of the Ascona was comprehensively wrecked, Henri had dislocated a thumb and Fred was completely winded with bruised ribs. However, the driver insisted on continuing. He struggled back to service in Jyväskylä, where the team had difficulty fitting lamps anywhere! Miraculously, the car was made road legal and Henri set off to the Harju town stage, where he set second fastest time, but without any water in the radiator the head gasket had gone by the time they limped out of Ruuhimäki. Retirement came as a relief for Fred Gallagher: "I was hurting like hell!" Harri Toivonen had been getting into the groove after a penalty for a jump start and was lying just outside the top ten when he had an enormous roll. Again, the biggest concern was what Pauli would say about the damage to the Escort. "It was very different now, when father was paying it all from his own pocket", Harri points out. "When Henri started, Dad was managing director of a car importer that had its own competition department." And so the 1000 Lakes ended with the brothers both having a hand in bandages!

 1982

Rothmans gab Henri Toivonen und Speedway-Weltmeister Bruce Penhall die Chance, Raul Boesels March-821-Formel-1-Auto zu testen. Der Mann im Bild links trägt zwar den Helm von Raul Boesel, ist aber in Wahrheit Henri Toivonen. Henris Helm hatte keine Sauerstoffzufuhr, die damals in der Formel 1 vorgeschrieben war.

Rothmans gave Henri Toivonen and world speedway champion, Bruce Penhall, a chance to try out Raul Boesel's March 821 Formula 1 car. Despite appearances, it is actually Henri driving down the pit lane but wearing Boesel's helmet. Henri's own helmet did not have the oxygen supply system then compulsory in F1.

Henri Toivonen Die nächste Station: Opel / Rallying with Opel

Die 1000 Seen 1982 war ein Großereignis für die Familie Toivonen. Harri (links) sollte im Ford Escort von David Sutton zeigen, dass er für den nächsten Schritt bereit war. Doch seine Fahrt endete genau wie die von Henri durch einen Unfall. Rauno Aaltonen stand damals bei Opel unter Vertrag, während Pauli Toivonen die Fortschritte seiner Söhne weiter im Auge behielt.

The 1982 1000 Lakes Rally was a big occasion for the Toivonen family. Harri had a Ford Escort RS from David Sutton to show that he was ready for the big time (left), but it all ended in an expensive accident. Henri, too, crashed his Opel Ascona. Rauno Aaltonen was an influence in the Opel team while Pauli Toivonen still liked to keep an eye on both of his sons.

Henri Toivonen Die nächste Station: Opel / Rallying with Opel

Wenn du es nach einem Unfall noch aus der WP schaffst, kannst du immer sagen, dass du wegen eines Technikdefekts ausgefallen bist …

When you manage to get out of the stage after an accident, you can always claim that it was retirement through a technical failure …

Erneut hatte Harri vor allem Angst vor Paulis Standpauke. „Mein Vater zahlte das alles aus der eigenen Tasche", erklärt Harri. „Als Henri anfing, war das etwas ganz anderes. Da war Pauli Geschäftsführer einer Importeursfirma, die ihre eigene Wettbewerbsabteilung hatte."

Die Sanremo war ein weiteres Highlight für Henri Toivonen, obwohl er auch bei diesem WM-Lauf kein gutes Resultat einfuhr. Vor der Rallye lag Optimismus in der Luft und Fred glaubte sogar an den Sieg. Henri stand bei den italienischen Fans hoch im Kurs, die Unterstützung der Tifosi war überwältigend. Aber es gab keinen Zweifel, dass die Audi Quattro auf Schotter im Vorteil waren. Bei der Ankunft in Pisa nach dem Ende der Schotterprüfungen lag Henri auf Rang Fünf, mehr als acht Minuten hinter Blomqvist. Der Schwede war als einziger Audi-Mann ohne Probleme durchgefahren. Mit vier Quattro vor sich zeigte Toivonen auf Asphalt sein ganzes Talent und holte einen nach dem anderen ein – und das trotz eines Drehers, der 20 Sekunden kostete. „Das Auto geht nicht richtig, der Motor hat nicht die volle Leistung. Bergauf ist das sehr schlecht, also muss ich bergab die Augen schließen und schneller sein", sagte der Mann der Stunde damals. Drei Prüfungen vor Schluss lag Henri nur noch 16 Sekunden hinter dem zweitplatzierten Mikkola, Blomqvists Vorsprung betrug nur noch zwei Minuten. Vor der letzten Prüfung kam Henri sogar bis auf fünf Sekunden an Mikkola heran. Toivonen setzte jetzt alles auf eine Karte: Ersatzrad und Wagenheber blieben im Service, um Gewicht zu sparen. Doch dann, sieben Kilometer vor dem Ende der Prüfung, war seine Attacke vorbei. Henri touchierte einen Randstein, schlitzte sich den superweichen Michelin-Reifen auf und fiel auf Platz Fünf zurück. Ein Geschenk von Stig Blomqvist war nur ein kleiner Trost: „Stig kaufte uns eine Flasche Cognac, weil er uns seinen Sieg zu verdanken hatte", schildert Gallagher. Michèle Mouton kämpfte damals um den WM-Titel und Audi hätte sie vermutlich gewinnen lassen, wenn die Quattro an der Spitze unter sich gewesen wären. Henri hatte diesen Plan vereitelt.

Nach der Sanremo zog es Henri auf die Rennstrecke. „Er sagte, er würde gerne mal ein Formel-3-Auto fahren", beschreibt Gallagher. „Also sprach ich mit Mike Greasley und er schlug vor, mich mit Eddie

Sanremo Rally was the other 1982 WRC highlight for Henri Toivonen even though he did not get a result to reflect it there either. There was a degree of optimism in the air and Fred even predicted his man to win. Henri's status with the Italian fans was immediately obvious and support for him was overwhelming. Yet there was no denying the Audi Quattro's advantage on gravel and by the time the rally had reached Pisa and was heading back to the asphalt stages, Henri was lying fifth and was over eight minutes behind Stig Blomqvist, who alone among the Audi drivers had escaped problems. With only Audis ahead and asphalt remaining Toivonen put in a stunning display. He was catching them hand over fist, notwithstanding a twenty seconds delay with a spin. "But the car is not right, the engine is not pulling properly. It is quite bad on the uphill sections, so on the downhill you just have to close your eyes and go faster …", reported the hero of the hour. With three stages left he was only sixteen seconds behind second-placed Mikkola. As day broke, Blomqvist was still ahead but now his advantage to the rival team had been reduced to two minutes while Henri was just five seconds behind Mikkola with one stage to go! Henri threw all excess weight out of his car: spare wheel, jack, etc. Then, seven kilometres from the end of the stage, his challenge was over. He clipped a verge, slashing the super soft Michelin tyre and dropped out of the battle to finish a dejected fifth. A present from Stig Blomqvist was mild consolation. "Stig bought us both a bottle of cognac, because he owed his win to us", cracks Gallagher. With Michèle Mouton fighting for the world title, it had been expected that Audi would swap the places of its drivers, if they occupied the leading positions, but Henri's charge had split them and put paid to that.

After Sanremo, Henri indulged in a bit of racing for a change. "He'd been saying he'd like to try Formula 3, so I got in touch with Mike Greasley, who suggested Eddie Jordan might be the guy to talk to", Fred Gallagher explains. "Eddie gave me a sum for the drive and Henri went chasing it in Finland. He got less than half of what was required from Finnlux [TV manufacturer], but Eddie asked how much he had and just said: 'OK, give me that and we'll

Das miese Wetter hielt Henris treue Fans in Italien nicht davon ab, an der Strecke auszuharren. Henri belohnte sie mit einer tollen Vorstellung besonders auf den Asphaltprüfungen der letzten Etappe. Er war drauf und dran, Mikkola von Platz Zwei zu verdrängen, als ihn ein Reifenschaden zurückwarf.

Gloomy weather did not discourage Henri's adoring fans in Italy and he gave them a magnificent display of driving especially on the tarmac stages of the last leg. For a while, he looked as if he would overhaul Mikkola for second place but sadly his efforts to do so ended thanks to a puncture.

Jordan in Verbindung zu setzen. Eddie nannte mir eine Summe und Henri zog los, um das Geld aufzutreiben. Henri bekam nicht einmal die Hälfte davon vom TV-Hersteller Finnlux. Dennoch sagte Eddie: ‚Okay, gib mir das Geld. Wir ziehen das durch.'" Also startete Henri zunächst bei einem Formula-Libre-Rennen in Silverstone, um sich an den Ralt-Toyota RT3 zu gewöhnen, bevor er am nächsten Tag beim Finale der britischen Formel-3-Serie in Thruxton mitmischte. In Silverstone startete Henri von der Pole, im Rennen fiel er anfangs auf Platz Drei zurück, gewann aber letztlich, nachdem der Lotus Esprit Turbo von Tony Sugden durch Probleme eingebremst wurde. Den Highspeedkurs von Thruxton am nächsten Tag fand Henri nicht sehr schwierig. „Das ist keine anspruchsvolle Strecke. Auf der Gegenseite kannst du alles voll fahren. Es geht nur um das optimale Setup für das Auto." Im Training erzielte Henri einen respektablen neunten Platz knapp hinter Teamkollege James Weaver. Auf Leute wie Martin Brundle und den künftigen Meister Tommy Byrne fehlte ihm aber eine Sekunde. Im Rennen konnte Henri durch Dreck auf dem Visier fast nichts sehen und wurde Zehnter. Brundle gewann den Lauf.

Im November nahm Henri auch am Thruxton TV Meeting teil, bei dem ein gewisser Ayrton Senna sein Formel-3-Debüt feierte. Diesmal war Henri Fünfter in der Qualifikation mit 1,2 Sekunden Rückstand auf den Brasilianer. Im langsameren zweiten Training holte Henri mit verändertem Setup Platz Drei. „Im Motodrom und in der Schikane bin ich wirklich schlecht unterwegs", beschrieb Toivonen. „Ich hätte öfter an die Box fahren sollen, um das Setup zu ändern. Schade, dass ich keinen besonders starken Motor habe." Nach stetiger Verbesserung erzielte Henri in einem von Senna dominierten Rennen die vierte Position.

Eddie Jordan wurde zu einem guten Freund, der später interessante Dinge über Henri sagte: „Er hatte dieses unglaubliche Talent und Charisma. Er hatte eine so starke Ausstrahlung. Du wusstest automatisch, dass da mal ein großer Star wird", beschrieb Jordan 1990, kurz nachdem er sein eigenes Formel-1-Team gegründet hatte. „Als Senna zum ersten Mal im Formel-3-Auto saß, auch in unserem Team, hatte ich ein ähnliches Gefühl wie bei Henri. Du konntest spüren, dass da jemand war, der sofort wusste, was er tat. Ich möchte

do it!'" It was decided to do a Formula Libre race in Silverstone at first to get the hang of Jordan's Ralt-Toyota RT3 before participating in the British F3 series finale the next day in Thruxton. In Silverstone Henri dropped to third after starting from pole, but won the race from Will Hoy's Clubmans Mallock when Tony Sugden's Lotus Esprit Turbo slowed with problems. Interestingly, the next day Henri did not find the Thruxton circuit very challenging. "This is not a very testing circuit, you can easily run flat around the back. It's just a case of getting optimum settings for the car", was his verdict. Ninth quickest in practice, just shy of team-mate James Weaver, was respectable enough although Henri was over a second away from the likes of Martin Brundle and champion elect, Tommy Byrne. In the race he was virtually unable to see for muck on the visor and ended up tenth while Brundle won. In November, Henri also took part in the end of season Thruxton TV meeting, which witnessed the F3 debut of Ayrton Senna. This time he was fifth in qualifying, 1.2 seconds from the Brazilian, but third in the slower second session after changes to the set-up. "I'm really bad through the complex and the chicane, so I should have stopped in the pits more often to change the settings. Pity I don't have a very powerful engine", he reflected. Steady improvement saw Henri drive to a good fourth in the Senna-dominated race and win his own battle with Davy Jones.

Eddie Jordan became a close friend who later had interesting things to say about Henri. "He had this unbelievable talent and charisma and the style of the person was so affectious [sic] that you automatically knew he was going to be a big star", said Jordan moments after launching his own F1 team in 1990. "When Senna drove an F3 car the first time that was also with us and it was a similar type of feeling with Henri. You could feel ... that here was someone who immediately knew what he was doing. I want to be very careful about my assessment, but I have to say that had he gone on a Grand Prix style route, nobody knows how good he could have been, other than that he would certainly have been a GP winner. But to be a World Champion would have been something for which you also need a great amount of luck, and in hindsight I'm not sure that he had all the luck ..."

Eddie Jordan war von Henris Vorstellung im Formel-3-Ralt schwer beeindruckt. Aber mit seinen 26 Jahren war er für eine Karriere im Formel-Rennsport zu alt. Vielleicht wären die Sportwagen jedoch eine Option gewesen.

Eddie Jordan was hugely impressed by Henri's exploits in his F3 Ralt, but at the age of 26 it was probably too late to diverge towards a parallel career in single-seaters.

mit meiner Beurteilung vorsichtig sein, aber wenn er in Richtung Grand Prix gegangen wäre – wer weiß, wie gut Henri geworden wäre. Er wäre sicherlich ein Grand-Prix-Sieger geworden. Aber um Weltmeister zu werden, braucht man auch eine Menge Glück. Und rückwirkend betrachtet hatte Henri ja nicht unbedingt Glück …"

Damit war die Saison 1982 für Toivonen aber noch nicht beendet. Wie üblich stand zum WM-Abschluss die RAC Rallye auf dem Programm, die mit einem Schock begann. Opels Nummer Eins Walter Röhrl wurde vor dem Start gefeuert, weil er am Abend vor der Rallye einen Empfang ausgelassen hatte. Jochi Kleint ersetzte Röhrl, außerdem verstärkte Ari Vatanen das Opel-Team. Doch als diese beiden ausgefallen waren, ruhten alle Hoffnungen auf Toivonen. Vor dem Kielder Forest ging Henri am Lancia Rally 037 von Markku Alén vorbei. Dann musste er aber Harald Demuth im Audi für vier Prüfungen den Vortritt lassen, bevor er Platz Zwei zurückeroberte. Der Deutsche ließ es in Yorkshire vorsichtiger angehen, dafür drückte Michèle Mouton von hinten. Hannu Mikkola war einsam an der Spitze, während sich Henri und Michèle ein unterhaltsames Duell um Platz Zwei lieferten. „Es ist zu matschig, ich habe am Kurvenausgang zu wenig Traktion", beschwerte sich Henri, als Michèle im Dalby Forest an ihm vorbeizog. Der Kampf wurde immer dramatischer, auf einer Prüfung unterboten beide sogar die Minimalzeit. Die Entscheidung fiel letztlich auf dem Asphalt von Oliver's Mount, wo Henri zu Beginn der Saison schon über Ari Vatanen triumphiert hatte. Toivonen war zwei Sekunden schneller als Mouton, das reichte aber nicht – er wurde mit neun Sekunden Rückstand Dritter.

Auf dem Heimflug von London war bei Henri ein Hauch von Resignation zu spüren. „Noch immer kein Allradantrieb im nächsten Jahr", seufzte er nach seiner Unterschrift bei Opel für 1983. „Ich weiß, meine Zeit wird kommen. Aber wann?"

The 1982 season was not quite done yet for Henri Toivonen. As usual, the RAC Rally capped the World Rally Championship season and that kicked off with a bit of a shock when Henri's team leader, Walter Röhrl, was sacked before the start for dodging a pre-rally reception. Ari Vatanen had been drafted into the team, but when he went off in Clocaenog, Henri was left to fly the Opel flag. He passed Markku Alén's Lancia Rally 037 into second before Kielder, but in the forest complex could not initially hold back the Audi of Harald Demuth who passed him for four stages before Henri was back in second. Later when the German took a cautious approach in Yorkshire it was Michèle Mouton who came through to challenge. Hannu Mikkola was again on his own up front, but Henri and Michèle now engaged in an entertaining duel over second. "Too muddy, I cannot get enough traction out of the corners", complained Henri and through Dalby Forest, Michèle edged ahead. There were some dramatic scenes as the two fought for seconds only to find that they had beaten the bogey time for a stage. The issue was decided on the tarmac of Oliver's Mount where, early in the season, Henri had triumphed over Ari Vatanen. This time he could only beat Michèle by two seconds, which was not enough – he lost second place to her by nine.

There was an air of resignation about the man as he was boarding the flight home from Heathrow airport. "Still no four-wheel drive for next year", he sighed after signing for another season with Opel. "I know my day will come, but when?"

Snapshots
by Fred

Toivonen
Pauli, Henri & Harri

RALLYE DE PORTUGAL VINHO DO PORTO

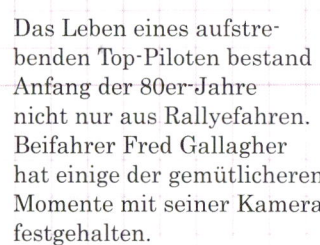

Das Leben eines aufstrebenden Top-Piloten bestand Anfang der 80er-Jahre nicht nur aus Rallyefahren. Beifahrer Fred Gallagher hat einige der gemütlicheren Momente mit seiner Kamera festgehalten.

The life of an international rally driver in the early 1980s was a lot more than just driving rallies. Co-driver Fred Gallagher caught some of the more leisurely moments of those times on film.

Henri Toivonen
Eine frustrierende Zeit
Frustration

Da der Manta 400 noch immer nicht homogiert war, musste für die Monte Carlo 1983 noch einmal der Ascona herhalten. Henri startete ungewohnt zurückhaltend und verlor gleich auf der ersten WP Zeit. Bis zur fünften Prüfung, dem Col des Garcinets, hatte er aber seinen Rhythmus gefunden und war nur eine Sekunde langsamer als Walter Röhrl, der jetzt einen Lancia 037 fuhr. Auf den größtenteils trockenen Straßen holte Toivonen schnell auf den drittplatzierten Stig Blomqvist im Audi Quattro auf. Henri setzte zwei Bestzeiten, ehe er auf der WP Trigance–Le Bourget einen „Big Moment" hatte. Im Service war Henri sichtlich mitgenommen: „Da war ein tiefer Abhang. Wenn wir da runtergefallen wären …" Das Rad hatte sich bei dem Zwischenfall im Bremssattel verhangen, Henri verlor acht Minuten. Rückblickend kostete das den möglichen dritten Platz.

Auf der letzten WP ging es für die Opel-Fahrer um nichts mehr, also schlossen Ari und Henri eine Wette. Sie machten eine Sollzeit aus und wer dieser Zeit am nächsten kam, würde das nächste Essen ausgegeben bekommen. „Ari hat versucht, die Zeit instinktiv zu treffen, während Henri absolut volle Lotte gefahren ist und kurz vor dem Ziel angehalten hat, um zur richtigen Zeit über die Linie zu fahren", schmunzelt Gallagher. „Ari hat dann das Essen bezahlt!"

Henri war gerade aus Monte Carlo zurückgekehrt, als Erja ihr erstes Kind bekam, Töchterchen Arla. Jetzt war die verspätete Homologation des Manta 400 ein Segen. Henri musste erst Ende Mai wieder in der WM mitmischen und hatte viel Zeit für seine Familie. Es gab Pläne, einige britische Formel-3-Rennen mit Eddie Jordan zu bestreiten, der auch Henris Manager werden wollte, aber aus diesen Ideen wurde nichts.

An Ostern flogen Henri, Erja und Arla nach Belfast. Beim Circuit of Ireland sollte der Ascona 400 ein letztes Mal bewegt werden. Zu Zeiten des Nordirlandkonflikts waren die Einheimischen überrascht, Erja mit ihrem Baby zu sehen. „Wir konnten hören, wie die Hotelbomben in der Nähe hochgingen", erinnert sich Erja. Henri war aber bald wieder bei ihr. Sein Ascona stoppte nach nur drei Prüfungen mit Achsschaden.

Zur Akropolis Rallye wechselte Henri endlich in den Opel Manta 400 – ein gutes Jahr später als ursprünglich geplant. Durch die Karosserieteile aus Kevlar war das Auto 80 Kilogramm leichter als der Ascona, außerdem lag der 275-PS-Motor weiter hinten als beim Vorgänger. Gegen die Audi und Lancia war der Manta trotzdem ein Underdog. In Griechenland kam erschwerend hinzu, dass es im Cockpit durch Plexiglas-Scheiben und einige andere Dinge fürchterlich heiß war. Die Temperatur pendelte sich bei gut 55°C ein.

Wenn das Auto lief, war der Manta für Top-Fünf-Zeiten gut. Doch Henri hatte Kupplungsprobleme und einen Reifenschaden, bei dem die Bremse beschädigt wurde. Nach Platz Neun auf der ersten Etappe verbesserte er sich im Laufe der zweiten Etappe auf die vierte Position, der Abstand zum Drittplatzierten war aber schon sehr groß. In der letzten Nacht prallte Henri jedoch frontal gegen einen Baum und schied aus. „Es war einer dieser Momente, wo Henri sagte, er habe die Ansage nicht gehört. Allerdings gab er zu, das ‚Achtung' gehört zu haben", erzählt Gallagher.

Wie so oft waren Pauli und Harri auch in Griechenland dabei, Letzterer sogar als Fahrer. Der kleine Bruder war zur rechten Zeit am

With the Manta 400 still not homologated, the Ascona had to be pressed into service again for the 1983 Monte Carlo Rally. After losing time on the very first stage, it was an unusually subdued start for Henri but, by stage five, Col des Garcinets, he was up to speed and only one second slower than Walter Röhrl who was now driving a Lancia Rally 037. In predominantly dry conditions, Toivonen was quickly catching third-placed Stig Blomqvist in his Audi Quattro but, having just set two fastest times, he then had a big moment in Trigance to Le Bourget. He was visibly shaken after reaching service: "It was a big drop and if we'd gone over the edge…" The wheel had got tangled around the brake caliper in the incident and some eight minutes were lost. With hindsight it could be seen that this cost Henri third place.

On the very last stage, with nothing to gain or lose for the Opel drivers, Ari and Henri decided to go for a wager: The one who got closest to a target time would pay the next lunch. Gallagher smiles at the memory: "Ari did his best to hit the time instinctively, whereas Henri went absolutely balls out, then stopped just before the finish to cross the line exactly on time! Ari paid the lunch."

Henri had barely got home from Monte Carlo, when Erja gave birth to their first child, daughter Arla. Happily, he now had some time to spend with the family as the ongoing delay with the Manta 400 homologation meant he would not be needed on WRC duty until late May. There were plans to do some more British F3 races with Eddie Jordan, who was also eager to manage Henri, but nothing ever came out of these.

At Easter, Henri, Erja and Arla flew to Belfast where the Opel Ascona 400 was going to be used one final time on the Circuit of Ireland. In an era of unrest in Ulster, the locals were surprised to find Erja arriving with a baby. "We could hear the hotel bombs going off not far away", she recalls. Henri was soon back with her, as the Ascona stopped with axle failure after only three stages.

For the Acropolis Rally, at long last, the Opel Manta 400 was ready for its WRC debut on gravel, more than a year later than originally intended. With extensive use of Kevlar panels it was 80 kg lighter than the Ascona and had its 275 bhp engine mounted further back in the chassis, but against Audi and Lancia it was still an underdog. It was unfortunate, too, that fixed Perspex-windows and some other features of this Group B machine made it uncomfortably hot in Greece with cabin temperatures regularly hovering around 55°C (131°F).

The Manta was good enough for top five times on the stages when all was going well, but it had clutch problems and Henri also had a puncture that damaged the brakes. From being ninth after the first leg he climbed to fourth after the second one but was still some way from third place. On the final night, he smashed the front of the car against a tree and was out. "It was one of those moments when Henri said he hadn't heard the note, although he did admit to hearing the 'danger' part of it", muses Fred Gallagher.

As was so often the case, Pauli and Harri were also present in Greece, the latter this time actually competing. He found himself in the right place at the right time, because with the introduction of new groups A and B, cars of old groups 2 and 4 could only

Die kleine Arla Toivonen reiste als Baby oft mit ihren Eltern zu den internationalen Rallyes. Über die Jahre zeigte sie mehr Interesse am Motorsport als ihr Bruder Marcus.

Young Arla Toivonen could often be seen with her parents at international rallies. She actually grew up to show more interest in motorised sports than did her brother Marcus.

Henri Toivonen Eine frustrierende Zeit / Frustration

Harri Toivonens erster Einsatz als Werksfahrer war für Mazda bei der Akropolis 1983. Henri, im Bild unten rechts mit Rita Vatanen, gab gleichzeitig sein Debüt im Manta 400 – eine frustrierende Premiere, denn gegen die Quattro hatte er keine Chance.

Harri Toivonen's first works drive came with Mazda in the 1983 Acropolis Rally. Henri, seen clowning with Rita Vatanen, was by that time somewhat frustrated by a lack of competitivity against the four-wheel drive Audi Quattros.

rechten Ort gewesen. Die FIA-Prioritätsfahrer durften nur noch Autos der neuen Gruppen A und B bewegen und nicht mehr die alten Wagen der Gruppen 2 und 4. Mazda aber setzte bei der Akropolis zwei RX-7 ein, die in der Gruppe 2 homologiert waren. Also suchte das Mazda Rallye Team Europe einen Fahrer ohne FIA-Status, der das zweite Auto neben Teamchef Achim Warmbold fuhr. Bei der Rallye hatte das Werksteam viele Probleme mit den Vorderradaufhängungen und Hinterachsdifferenzialen, dennoch holten sie einen Doppelsieg in der Gruppe 2. Warmbold gewann vor Toivonen.

In Finnland wurde Harri, der junge Hoffnungsträger, in das neu gegründete „Finnish Junior Rally Team" aufgenommen. Unter der Leitung von Simo Lampinen sollte er an ausgewählten internationalen Rallyes teilnehmen. Die geplanten Termine des Junior-Teams, dem auch Juha Kankkunen angehörte, waren die 1000 Seen und die RAC Rallye.

Kurz vor dem alljährlichen Sommerfest der Toivonens in Jyväskylä, der 1000 Seen Rallye, startete Henri bei der MIRA Rallye als Ersatz für Walter Röhrl. Diese Allstar-Veranstaltung war kurz, die Gesamtzeit auf den Prüfungen betrug nur zwölf Minuten. Auf der ersten WP blockierte die Handbremse an Henris Manta, damit waren die Chancen auf den Sieg schon verflogen. Letztlich wurde er dennoch Dritter mit nur zehn Sekunden Rückstand auf Stig Blomqvist im Quattro.

Auf den schnellen, hügeligen Straßen Mittelfinnlands wollten Henri und Harri ihr Können zeigen. Wobei nicht ganz klar war, was das in Bezug auf das Endergebnis zu bedeuten hatte. Harri durfte in einem Mitsubishi Lancer 2000 Turbo mit 260 PS starten. Im Vorjahr hatte Pentti Airikkala mit diesem Gruppe-4-Auto Platz Drei erreicht. Seitdem war der Lancer durch den Wechsel des Einsatzteams aber wenig weiterentwickelt worden. Harri verlor Zeit wegen einer defekten Benzinpumpe. Der Schaden brachte ihm am ersten Tag anderthalb Strafminuten ein. Später schied er an zwölfter Stelle liegend durch Getriebe- und Elektrikprobleme aus – eine gute Leistung unter diesen Umständen.

Unterdessen verblüffte Henri die Experten mit Platz Drei während der ersten beiden Tage, ehe ihn ein Dreher in diesem dicht beisammenliegenden Feld auf Rang Sechs zurückfallen ließ. Beim Regrouping auf der Schleife nach Süden verschlechterte sich das Wetter und Henri sagte zu seinem Beifahrer, es wäre „Zeit zu attackieren". Henri verbuchte unglaubliche fünf Bestzeiten in Folge und halbierte seinen Rückstand auf den führenden Blomqvist um eine Minute auf 47 Sekunden – bis der Motor hochging.

Rothmans wollte als Sponsor der britischen Meisterschaft und des Opel-Werksteams, dass Toivonen/Gallagher bei der Manx Rallye starten. So hatten sie die Möglichkeit, das Drama aus dem vergangenen Jahr vergessen zu machen. Die erste WP wurde bei Regen und Nebel ausgetragen. Henri fuhr eine Fabelzeit und war auf und davon. In der Mitte der dritten Etappe war Teamkollege Vatanen Zweiter und Opel gab durch: „Positionen halten." Doch es gab noch eine letzte Wendung. Kurz vor Ende schied Stig Blomqvist aus. GM-Kollege Russell Brookes lag im Vauxhall Chevette jetzt auf Platz Drei und hätte mit einem Sieg den Titel gewonnen. „Ich weiß nicht, ob uns Tony Fall einfach nur ärgern wollte", erklärt Gallagher. „Aber er sagte, GM würde verlangen, dass Brookes gewinnt. Das kam für uns überhaupt nicht infrage! Auf der Zielrampe in Douglas sahen wir, wie Stig uns aus seinem Hotelzimmer zuwinkte. Diesmal gab es für jeden eine Flasche Whisky."

Das Training zur Sanremo Rallye war besonders spannend, weil Toivonen/Gallagher ihre Zukunft planen. „Wir saßen im Hotel und dachten über die Angebote für 1984 nach", beschreibt Fred. „Es

be driven by non-seeded drivers. This opened the door for Harri to what was in effect Mazda's works team. In Belgium at Mazda Rallye Team Europe (MRTE), Achim Warmbold had prepared two Mazda RX7 coupés to Group 2 specification, one for himself and one for Harri Toivonen. In Greece the team ran into many problems particularly with front suspension and rear differentials, but both crews made it to the finish to clean up in Group 2, with the boss ahead of Harri.

In Finland, Harri – the bright young hope – was included in a new initiative called the Finnish Junior Rally Team, where he was to be coached by Simo Lampinen and represent his country in selected international events. Planned outings for the team, which also boasted Juha Kankkunen among its members, were the 1000 Lakes and RAC rallies.

Before it was time for the traditional Toivonen Jyväskylä summer fest, Henri had been a last minute replacement for Walter Röhrl in Sweden's all-star MIRA Rally. This was a short event with a total time of just some twelve minutes spent on the stages. Henri lost any chance of victory when the handbrake of his Manta jammed on in the first test, but he still came through to end up third, no more than ten seconds behind the winner, Stig Blomqvist in an Audi Quattro.

On the fast switchback roads of Central Finland, both Henri and Harri were keen to show their stuff, even though it was hard to say just what this might mean in terms of results. Harri was now given a chance in a 260 bhp Group 4 Mitsubishi Lancer 2000 Turbo, which had been driven to third by Pentti Airikkala the year before. However, little development had taken place since then despite the operation finding a new home in Britain as Team Ralliart. Harri was to lose time with fuel pump failures, which burdened his tally with one and a half minutes of road penalties on the first leg, and he then retired with gearbox failure and electrical problems while running twelfth – a good showing in the circumstances.

Meanwhile Henri astounded experts by holding third during the first two legs until a spin dropped him to sixth in the tightly bunched field. After regrouping around midnight at the southern tip of the route, the weather turned nasty and Henri said to his co-driver it was "time to have a go". Quite incredibly he was fastest over the next five stages! His deficit to leader Blomqvist was cut by one minute to just forty-seven seconds. And then the Cosworth engine blew …

UK championship sponsor Rothmans wanted the Toivonen/Gallagher partnership back for its Manx Rally, which presented them with an opportunity to redress the grievance suffered on the island the year before. In the rain and fog of the first stage, Henri set a mind-blowing time and never looked back. In the middle of the third leg it was decided to freeze the Opels' positions with team-mate Vatanen lying second. There was still a twist to come though. When Stig Blomqvist retired near the end Russell Brookes in a Vauxhall Chevette was lying third and could pip the Swede to the British title if he won the rally. "I don't know whether it was just Tony Fall winding us up, but he did suggest that GM demanded Brookes to win", says Fred Gallagher. "No way would we have that! On the finish ramp in Douglas we could see Stig waving from his hotel room window and this time there was a bottle of whisky for each of us."

The recce period for the Sanremo Rally was interesting since the future of the crew was at stake. "We were sitting in the hotel and considering Henri's offers for 1984", explains Fred. "There was

Henri Toivonen Eine frustrierende Zeit / Frustration

Die finnischen Fans waren eigentlich für ihr gutes Verhalten bekannt. Aber wenn sie Henri Toivonen erwarteten, konnte es auch schon mal anders aussehen. Leider endete seine Serie an Bestzeiten bei der 1000 Seen 1983 durch einen Motorschaden.

Finnish spectators at the 1000 Lakes Rally were normally well behaved, but the arrival of Henri Toivonen always got them highly excited. Unfortunately, a sensational sequence of fastest stage times in 1983 was brought to an end by engine failure.

Henri Toivonen Eine frustrierende Zeit / Frustration

gab eins von Peugeot. Aber wir dachten, dass deren Auto erst in der zweiten Saisonhälfte fertig sein würde. Also rief Henri Jean Todt an und sagte: ‚Nein, danke.' David Richards bot ihm einen Platz im Rothmans-Porsche an. Die hatten auch keinen Allradantrieb und es fühlte sich irgendwie zweitklassig an. Also sagte Henri auch ihm ab. Cesare Fiorio tauchte auf und nahm uns auf seiner Yacht mit nach Portofino, wo wir von einigen seiner Freunde unterhalten wurden. Das Resultat war, dass wir 1984 für Lancia in der Rallye-WM fahren würden. Nur gab David Richards nicht klein bei. Er flog nach Siena, um Henri die Porsche-Pläne zu unterbreiten und schaffte es, seinen Wunschpiloten umzustimmen."

Neben dem Vertragspoker ging Henri auch eine andere Sache durch den Kopf. In Finnland gab es und gibt es bis heute eine allgemeine Wehrpflicht. Da Pauli die richtigen Leute kannte, konnte der Militärdienst bisher immer verschoben werden. Doch die Einberufung war unausweichlich und machte das Leben für Henri nicht leichter. „Henri verabscheute den Militärdienst", bestätigt Fred. Mit einem vollen Terminkalender würde er das Unvermeidbare aber noch ein bisschen länger herauszögern können.

Die Rallye Sanremo begann mit Toivonen in der Verfolgerrolle hinter den Lancia 037 von Röhrl und Alén. Nach einem zeitraubenden Plattfuß in der Toskana eroberte er vor der abschließenden Asphaltetappe den dritten Platz zurück. In den Bergen oberhalb von Sanremo konnte Henri aber nicht sein übliches Feuerwerk zünden, denn er musste immer die Motortemperatur im Auge behalten. Mit einer defekten Zylinderkopfdichtung schleppte er den Manta an vierter Stelle ins Ziel.

one from Peugeot, but we didn't think their new car would be ready before the latter part of the season, so Henri called Jean Todt to say 'Thanks, but no thanks'. David Richards was offering a Rothmans drive in a Porsche, but they would not have 4WD ready either and it felt a bit second-rate, so Henri called him to refuse the offer. Cesare Fiorio turned up at some point and took us in his yacht to Portofino, where we were entertained with some of his friends. The outcome was that there was an understanding we'd be driving for Lancia in the 1984 World Rally Championship. Only David Richards did not give in so easily. He flew to Siena to show Henri some brochures about the Porsche plans and somehow managed to turn his head."

Quite apart from contractual considerations there was something else weighing on Henri's mind too. Military Service is compulsory in Finland and so far he had been able to put that off through Pauli having connections in the right places. The call up was looming for him and it did not make things any easier. "Military Service was definitely a disgust for Henri", affirms Fred. A busy programme of events would allow him to delay the inevitable a little bit longer.

The Sanremo Rally began with Toivonen giving chase to Röhrl and Alén in their Lancia Rally 037s. After a time-consuming puncture in Tuscany, he was back in third again for the final mountain stages. This time that last night did not produce the customary sparkle, however, because Henri had to keep one eye on engine temperatures. The reason was that the head-gasket had blown and the car only just crawled to the finish in fourth place.

Die 1000 Seen Rallye war wieder einmal eine Familienangelegenheit der Toivonens. Henri ließ Töchterchen Arla (links) ein bisschen Rallyeluft schnuppern. Harri (oben) gab im Mitsubishi Lancer Turbo sein Bestes. Durch fehlende Entwicklungsarbeit war der Hecktriebler aber chancenlos. Henri hingegen war bestens im Geschäft, ihm lagen für 1984 mehrere Angebote vor.

The 1000 Lakes Rally was once again a family affair for the Toivonens. Henri gave his daughter Arla, opposite page, a taste of rallying. Harri, above, meanwhile tried to make the best of a Mitsubishi Lancer 2000 Turbo, but the car's lack of development had let it fall behind the others. Meanwhile, there was no shortage of offers for Henri's driving services.

Henri Toivonen Eine frustrierende Zeit / Frustration

Bei der Rallye Sanremo 1983 fuhr Henri ungewöhnlich zurückhaltend. Dennoch war er der größte Gegner der Audi, bevor er durch eine defekte Zylinderkopfdichtung ausfiel.
The 1983 Sanremo Rally was an uncharacteristically subdued event for Henri but, before a blown head-gasket sidelined him, he had been the main threat to the Audis.

Henri Toivonen Eine frustrierende Zeit / Frustration

Derek Bell und Henri Toivonen begegneten sich 1983 oft bei Promotion-Events, wo Rothmans Mitfahrten und ähnliches veranstaltete. Im Herbst fuhr Henri den Porsche 956 auch bei Rennen.

Derek Bell and Henri Toivonen spent some time together at Rothmans promotional events during 1983, giving passenger rides and suchlike. Henri also got to race a Porsche 956.

Nach einem sonnigen Tag auf der Rennstrecke verspürte Henri wieder den Reiz am Rennfahren.

A sunny day at a race track tended to give Henri an itch to go circuit racing again.

Toivonen verbrachte den Herbst 1983 größtenteils in Italien. Nach der Sanremo bekam er die Chance, einen Porsche 956 beim Lauf der Langstrecken-Europameisterschaft in Imola zu fahren. Dort durfte er den Gruppe-C-Rennwagen von Richard Lloyd Racing aber nur im Training bewegen. Eine Woche später absolvierte er in dem Porsche einen von sechs Stints beim Sechs-Stunden-Rennen von Mugello. Jonathan Palmer und Derek Bell fuhren die anderen fünf Stints. Palmer hatte die Pole-Position erzielt, danach musste das Team jedoch auf den Ersatzmotor ausweichen, der weniger PS hatte und mehr Sprit verbrauchte. In der ersten Stunde fiel der Porsche auf Platz Sechs zurück. Vier Runden hatten sie verloren, als sich etwas am Unterboden gelöst hatte und mit Tape fixiert werden musste. Außerdem gab es Vibrationen in den Reifen. Am Ende wurden sie Dritte hinter Bob Wollek/Stefan Johansson im 956 und Riccardo Patrese/Alessandro Nannini im Lancia.

Damit war die Italien-Reise noch nicht vorbei. Für Mauro Manninis Team ProMotor Sport pilotierte Henri einen Ferrari 308 GTB bei der Rallye di San Marino. Ein Teil des Deals war, dass Harri als Teamkollege in einem Gruppe-4-Ferrari startete. Beide Brüder fuhren mit neuen Copiloten. Den Platz neben Henri nahm Juha Piironen ein, während Harri dem jungen und weltoffenen Cedric Wrede die erste Rallyeerfahrung gönnte. Miki Biasion dominierte die Rallye im Lancia 037. Henri fuhr auf WP Eins die drittbeste Zeit und begeisterte die Fans mit einer Bestzeit auf WP 13, bevor er das Auto auf der Seite liegend in einem Graben parkte, nachdem ein Kugelgelenk in der Lenkung den Geist aufgegeben hatte. Harri schied mit Motorschaden aus.

Henri Toivonen actually spent much of autumn 1983 in Italy, because soon after Sanremo he realized an ambition when given a chance to race a Group C Porsche 956. He first went to Imola for a round of the European Endurance Championship, but had to be content with just practicing the Richard Lloyd Racing car there. A week later in Mugello he got to do one of the six stints in a six-hour race in the same car. Jonathan Palmer had qualified it on pole but when the team had to switch to a spare engine that had less power and was thirstier, the crew – Derek Bell as the third member – dropped to sixth in the first hour. Having lost four laps with loose underside bodywork that needed to be taped up and then more time with tyre vibrations, they eventually finished third behind Bob Wollek/Stefan Johansson in a similar 956 and Riccardo Patrese/Alessandro Nannini in a Lancia.

More Italian jobs followed, as Henri agreed to drive a Ferrari 308 GTB for Mauro Mannini's ProMotor Sport team in the San Marino Rally. Part of the deal was an opportunity for brother Harri to get a seat in the team's Group 4 Ferrari. Both had new co-drivers for this little episode. Henri teamed up with Juha Piironen and Harri gave a first taste of the sport to an entrepreneurial young cosmopolitan called Cedric Wrede. The rally was dominated by Miki Biasion in a Lancia Rally 037, but Henri was third on the first stage and finally delighted his local fans by being fastest on stage thirteen, before retiring with the car deep on its side in a ditch after a steering ball-joint had given up. Harri retired his Ferrari with engine problems.

Henri Toivonen Eine frustrierende Zeit / Frustration

"In Griechenland war ich Harris Beifahrer und da sprach ich mit Henri erstmals darüber, ob wir in Zukunft zusammen fahren sollten", sagt Juha Piironen. „In San Marino wollten wir prüfen, ob das funktioniert mit seinem englischen Aufschrieb und so weiter. Danach nahmen wir noch in einem sehr freizügig gebauten Ferrari 308 an der Rallye di Monza teil. Die Rallye endete aber mit einem Diff-Schaden."

In der Nacht vor der RAC Rallye verkündete Rothmans, dass Henri Toivonen 1984 im Porsche an der Europameisterschaft teilnehmen würde. Die Nachricht des Tages war aber, dass Fred Gallagher nicht mehr zum Team gehören würde. „Ich wollte einen Beifahrer, der mit vollem Einsatz hinter dem Programm steht und hatte nicht den Eindruck, dass Gallagher das tun würde", rechtfertigte sich David Richards, der zur Saison 1984 sein eigenes Team gründete. Henri kritisierte Fred übrigens nie öffentlich.

Henri begann die RAC nachdenklich, übernahm aber bald Platz Zwei hinter Stig Blomqvist, der mit seinem Quattro allen davon fuhr. Dann rutschte Toivonen an einer Feuerschleuse von der Strecke und verlor mehrere Minuten, das Auto blieb aber fast unbeschädigt. „Die Stimmung im Auto war recht gespannt", gibt Fred zu. „Leider hat sich unsere Beziehung nie mehr richtig davon erholt." Nach einem Motorschaden im Grizedale Forest trennten sich ihre Wege.

Direkt nach der Rallye hatte Gallagher die Vermutung, dass es Henri bei seinen Rallyes im Rothmans-Porsche vielleicht zu leicht haben würde. Er fürchtete, dass dies Henris Selbstdisziplin schaden könnten. Denn in der gemeinsamen Zeit hatte Toivonen immer mehr die Allüren eines internationalen Rallyestars gezeigt.

Aber Fred lag damit zumindest teilweise falsch. Die EM-Läufe waren kein Spaziergang für „ein kleines Team, das aus dem Nichts kam", wie es Teamkoordinator Charles Reynolds formuliert. „Am Anfang gab es fünf Mechaniker und mich. Wir hatten nicht einmal einen Ingenieur, bis David Lapworth irgendwann zu uns stieß. Es dauerte einige Monate, ehe wir unsere eigene Werkstatt in Silverstone bezogen. Die Autos hatten unsere Leute noch im Porsche-Werk in Weissach zusammengebaut."

Henri hatte der Traum gelockt, 1985 am Steuer des beeindruckenden Porsche 959 mit Allradantrieb zu sitzen und das WM-Comeback der Stuttgarter anzuführen. In der Zwischenzeit wollte er in die Fußstapfen seines Vaters treten und – genau wie Pauli 1968 – den EM-Titel auf einem Porsche 911 gewinnen. Henri fuhr den gerade erst homologierten 911 SCRS. Rothmans hatte für Toivonen auch die Gruppe-C-Rennen in Monza, Le Mans, Spa und Kyalami vorgesehen, alle im Porsche 956.

Obendrauf wurde im Dezember ein WM-Programm mit Lancia verkündet, das fünf Läufe beinhaltete. Damit konnte Henri den Militärdienst für ein weiteres Jahr verschieben. Außerdem zog er mit seiner kleinen Familie nach England in das Örtchen Marsh Gibbon, also in die direkte Nachbarschaft von David Richards.

"Ich kannte Henri schon eine Weile", erklärt Richards. „Neil Wilson war einige Male sein Beifahrer und Neil ist ein guter Freund von mir. Wir kommen aus derselben Gegend. Ich dachte schon immer, dass Henri mal ein großer Star wird. Also war es eines meiner großen Ziele, dass er Teil meines Teams wird, wenn ich es gründe." Zwischen den Familien entwickelte sich eine Freundschaft. Erja verbrachte viel Zeit mit Karen Richards, die auch junge Kinder hatte.

David Richards gab sein Bestes, damit sich Henri in der neuen Umgebung wohlfühlt. „Ich habe gesehen, wie Karen in einem neuen, schwarzen Porsche herumgefahren ist und meinte zu Henri scherz-

"I'd been in Greece as Harri's co-driver and it was there we'd started talking with Henri about possibly joining forces in the future", says Juha Piironen. "The San Marino outing was really to check whether it would work, what with his English pacenotes and so on. As a follow-up we also did the Monza Rally in a more liberally built Ferrari 308, but that ended in diff failure."

On the night before the RAC Rally, Rothmans announced that Henri Toivonen would be driving a Porsche for them in a programme of European Championship rallies in 1984. The bombshell of the occasion was the dropping of Fred Gallagher from the outfit. "I wanted a co-driver who would give his full commitment to the programme and did not think that Gallagher would give that", justified David Richards, who'd be setting up a new team to run the show. Henri refused to criticize Fred in public.

Henri started the RAC Rally in pensive mood, but got up to second as Stig Blomqvist sailed into the distance in his Audi Quattro. He then lost several minutes with an off down a firebreak, but the car did not suffer much damage. "It was fairly tense in the car", Fred admits. "Unfortunately our relationship never really recovered to what it had been." Eventually their ways parted after the engine blew – in Grizedale Forest of all places.

Immediately after the rally, Gallagher privately suspected Henri might be going to have it too easy in the rallies he was meant to do with Rothmans Porsche. That could free up his self-discipline as, during their time together, Henri had been indulging more readily in the spoils of an international rally star.

Fred Gallagher would be at least partially wrong. Those European rallies would be no piece of cake, especially for "a small team starting from nothing", as team co-ordinator Charles Reynolds puts it. "It was just five mechanics and myself at first, we didn't even have an engineer until David Lapworth joined a bit later. It took some months before we got any premises of our own at Silverstone and the cars had been initially built by our mechanics in Porsche's Weissach facility."

Henri had been lured by the dream of taking the wheel of the awesome 4WD Porsche 959 in 1985, when he would lead the Stuttgart manufacturer's return to rallies on the world stage. Meanwhile he'd follow in his father's footsteps and hopefully collect the 1984 European title in a Porsche 911 SCRS, a freshly homologated evolution of the classic model. Rothmans also had plans to include some racing with Group C entries mooted for Monza, Le Mans, Spa and Kyalami; all with a Porsche 956.

Furthermore, there was a five event WRC programme with Lancia that was announced in December. These commitments meant Henri could brush aside any thoughts of National Service for another year or so. He also moved his small family to England to live in a house found for him in Marsh Gibbon by David Richards, now a close neighbour.

"I'd known Henri for some time, because Neil Wilson had made appearances as his co-driver and Neil's a good friend of mine as we come from the same area. I always thought Henri was a real star in the making and one of my main objectives was to get him in my team when I set it up", says Richards. The two families became very close, as Erja started to spend a lot of time with Karen Richards, who also had young children.

David Richards certainly did his best to make Henri feel comfortable in his new environment, as Erja testifies: "I'd noticed Karen

David Richards und Henri Toivonen hatten große Pläne für die Zukunft, doch zunächst musste der Porsche 911 SCRS weiterentwickelt werden. Bei der Rallye Costa Brava fuhr Henri nach seinem Ausfall als Nullwagen weiter, um Testkilometer zu sammeln.

David Richards and Henri Toivonen held high hopes for the future, but first the Porsche 911 SCRS needed development. Any testing helped, such as rejoining the Costa Brava Rally as a course car after retiring.

haft, was für ein schönes Auto sie doch hat", erzählt Erja. „Es stellte sich heraus, dass der Porsche eigentlich für Henri bestimmt war."

Im Winter verbrachte Toivonen einige Zeit in Weissach bei Tests mit einem Porsche 911. „Der geht zwischen 3.000 und 8.000 Touren sehr gut", berichtete der Finne. „Aber mit dem jetzigen Differenzial braucht man das ganze Drehmoment, damit das Auto in Bewegung bleibt. Im dritten Gang fährt das Auto 170 km/h, das ist mehr als genug. Es fährt sich wirklich gut, wobei ich hart arbeiten muss, um einen sanften Fahrstil zu erreichen. Wenn ich nicht aufpasse, wird das Auto sehr hecklastig, besonders auf Schotter."

Das Problem war, dass Henri die Testarbeit in einem Gruppe-4-Porsche ohne Stabilisator machte. Als die Saison in Spanien begann, war das Handling komplett anders. Das Gruppe-B-Auto war ohne Schraubenfedern an der Hinterachse homologiert worden – für das Team eine böse Überraschung. „Die Torsionsstäbe haben den Effekt, dass sie das Auto anheben, und das beeinflusst die Fahrstabilität", erklärte Henri. Die Torsionsstab-Hinterachse blieb ein Schwachpunkt des 911 SCRS, genau wie das Getriebe.

Die ersten beiden Einsätze des Rothmans-Porsche – die Rallye Costa Brava, die später zur Rallye Catalunya wurde, und die RACE Rallye Costa Blanca – endeten beide durch technische Defekte. Schlimmer war jedoch, dass Henri entgegen seiner Erwartungen nicht in Führung gelegen hatte. „Wir waren alle noch in der Lernphase, sogar David Richards", gibt Charles Reynolds zu.

Henris neuer Beifahrer im Porsche war der Engländer Ian Grindrod. Zwischen den spanischen EM-Läufen bestritt er mit Juha Piironen die Rallye Portugal im werkseingesetzten Lancia. „Auf Asphalt ist der 037 wirklich wie ein Gruppe-C-Auto", schwärmte Henri. „Das ist das absolut schnellste Auto, das Gefühl ist unbeschreiblich." Trotzdem gab es für Henri noch gewisse Unsicherheiten: „Jedes Mal, wenn ich dieses Auto in Italien getestet habe, hat es geschneit. Ich weiß nicht, wo das Limit ist."

Trotzdem ärgerte Henri in Portugal seine Konkurrenten. Auf den ersten fünf Asphaltprüfungen von Sintra fuhr er jeweils Bestzeit. Dann kam die sechste WP. „Zwischen den Steinmauern ließ er das Heck leicht raushängen, ohne die kleinste Lücke zu lassen", erinnert sich Piironen. „Auf der Außenseite einer Kurve ragte ein Baum aus der Mauer heraus. Das Heck schlug dagegen, woraufhin das Auto von einer Mauer zur nächsten prallte. Bei jedem Aufprall fielen Karosserieteile ab."

Henri hatte alle Hoffnungen weggeworfen und war am Boden zerstört. „Dieses Erlebnis eröffnete einen genauen Blick in die Psyche des Fahrers", sagt Piironen. „Er hatte dieses absolut unheimliche Selbstvertrauen auf Asphalt. Aber der Ausgang zeigte, wie nah er am Limit unterwegs war."

Grindrod musste nach den Rallyes in Spanien wegen Nierenbeschwerden pausieren und so nahm Piironen seinen Platz im Porsche ein: „Meine Frau hatte mir gerade gesagt, dass sie zum ersten Mal schwanger war, als Henri anrief und fragte, ob ich ihm in Frankreich beim Training helfen könnte. Eigentlich sollte es nur ein paar Tage dauern, aber am Ende war ich über einen Monat weg. Meine Frau war nicht gerade erfreut!"

Piironen bemerkte schnell, das die EM-Läufe eine harte Nuss waren. „Es gab einige sehr gute Fahrer und Teams, die viel Erfahrung bei den Rallyes hatten. Die wussten, welche Getriebeübersetzung sie am besten fahren und solche Dinge. Wir mussten das alles erst lernen. Und wir hatten auch nicht viel Zeit zum Testen."

driving about in a new black Porsche and a bit sarcastically mentioned to Henri what a nice car she'd got. It turned out that the Porsche was actually meant for him!"

Over the winter, Henri Toivonen spent some time testing a Porsche 911 in Weissach. "It pulls very well between 3,000 and 8,000 rpm but, with the current differential we have fitted, it needs all the torque available to keep it moving", he reported. "At present the car is capable of 170 kph in third, which is more than enough for what I want. It handles very well at present, although I have had to work hard at achieving a smooth driving style. If I'm not careful, it becomes very tail-happy, particularly on the loose."

Trouble was he did all the early work in a Group 4 version without an anti-roll bar and when the season started in Spain he found that the handling was completely different. The Group B version had been homologated without the rear coil spring suspension, which came as a nasty surprise to the team. "The torsion bars tend to produce a sort of jacking effect on the car and this affects its stability", Henri explained. The torsion bar system was to remain a weak link, as was the gearbox.

The first two outings with the Rothmans Porsche – the Rally Costa Brava, which later morphed into Rally Catalunya, and the RACE Rally Costa Blanca, basically the same event that Pauli had won back in 1968 – both ended in mechanical failures. Worse was the fact that much against his expectations Henri had not been leading either of them. "We were all on a learning curve, including even David Richards", admits Charles Reynolds.

Henri's new co-driver in the Porsche was Englishman Ian Grindrod, but between those two European series rallies he linked up with Juha Piironen in a works Lancia Rally 037 for the WRC round in Portugal. "Really, this is like a Group C car on tarmac", he enthused. "It is absolutely the fastest thing and the feeling is incredible." Still, he admitted to a degree of uncertainty: "It has been snowing in Italy every time I have been to try this car, so I don't know its limits."

Apparently pushing all doubts aside, Henri set off to scorch the opposition, fastest on all the Sintra asphalt tests until stage six, the last one of the second loop. "He was hanging the tail out slightly between stone walls, without leaving any margin", recounts Juha Piironen. "There was a tree growing out of the wall on the outside of a bend and the rear corner swiped that, which sent the car bouncing between those walls, shedding bodywork on every hit."

Having thrown away his chances, Henri was distraught. "That experience opened a fascinating landscape into the psyche of the driver", says Piironen. "He seemed to have an absolutely uncanny touch and confidence on asphalt, and yet, the outcome showed just how close he was to the edge."

Ian Grindrod was ordered to rest after the Spanish rallies due to a kidney complaint, which meant Juha Piironen stepped in to replace him in the Porsche: "My wife had just told me she was pregnant for the first time, when Henri called and asked me to fly to France to help with the recce. It was supposed to be for just a few days, but I ended up staying away from home for over a month. She was not amused!"

Piironen rapidly discovered that European Championship rallies were a tough nut to crack. "There were some very good drivers and teams who had vast experience of the events. They knew

Eine bittere Pille: In Portugal fuhr Henri auf den ersten fünf Prüfungen Bestzeit, dann krachte er mit dem Heck in eine Mauer.
A bitter blow! Having set a string of fastest stage times, Henri was thoroughly dejected after crashing out in Portugal.

Für viele war es nur eine Frage der Zeit, bis Henri für Lancia fahren würde. Als es dann so weit war, fühlte sich Henri bei den Italienern sofort heimisch.

It had always been on the cards that one day Henri would drive for Lancia and, when he did, he immediately felt at home in the team.

1984

In Henri Toivonen steckte mehr als nur ein kleiner Showman. Auf den Sintra-Prüfungen, die wie immer von Tausenden Fans belagert wurden, setzte er sich perfekt in Szene.

There was more than just a little of the performing artist in Henri Toivonen and the Sintra stages, lined with their usual crowds, gave him the perfect chance to indulge.

Henri Toivonen Eine frustrierende Zeit / Frustration

Bei der Rallye des Garrigues war die Reifenwahl auf der letzten WP wegen eines plötzlichen Schauers schwierig. Dadurch ging Henri an François Chatriots Renault 5 Turbo vorbei an die dritte Position. Dennoch lag er hinter dem Lancia 037 von Jean-Claude Andruet und Guy Fréquelins Opel Manta 400. Bei der Critérium Alpin kämpfte Toivonen mit den R5 Turbo von Jean Ragnotti und Bruno Saby sowie Bernard Béguins BMW M1 um den Sieg. Am Ende unterlag er Ragnotti um 48 Sekunden. Es sagt einiges über das Niveau, dass Fréquelin diesmal deutlich geschlagen wurde und Bernard Darniche im Audi Quattro als Sechster chancenlos war.

Vier Tage später kehrte Ian Grindrod beim Circuit of Ireland in Henris Cockpit zurück. Piironen flog direkt nach Sardinien, wo er bis zum Start der Rallye Costa Smeralda auf seinen Fahrer wartete. In Irland rechnete sich Henri keine großen Chancen auf eine vordere Platzierung aus. Er fand, dass es dem Porsche an Leistung fehlte und dass die Hinterradaufhängung zu niedrig war, und „wenn wir sie anheben, ist das Auto schwer zu fahren". Trotzdem fuhr er auf den ersten beiden Prüfungen Bestzeit, bevor er eine Mauer touchierte, woraufhin komischerweise beide Hinterreifen Luft verloren. Einer musste gewechselt werden, was sechs Minuten kostete. Henri setzte danach 18 Bestzeiten in Serie und eroberte die Führung zurück! Beobachter verdrehten die Augen, als sie sahen, wie Toivonen zwischen Steinmauern quer um Kreuzungen driftete. Die Portugal-Erfahrung hatte ihn wohl nicht beeinflusst.

Doch um die Ecke wartete schon das Drama. Da Henri fast uneinholbar in Führung lag, nutzte er am Ende einer Etappe die Gelegenheit, an einem Promi-Kartrennen teilzunehmen. Dabei krachte Toivonen rückwärts in einen Mast und musste mit dem Krankenwagen abtransportiert werden – Erinnerungen an 1982 wurden wach! Die Diagnose der Ärzte: eine Rückenverletzung und ein verstauchter Knöchel. Trotzdem setzte Henri die Rallye fort. Doch auf der ersten WP am nächsten Morgen steckte der vierte Gang seines Porsche fest. Die Getriebeprobleme dauerten an, bis die Mechaniker beim Getriebewechsel die Maximalzeit überschritten.

Als Toivonen mit einem Privatjet in Sardinien ankam, sah er nicht so aus, als wäre er fit für den bis dato am stärksten besetzten EM-Lauf, bei dem allein die WP-Gesamtzeit sieben Stunden betrug. „Henri dachte sicher, er wäre es dem Team schuldig, nachdem er in Irland so leichtsinnig gewesen war", erklärt Juha Piironen. „Ich musste auf den längeren Verbindungsetappen ans Steuer, aber auf den Prüfungen fuhr Henri wie ein Verrückter."

Henri beschädigte die Vorderradaufhängung seines Porsche bei einer harten Landung und lag hinter den Lancia von Adartico Vudafieri und Carlo Capone. Dann hatte Capone ein Problem und Henri rückte auf Platz Zwei vor. Am nächsten Tag machte er Jagd auf den Führenden und zog vorbei, als Vudafieri einen Reifenschaden hatte. Am Start der Schlussetappe steckte bei Vudafieris 037 der Gang fest, während der Porsche Öl verlor. Vudafieri schied kurz darauf mit Motorschaden aus, aber auch Toivonen kämpfte weiter mit Problemen: Ein Querlenker an der Hinterachse war abgeschert. Durch die Reparatur kassierte Henri eine Strafminute, doch er schaffte es ins Ziel und gewann mit 57 Sekunden vor Capone.

Die Siegesfeier war unvergesslich. Während Henri den Champagner versprühte, winkte er mit seiner Krücke. „Ich glaube, der Sieg in Sardinien war für mich das Highlight", sagt David Richards. „Es war eine harte Rallye und es ging eng zu. Henri fuhr grandios, es war ein verdienter Sieg."

what ratios to use in the gearbox and things like that, whereas we had it all to learn. We didn't have much time to test either." In the Garrigues Rally, a sudden shower on the last stage made tyre choice critical and allowed Henri to pass François Chatriot's Renault 5 Turbo into third, but he still lost to Jean-Claude Andruet's Lancia Rally 037 and Guy Fréquelin's Opel Manta 400, although it was all very close. On the Critérium Alpin, he battled with the Renault 5 Turbos of Jean Ragnotti and Bruno Saby plus Bernard Béguin's BMW M1, losing victory to Ragnotti by forty-eight seconds. It says something of the level of competition that this time Fréquelin was beaten fair and square, while Bernard Darniche in an Audi Quattro never stood a chance and ended up sixth.

Just four days later Ian Grindrod returned to guide Henri on the Circuit of Ireland, while Piironen went straight to Sardinia, where he would be waiting for the man to start the Costa Smeralda immediately afterwards. Henri was not too confident about his chances in Ireland. He felt the Porsche was down on power and "its rear suspension is too low and, when we raise it, it's difficult to drive". He was fastest on the first two stages anyway, but then clipped a wall, which somehow led to both rear tyres going flat. One had to be changed and six minutes were lost. On each of the next eighteen stages he was fastest, inexorably charging back to first place! Onlookers rolled their eyes at the sight of Toivonen sliding sideways into junctions between solid stone walls – the Portugal experience obviously had not dented his resolve!

The drama was only just beginning, however. Enjoying an apparently insurmountable lead, Henri grabbed the opportunity to have some fun in a celebrity kart race at the end of a leg. He crashed backwards into a post and had to be taken to hospital by ambulance – echoes of 1982! Back injury and a sprained ankle were diagnosed, but Henri opted to carry on only for the Porsche to get stuck in fourth gear in the first stage the next morning. Dire gearbox trouble then persisted until the mechanics ran out of time in an attempt to change the unit.

Arriving in Sardinia by private jet, the limping Henri Toivonen did not look fit to take on the season's best ERC entry yet in a rally where nearly seven hours would be spent on special stages. "I think Henri felt he owed the team for having been frivolous in Ireland", opines co-driver Juha Piironen. "I had to drive some of the longer liaison sections, but on the special stages Henri drove like a man possessed."

He first followed the Lancias of Adartico Vudafieri and Carlo Capone after damaging the Porsche's front suspension in a heavy landing. When Capone had an incident of his own, it let the Finn into second and following an overnight rest he began to catch the leader, soon edging ahead when the Italian suffered a puncture. At the start of the final leg, Vudafieri's Lancia jammed in a gear but now the Porsche was losing oil. When Vudafieri dropped out with engine failure, again Toivonen too had more trouble as a rear suspension arm had sheared. Changing it brought a one-minute road penalty, but Henri just made it to the end without further time loss to win by fifty-seven seconds from Capone.

Celebrations were memorable with the winner spraying champagne and waving his crutch for theatrical effect. "I think winning in Sardinia was the highlight for me", says David Richards. "It was a very tough rally, it was quite close. Henri drove superbly and it was a really genuine win."

Henri Toivonen Eine frustrierende Zeit / Frustration

Trotz einer selbstverschuldeten Verletzung fuhr Henri bei der Rallye Costa Smeralda wie ein Verrückter. Selbst zahlreiche Rückschläge hielten ihn bei diesem harten EM-Lauf nicht vom Siegen ab.

After a self-inflicted injury, Henri Toivonen drove like a man possessed on the Costa Smeralda Rally. Even repeated setbacks could not deny him victory on this gruelling round of the European Championship.

Auch Piironen war beeindruckt: „Der Porsche war ein altmodisches Auto. Wir hatten überhaupt keinen Grip, besonders auf Schotter. Der Tacho war mit den Hinterrädern verknüpft und konnte 250 km/h anzeigen, während das Auto noch stand. Beim Drift um die Ecken hatte der 911 das Handling eines Hammers. Aber Henri hatte ein wunderbares Gefühl dafür. Auf losem Untergrund fühlte es sich an, als würde man von einer Seite zur andern schweben."

Danach kehrte Piironen endlich in die Heimat zurück. Bei der Rallye Zlatni Piassatzi saß Ian Grindrod im Porsche. In Bulgarien gaben Toivonen/Grindrod das Tempo vor. Der Porsche war weiterentwickelt worden und hatte jetzt eine Chance gegen den Lancia von Carlo Capone, der sich als größter Rivale in der Europameisterschaft herausstellte. Am Ende von Tag Eins stempelte die Porsche-Crew wegen eines Fehlers des glücklosen Grindrod fünf Minuten zu früh. Bei unerwartetem Schneefall machte Henri viel Boden gut und lag am Ende nur noch 32 Sekunden hinter dem Italiener. Diese Rallye war aber sicher eine verpasste Chance.

Piironen hatte nicht viel Zeit, um seine Frau zu beruhigen. Er musste zum Akropolis-Training aufbrechen. Bei der Rallye waren die heckgetriebenen Lancia den Allrad-Audi hoffnungslos unterlegen. Immerhin war Toivonen der schnellste der Lancisti, bis er zur Halbzeit von einer Änderung in der Straße durch Bauarbeiten überrascht wurde und verunfallte. „Das war ein dummer Fehler", ärgert sich Piironen. Durch zwei Unfälle bei zwei Rallyes für Lancia machte die Presse mächtig Feuer. Sie beschuldigte Henri, zu wenig Selbstbeherrschung und Geduld zu haben.

Wobei es bei Henris vollem Programm sicher nicht leicht war, zwischen den Autos hin und her zu springen. Henri verbrachte kaum Zeit in Marsh Gibbon, wo Erja eines Tages Besuch vom Pfarrer bekam. „Er sagte, dass unsere Nachbarn verärgert wären, weil unser Garten so unordentlich aussah. Ich musste mir von Karen Richards einen Rasenmäher leihen, um das zu ändern."

The co-driver was impressed too: "That Porsche was an old-fashioned car by then. Its grip was non-existent particularly on gravel. The speedo was connected to the rear wheels and could show 250 kph while the car was standing still … Sliding in the corners, it had the handling characteristics of a hammer. But Henri had a fantastic grip on it – on loose surfaces it felt like he had it floating from side to side."

So, Piironen finally got to return home to Finland and it was Ian Grindrod back in the right-hand seat for the Zlatni Piassatzi Rally where the pair set the pace. The Porsche had now been sufficiently developed to offer a fighting chance against the Lancia of Carlo Capone who was emerging as Henri's main protagonist in the European series. At the end of the first day, a mistake by the hapless Grindrod caused the pair to clock into a time control five minutes early. Unseasonal snow later in the rally allowed Henri to claw back much of the deficit and only lose by thirty-two seconds to the Italian, but this had definitely been a missed opportunity.

Piironen did not have long to soothe his wife before leaving again for the Acropolis Rally recce. The Greek event was something of a lost cause for the 2WD Lancias now, and even though Toivonen was quickest among them, in his turn he was totally outclassed by the Audis. He crashed halfway through the event when faced with a minor deviation caused by road works. "That was a silly mistake", grunts Piironen. Two shunts in two events for Lancia got Henri a lot of flak in the press that castigated him for lack of self-control and patience.

It cannot have been easy to jump from one car to another in Henri's hectic schedule. He rarely got to spend time in Marsh Gibbon, where Erja one day got a visit from the Vicar. "He came to say the neighbours were upset, because our garden was in such an uncared-for state. I had to borrow a lawn mower from Karen Richards to sort it out!"

Viel Freude – und ein bisschen Show – auf dem Podium.
Pure joy – and some showmanship – on the podium!

In der Europameisterschaft war durch die Nullnummern zu Beginn und durch Capones starke Form Flexibilität gefragt. Neue Läufe wurden in den Terminkalender aufgenommen und die Gruppe-C-Pläne erst einmal auf Eis gelegt. Mit einer Ausnahme: Ein Porsche 956 wurde für ein „Special Saloon"-Rennen nach Ahvenisto, Finnland gebracht. Henri gewann gegen diese Spezialtourenwagen mit irrwitzigem Vorsprung.

Ende Juni fand bei der Ypern Rallye das nächste Duell Toivonen gegen Capone statt. In Belgien gaben zunächst die Lancia von Jean-Claude Andruet und Capone den Ton an, weil Henri durch einen Dreher und die falsche Reifenwahl Zeit verlor. Doch dann fiel Capone durch einen Reifenschaden zurück und Andruet kassierte eine Strafzeit durch einen Getriebetausch. Porsche feierte einen wichtigen Sieg und Toivonen übernahm erstmals die Meisterschaftsführung.

Flexibility needed to be adopted in the ERC programme depending on the situation in the championship. With the early no-scores and Carlo Capone's strong form, events had to be added and any ideas of Group C racing could be forgotten for the time being. There was one exception: a Porsche 956 was sent to Finland for a two-heat Special Saloon race in Ahvenisto, which Henri won by a ridiculous margin.

Late June saw another encounter between Toivonen and Capone in Belgium's Ypres Rally. It was the Lancias of Jean-Claude Andruet and Capone that set the early pace as Henri lost time with a spin and a wrong tyre choice, but then Capone dropped back with a puncture. When a gearbox change for Andruet brought him road penalties, the Porsche came through to collect a prestigious win. The result also put Henri Toivonen in the lead of the series for the first time.

Henri Toivonen Eine frustrierende Zeit / Frustration

Juha Piironen leistete einen großen Beitrag zum Sieg bei der Costa Smeralda 1984. Wegen Henris Verletzung übernahm der Copilot auf den meisten Verbindungsetappen das Steuer.

Co-driver Juha Piironen played a big part in the Costa Smeralda victory of 1984. Henri's painful injury forced Juha to take the wheel on most of road sections between stages.

1984

Henri Toivonen Eine frustrierende Zeit / Frustration

Auf Bitten seines Sponsors Rothmans wurde die Mille Pistes Rallye ins Programm genommen. Dort folgte der nächste Sieg vor einer Horde Renault 5 Turbo, die von Chatriot, Saby, Thérier und Ragnotti gefahren wurden. Dahinter folgten die Opel von Guy Fréquelin und Erwin Weber sowie Darniches Audi Quattro. Jetzt war Henri sein Geld wirklich Wert.

Daheim in Marsh Gibbon war Erja erneut schwanger. Sie fühlte sich in dem großen Landhaus einsam und sehnte sich nach der Rückkehr nach Finnland. „Henri war kaum zu Hause und es gab ein paar beunruhigende Verbrechen in der Gegend. Eines Tages fasste ich den Entschluss und ließ eine Notiz auf dem Küchentisch: ‚Ich bin nach Hause – du findest mich in Finnland.' Am 14. Juli haben wir mit Ulla und Pauli eine Party veranstaltet, als ich plötzlich die Wehen bekam. Henri bot an, mich ins Krankenhaus zu fahren. Aber ich habe gesagt: ‚Das geht nicht, du hast getrunken.' Also fuhr ich selbst."

Glücklicherweise hatte Henri im Juli mehr Zeit, die er mit Erja, Arla und dem neugeborenen Sohn Markus verbringen konnte. Henri wusste zwar noch nichts davon, aber er sollte die nächsten sechs Monate deutlich weniger reisen. Doch erst einmal ging es zur Madeira Rallye, wo Juha Piironen Beifahrer war. Nach dem Fehler in Bulgarien hatte Henri das Vertrauen in Ian Grindrod verloren.

In Madeira rutschte Carlo Capone kurz nach dem Start bei Regen und Nebel von der Bahn. Henri litt unter Motorproblemen und musste in der ersten WP dreimal anhalten. Was folgte, war ein Toivonen in Bestform: Mit 23 Bestzeiten auf 28 Prüfungen holte er den Rückstand auf Patrick Snijers in einem weiteren Porsche 911 SCRS wieder auf. Dann musste Henri auf einer Prüfung einem Taxi ausweichen und Snijers hatte zwei Reifenschäden. Schlussendlich gab die Aufhängung des Belgiers den Geist auf und Henri hatte den Sieg fünf Prüfungen vor Schluss sicher. Auf Madeira gab es reichlich EM-Punkte, die Führung vor Capone war jetzt beträchtlich.

Durch das verrückte EM-Programm reduzierte sich die Zeit fürs Training zur 1000 Seen. „Ich bin 5.500 Kilometer gefahren, weniger als je zuvor", sagte Henri schmunzelnd. „Es war sehr intensiv, ich bin viel bei Nacht gefahren." Doch es gab Bedenken wegen Henris Rückenschmerzen, die er auf die anstrengenden Fahrten im Porsche in der Europameisterschaft zurückführte. Beim „Großen Preis von Finnland" war Toivonen seit dem fünften Platz von 1977 nicht mehr ins Ziel gekommen, deswegen wollte er es ruhig angehen lassen. Teamchef Cesare Fiorio machte nach den beiden Unfällen auch klar, dass Henri das Auto unbedingt ins Ziel bringen sollte.

Henri hielt sein Wort und fuhr zurückhaltend, während Teamkollege Alén seinem Markenzeichen „Maximum Attack" alle Ehre machte. Doch auch Markku konnte Ari Vatanen nicht stoppen, der den neuen Peugeot 205 T16 zum ersten Sieg führte. Dahinter hatte Toivonen den Audi Quattro von Stig Blomqvist langsam eingeholt. Auf den Prüfungen, wo Henri im Vorjahr eine Reihe von Bestzeiten gesetzt hatte, wiederholte er das Kunststück und ging vorbei. Ein Dreher warf ihn kurzfristig hinter Stig zurück, doch am Ende war der Audi gegen den Lancia machtlos. Platz Drei nach einer besonnenen Leistung war ein willkommenes Geburtstagsgeschenk für Henri, der sich damit wieder das FIA-A-Prädikat sicherte.

Montags fühlte sich Henris Rücken schlecht an. Der Arzt stellte einen Bandscheibenvorfall fest. Die Verletzung war vermutlich eine Folge des Kartunfalls in Irland, die sich durch eine harte Landung am Wochenende verschlimmert hatte. Auf der berühmten Ruuhimäki-Prüfung war Henri doppelt so weit geflogen wie alle anderen. Jetzt musste Henri erst mal pausieren.

To appease the interests of Rothmans, the French Mille Pistes event was again fitted in and another win was claimed there ahead of a horde of Renault 5 Turbos driven by the likes of Chatriot, Saby, Thérier and Ragnotti, as well as the Opels of Guy Fréquelin and Erwin Weber and the Audi Quattro of Darniche. Henri was truly earning his money now.

At home in Marsh Gibbon, Erja was expecting their second child. She was beginning to feel a bit desolate in the big country house and longed to get back to Finland: "Henri was hardly ever in the house and there had been some worrying crime in the area. One day I made up my mind and left a note on the kitchen table: 'Gone back home – you'll find me in Finland'. On July 14th, we were having a party with Ulla and Pauli, when I started to feel contractions. Henri volunteered to drive me to the hospital, but I said 'You can't do it, you've had drinks'. So I drove myself."

Happily Henri did have more time off in July, so he could share it with Erja, Arla and newborn son Markus. Without knowing it at the time, he would in fact be travelling a lot less for the next six months. But first it was time for the Madeira Rally where Juha Piironen was to co-drive. Henri had lost faith with Ian Grindrod after the Englishman's unfortunate mistake in Bulgaria.

In Madeira, Carlo Capone almost immediately crashed out in rain and fog, while Henri suffered from an engine malady and stopped three times on the opening stage thus dropping well back. What followed was vintage Toivonen: Twenty-three fastest times out of twenty-eight stages closed the gap to the similar car of leader Patrick Snijers. Going off to avoid a taxi on a stage was a setback to progress, but two punctures for Snijers more than balanced this out. Finally when the Belgian's suspension failed, Henri claimed the lead with five stages to go. This was a high-scoring round of the series, so he now had a healthy lead over Capone.

The mad European campaign had reduced time available for a 1000 Lakes Rally recce. "I've done about 5,500 km, which is less than ever before", said Henri with a wry smile. "But it's been quite intensive with much night-time driving." Back pains that he attributed to the hard ride of the Porsche on those European Rally Championship events caused a slight worry. Having not finished the "Finnish Grand Prix" since that fifth place back in 1977 he was now determined to take a sensible approach. Lancia team boss Cesare Fiorio also made it very clear that after two crashes, his priority had to be on bringing the car home.

True to his word, Henri settled in while team-mate Alén got into a trademark 'maximum attack'. Even Markku could not stop Ari Vatanen from coming through for a first win in the new Peugeot 205 T16, but, behind these two, Toivonen gradually hauled in the Audi Quattro of Stig Blomqvist. When the route revisited those stages where he had stunned with a sequence of fastest times the year before, a repeat performance gave him the advantage. A spin swapped their placing momentarily, but in the end there was nothing Stig could do to keep the Lancia behind. Third place after a mature performance was a welcome birthday present for Henri, who regained his A-seeding with the FIA as a result.

On the Monday, Henri's back felt worse and he went to have it examined. A slipped disc was diagnosed, very likely a consequence of that karting accident in Ireland and then aggravated by a rough landing at the weekend when he had flown twice as far as anyone else from one particular crest on the classic Ruuhimäki stage. He was ordered to rest.

Auf dem steinigen Schotter der Mille Pistes Rallye fuhr Henri erneut zum Sieg. Die Rallye gehörte zwar nicht der Europameisterschaft an, da Rothmans jedoch Sponsor des Events war, durfte ihr Star natürlich nicht fehlen.

Another win was notched up on the rough roads of the Mille Pistes Rally in France. It was not a round of the European series, but Rothmans wanted their star driver to put in an appearance at the rally they sponsored.

Henri Toivonen Eine frustrierende Zeit / Frustration

Das 1000-Kilometer-Rennen in Spa am folgenden Wochenende wurde gestrichen. Dort sollte Henri mit Vern Schuppan einen Rothmans-Porsche-956 fahren. John Watson ersetzte den Finnen. Durch die Verletzung geriet auch das WM-Programm aus der Bahn. Um die Titelchancen zu wahren, nahm David Richards Manx, Tour Auto, Antibes und Catalunya in den Kalender auf, sowie – wenn nötig – San Marino. Capone lag zwar noch einen Punkt hinter Toivonen, hatte aber trotzdem einen Vorteil, weil Henri bald die ersten Resultate streichen musste. Das hatte aber auch sein Gutes: Dass Henri ein paar Läufe hatte auslassen müssen, war wegen der Streichresultate nicht das Ende seiner EM-Hoffnungen.

Capone hatte sich diesen Vorteil bei der Halkidikis Rallye herausgefahren, wo Harri Toivonen einem untergeordneten EM-Titel hinterherjagte. Die FIA hatte für 1984 eine Gruppe-A-Challenge ins Leben gerufen, die Harri gewinnen wollte, nachdem ihm das Team Ralliart nach dem Ausfall bei der RAC 1983 kein Cockpit mehr anbieten konnte. Pauli Toivonen leitete mittlerweile drei verschiedene Autohäuser, er verkaufte jetzt also auch Opel und Audi. Da überraschte es nicht, dass er seinem Sohn einen Audi 80 Quattro gab.

Mit dem Allradler hatte Harri im Winter bei der Hanki Rallye die Gruppe A gewonnen und den zweiten Gesamtrang eingefahren. Dafür gab es die Maximalpunktzahl in der Gruppe-A-Challenge, in der kein Team konstant punktete. Also hatte Harri im Spätsommer noch Chancen auf den Titel. Für den Lauf in Griechenland bekam er einen Opel Ascona, mit dem er bis auf Platz Sechs nach vorn fuhr, ehe er mit defekter Kraftübertragung ausfiel. Zum Saisonende war Harri immer noch Zweiter in der Gruppe-A-Challenge.

Seit einiger Zeit bekam Harri große Unterstützung von Henri, der immer wieder betonte, wie vielversprechend sein Bruder fuhr: „Ich habe noch nie jemanden gesehen, der so viel Talent hat wie Harri. Physisch kann er alles. Die Hände machen das, was sie sollen, die Füße auch. Das ist alles da. Das Problem ist, dass er ein bisschen zu heißblütig ist. Er konzentriert sich nicht stark genug und er kann das Tempo bei einer langen Rallye nicht halten."

Während der Zwangspause dachte Henri über seine Zukunft nach. Es gab ein Tauziehen zwischen Rothmans und Lancia, das Ende September vermutlich seinen Höhepunkt erreichen würde. Das Problem war die Terminüberschneidung der Sanremo mit der Tour de France Automobile. Henri hatte den Glauben an den allradgetriebenen Porsche 959 verloren und war besorgt, dass er kein siegfähiges Auto in der WM fahren würde. „Henri schickte mich zu David Richards, um ihm mitzuteilen, dass Henri den Vertrag beenden möchte", verrät Juha Piironen. „Es gab eine Art Ausstiegsklausel im Vertrag und Henri glaubte, dass er die nutzen könnte, wenn der 959 nicht zu Stande käme."

„Der 911 SCRS sollte nur eine kurzfristige Lösung sein, aber im Endeffekt mussten wir das Auto länger einsetzen als geplant", gibt David Richards zu. „Es war klar, dass der 959 verspätet war. Außerdem war das Auto ein bisschen zu groß und nicht gerade für den Rallyesport geeignet."

In Sanremo war Henri wegen seiner Rückenverletzung nur Zuschauer. Cesare Fiorio machte keinen Hehl daraus, dass er den Rekonvaleszenten gerne in seinem Team hätte: „Ich hoffe, er unterschreibt für zwei Jahre, aber erst muss er seine Vertragsangelegenheiten regeln." David Richards hingegen bestand darauf, dass er eine Option für 1985 besitzt und dass jede Freistellung für WM-Läufe erst einmal besprochen werden muss. Doch zunächst ging es mit dem EM-Programm weiter.

This meant pulling out from the following weekend's Spa 1000 km race, where Henri had been entered in a Rothmans Porsche 956 with Vern Schuppan, a late call arranging for John Watson to stand in for the Finn. It also threw the European rally campaign off the rails. To keep their points chase on track, David Richards had pencilled in Manx, Tour Auto, Antibes and Catalunya for Henri, plus San Marino if needed. Despite Capone closing within one point of Toivonen, the Italian would still hold the upper hand because his rival would soon need to drop scores. Thus missing some of these rallies did not immediately spell the end of Henri's championship hopes.

Capone's advance had come in the Halkidikis Rally, where coincidentally Harri Toivonen was chasing a secondary European title. The FIA had launched a Group A Challenge for 1984 and, when there was no longer a berth available at Team Ralliart after Harri had retired his Mitsubishi from the 1983 RAC Rally, he focused on this trophy. Pauli Toivonen was by now running three different car dealerships and having added Opel and Audi to his portfolio, the choice of a Group A Audi 80 Quattro for the younger son was quite natural.

With the 4WD Group A Audi, Harri had won the group and finished second overall in a hotly contested Hankiralli in the winter. This gave him maximum points in the Challenge and when nobody else managed to score consistently all year, he was in with a chance of the title by late summer. An Opel Ascona was sourced for the Greek event, where Harri again led Group A and got as high as sixth overall before retiring with broken transmission. At the end of the year, he was still runner up in the Challenge.

For some time Harri had been receiving very enthusiastic support from Henri, who repeatedly made remarks of how promising his brother was. "I've never seen anyone who had so much raw driving talent as Harri; physically he's got it all. The hands work like they should, the feet work like they should … It's all there! The problem is that he's a bit hotheaded. He doesn't concentrate hard enough and he can't keep up the pace all through a long event."

During the enforced rest in Finland, Henri was mulling over his future. There was a tug-of-love over his services between Rothmans and Lancia, which had been threatening to come to a head in late September, with a date clash between the Sanremo Rally and the Tour de France Automobile. He had started to lose faith with the promises of a 4WD Porsche 959 and was anxious to get a winning chance in the WRC. "Henri sent me to see David Richards to deliver the news that he wanted to terminate that relationship", reveals Juha Piironen. "There was some kind of get-out clause in the contract and he believed it could be exploited if the 959 did not materialize."

"The 911 SCRS was supposed to be just a short term fix, but it turned out that we had to run it for longer than we'd anticipated", admits David Richards. "It became very clear that the 959 was delayed. It was going to be a little bit too big and it wasn't ideally suited for what we did in rallying."

Henri Toivonen was present in Sanremo as a spectator, still suffering back pains. Cesare Fiorio made no bones about his ambition to have the convalescent in his team. "I hope he will sign for two years, but first he must put his affairs in order", said the Lancia boss. David Richards insisted he had Toivonen under option for 1985 and any release for WRC events would have to be discussed. But first, there was still the 1984 European programme to think of.

Bei der 1000 Seen 1984 stand Henri unter Druck, er musste den 037 unbedingt ins Ziel bringen. Mit Platz Drei erfüllte er sein Soll, bei einer Landung brach aber die alte Rückenverletzung wieder auf. Diese sollte sein weiteres Programm stark einschränken.

Henri Toivonen was under pressure to bring the car to the finish in the 1984 1000 Lakes Rally. He duly obliged and finished third, but had managed to injure his back in a heavy landing. That injury was to curtail his busy season.

Henri Toivonen Eine frustrierende Zeit / Frustration

Am Vorabend der 1000 Seen Rallye 1984 feierte Henri seinen 28. Geburtstag. Die Ehrentage von Henri und Pauli fielen oft mit ihrer Heimrallye zusammen.

Henri celebrated his twenty-eighth birthday on the eve of the 1000 Lakes Rally. The birthdays of both Henri and Pauli often coincided with their big home event.

Von Sanremo fuhren Toivonen und Piironen zum Training der Antibes Rallye nach Nizza. Das mussten sie jedoch nach dem ersten Tag abbrechen, weil sich Henris Rückenleiden wieder verschlechterte. Er flog nach Finnland, um sich operieren zu lassen. So sollte das Problem ein für alle Mal behoben werden. Damit wurden zwar alle Hoffnungen auf den Gewinn des EM-Titels 16 Jahre nach seinem Vater begraben, aber vielleicht war es für Henri auch eine Erleichterung, denn so konnte er sich komplett auf die nächste Saison konzentrieren. Vorher musste jedoch die Vertragssituation geklärt werden.

Im Dezember nahm er an der Vorstellung von Lancias Allradauto teil, dem Delta S4, und er wurde als Werksfahrer für 1985 präsentiert. Dennoch machte David Richards klar, dass Henri Toivonen einen gültigen Vertrag mit Rothmans hatte. „Nach den Gesetzen unseres Landes begeht er einen Vertragsbruch. Wir haben ihm ein Angebot unterbreitet und er hat darauf nicht reagiert, jetzt liegt die Sache beim Rechtsanwalt." Das Angebot, auf das sich Richards bezog, garantierte nur drei WM-Läufe zusätzlich zu einer weiteren EM-Saison, und das im „alten" Porsche 911.

„Es war für alle eine frustrierende Zeit", erinnert sich DR. „Henri war damals ein junger Bursche. Ich bin sicher, dass wir uns gelegentlich gestritten haben – so war es bei mir später auch mit Colin McRae, Richard Burns und Petter Solberg. Wir waren eine Weile zerstritten, aber wir blieben Freunde."

Letztlich wurde die Sache einvernehmlich aus der Welt geschafft. Henri verkaufte sein Haus in Marsh Gibbon und seine Zukunft lag ausschließlich bei Lancia. Erja war anfangs sehr dagegen, dass Henri für die Italiener fährt. An die Gründe kann sie sich nicht mehr

Right after Sanremo, Toivonen and Piironen arrived in Nice to start their recce for the Antibes Rally. This had to be abandoned after the first day, however. Henri's back had got worse again and he flew to Finland where an operation was suggested as a permanent cure to the problem. Although this meant that any chances of clinching the European title sixteen years after Pauli's win were now gone, this was probably a relief for Henri because it allowed him to focus fully on the next season. But the contractual situation still had to be sorted out.

In December, he participated in the launch of Lancia's 4WD supercar, the Delta S4, and was announced as one of the team's official works drivers for 1985. David Richards still pointed out that Rothmans had a valid contract with Henri Toivonen: "He is in breach of contract as the law stands in this country. We have made an offer, he has not come back, and the matter is in the hands of the solicitors." The offer that Richards referred to only guaranteed three WRC rounds in addition to another season in the European series, and the old, rear-wheel drive Porsche 911 SCRS would still have been the car used.

"It was a frustrating time for us all", recalls David Richards. "Henri was a young lad at the time and I'm quite sure we fell out on occasions, like I did with Colin McRae, Richard Burns, Petter Solberg… all of them for a while, but in the end we remained friends."

Eventually, it was all sorted out amicably. Henri had sold his house in Marsh Gibbon and a future now beckoned exclusively with Lancia. Erja had been very much opposed to him joining the Italian team in the first place, for reasons she can no longer quite

genau erinnern. „Es hatte irgendetwas zu tun mit ihrem Willen, um jeden Preis zu gewinnen", erzählt Erja. „Ich bin mir aber nicht sicher, warum ich dabei so hartnäckig war."

Henri hingegen blühte in der entspannten Atmosphäre der Italiener auf. „Er hasste es, wenn Leute ihn beherrschen wollten", sagt Erja. „Er reagierte dann auf eine Art und Weise, die die Situation noch schlimmer machte, vielleicht mit Absicht, vielleicht sogar instinktiv. Wenn man Henri für eigenwillig oder unorganisiert hielt, dann lag es vielleicht daran und nicht an seiner launigen Art oder so etwas."

remember. "It was something to do with their perceived will to win at any cost, but I'm not sure why I was so adamant about it all", she concedes.

Yet, Henri seemed to thrive in the laid-back atmosphere of the Italian team. "He detested it when people tried to contain him", says Erja. "He could then react in a way, which maybe made the situation worse, either deliberately or perhaps even instinctively. If someone thought he was wayward or disorganized, it might have been because of this, rather than petulance or anything like that."

Darauf hatte er so lange gewartet: Im Dezember 1984 präsentierte Lancia sein langersehntes Allradmonster. Henri schmachtete genau wie Markku Alén danach, den Delta S4 endlich zu bewegen. Doch bis der S4 sein Debüt geben würde, sollte noch viel Zeit vergehen. Für Attilio Bettega leider zu viel Zeit …

What he'd been waiting for! In December 1984 Lancia finally presented their long-awaited four-wheel drive supercar. Like Henri, Markku Alén had been yearning to get his hands on it. However, the car still had a long development period ahead and sadly Attilio Bettega never got to drive it in anger.

Henri Toivonen

Großes Finale, tragisches Ende
Crescendo

Zur Saison 1985 musste Cesare Fiorio eingestehen, dass der Lancia 037 zum alten Eisen gehörte, deshalb konzentrierte er seine Anstrengungen auf die Entwicklung des neuen Delta S4. Erst kurz vor Toresschluss entschied sich Lancia für die Teilnahme an der Rallye Monte Carlo, noch immer mit dem alten 037. Wochen vor dem Start sah es so aus, als würde in den Seealpen wenig Eis und Schnee liegen und unter diesen Bedingungen hatte der Zweiradler eine kleine Chance gegen die Allradwaffen von Peugeot und Audi. Die Motorleistung des 037 war auf 340 PS angewachsen und durch neue Reifenbestimmungen durfte das Auto hinten jetzt breitere Reifen fahren als vorn.

Die Wettervorhersage der Italiener erwies sich jedoch als falsch. Gerade erst von seiner Operation genesen, nahm Henri Toivonen den Kampf gegen die Allrad-Fraktion auf. Doch selbst Reifenwechsel in den Prüfungen konnten den Nachteil des 037 nicht wettmachen. Lancia wollte damit das Traktionsproblem umgehen, allerdings funktionierte bei Toivonen ein Schlagschrauber nicht richtig und so musste Henri die WP auf falschen Reifen beenden, die dazu noch abgenutzt waren. Dadurch verlor er das Duell mit Stig Blomqvists Audi. Platz Sechs war nicht das gewünschte Resultat, obwohl Toivonen im Schatten von Audi und Peugeot immerhin drei Bestzeiten fuhr. Auf den kürzeren Prüfungen kam er in den Genuss der neuen superweichen Pirelli-Pneus. „Die sind abgeleitet von den Qualifying-Reifen aus der Formel 1", erklärte Henri. „Unglaublich in den Kurven. Auf einer Prüfung haben wir Röhrl eingeholt und ich war mir sicher, dass ich ihn überholen kann. Aber dann waren die Reifen hinüber und er zog uns wieder davon."

Nach dem Monte-Erlebnis strich Lancia Portugal aus dem Kalender, um die Entwicklung des Delta S4 zu forcieren. Im Frühjahr wurde

By 1985, Cesare Fiorio had acknowledged that the Lancia Rally 037 was at the end of its life and therefore he concentrated his efforts behind the development of the new Delta S4. Very late in the day it was decided to put in an entry for the Monte Carlo Rally, still with the old 037. This was simply because the early indications were that the roads might stay free of snow and ice, in which case, the two-wheel drive car just might have some kind of chance to challenge the latest 4WD projectiles from Peugeot and Audi. Engine developments had boosted the 037's power output to 340 bhp and a change in regulations now allowed the team to run different tyre widths front and rear when required.

Predictions of a dry rally turned out to be wrong. Barely recovered from his operation, Henri tried to take the fight to the all-wheel-drive opposition, but even mid-stage tyre changes could not wipe out their advantage. Lancia used this new trick to overcome its grip deficit but, on the last night, a jammed tyre gun meant Toivonen had to complete a test on tyres that were both wrong and worn, which lost him a battle with Stig Blomqvist's Audi. Sixth place was not much to shout about, although Henri had managed to score three fastest times in the shadow of the mighty battle between Peugeot and Audi. On some of the shorter stages, he had greatly enjoyed the delights of Pirelli's latest super-soft rubber. "It's derived from a Formula 1 qualifying compound", Henri explained. "Incredible cornering. On one stage we caught right up with Röhrl and I was sure I could overtake him, but then the tyres went off and he went away from us again."

After the Monte experience, Lancia cancelled its entry in Portugal so that they could speed up the development of the Delta S4. In the spring, the new car was shown to the public when Markku Alén drove it at the head of the field on the Costa Smeralda Rally. For comparison purposes, Toivonen was entered in the actual competition with the old Lancia Rally 037. He was holding a comfortable lead when he approached a 90-degree bend, well-known to all event regulars, at "100 kph too fast" according to co-driver Juha Piironen. Henri just managed to turn the car around to hit a dry-stone wall backwards.

Gute Miene zum bösen Spiel: Bei der Rallye Monte Carlo 1985 hatte Henri Toivonen mangels Allrad auf Eis und Schnee keine Chance gegen die Peugeot und Audi. Auf trockenem Asphalt fuhr er dagegen einige beeindruckende Zeiten.

In some ways, the 1985 Monte Carlo Rally was just a laugh for Henri Toivonen. In the mixed conditions, he stood no chance against the Peugeots and Audis on snow and ice, but he made some stunning times on the clear asphalt stages.

Lancia zog bei der Wetterlotterie von Monte Carlo ein schlechtes Los. Nicht einmal die Lancia-typischen Reifenwechsel auf den Wertungsprüfungen, die den Vorteil im Trockenen erhöhen sollten, zahlten sich aus. Henri wurde nur Sechster.

Lancia's gamble on the weather went wrong in Monte Carlo. They still tried to maximize their advantage on dry roads by performing mid-stage tyre changes, but this backfired and Toivonen had to be content with sixth place.

Henri Toivonen Großes Finale, tragisches Ende / Crescendo

Der Sommer und Herbst 1985 war für beide Toivonen-Brüder eine schwierige Zeit. Henri kämpfte in der WM mit stumpfen Waffen – mit dem alternden Lancia 037 – und litt später unter seiner alten Verletzung. Harri quälte sich mit dem unzuverlässigen Fiat Ritmo herum.

The spring and summer of 1985 was a trying time for the Toivonen brothers. Henri was in any case fighting impossible odds with the ageing Lancia Rally 037 and then later recuperating from serious injury, while Harri struggled with an unreliable Fiat Ritmo.

das neue Auto der Öffentlichkeit gezeigt. Markku Alén fuhr damit als Nullwagen bei der Rallye Costa Smeralda. Zum Vergleich nahm Henri Toivonen im alten 037 am Wettbewerb teil. Der Finne führte die Rallye mit komfortablem Vorsprung an, als er auf eine 90-Grad-Kurve zusteuerte, die den „Stammgästen" der Rallye bestens bekannt war. Laut Beifahrer Juha Piironen war Henri „100 km/h zu schnell". Er konnte das Auto nur noch herumdrehen und prallte rückwärts in eine Mauer.

„Als wir zum Stehen kamen, hörte ich Henri über die Gegensprechanlage jammern: ‚Ich habe Schmerzen'", erinnert sich Piironen. „Es war beängstigend." Zum Glück war ein Hubschrauber in der Nähe, der Henri ins Krankenhaus brachte. Er hatte sich zwei Halswirbel gebrochen. Der Unfall hätte aber auch schlimmere Folgen haben können. Glücklicherweise trug Henri keine Behinderungen davon, aber er musste erneut lange pausieren, und das gerade vier Monate nach seiner vorherigen Zwangspause.

„Ich habe die Kurve lange vorher angesagt und Henri hat zugegeben, mich gehört zu haben. Ich kann nicht verstehen, warum er nicht reagiert hat, ehe es zu spät war", wundert sich Piironen. Der verhängnisvollen Kurve war ein leichter Knick vorausgegangen und bei der Rallye war dieser Knick durch Zuschauer verdeckt. Henri selbst glaubte, dies sei die Unfallursache gewesen. Er hielt die 90-Grad-Kurve für den vorherigen Knick.

Anfang Mai erfuhr Henri in seinem Krankenbett in Helsinki die traurige Nachricht, dass sein Teamkollege Attilio Bettega in Korsika tödlich verunglückt war. Hannu Mikkola war zu Besuch und schilderte Henri die Details des Unfalls, danach war Henri in einer düsteren, nachdenklichen Stimmung. Stefan Johansson, ein alter Freund aus Kart-Zeiten, hatte kürzlich einen Vertrag beim Formel-1-Team von Ferrari als Ersatz von René Arnoux unterzeichnet. Diese unterschiedlichen Schicksale ließen ihn grübeln: „Das Leben kann so verrückt sein. Der eine erlebt alle Weihnachten an einem Tag und für den anderen ist plötzlich alles vorbei ..."

Bevor Henri aus dem Krankenhaus kam, wurde ein Metallgestell an seine Schläfen und Schultern geschraubt. Damit konnte er seinen Kopf nicht einen Millimeter bewegen. Es war ein erschreckender Anblick, es hielt den Finnen aber nicht davon ab, in der Öffentlichkeit aufzutauchen und sogar PR-Termine wahrzunehmen. Zu Beginn des Sommers war ein Nachbar geschockt, als er sah, wie Henri Tennis spielte: mit fixiertem Kopf, als würde er starr nach vorn schauen.

Die Rallye Costa Smeralda war auch für Harri Toivonen brutal, wenn auch in völlig anderer Hinsicht. Der jüngere Bruder schied nach weniger als einem Kilometer mit Differenzialschaden aus. Harri hatte sich zum ersten Mal einen Stammplatz in einem internationalen Team gesichert. Im Fiat Ritmo Abarth 130TC nahm er dank Sponsor West an der Gruppe-A-Challenge teil. Cedric Wrede war als Beifahrer voller Begeisterung dabei. Für beide war es ein Schritt hin zu einer internationalen Profikarriere.

Bis dato verliefen die Auftritte allerdings frustrierend. Im Februar waren sie bei der Rallye Costa Blanca in Spanien nach WP Drei mit Zündungsproblemen ausgefallen. Nach Sardinien lief es bei der Hunsrück-Rallye viel besser, bis der Auspuff am zweiten Tag brach. Die Crew war plötzlich von Flammen umgeben und musste aufgeben.

Als Wiedergutmachung durfte Harri zur Madeira Rallye in den Lancia 037 des West-Teams wechseln. Obwohl er zum ersten Mal in einem Gruppe-B-Auto saß, gab er eine sehr gute Probe seines Könnens ab. Am letzten Tag behauptete er Platz Vier hinter Salvador Servià, Andrea Zanussi und Dario Cerrato in vergleichbaren 037. Doch dann

"After we'd come to a stop it was chilling to hear the whine 'I'm in pain' on the intercom", recalls Piironen. Luckily there was a helicopter close by, so Henri could be quickly airlifted to hospital. He had suffered two cracked vertebrae in the neck, which might have had very serious consequences indeed. As it was, he escaped permanent disability but was again consigned to a lengthy period of convalescence, barely four months after the previous one.

"I called the bend well in advance and Henri later admitted he had heard me. I cannot understand therefore why he didn't react until it was too late", wonders Piironen. The fateful corner had been preceded by a slight kink detailed in the pacenotes, but during the rally this had been obscured by spectators and Henri personally believed that this was the reason for the accident. Arriving at the second bend, he had taken it to be the preceding kink.

In early May, Henri was lying in his hospital bed in Helsinki when he got the news that Lancia team-mate Attilio Bettega had been killed in Corsica. As a visiting Hannu Mikkola was giving him the details of what had happened, Henri was in sombre and reflective mood. Stefan Johansson, an old friend from karting days, had just recently been signed by Ferrari to replace René Arnoux and the contrasting fortunes made him whisper: "Life can be so strange: For one person it's like all his Christmases coming at once, and for the other it's suddenly all over …"

Before Henri was released from hospital, a metallic crib was bolted to his temples and fitted onto his shoulders such that the head could not be moved by as much as one millimetre. It made for quite a startling sight, but did not stop the man from soon being out and about and even making PR appearances. Not long into the summer, a neighbour of Pauli and Ulla Toivonen was in fact quite shocked to see their son playing tennis with his head rigidly fixed so as to stare straight ahead!

The Costa Smeralda Rally had also been cruel – albeit on a completely different level – to Harri Toivonen, who retired after less than a kilometre with differential failure. For the first time, Harri had secured a regular drive in an international team when he was included in a West-sponsored outfit running Fiat Ritmo Abarth 130TCs in the FIA Group A Challenge. Energetic co-driver Cedric Wrede seized the opportunity with enthusiasm and the pair definitely saw this as a step into full-time international rallying.

So far the campaign had been dispiriting, however. In February their effort in Spain's Costa Blanca Rally had been over after three stages with ignition failure. After Sardinia they had a much better run on the Hunsrück Rally until the exhaust broke on the second day. The crew were overcome by fumes and consequently had to withdraw.

By way of compensation, Harri was promoted to the team's Lancia Rally 037 for the Madeira Rally where he gave a very good account of himself, despite driving a Group B car for the first time. Holding a competitive fourth place on the last day behind the similar cars of Salvador Servià, Andrea Zanussi and Dario Cerrato, luck nevertheless again deserted him as the Lancia's transmission seized. An unhappy end to Harri's season came in Cyprus where, back in the Fiat, he took the lead of Group A but then retired very early with steering failure.

Henri Toivonen was ready to return in the 1000 Lakes, which many people felt to be the most unforgiving place imaginable for overcoming any possible mental hang-ups after an accident. Henri admitted as much, saying: "Apparently I still have that incident in

verließ ihn das Glück: Die Kraftübertragung streikte. Harris Saison endete mit einem Tiefpunkt. In Zypern führte er im Fiat die Gruppe-A-Wertung an, als er mit defekter Lenkung ausrollte.

Sein großer Bruder kehrte zur 1000 Seen Rallye ins Cockpit zurück. Es gibt wohl kaum eine schlechtere Rallye, um mögliche mentale Blockaden nach einem Unfall zu lösen. Henri verriet nur so viel: „Offensichtlich habe ich den Zwischenfall noch im Hinterkopf. Ich muss das schnelle Autofahren erst wiederentdecken." Bei seiner Heimrallye fuhr Toivonen das Auto, mit dem er auf Sardinien verunfallt war. Das Chassis war scheinbar noch intakt.

Doch schon auf der ersten WP rutschte Henri beim Anbremsen von der Straße in einen Graben: „Ich war komplett in Panik. Ich wusste nicht, was ich tun soll. Also bin ich voll auf die Bremse und wir sind geradeaus geschossen." Toivonen verlor anderthalb Minuten und weitere Sekunden auf den nächsten Prüfungen, ehe die Mechaniker den Schrotthaufen wieder in einen Lancia verwandelt hatten. Es dauerte bis in die zweite Rallyehälfte, bis Henri seinen Rhythmus fand. Nachdem er Teamkollege Alén auf einigen Prüfungen geschlagen hatte, sah er den Schaden in einem besseren Licht: „In Linkskurven ist der 037 wie ein Talbot Sunbeam und in Rechtskurven untersteuert das Auto stark. Das macht viel Spaß!" Im Kampf um Platz Vier setzte sich Henri gegen Kalle Grundel (Peugeot 205 T16 E2) und Per Eklund (Audi Quattro) durch, damit waren die bösen Geister von Sardinien endgültig verflogen.

In Sanremo war Henri wieder ganz der Alte. Er fuhr erneut das Auto von Sardinien, war mit dem Handling des 037 aber nicht zufrieden. Auf dem Schotter hatte er gegen Röhrls Audi Sport Quattro E2 oder Salonens Peugeot 205 T16 E2 ohnehin keine Chance, doch als die Rallye in der Berge oberhalb von Sanremo zurückkehrte, erwachte Henri zum Leben. Auf den letzten sieben Prüfungen fuhr er sechs Bestzeiten. „Das war magisch", bestätigt Juha Piironen. „Ich kenne niemanden, der auf Asphalt so viel Gefühl fürs Auto hatte wie Henri. Aber er gab auch beunruhigende Kommentare von sich, wie: ‚Die Reifen sind am Ende, ich weiß nicht, ob wir es bis zum Ende der Prüfung schaffen. Halt dich beim Bremsen gut fest!'" Auf dem Asphalt zog Henri an seinem entmutigten Teamkollegen Alén vorbei und wurde Dritter.

An seinen Leistungen im Rallyeauto gab es wenig auszusetzen, dafür wurden einige Dinge in Henris Privatleben komplizierter. An einigen war er selbst schuld. Im Spätsommer ging Henri eine Beziehung mit einer Prominenten ein, einer früheren Miss Finnland. Bis jetzt hatte Erja den Tratsch über ihren Mann als „Womanizer" als Berufsrisiko abgetan. Aber das hier war etwas anderes. Die Affäre wurde von den Boulevardzeitungen aufgenommen und verletzte sie sehr. Während des ganzen Tumults musste Henri auch noch zum Militär. Nach dem finnischen Gesetz müssen Männer ihren Wehrdienst vor ihrem 30. Lebensjahr ableisten, für Henri war es also höchste Zeit. Rekrut Toivonen trat am 15. Oktober in der Transportabteilung der Finnischen Armee in Helsinki seinen Dienst an.

Wenn er nicht in der Kaserne war, verbrachte Henri seine Nächte im Hotel und nicht zu Hause. Das Hotel war nicht weit von dem großen, noblen Domizil entfernt, in das Henri und Erja nach ihrer Rückkehr aus England gezogen waren. Es war zwar keine Trennung, aber trotzdem eine unangenehme Zeit für alle Beteiligten. Mitten in diesem Durcheinander kam der Anruf von Martini, für Lancia an der Rallye Catalunya teilzunehmen.

In Spanien ging Henri in Führung, doch auf WP Drei hatte er einen Platten und krachte in einer engen Linkskurve in eine Betonmauer. Es war ein brutaler Unfall, der bis dato schlimmste für Beifahrer Piironen:

the back of my mind. I have yet to rediscover the flow for driving fast." He was given the same car that he had crashed in Sardinia, as the main chassis seemed to be intact.

And then he plunged off the road on the opening stage, braking downhill into a ditch: "I was in a complete state of panic. I didn't know what to do but locked up and went straight off." A minute and a half was lost plus more on the next stages before Lancia mechanics got the car into some kind of shape. It took until the second half of the rally for Henri to hit a proper rhythm. Beating team-mate Alén on stages made him now see the car's damage in a more favourable light: "It's like a Talbot Sunbeam on lefthanders and it understeers a lot on right hand corners. It's a lot of fun!" Winning the battle for fourth with Kalle Grundel (Peugeot 205 T16 E2) and Per Eklund (Audi Quattro) must have finally exorcised the ghosts of that Sardinia accident.

In Sanremo it became very obvious that Henri Toivonen was back to his sublime best. Still having to use the same car, he was complaining of its handling which the team attempted to cure by adjusting wheel angles. There was nothing the Lancias could do against Röhrl's Audi Sport Quattro E2 or Salonen's Peugeot 205 T16 E2 on the gravel stages of Tuscany but yet again, when the rally returned to asphalt in the mountains behind Sanremo, Henri came alive, setting six fastest times on the last seven stages. "It was magic", confirms Juha Piironen. "On tarmac Henri could feel a car like no one else I've known. But he could also make disturbing comments like: 'The tyres are finished, I don't know how we're going to make it to the end. Hold on tight under braking!'" On those last stages Henri moved past dispirited team-mate Alén to take third.

While there seemed to be no worries about his driving, various things were complicating the private life of Henri Toivonen at this time, some of them of his own doing. In late summer, he had strayed into a relationship with a girl who was something of a celebrity, in fact, a former Miss Finland. Until now, Erja had shrugged off any gossip of womanizing as an occupational hazard, but this was different. The affair got into the tabloids and it hurt her considerably. In the emotional turmoil of the autumn, Henri also could no longer postpone his National Service. According to Finnish law, men had to serve their time before the age of thirty, so this made it the time for Henri. Conscript Toivonen reported on October 15th to serve in the Transport Company of the Finnish Army in Helsinki.

For some weeks he did not live at home, instead checking in a hotel when on leave from the army. The hotel was not far from the big posh house Henri and Erja had got themselves on their return from England and though they did not actually break up, the situation was obviously awkward to all. Amongst this confusion came the call from Martini to make an appearance for Lancia in the Catalunya Rally.

Henri took the lead in Spain, but on the third stage an apparent puncture before a tight left sent the car into a large concrete well. It was a violent crash, the biggest yet for co-driver Piironen: "Even the roll cage was snapped on my side, but still Henri tried to restart the car, which was a bit hopeless, because the pedals had been pushed over to where I was sitting ..." He was lucky to get away with a sprained ankle while Henri had bruised his ribs.

Once back in Finland, Juha Piironen decided to severe his ties with Lancia and Toivonen. "It was not so much to do with worrying about my health. Juha Kankkunen had called me and proposed the idea of joining Peugeot with him for 1986.

Sanremo war für Henri wieder ein tolles Pflaster. Auf dem Schotter der Toskana begeisterte er die Tifosi, auf Asphalt legte er noch eine Schippe drauf und beeindruckte Beifahrer Juha Piironen sowie Teamkollege Markku Alén nachhaltig.

San Remo again brought out the best of Henri. His performance on the Tuscan gravel stages thrilled the crowds, but his later heroics on asphalt particularly impressed co-driver Piironen, as well as his team-mate Markku Alén.

„Auf meiner Seite war sogar der Käfig eingeknickt. Henri versuchte zwar noch, das Auto zu starten, aber es war hoffnungslos. Die Pedale hatte es auf meine Seite verschoben." Pironen kam mit einem verstauchten Knöchel davon, Henri hatte sich die Rippen geprellt.

In Finnland beschloss Juha Piironen, die Zusammenarbeit mit Lancia und Toivonen zu beenden. „Es lag weniger daran, dass ich Angst um meine Gesundheit hatte. Juha Kankkunen hatte mich gefragt, ob ich 1986 mit ihm zu Peugeot gehen möchte. Außerdem wurde ich zu sehr in die problematischen zwischenmenschlichen Beziehungen der Familie meines Fahrers verwickelt. Das kam alles zusammen." Piironen kündigte bei Lancia, blieb mit Henri aber befreundet.

Die dunklen Wolken über Henri Toivonen sollten sich aber schon bald in Luft auflösen. Bei der RAC Rallye feierte er seine Wiederauferstehung. Die Affäre, die seine Ehe belastet hatte, hatte er beendet und auch den lästigen Militärdienst hatte er ein für allemal hinter sich gelassen. Wegen seiner Verletzungen wurde Henri vom Dienst befreit. Zudem gab der Lancia Delta S4 in Großbritannien sein Debüt. Jetzt hatte Toivonen die Waffe, auf die er so lange gewartet hatte. „Ich bin sicher, dass mir ein Allradauto sehr gut liegen wird", hatte er prophezeit. „Ich habe mein ganzes Leben mit dem linken Fuß gebremst, um das Auto auszubalancieren, damit es die ganze Zeit leicht driftet. Ich bin immer bereit, das Heck herauszuhängen, einfach aus Gewohnheit."

Diese Begabung brauchte er beim Delta S4 auch, denn das Auto war ein Biest, besonders in dieser frühen Phase der Entwicklung. Mit 100 PS mehr als der 037 in einem erheblich leichteren Chassis hatte der S4 eine unglaubliche Leistung. Aber es war auch eine komplexe Maschine, die nicht gerade gut für das Selbstvertrauen des Fahrers war. Mit 880 WP-Kilometern war die RAC eine sehr lange Rallye für Lancia, die Neil Wilson wegen seiner Streckenkenntnisse neben Toivonen setzten.

Die RAC begann an einem düsteren Sonntagmorgen in Nottingham. Der Kontrast zwischen dem Wetter und der Stimmung im Lancia-Lager hätte kaum größer ausfallen können: Markku Alén fuhr auf der Auftaktprüfung Bestzeit, Toivonen wurde Zweiter. Alén gab ein beeindruckendes Tempo vor und führte mit 19 Sekunden, als die Rallye auf die Waldprüfungen wechselte. Henri war etwas vorsichtiger und behauptete Rang Zwei.

Henri hatte vor dem Start nur 40 Kilometer im S4 abgespult und musste auf losem Untergrund noch viel über das Auto lernen. Zudem hatte er Probleme mit dem Kompressor und fiel auf Rang Fünf zurück, während Hannu Mikkola im Audi die Führung übernahm. In Wales schied der Sport Quattro E2 durch ein fehlerhaftes Motormanagement aus und als dann auch noch beide Peugeot aufgaben, lagen die beiden Lancia plötzlich wieder an der Spitze.

Lancia hatte beim Debüt des S4 keineswegs mit einer fehlerlosen Vorstellung gerechnet und schon bald sorgten Elektrikprobleme für Stirnrunzeln: Die Motoren gingen ohne Vorwarnung aus. Als Henris Auto in einer Prüfung stoppte, fiel er hinter den MG Metro 6R4 von Tony Pond zurück. Nach Wales war Toivonen mit vier Minuten Rückstand auf Alén Dritter. Hier bemerkte das Team, dass die Motorprobleme mit sinkenden Temperaturen schlimmer wurden, also klebten sie die Kühlöffnungen mit Klebeband zu.

Doch es sollte noch genug Schrecksekunden für die Lancisti geben. In Yorkshire rutschte Alén im ausgedrehten fünften Gang eine Feuerschneise herunter. Auf den nächsten vier Prüfungen hatte Toivonen wegen eines defekten Differenzials nur Heckantrieb. Pond fuhr im Metro als Dritter über die Prüfungen und sah ihre Spuren: „Elende

I also felt myself a bit tangled into the recently problematic human relations of my driver's family and it all just added up." Juha conveyed his resignation to Lancia, but remained friends with Henri.

All the clouds hanging over Henri Toivonen were about to be dispelled however. The RAC Rally in late November 1985 turned out to be almost like a new dawn for the man. By then he had put an end to the affair that strained his marriage. The burden of National Service was also lifted once and for all, because he got exemption on the grounds of his earlier injury. And finally, Lancia's Delta S4 was homologated for a debut in Britain. Here was the weapon Henri had been craving for all these years. "I'm sure a 4WD car will suit me very well", he had professed. "All my life I've driven with left foot braking to balance the car, to keep it slightly sideways almost all the time and I'm always ready to get the tail out, just out of shape."

He needed such aptitude, because the Delta S4 was a beast to handle, especially in this early stage of its development. Boasting at least 100 bhp more than the 037 in a considerably lighter chassis, it had electrifying performance, but it was also a complex machine that did not readily boost a driver's confidence. With its 880 km of special stages, the RAC was going to be a very long rally for Lancia, who recruited Neil Wilson as a specialist co-driver for Henri Toivonen.

Early on a murky Sunday morning the rally got underway from Nottingham's Wollaton Park. The surrounding gloom was in stark contrast to spirits in the Lancia camp, when Markku Alén blasted to fastest time on the short opening sprint, followed by Toivonen. Markku Alén set off at his usual cracking pace to lead by nineteen seconds as the rally headed into the forests, with a slightly more cautious Henri in second.

He had only driven the Delta on gravel for 40 km before the start and now had lots to learn about its quirks on the loose. At the same time, his Lancia ran into supercharger trouble and he dropped to fifth as Hannu Mikkola came through to lead in Wales. Before the rally left the Principality, however, the Sport Quattro E2 had succumbed to engine management problems and, when both works Peugeots were also sidelined, the Italian team again found both its cars at the head of the leader board.

Lancia never expected faultless reliability on the new car's debut and sure enough an electrical gremlin raised its head, causing the engines to cut out without warning. When Henri's car stopped on a stage, he dropped behind the MG Metro 6R4 of Tony Pond. With Wales left behind, he was in third, trailing leader Alén by four minutes. The team discovered their engine problems were worst in cold temperatures and started to block off the radiator openings with tape.

There were still plenty of other scares in store for them. In slippery Yorkshire, Alén went down a Dalby firebreak flat in fifth. For the next four stages, Henri Toivonen was left with rear-wheel drive only when his front differential failed. Following these two on the road, Tony Pond could witness some of their moments. "Bloody Lancias, all through the stages you can see where they have been going off. There are skid marks here, bits missing there. They spin, go off, hit things all the time, but they still keep going", commented the British driver.

Up in Scotland, Toivonen was back past Pond into second, this despite a flip in Kilburn: "It was happening so fast I didn't realize that it had happened until we stopped", Henri said. "I had just

Mit einem Sieg bei der RAC 1985 hätte wohl niemand gerechnet. Das Lancia-Team leistete Schwerstarbeit, um die neuen Autos trotz der vielen Probleme ins Ziel zu bringen.
The victory on the 1985 RAC Rally was another triumph against the odds. Through various hardships with their new car, the whole Lancia team had to fight for that win.

Henri Toivonen Großes Finale, tragisches Ende / Crescendo

1980 war es Bath, 1985 war Nottingham der Schauplatz des großen Triumphs von Henri Toivonen. Und wieder konnte er den Moment mit vielen Freunden und Förderern teilen.

As with his 1980 win in Bath, 1985 in Nottingham was a scene of jubilation as Henri received the spoils of victory. Again, he was happy to share it all with friends and supporters.

Lancia. Überall auf den Prüfungen siehst du, wo sie abgeflogen sind. Hier sind Bremsspuren, da liegen Teile. Sie drehen sich, fliegen ab oder rammen irgendetwas, aber sie fahren immer weiter."

In Schottland war Toivonen wieder an Pond vorbeigezogen auf Platz Zwei, trotz eines Überschlags in Kilburn: „Es ging so schnell. Ich habe es erst realisiert, als wir zum Stehen kamen. Ich war gerade erst aus der Kurve raus und gab Gas, als das Heck auf Eis in einen Graben rutschte." In Kielder verlor Henri erneut den Vorderradantrieb, doch Alén erwischte es noch schlimmer: Er verlor durch einen Ausrutscher an einer Stelle, wo keine Zuschauer standen, viel Zeit. Markku fiel auf Platz Drei hinter Pond zurück. Aber es ging immer noch knapp zur Sache, das Führungstrio trennte nur eine Minute.

Auf dem Weg nach Süden wurde Toivonen durch einen defekten Kompressor und Probleme mit der Kraftübertragung eingebremst. Henri hatte wieder nur Zweiradantrieb. Nach der Reparatur musste er kämpfen, um nicht die Karenzzeit zu überschreiten. Der S4 fuhr jetzt als 21. Fahrzeug. Zu allem Überfluss stempelte Neil Wilson an einer Kontrolle zu spät, doch trotz der Zeitstrafe lag Toivonen weiter in Führung.

Glücklicherweise war dies das letzte Drama für Toivonen/Wilson. Alén schob sich noch an Pond vorbei und so feierte Lancia einen überraschenden Doppelsieg. Nach fünf Jahren Abstinenz versprühte Henri endlich wieder Siegerchampagner in der WM. Aber bei der Rallye war es drunter und drüber gegangen. In den Augen des Siegers hatte das Format zumindest eine Teilschuld: „Diese Rallye ist zu hart. Sie muss geändert werden, wenn wir mit diesen Autos sicher fahren sollen."

Trotz dieses schönen Erfolgs gab es beim Delta S4 noch eine Menge zu tun. Zur Monte Carlo 1986 stieg die Leistung auf 450 PS an und das Ansprechverhalten des Motors bei niedrigen Drehzahlen wurde verbessert. Im Fürstentum hatte Lancia zudem den neuen, schmalen Mischreifen namens Pirelli S1 als Ass im Ärmel. Dieser Pneu bestand aus einer harten Mischung, in der die Spikes auf Asphaltstücken besser hielten. Zur neuen Saison tat sich Henri mit Beifahrer Sergio Cresto zusammen. Beide kannten sich von 1984, als Cresto mit Carlo Capone gefahren war. Cresto hatte italienische Wurzeln, war aber in New York geboren worden. Der Italo-Amerikaner las die Noten in einem interessanten Sprachmix.

Der Saisonauftakt fand bei typischen Monte-Bedingungen statt und wurde zu einem Duell der Giganten: Neben Lancia waren die Werksteams von Peugeot, Audi, Austin Rover und Citroën mit ihren Gruppe-B-Monstern vor Ort. Auf den ersten sechs Prüfungen schmolz der Schnee und Lancia übernahm die Initiative. Henri Toivonen drückte der Rallye sofort seinen Stempel auf. Auf der 44 Kilometer langen WP Chartreuse war er 30 Sekunden schneller als der Rest des Feldes, sein Vorsprung wuchs auf über eine Minute an. Teamkollege Alén war trotz Fehlzündungen Zweiter vor Biasion, Saby, Röhrl und Salonen.

Henri hatte zwar ein paar Bremsprobleme, dennoch hatte er nach elf Prüfungen 1.41 Minuten Vorsprung auf Röhrl im Audi. Sein Bruder Harri und Neil Wilson waren als Eisnotenfahrer für Henri unterwegs. Neil erinnert sich an ein kurzes Gespräch bei der Rallye: „Als wir nach der RAC auf dem Auto standen, hatte Henri gesagt, wie sehr er diesen Sieg gebraucht hatte. Ich sagte zu ihm: ‚Ab jetzt wird alles einfach.' Vor der Burzet kam er auf das Gespräch zurück: ‚Du hattest Recht, jetzt ist alles so einfach!'"

come out of the corner and was going again, when the back slid into a ditch because of the ice." In Kielder, he again lost drive to front wheels but it was worse for Alén, who dropped a lot of time with an off in a place where there were no spectators to help. Markku slipped to third about one minute behind Henri, but, with Pond between them, it was all very close.

Heading south from Carlisle, Toivonen was hampered by a malfunctioning supercharger as well as transmission trouble that again reduced him to 2WD. After repairs, Henri was fighting to stay within allowed lateness. Now running twenty-first on the road, Neil Wilson was not aware of their position and this led to a penalty for starting a stage late, because the first twenty cars were given two-minute gaps, but later runners only one. It did not cost them the lead, though.

Luckily that was to be the last drama for Toivonen/Wilson and, as Alén pushed past Pond, Lancia got to celebrate a most unexpected 1-2. After a five-year hiatus, Henri was spraying champagne as a WRC winner again, but it had been a topsy-turvy rally. The winner wanted to remind everyone that the event format was at least partly to blame for that. "This rally is too hard and it needs to be changed, if we are to drive these cars safely", Henri warned.

The success had been sweet, but there was still a lot of work to do with the Lancia Delta S4. For the 1986 Monte Carlo Rally, engine output was boosted to 450 bhp and, more importantly, response was improved lower down the rev range. A definite ace up Lancia's sleeve was the new, narrow S1 tyre introduced by Pirelli for mixed conditions. This had a strong compound to hold the studs when bare tarmac was encountered. For the new season, Henri Toivonen joined forces with Sergio Cresto, whom he had got to know well in 1984 as Carlo Capone's co-driver. The New York-born Italian's American English turned out to nicely accentuate Henri's pace-notes.

The conditions in the French Alps proved mixed indeed for what was touted as a true battle of giants. In addition to Lancia, there were full factory squads from Peugeot, Audi, Austin Rover and Citroën all with Group B "supercars". However it was the Italians who seized the initiative as snow was quickly disappearing from the first six stages above Aix-les-Bains. Henri Toivonen was soon in the lead and on the 44 km Chartreuse stage stamped his authority with a time over half a minute better than the rest, to lead by a full minute. Team-mate Alén in second had been suffering from a persistent misfire and thus he had Biasion, Saby, Röhrl and Salonen all hot on his heels.

Henri endured some brake problems, but after eleven stages held a 1min 41sec advantage over Walter Röhrl's Audi Sport Quattro E2. Harri Toivonen and Neil Wilson had been recruited to work on Henri's ice-notes and Neil recalls a brief exchange at this stage: "When we'd been standing on the car after the RAC, Henri mentioned how he'd needed that win so much. I then said to him it'll be easy from now on. At the bottom of Burzet he now said to me: 'You were right, it's so easy now!'"

Perhaps that was tempting fate a bit. In Burzet, a puncture dropped Röhrl down the order but, driving away from the same stage, there was an incident that seemed to spell the end of Toivonen's hopes as well. He came across a spectator's Peugeot hurtling around a corner on the wrong side of the road and hit it head-on …

Henri Toivonen Großes Finale, tragisches Ende / Crescendo

Ob Henri damit sein Schicksal herausforderte? Auf der Burzet-Prüfung fiel Röhrl durch einen Reifenschaden zurück. Auf dem Weg zur nächsten WP war wiederum Henri in einen Zwischenfall verwickelt, der seine Siegeshoffnungen fast begraben hätte: Als er um eine Kurve bog, kam ihm der Peugeot eines Zuschauers auf der falschen Seite entgegen. Die Autos krachten frontal ineinander.

Der Aufprall war so heftig, dass jedes Rallyeauto mit einem normalen Monocoque-Chassis in der verbliebenen Zeit nicht mehr reparabel gewesen wäre. Durch den Gitterrohrrahmen des Delta konnten die Mechaniker jedoch in einer halben Stunde einzelne Rohre herausflexen und neue einschweißen. Die ganze Frontpartie inklusive Aufhängung, Lenkgetriebe, Kühler usw. wurde neu gebaut. Das Chassis war links zwar um zwei Zentimeter nach hinten verschoben, aber immerhin war der S4 wieder fahrtauglich. Auch der Fahrer war angeschlagen: Henri hatte sich an der Hüfte verletzt und wurde fortan mit Schmerzmitteln behandelt.

In Rechtskurven untersteuerte Toivonens Lancia jetzt, in Linkskurven fuhr er sich fast wie immer. Erstaunlicherweise verteidigte Henri seine Führung, bis ihn zwei Missgeschicke heimsuchten. Erst spießte ein Nagel auf dem Col des Garcinettes einen seiner Reifen auf, was anderthalb Minuten kostete. Danach führte Lancia in der Sisteron-Prüfung einen Reifenwechsel durch. Die anfangs gefahrenen Slicks waren jedoch zu hart und kamen nicht auf Temperatur. Durch diese

The impact was so heavy that any rally car with a normal monocoque chassis would have been beyond repair in the time available. The Delta's tubular space frame, however, allowed the mechanics to cut out tubes and weld new ones in their place in half an hour. In effect, the entire front section of the car was rebuilt with new suspension, steering gear, radiator, etc. This still left the chassis pushed back by two centimetres on the left side, but at least the S4 was roadworthy. The crew required some attention too for Henri had hurt his hip and was in need of pain-killing injections for the rest of the rally.

The Toivonen Lancia now understeered on right hand corners, but was nearly normal on left-handers. Remarkably, the driver still managed to keep his lead intact until facing a double whammy. First a stud pierced one of his tyres on the Col des Garcinettes test causing a loss of about one and a half minutes. Next a Lancia tyre stop was performed in Sisteron, but this time the slicks they started with were too hard and never reached full working temperature before being exchanged for narrow snow tyres. These mishaps meant that Toivonen lost the lead to Peugeot's Timo Salonen, who had an advantage of thirty-three seconds when the crews arrived in Monte Carlo. While others took a well-earned rest, Henri boarded a helicopter to the mountains. He wanted to drive the first two stages of the last loop, maybe just to gain a psychological advantage.

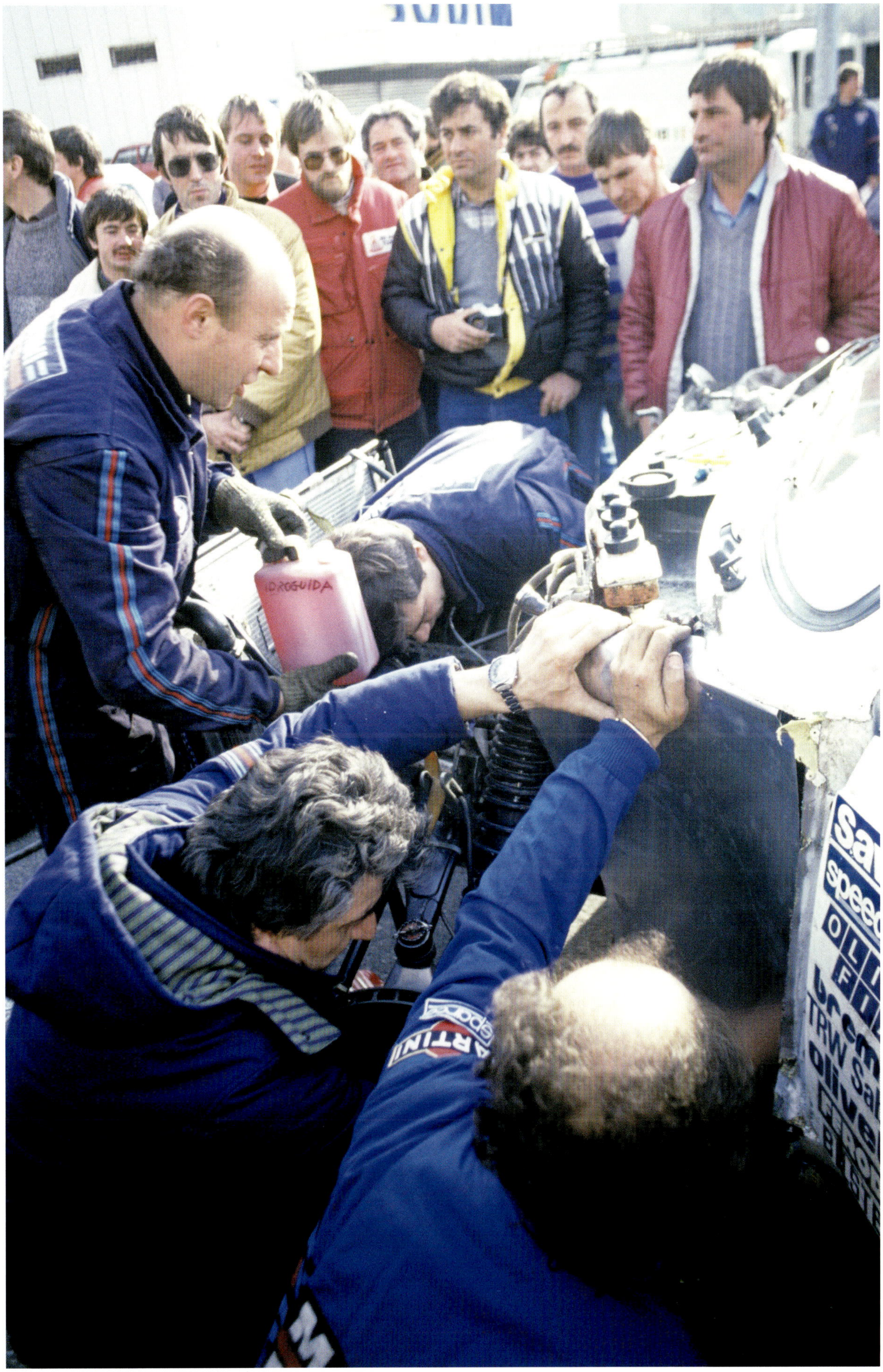

Nach dem Unfall bei der Monte schraubten die Mechaniker bei jeder Gelegenheit am Delta S4, um das Auto wieder in seine Ursprungsform zurückzuversetzen.

After the accident, the mechanics had to carry out ongoing repairs all the way to Monte Carlo to put Henri's Delta S4 into proper shape.

Malheure verlor Toivonen die Führung an Timo Salonen. Der Peugeot-Pilot hatte bei der ersten Ankunft in Monte Carlo 33 Sekunden Vorsprung. Während sich die anderen Fahrer eine Pause gönnten, flog Henri mit dem Helikopter in die Berge. Er wollte die ersten beiden Prüfungen der letzten Schleife abfahren – vielleicht nur um einen psychologischen Vorteil zu haben.

Die trockenen Bedingungen kamen den Peugeot entgegen, das bestätigte Salonen mit einer Bestzeit auf der nächsten WP. Er war 15 Sekunden schneller als Toivonen. Aber danach war Henri unaufhaltsam: Auf dem Turini schlug er Salonen um 24 Sekunden, auf dem Col de la Couillole gar um 48. Damit übernahm er auch die Spitze. Wegen seiner Führung beschloss Henri, auf den weiteren Prüfungen keine Slicks mehr aufzuziehen: „Die werden einfach nicht warm."

Ein Gegenangriff von Timo Salonen auf der letzten Schleife war spätestens dann Geschichte, als Salonen auf dem Col de la Madone nassen Asphalt vorfand – ein Untergrund, den er hasste. Der Peugeot-Fahrer gab sich mit Rang Zwei zufrieden und wurde zwei Prüfungen später auf dem Couillole gar von Henri eingeholt. „Das war der Moment, wo ich wusste: Wir haben gewonnen", erzählte Toivonen im Hafen von Monte Carlo. 20 Jahre nach dem kontroversen Triumph seines Vaters Pauli feierte Henri einen der größten Siege in der Monte-Geschichte. Er konnte die Freude sogar mit Erja und den Kindern teilen, denn er hatte eine Wohnung in Monte Carlo angemietet, um näher bei Lancia zu sein.

Dry conditions supposedly tipped the scales in Peugeot's favour and this seemed to be borne out by Salonen being fifteen seconds faster on the next stage. But there was no stopping Henri now. He beat Timo by twenty-four seconds on the Turini and a whopping forty-eight on the Col de la Couillole, which swapped their positions. Contemplating his regained lead, Henri revealed Lancia would not be using slicks at all on the remaining stages. "They just do not warm up", he shrugged.

Any ideas Timo Salonen may have had of challenging his countryman on the last mountain section were soon forgotten when he reached the Col de la Madone to find wet tarmac, a condition he detested. The Peugeot driver would settle for points. Two stages later Henri caught Timo on the Couillole. "That was the moment when I knew we had won", Henri declared triumphantly back in Monte Carlo harbour. Twenty years after Pauli Toivonen had given Citroën that controversial success, his son was now celebrating one of the greatest wins ever in the same event. Henri got to share the emotion with Erja and the kids, since he had just rented a flat in Monte Carlo to stay closer to Lancia.

Not even this climactic moment of joy was quite free of drama for Henri. He had to to hospital to have the hip injury from the collision checked and later fly to Rome for more examinations. Briefly there were doubts about his fitness to start the Swedish Rally in three weeks time, but those worries were overcome.

Die letzte Nacht der Rallye Monte Carlo 1986 war unvergesslich – auch für die Fans an der Strecke.
The last night of the 1986 Monte Carlo Rally was unforgettable and the fans really appreciated it.

Henri war einfach unschlagbar. Auf dem Col de Turini schlug er seinen Rivalen Timo Salonen um 24 bzw. 17 Sekunden.
Henri simply could not be denied. On the two runs over Col de Turini, he beat rival Salonen first by 24 and then by 17 seconds.

Doch nicht einmal dieser Moment der Euphorie ging für Henri ohne Drama über die Bühne. Er musste schnell ins Krankenhaus, um seine Hüftverletzung untersuchen zu lassen. Später flog er für weitere Untersuchungen nach Rom. Es gab kurz Zweifel, ob er fit sein würde für den Start bei der Schweden Rallye in drei Wochen, aber diese Sorgen waren unbegründet.

Die Fahrer fühlten sich auch in Schweden noch nicht richtig wohl im Delta S4. Während Salonen das Tempo vorgab und allen davonzog, hatten die S4 das Problem, dass sie in den tiefen Fahrspuren von einer Seite zur nächsten hüpften. Lancia war nicht sicher, ob die neuesten Pirelli-Reifen daran schuld waren. „Die Front zieht in alle Richtungen. Nicht nur dort, wo Spurrillen sind, sondern auch wenn die Fahrbahn eben ist", beschwerte sich Henri, der bei seiner ersten Schweden Rallye auf Rang Zwei lag.

Auf WP Sieben endete Salonens ungebrochene Serie von Bestzeiten: Nach einem Motorschaden fing der Peugeot Feuer. Das Ende seiner Rallye. Henri profitierte davon und bestimmte jetzt das Tempo. Beim Nachtstopp hatte er eine komfortable Führung. Lancia reduzierte jetzt sogar die Motorleistung und senkte das Drehzahllimit, trotzdem war für Toivonen in der nächsten Prüfung Feierabend wegen eines Ventilschadens. „Jetzt frage ich mich, ob Salonen noch immer an der Bar sitzt", wurde Henri damals zitiert.

In Schweden war Harri Toivonen noch als Schotterspion für seinen großen Bruder unterwegs, aber nur eine Woche später saß Harri selbst in einem Gruppe-B-Monster. Für das R-E-D-Team bestritt er die britische Meisterschaft in einem MG Metro 6R4. Die National Breakdown Rallye war sein erster Auftritt in einem rechtsgelenkten Auto. Abgesehen vom Dogbox-Getriebe kam sein Metro im vollen Werkstrimm daher. Harri gewöhnte sich schnell an das neue Auto und lag auf Platz Sechs, nachdem er wegen nicht funktionierender Scheibenwischer einen Rang eingebüßt hatte. Fünf Prüfungen vor dem Ziel rammte er jedoch einen Torpfosten und zerstörte den Kühler des Metro.

Die nächste Station für das Lancia-Werksteam war Portugal, wo normalerweise die Kräfteverhältnisse für die restliche Saison offengelegt werden. Wie üblich begann die Rallye auf dem Asphalt von Sintra. Nach der ersten Schleife führten die Lancia von Biasion, Toivonen und Alén knapp vor Peugeot-Neuling Kankkunen sowie Röhrl im Audi. Weiter sollten all diese Piloten wegen des schlimmen Unfalls von Joaquim Santos nicht fahren. Der Ford RS200 des Portugiesen war in WP Eins von der Straße gerutscht und hatte dabei vier Zuschauer getötet. Aus Protest gegen die unzureichenden Vorkehrungen zur Zuschauersicherheit beschlossen die Werksfahrer von Lancia, Peugeot, Audi, Ford und Austin Rover, nicht weiter an der Rallye teilzunehmen.

Durch das frühe Ende in Portugal hatte Henri Zeit für Urlaub mit Erja und seinen Eltern, die sich für den Winter eine Immobilie in Benalmádena an der Südküste Spaniens zugelegt hatten. Für die Safari Rallye brauchte Lancia Henris Dienste nicht, dort setzten sie den 037 ein letztes Mal ein. Stattdessen testete er um Ostern herum den Delta S4 auf Korsika.

Henri probierte breitere Pirelli-Reifen und die neuesten Modifikationen am Auto aus, wie veränderte Anlenkpunkte für die Aufhängung, neue Federn, Dämpfer und Stabilisatoren. Von den Veränderungen war er begeistert: „Erst jetzt fange ich an, das Auto zu verstehen. Es liegt 2,5 Zentimeter tiefer als in Monte Carlo und ist 1,6 Sekunden pro Kilometer schneller. Damit sind wir auf trockenem Asphalt zumindest gleichauf mit Peugeot."

The drivers were still not completely at ease with the Delta S4 in Sweden where no one could live with the pace of Timo Salonen, who pulled out a lead right from the start. Lancia were concerned about their cars bouncing from side to side in the deep ruts and were not sure whether the latest Pirellis were to blame. "The front is pulling everywhere, not just on the rutted sections, but even on the smooth", complained Henri, who still held second in this, his first Swedish Rally.

The long seventh stage brought an end to Salonen's unbroken string of fastest times – his rally being over with engine failure and the Peugeot on fire. Following his countryman's demise, Henri now set the pace to hold a strong lead into the overnight halt. The Lancia team was confident enough to turn down the boost in his engine and restrict revs for the morning but, even so, Toivonen was brought to a stop by a dropped valve on the very next stage. "The only thing now is whether Salonen is still in the bar", he was last heard musing.

Harri Toivonen had been making gravel notes for big brother in Sweden, but less than a week later stepped up to the "supercar" ranks himself in the British Championship with an MG Metro 6R4 run by the well-established R-E-D team. Yorkshire's National Breakdown Rally was to be his first outing in a right-hand drive car, the Metro in full works specification except for a dog-clutch gearbox. Harri acquitted himself well, holding sixth place, but having slipped one position when the wipers failed in a blizzard. He then blotted his copybook by smashing the car's radiator against a gatepost just five stages from the finish.

Next stop for Lancia's works team was Portugal, which normally offered a fairly reliable pointer to form over the rest of a season. As usual, the rally began with asphalt stages in Sintra where, after the first loop, the Deltas of Biasion, Toivonen and Alén led narrowly from Peugeot's new boy Kankkunen and Audi's Röhrl. This was as far as any of them would get however. There had been a very serious accident on the very first stage when local driver Joaquim Santos speared off into a crowd of spectators with his Ford RS200, killing four of them. All the works drivers from Lancia, Peugeot, Audi, Ford and Austin Rover unanimously decided to withdraw from the event in protest at the inadequate safety precautions provided by the organisers for the spectators.

The early exit from Portugal allowed Henri to join Erja for a holiday with his parents, who had bought themselves a place in Benalmádena on the southern coast of Spain in which to spend the winter months. Lancia did not require him for the Safari Rally where the team used the old 037 for one final time. Instead, at Easter time, Toivonen focused on tarmac development of the Delta S4 in Corsica.

Henri tried wider tyres from Pirelli with all the latest modifications to the car that included revised suspension pick-up points, new springs, dampers and rollbars at both ends. He enthused about the changes: "I'm only now beginning to understand the car. It is two and a half centimetres lower than in Monte Carlo and 1.6 seconds per kilometre faster, which puts us at least equal with the Peugeot on dry tarmac."

During the week-long test period, he often made phone calls to check on Harri's progress in the Circuit of Ireland. He told his brother to calm down and ease off after early problems like a puncture and inability to hear the notes properly on the intercom. Towards the end of the long event, Harri was charging regardless

Frankreich gegen Italien, Peugeot gegen Lancia oder Salonen gegen Toivonen. Die Lancisti setzten alle Hebel in Bewegung. Während der Pause in Monte Carlo ließen sie Henri noch einmal die Prüfungen der letzten Nacht abfahren.

A rally to be won – France held its hopes for Peugeot and Salonen, Italy for Lancia and Toivonen. The Italian side left no stone unturned, Henri even hopping off for a last-minute recce instead of resting before the last night's action.

Henri Toivonen Großes Finale, tragisches Ende / Crescendo

Unvergessliche Momente! An den Monte-Triumph wird sich höchstens die kleine Arla, die auf Henris Schoß saß, nicht mehr erinnern.
Moments never to be forgotten! Perhaps the only one who cannot remember is little Arla who is sitting on Henri's lap.

Rallye Monte Carlo 1986

Während des Tests war Henri häufig am Telefon, um sich über Harris Fortschritt beim Circuit of Ireland zu informieren. Er riet seinem Bruder, es nach Problemen mit der Gegensprechanlage und einem Reifenschaden ruhig angehen zu lassen. Gegen Ende dieser langen Rallye attackierte Harri rücksichtslos und lag auf Kurs zu Platz Drei hinter David Llewellin im Schwesterauto und Russell Brookes im Manta, bis er einen Unfall baute und die Lenkung stark beschädigte. Bis zu seinem Ausfall war Harri sehr beherzt gefahren.

Ein paar Tage nach seiner Rückkehr aus Korsika traf Henri einen alten Freund. „Das Leben ist großartig", strahlte Henri. „Endlich habe ich ein siegfähiges Auto und die Ergebnisse stimmen. Und jetzt, wo Erja und ich uns wiederentdeckt haben, ist auch zu Hause wieder alles bestens. Meine einzige kleine Sorge sind mögliche Nachwirkungen des Sardinien-Unfalls – etwas in meinem Nervensystem. Ich habe immer wieder Blackouts." Der Freund riet ihm, schnell den Teamarzt von Lancia zu konsultieren. „Nein, nein", sagte Henri. „Das mache ich nicht. Vielleicht lassen die mich nicht fahren."

Vor dem nächsten WM-Lauf kehrte Henri Toivonen nach Sardinien zurück, um bei der Rallye Costa Smeralda die Erinnerungen an den Unfall vergessen zu machen. Im Delta S4 war er mit Abstand der schnellste Fahrer und gewann. Sein enormer Vorsprung schmolz am zweiten Tag aber wegen Problemen mit dem Volumex-Kompressor zusammen. Henri musste auf einer WP anhalten und den Kompressor überbrücken, um weiterfahren zu können. Der Motor lief danach nur noch zwischen 7.000 und 8.500 Touren und so hatte Toivonen im Ziel magere 36 Sekunden Vorsprung auf Andrea Zanussi im Peugeot.

Zwei Tage vor dem Start der Tour de Corse feierten Erja und Henri ihren Hochzeitstag. Sie flog extra für ein Candle-Light-Dinner nach Ajaccio, danach kehrte sie nach Monaco zurück. Es war nie geplant gewesen, dass sie für die Rallye bleibt. Henri hatte sich eine Grippe eingefangen, die sogar zur Angina wurde. „Mein Hals ist stark entzündet und ich habe Fieber, aber sonst ist alles bestens", sagte er in einem TV-Interview, das jahrelang zurückgehalten wurde. „Ich habe fast alle Prüfungen dreimal abgefahren. Das wird eine sehr harte Rallye, weil die Straße immer nur links und rechts geht. Es gibt nur wenige Geraden, wo du den vierten Gang einlegen kannst, und ganz wenige, wo du bis in den fünften kommst." Nach den Tests hatte

and seemed poised to finish third behind the sister car of David Llewellin and the Opel Manta of Russell Brookes, until he shunted and damaged the steering too badly to continue. He had shown some spirited driving, though.

A couple of days after returning from Corsica, Henri ran into an old friend that he had not seen for a while. "Life is good", he smiled. "At last I've got a winning car and the results are coming. And now that we've rediscovered each other with Erja, everything is fine at home. My only slight concern is that there may still be some after-effects of that Sardinia accident ... something in the nervous system maybe, because I get black-outs." The friend advised him to urgently consult Lancia's team doctor about such worries. "No, no! I daren't do that", dismissed Henri. "They might not let me drive ..."

Before the forthcoming WRC event, Henri Toivonen still returned to the Costa Smeralda Rally to wipe off the memory of his accident. In a Delta S4, he was fastest by far but yet again only won despite adversity as an enormous lead was whittled away on the second day when the Volumex supercharging system started playing up. He stopped on a stage, but bypassing the supercharger got the car going. With the engine only working properly between 7,000 and 8,500 rpm, Toivonen was no more than thirty-six seconds ahead of Andrea Zanussi's Peugeot at the finish.

Two days before the start of the Tour de Corse, Erja and Henri had a wedding anniversary. She flew down to Ajaccio to celebrate the occasion with a candle-lit dinner, but there were no plans for her to stay for the rally. As Erja returned to Monaco, Henri was left pondering his chances, having picked up 'flu which then developed into angina. "My throat is really sore and I have fever, but otherwise everything is fine", he said in a video interview, which was subsequently held back for years. "I've practiced nearly all the stages three times. This is going to be a very hard rally, because the roads are constantly twisting and turning. There are very few straights, where you can snatch fourth gear, just maybe fifth." Weeks ago, he had singled out one particular concern after the test period: "Saby has been practicing the stages since March. There's no way those of us with full programmes can afford to do something like that."

1986

Porto Cervo, 18. April 1986: Henris letzter Sieg. Hier gratuliert ihm der drittplatzierte Dario Cerrato. Der nächste Stopp lautete Korsika.
Last victory: Porto Cervo on April 18th, 1986. Third-placed Dario Cerrato was one of the well wishers. Next stop Corsica.

Henri Toivonen Großes Finale, tragisches Ende / Crescendo

Bei der Rallye Costa Smeralda 1986 war Henri der mit Abstand schnellste Fahrer. Obwohl sein Vorsprung durch technische Probleme stark schrumpfte, war die Botschaft klar: Toivonen war bereit, auch in der Weltmeisterschaft zu dominieren. Das Fahrverhalten des Delta S4 kam ihm jetzt mehr entgegen und ihm kamen die ersten Gedanken an den WM-Titel in den Sinn.

In 1986 Henri Toivonen was by far the fastest driver during the Costa Smeralda Rally. His winning margin did not reflect that thanks to mechanical trouble, but the message was clear: He was ready to dominate even on the world scene. The behaviour of Lancia's Delta S4 now appeared to be more to Henri's liking and thoughts of a world title started to creep into his mind.

Toivonen eine spezielle Sorge geäußert: „Saby hat die Prüfungen seit März trainiert. Fahrer wie ich, die die ganze Saison bestreiten, haben keine Chance, so etwas zu machen."

Henris Angst vor Bruno Sabys „unfairem Vorteil" war berechtigt. Der Franzose war auf der ersten WP zwölf Sekunden schneller als der Rest. Auf Prüfung Drei erzielte jedoch Toivonen die Bestzeit und von da an fuhr er ein gnadenloses Tempo. Er setzte eine Bestzeit nach der anderen und hatte sich bis zum Etappenziel in Bastia einen Vorsprung von 1.42 Minuten herausgefahren. Saby war Zweiter, der Rest komplett abgeschlagen. Trotzdem hatte Henri Sorgenfalten auf der Stirn. „Das ist eine verrückte Rallye. Wir haben die WP-Länge einer kompletten 1000 Seen Rallye an einem Tag zurückgelegt. In diesen Autos ist das überwältigend. Das Gehirn kommt da einfach nicht mit …"

Auf der ersten WP am nächsten Morgen reduzierte Saby den Vorsprung um elf Sekunden, ehe Henri wieder das Zepter übernahm. Er setzte vier Bestzeiten in Folge und war auf der letzten WP unglaubliche 47 Sekunden schneller als sein Gegner. Den vorherigen Rekord auf dieser Prüfung unterbot Toivonen um drei Minuten! Beim Mittagsstopp in Corte hatte sich der Finne ein Polster von 2.45 Minuten herausgefahren. Die Schlacht schien gewonnen. Am ersten Tag hatte Henri den MG Metro 6R4 von Tony Pond mehrmals überholt. Der Brite konnte den Lancia-Fahrer so genau beobachten: „Er ging keine Risiken ein", lautete Ponds Urteil.

Auf dem Weg von Corte nach Calvi wartete zunächst die WP Col d'Ominanda auf die Teams. Auf dieser Prüfung gab es nach fünf Kilometern eine schnelle Bergab-Passage, die in einer zumachenden Linkskurve endete: Links Berge, rechts ein Abhang. Diese Kurve war als eine der gefährlichsten Stellen der Rallye bekannt. Eine Kurve, an die sich die Fahrer erinnern, sogar wenn der Beifahrer die Ansage vergisst. Unerklärlicherweise und unglaublicherweise fuhr Henri in dieser Kurve geradeaus. Es gab keine Anzeichen dafür, dass

Henri's fears of Bruno Saby's "unfair advantage" proved justified, when the Frenchman was fastest by twelve seconds on the first stage. On stage three, Toivonen posted the best time however, and from then on his pace was relentless. Setting one fastest time after another he had built up a lead of 1min 42sec by the time the rally reached Bastia for an overnight rest after completing a dozen stages. Saby was second and the rest were nowhere. Yet Henri was wearing a frown: "This is a crazy event! We have covered the equivalent of one full 1000 Lakes Rally's worth of stages in one day and in these cars it's overwhelming. The brain simply cannot keep up …"

On the first stage the next morning Bruno Saby managed to claw back seven seconds, but then Henri was back on it again. He cleaned up on the next four stages, an amazing forty-seven seconds faster than the main opponent on the last one of them. That time undercut the old record for the long stage by three minutes! Reaching the lunchtime regrouping in Corte, the Finn's advantage was 2min 45sec and the battle appeared to be won, the rally in his pocket. On the opening day, Henri had overtaken Tony Pond's MG Metro 6R4 on several stages thus giving the Briton an opportunity to watch him from behind. "He was not taking chances", was Pond's verdict.

Heading from Corte towards Calvi, the next stage awaiting was the Col d'Ominanda, where after some five kilometres is a flat-out downhill section ending in a tightening left-hander with a mountainside on the left and a drop on the right. This was recognized as one of the rally's most dangerous places; one that the drivers could remember even if the co-driver missed a note. Inexplicably – unbelievably – Henri went straight on, without any apparent signs of having tried to slow down the Lancia. It left the road, hit some treetops and ended up about three metres below road level, bursting into flames that quickly became an inferno. Henri and Sergio Cresto were believed to have been dead on impact.

Beim Start zur Tour de Corse fühlte sich Henri nicht gesund. Nach dem Unfall wollte sich Pauli Toivonen das letzte Videointerview seines Sohnes nicht anschauen, weil er darin genau erkannt hätte, ob Henri fit genug gewesen wäre oder nicht.

Henri was not well at the start of the Tour de Corse. Later, Pauli Toivonen did not want to watch the last video interview of his son, because he said he would immediately detect whether Henri was fit to drive or not.

Zur Halbzeit der Tour de Corse lag Henri souverän in Führung. Er hätte er sich auf seinem Polster bequem ausruhen können.

By halfway, Henri had the Tour de Corse in his pocket. With a lead of close to three minutes he could have just stroked home, had he wanted to.

er versucht hat, den Lancia abzubremsen. Das Auto kam von der Straße ab, krachte in die Baumwipfel, kam etwa drei Meter unterhalb der Straße zum Stehen und ging in Flammen auf. Es war ein Inferno. Es ist davon auszugehen, dass Henri und Sergio Cresto schon beim Aufprall tot waren.

Saby, Biasion, Chatriot, Alén und andere Fahrer kamen an die Unfallstelle. Kurz darauf traf Lancia-Ingenieur Giorgio Pianta im Helikopter ein. Er versuchte verzweifelt, die Flammen mit dem Abwind der Rotoren auszublasen. Aber alle Versuche waren vergeblich. Das Auto brannte komplett aus, die Zeugen waren von diesem Anblick schockiert. Lancia zog sich aus dem Wettbewerb zurück – genau wie ein Jahr zuvor, als Attilio Bettega ums Leben gekommen war. Der ganze Sport versank im Schockzustand. Der Motorsportverband handelte schnell. Die FIA verbot die Gruppe-B-Monster und änderte die Formate der Rallyes.

An jenem Nachmittag war Erja Toivonen in Monte Carlo gewesen. In den vorherigen Monaten war viel passiert und sie wollte ihren Kopf bei einem langen Spaziergang frei bekommen. Als sie nach Hause kam, klingelte das Telefon schon eine ganze Weile. „Sitzt du?", fragte die Stimme am anderen Ende der Leitung.

Ulla Toivonen verfolgte die Rallyeeinsätze ihrer Söhne normalerweise nicht. „Ich habe mir immer Sorgen gemacht. Als Henri anfing und wir alle zu den Rennen gefahren sind, konnte ich mir nie den Start anschauen." Ulla ließ sich nur die wichtigen Informationen von Pauli durchgeben, der täglich mit den Jungs telefonierte, wenn er nicht selbst vor Ort war. Doch an diesem schicksalhaften Tag hatte Ulla den Videotext des Fernsehers angeschaltet. Dort las sie die Nachricht von Henris Tod.

Pauli Toivonen war bei der Wales Rallye gerade kurz davor, zur Technischen Abnahme zu fahren. Er kümmerte sich jetzt mehr um seinen jüngeren Sohn, da Harri offensichtlich mehr Unterstützung brauchte als Henri. „Wir bemerkten, wie sich die Mechaniker um uns herum

Saby, Biasion, Chatriot, Alén and others arrived. Soon also Lancia's team engineer, Giorgio Pianta, came in a helicopter, desperately trying to use the downwash from its rotors to put out the flames. Nothing could be done. The car burnt out to a charred frame, the onlookers shattered by what they had witnessed. Lancia withdrew from the competition as they had done when Bettega was killed on the same rally, just one year to the day before. Shockwaves went through the whole sport. The international federation quickly moved to outlaw Group B "supercars" and to re-configure rally formats.

In Monte Carlo, Erja Toivonen had spent the afternoon out. A lot had been happening in the past months and she wanted to clear her thoughts so she had gone for a long walk. Coming back home, the phone rang, as it had been doing for some time: "Are you sitting down", said the voice at the other end.

In Finland, Ulla Toivonen was not in the habit of following the rallies in which her sons competed. "I'd always been worried. When Henri started and we all went to the races, I could never watch the start." She relied on hearing the essential bits from Pauli, who would talk to the boys daily on the phone, if he was not present actually watching them. On this fateful day, poor Ulla had tuned into the TV text-pages where she read the news of Henri's death.

In Wales, Pauli Toivonen was about to drive to scrutineering for the Welsh Rally with Harri. His focus had now slightly shifted to the younger son's efforts with Harri obviously more in need of his support than Henri. "We somehow became aware of the mechanics around us turning away and started to wonder what was the matter" relates Harri. "Then one of them said we should go to the Rally Office where my team-mate's co-driver, Phil Short, told us what had happened."

"The worst moment of my professional life was when I had to call Pauli a couple of hours after the accident", says Cesare Fiorio.

umdrehten, und fragten uns, was das zu bedeuten hat", erzählt Harri. „Dann sagte einer von ihnen, dass wir ins Rallyebüro gehen sollen. Dort erklärte uns Phil Short, der Beifahrer meines Teamkollegen, was passiert war."

„Der schlimmste Moment in meiner Karriere war, als ich Pauli ein paar Stunden nach dem Unfall anrufen musste", sagt Cesare Fiorio. „Ich weiß nicht mehr, was ich damals gesagt habe, aber es gab für mich noch nie eine schwierigere Aufgabe. In meinen Augen hatten Henri und Pauli beide diese absolute Hingabe für ihren Job. Sie waren voll dabei. Ich sage immer wieder, dass Henri im Rallyesport der beste und talentierteste Fahrer war, mit dem ich je zusammengearbeitet habe. Er konnte immer 100% des Potenzials von seinem Auto nutzen. In der Formel 1 war Fernando Alonso der beste Fahrer, den ich gemanagt habe. Das sind die Fahrer, die mir das unglaublichste Gefühl vermittelt haben."

Die Tragödie brachte viele Leute und sogar ganze Gemeinschaften durcheinander. Aber kaum jemand kann sich vorstellen, wie es sich für die Familie angefühlt haben muss. In Cardiff organisierten sich Pauli und Harri auf die Schnelle einen Heimflug im Privatjet. In Monte Carlo musste sich Erja dazu zwingen, die wichtigsten Alltagsdinge zu erledigen. „Die Realität traf uns hart. Ein Beispiel: Ich hatte zu dem Zeitpunkt kein Geld auf dem Konto, aber Keke half mir. Er hat mich fantastisch unterstützt", beschreibt sie. „Erja war in einer Situation, die ganz schwierig zu ertragen ist, wenn man alleine ist und weg von der Heimat. Da ich älter bin, dachte ich, ich könnte ihr helfen", sagt Keke Rosberg. „Jean Todt rief ebenfalls an und fragte, ob ich irgendetwas bräuchte. Das war sehr rücksichtsvoll für den Chef eines rivalisierenden Teams", betont Erja.

Die Messe und Weihung fand in der römisch-katholischen Kirche von Helsinki statt. Wenige Tage später wurde Henri Toivonen auf dem Friedhof von Espoo beerdigt. Bei der gut besuchten Trauerfeier wurden Stücke von Schubert und Sibelius gespielt sowie eine Cello-Version von Paul McCartneys Song „Yesterday". Besonders ergreifend war der Moment, als Des O'Dell seinen Kranz auf den Sarg legte. Henri war für Des so etwas wie ein eigener Sohn.

Der Verlust von Henri war immens, weil er im Leben von so vielen Menschen eine große Rolle gespielt hatte. Vor allem in Erjas: „Wir haben zwölf Jahre zusammen verbracht. Er war ohne Zweifel der richtige Mann für mich. Er hatte zwar seinen eigenen Kopf, aber er konnte mich auch auf Händen tragen. Ich habe ihn so sehr geliebt." Mit ihren beiden Kindern zog sie sich für ein Jahr nach Spanien zurück. Danach zog sie wieder nach Finnland und begann zu arbeiten, wie sie es in ihrer Zeit mit Henri auch die meiste Zeit getan hatte.

Die Tragödie hinterließ auch bei Pauli Spuren. Er hatte danach ein Herzleiden, ein sogenanntes Vorhofflimmern. „Bei der Behandlung hat sein Herz sogar dreimal aufgehört zu schlagen", verrät Ulla Toivonen. Pauli hielt die Krankheit lange Zeit geheim. Nur seine engsten Vertrauten wussten davon. Aber er musste sich ja noch um seine Geschäfte kümmern – und um Harris Zukunft.

Harri wollte sich erst aus dem Motorsport zurückziehen. „Ich kann auf keinen Fall weitermachen, ich muss an die Gefühle von Mutter und Vater denken", hatte er voller Verzweiflung in Cardiff gesagt. Doch in den nächsten Wochen bekamen Ulla und Pauli seinen Ärger darüber mit. „Zu Hause habe ich mit meinen Fäusten Löcher in die Wände geschlagen", so Harri. „Irgendwann schlug Pauli vor, dass wir in die Sauna gehen und reden. Er sagte, dass mir das Fahren wohl noch viel bedeute und dass es offensichtlich genauso teuer wäre, wenn ich zu Hause bliebe, weil ich am Haus so viel kaputt machen würde …"

"I cannot remember what I said at the time, but there has not been another task as difficult as that for me. From my point of view, Henri and his father Pauli were the same in that they both had total commitment to the job they were asked to do. They gave it everything. I have been saying that in rallies Henri was the best and most talented driver I ever worked with, because he could always express 100% of the potential of his car. Like in Formula 1, the best driver I have had the experience to manage was Fernando Alonso. Those two are the drivers who have made for me the most incredible feeling."

The tragedy threw lots of people and whole communities into disarray, but hardly anyone can imagine what it must have felt like to be within the family. In Cardiff, Pauli and Harri made hasty arrangements to fly home by private jet. In Monte Carlo, Erja had to steel herself to take care of various essential routines. "The realities hit hard. For example, I did not have any money in my bank account at that moment, but Keke came to help me out. He was fantastically supportive", she praises. "Erja found herself in a situation that was horrible to bear for someone on her own, away from home. Being older, I thought I could somehow help", says Keke Rosberg. "Jean Todt too phoned to ask if I was in need of anything. That was most considerate from the manager of a rival team", Erja points out.

After Mass and Consecration in Helsinki's Roman-Catholic Cathedral, Henri Toivonen was buried a few days later in the cemetery of Espoo's Church following a widely attended funeral service. Tunes of Schubert and Sibelius were heard in the service, as well as a cello rendition of Paul McCartney's "Yesterday". A poignant sight was the silver-haired Des O'Dell laying his wreath on the coffin. Des had come to consider Henri almost like a son of his own.

The loss of Henri had been immense since a defining chapter was closed in so many lives, above all Erja's: "We had twelve years together and there can be no doubt Henri was the right man for me. Enough of an independent soul, but also inclined to keep me like a flower on his palm. I was so fond of him." With two young children she initially retired to Spain for a year, but subsequently returned to Finland and went back to work, as she had done for most of the time with Henri.

The tragedy took its toll on Pauli, who developed a heart condition called atrial fibrillation. "Three times he even had his heart stopped in an attempt to cure it", reveals Ulla Toivonen. For a very long time he managed to keep this a secret to all but his nearest and dearest. He had the business to put his mind to – and there was also Harri's future to think of.

Harri's immediate reaction had been to quit competing. "There's no way I can carry on, I have to consider the feelings of Mother and Father", he had said in distress while still in Cardiff. In the next weeks, his aggravation became very obvious to Ulla and Pauli. "At home I had been banging holes in the walls with my fists when one day Dad suggested we go to the sauna and talk things over. He said driving still clearly meant a lot to me and that keeping me home would apparently be just as costly, because I was doing so much damage to the house …"

Warum sollte jemand hier verunglücken? Doch leider geschah eben das und die Folgen waren verheerend. Markku Alén und Seppo Harjanne gehörten zu den Sargträgern.

Why would anyone crash here? But if it happened, the consequences would be devastating. Markku Alén and Seppo Harjanne led the pall bearers.

Henri Toivonen Großes Finale, tragisches Ende / Crescendo

Harri Toivonen

* 22. Oktober 1960 in Jyväskylä, Finnland
* October 22, 1960 in Jyväskylä, Finland

Harri Toivonen

Der Unvollendete
Unfulfilled promise

John Davenport, damals Motorsportdirektor bei Austin Rover, rief Harri an, um ihn zu fragen, ob er bereit wäre, das Rallyeprogramm fortzuführen. „Er drängte mich dazu weiterzumachen und letztlich bemerkte ich auch, dass ich das musste. Ich bin zur Schottland Rallye gereist, aber ich habe zu John gesagt, dass ich nicht weiß, wie gut ich sein werde. Er war fantastisch zu mir: ‚Vergiss die Zeiten. Fahr einfach und schau, wie du dich fühlst', sagte er."

Die Schottland Rallye wurde für Austin Rover zum Desaster. Der Staub auf den Prüfungen führte bei allen Werks-Metro zu Motorschäden. Bei der Ulster Rallye zwei Monate später fühlte sich für Harri alles wieder recht normal an. Er zeigte eine selbstbewusste Leistung, eroberte früh die vierte Position und behauptete diese bis ins Ziel. Vor ihm lagen nur Jimmy McRae (Metro), Mark Lovell (Ford RS200) und Mikael Sundström (Peugeot 205 T16). Russell Brookes im Opel Manta 400, der beim Circuit of Ireland noch weit vor Harri gelegen hatte, reihte sich diesmal hinter Toivonen ein.

Bei seiner Heimrallye nahm Harri eine wichtigere Rolle ein: Vom Werksteam bekam er einen Linkslenker-Metro. Zudem war er ein zentrales Element in den Vorbereitungen des Teams, da Stammpilot Malcolm Wilson zum ersten Mal an der 1000 Seen Rallye teilnahm. „Der Einsatz ist schon recht aufwändig", staunte Harri. „Ich habe ganz unschuldig gesagt, dass ich beim Test gerne mal Reifen mit einem sanften Profil ausprobieren würde. Also wurde ein Satz aus Großbritannien eingeflogen."

Während der Rallye jagte Harri den werksunterstützten Metro von Per Eklund und lag zwischendurch auf Platz Sechs, ehe die schnelleren Lancia-Piloten, die anfangs Zeit eingebüßt hatten, wieder an ihm vorbeizogen. Erst gegen Ende der Rallye verlor Toivonen den Anschluss an Eklund, als der Träger des Vorderachsdifferenzials vom Chassis abbrach und geschweißt werden musste. Die Reparatur brachte ihm zwar eine Strafzeit ein, dennoch erreichte Harri das Ziel direkt hinter dem Schweden als Achter. Viele Beobachter fanden diese Vorstellung couragiert.

Bei der Manx Rallye schied Harri durch einen Motorschaden aus. Zur RAC Rallye, wo ihn Pauli eifrig unterstützte, kehrte er ins Werksteam zurück. Mit Beifahrer Neil Wilson fuhr er ein beständiges Tempo, allerdings verlor er im Kielder Forest viel Zeit, als der Wagenheber beim Reifenwechsel streikte. Auf dem Weg nach Wales lief der Metro nur noch auf fünf Zylindern und schon kurz darauf war das Triebwerk ganz hinüber.

Am Saisonende steckte Harri Toivonen in einer Zwickmühle: „Der Plan war, 1987 bei Austin Rover zu bleiben. Aber durch das Verbot der Gruppe gab es kein Auto und kein Programm. Der MG Metro 6R4 mit seiner eckigen Form ließ sich sehr eigenartig fahren. Aber er war vielversprechend. Doch jetzt musste ich etwas anderes finden."

Dieses „etwas andere" war ein Gruppe-A-Mazda-323-4WD, den Harri mit Hilfe des finnischen Mazda-Importeurs einsetzte. In dieser Konstellation mussten die internationalen Karrierepläne hinten anstehen, dafür war die Saison im heimischen Finnland intensiver als je zuvor. Bei der Arctic Rallye holte er im Mazda den dritten Rang. Bei der Hanki Rallye hatte er zunächst Turboprobleme, dann kämpfte er sich wie entfesselt nach vorn und landete am Ende immerhin in den Top Ten.

The Austin Rover Motorsport Director, John Davenport, had been calling Harri Toivonen to check whether he was prepared to continue with the rally programme after Henri's tragic accident. "He urged me to go on and eventually I realised I needed to. I went to the Scottish Rally but said to John I wasn't sure how I'd perform. He was fantastic about it. 'Forget about the times, just drive and see how you feel', he said."

The Scottish Rally was a disaster for Austin Rover as a whole because dust on the stages caused engine failures with all the works Metros. Two months later in the Ulster Rally, things felt pretty normal again for Harri Toivonen. He was in confident form taking fourth place quite early and finishing in that position, beaten by Jimmy McRae in another Metro, Mark Lovell in a Ford RS200 and Mikael Sundström in a Peugeot 205 T16, but leaving behind the Opel Manta 400 of Russell Brookes who had been well ahead of him during the Circuit of Ireland.

For his home event, Harri Toivonen assumed a bigger role. In the works team he got to use a left-hand-drive car and was also central to the team's preparations since regular driver Malcolm Wilson had not taken part in the 1000 Lakes Rally before. "It was all quite lavish", Harri marvelled. "I innocently said, when asked, that I might like to try tyres with a smooth tread pattern in testing and, sure enough, a set was flown in from Britain."

During the rally he gave chase to the works supported but privately entered Metro 6R4 of Per Eklund and was running in sixth at best, but lost a couple of places when the Lancia Delta S4 drivers who had been delayed recovered to positions that better reflected their level. During the later stages, Harri lost touch with Eklund when his front differential carrier broke from the chassis and required welding. The repairs brought road penalties, but Harri still brought the car home in eighth position right behind the Swede. Several observers felt this performance of Harri had been a courageous one.

Harri retired from the Manx Rally, where his engine blew up, but was back in the works fold for the RAC Rally where Pauli was eagerly supporting him. This time paired with Neil Wilson, he settled into a steady pace, but a lot of time was wasted in Kielder when the jack broke while the crew changed a puncture. As the rally was heading to the Welsh stages, the car started running on five cylinders and it expired soon after.

At the end of the season Harri Toivonen was in a quandary: "The idea had been to stay with Austin Rover into 1987, but with the cancellation of Group B there was no car and no programme for the team. The MG Metro 6R4 had been a peculiar car to drive with its cubic shape and all, but it had promise. Now I needed to find something else."

That 'something else' was a Group A Mazda 323 4WD for which Harri received support from the manufacturer's Finnish importer. With such a set-up, international aspirations had to take a back seat, but the domestic season turned into his busiest ever. He took the Mazda to third in the Arctic Rally while he put in a heroic comeback drive after turbo problems in the Hankiralli but barely climbed back into the top ten finishers.

Cedric Wrede, seit 1983 Harris Beifahrer, schien der perfekte Partner für eine internationale Rallyekarriere zu sein. Dennoch blieb der achte Platz bei der 1000 Seen Rallye 1986 das beste Ergebnis der beiden in der Weltmeisterschaft.

Cedric Wrede, Harri's co-driver from 1983, seemed to be the perfect partner for someone pursuing an international rally career. However, eighth place in the 1986 1000 Lakes Rally would remain the pair's best result at World Championship level.

Harri Toivonen Der Unvollendete / Unfulfilled promise

Harri kehrte anschließend zur Rallye Costa Smeralda nach Sardinien zurück. Sein Auftritt dort führte zum gleichen Ergebnis wie zwei Jahre zuvor bei seinem Bruder: Harri musste im Krankenhaus von Helsinki operiert werden. Vor dem Start der Rallye rettete er den Vertreter eines italienischen Sponsors aus dem Meer, beim Sprung aus dem Boot verletzte er sich am rechten Knöchel. Toivonen begann die Rallye mit starken Schmerzen und war vielleicht gar nicht so unglücklich, als sein Auto den Geist aufgab. In Finnland bekam er vom Arzt eine Standpauke, denn seine Bänder waren gerissen und eine OP unvermeidbar.

Das Jahr verlief für Harri in vielerlei Hinsicht enttäuschend: „Das Auto war eine Gurke. In der Anfangszeit der Gruppe A konnte man es nicht zuverlässig machen. Ein geradverzahntes Xtrac-Getriebe wurde als zu teuer angesehen und das Getriebe, das wir hatten, machte immer Probleme." Im Sommer erreichte Harri nicht einmal bei einer kleinen nationalen Rallye das Ziel. Dort saß Marja Kinnunen auf dem Beifahrersitz, die Miss Finnland von 1985 war seit einiger Zeit Harris Freundin.

A return to Sardinia for the Costa Smeralda Rally was fitted in, but it led to Harri Toivonen being operated in the same Helsinki hospital where his brother Henri had been treated exactly two years earlier! Before the rally had even got underway, Harri ended up rescuing an Italian sponsor from the sea. In doing so, he jumped into a boat and hurt his right ankle. It gave him agonizing pain in the rally that, perhaps luckily, did not last long before the car failed. Back in Finland, he got a telling-off from the doctor who found that the ligaments were broken and ordered his patient to check in for surgery.

In most respects, the year was a disappointment. "That car was a lemon; in those early days of Group A it could not be made reliable", says Harri. "An Xtrac gearbox with straight-cut cogs was deemed too expensive for us and the box we had was always giving trouble." He did not even manage to finish a minor national rally in the summer, where Marja Kinnunen, Miss Finland 1985 and who had been Harri's girlfriend for some time, occupied the co-driver's seat.

1986

Vom Pech verfolgt: Bei Harris letzten Auftritten im MG Metro 6R4 ging immer irgendetwas schief. Es blieb das Gefühl, dass er mehr hätte erreichen können.
Something always went wrong for Harri in his last drives with the MG Metro 6R4. There was a feeling he could have achieved more.

Ab 1987 war Harri wieder auf die Unterstützung seines Vaters angewiesen. International sah man den jüngeren Bruder nur noch selten.

From 1987 on Harri again relied on backing from his father. It meant he was seen less on international events.

Harri und Pauli waren sich einig, dass man wettbewerbsfähiges Material am besten in Form eines Lancia Delta HF 4WD bekam. Also holten sie Anfang Dezember einen Ex-Werkswagen in Turin ab. Da gleichzeitig die Bologna Motor Show und das Bettega Memorial veranstaltet wurden, gab Harri hier sein Debüt im Delta. Das Bettega Memorial war ein Showrennen im Stile des Race of Champions, dem 1987 ein Delta-Markenpokal angehörte. Dort unterlag Harri im Finale Patrick Snijers, weil er im zweiten Lauf mit dem Vorderrad einen mit Beton gefüllten Traktorreifen traf.

Für die finnische Meisterschaft war der Lancia schnell genug. Harri Toivonen wurde zum großen Herausforderer von Titelverteidiger Mikael Sundström, der den Mazda selbst weiterentwickelt hatte. Das Duell Toivonen/Sundström war auch das Highlight bei der Hanki Rallye 1988. Sundström hatte sich einen kleinen Vorsprung herausgefahren, bis seine Kraftübertragung Probleme machte. Drei Prüfungen musste er mit Zweiradantrieb auskommen und so ging Harri mit einer Minute in Führung.

„Ich habe ganz schlecht geschlafen", gab der Führende am letzten Morgen zu. „Ich bin immer wieder aufgewacht, weil ich Angst hatte zu verschlafen." Der Druck war offensichtlich groß, aber letztlich war es Sundström, der den entscheidenden Fehler machte und abflog. Harri Toivonen gewann mit über zwei Minuten Vorsprung. Das war der größte Triumph seiner Karriere, und das sollte er auch bleiben. Zumindest im Rallyesport.

Harri war auf das Geld seiner Familie angewiesen und nach einem Motorschaden bei der 1000 Seen Rallye war die Saison beendet. „Pauli sagte, wir hätten nicht genug Geld für eine richtige Rallyesaison im Jahr 1989. Also habe ich mich auf der Rundstrecke umgesehen. Da ich auf den Highspeed-Prüfungen immer schnell war, meinte Henri, dass ich das Rennfahren mal ausprobieren sollte."

Juha Paajanen machte als Beifahrer beider Toivonen-Brüder eine interessante Beobachtung: „Wenn sie blind auf eine lange, schnelle

Harri and Pauli decided that the best way to ensure competitive equipment was to buy an ex-works Lancia Delta HF 4WD and one was collected from the factory in early December. That was the time of the Bologna Motor Show, so the Lancia was conveniently debuted in the Bettega Memorial knockout competition that was run concurrently with the show. Harri made the final in the supporting one-make race for Deltas but, in a second run against Patrick Snijers, he bent his front wheel against a tractor tyre marking the edge of the track that was filled with concrete.

In Finland, the car certainly proved quick enough for the domestic series where Harri Toivonen became the main challenger to reigning champion, Mikael Sundström, who had been developing the Mazda in a direction of his own. The battle between these two was the highlight of the 1988 Hankiralli. Sundström had established a slight advantage until his transmission began showing signs of weakness. He had to tackle three stages with 2WD only, which helped Harri to a lead of just over one minute.

"I had a terrible night's rest", confessed the leader on the last morning. "I kept waking up afraid that I'd oversleep!" The pressure was perhaps telling here but it was in fact Sundström who cracked first and went off, handing Harri Toivonen a final winning margin of over two minutes. Easily the biggest triumph of his career so far, it was unfortunately to remain so – in rallies.

Now reliant on family funding, Harri's season was cut short after an engine failure in the 1000 Lakes Rally: "Father said there wasn't really enough money to throw at a proper rally season in 1989, so I decided to look into racing instead. Henri had been saying that, as I was always quick on the faster special stages, I should try the circuits sooner or later."

Juha Paajanen makes an interesting observation comparing the two Toivonen brothers as rally drivers: "If there was a long, fast bend that was blind, Henri's foot stayed firmly planted to the loud

Harri Toivonen Der Unvollendete / Unfulfilled promise

Kurve zufuhren, blieb Henris Fuß fest auf dem lauten Pedal. Harri hat da manchmal gezögert. Er ist vom Gas runter, hat geschaut, und ist dann wieder aufs Gas. Henri hatte dieses Selbstvertrauen, das Harri noch aufbauen musste." Die Vorzeichen für eine große Zukunft im Rennsport standen also gut. Dort wusste Harri ja, wo es langgeht.

Die Erinnerungen an Henri Toivonen waren in der Rallyeszene noch sehr lebendig, als Michèle Mouton im Dezember 1988 das erste „Race of Champions" veranstaltete. Die Geburtsstunde einer Show-Veranstaltung, die bis ins neue Jahrtausend überlebt hat. „Wir wollten ein Rennen mit allen Weltmeistern auf identischem Material veranstalten", erklärt Michèle. „Als wir unsere Liste der ‚Champions' machten, wurde auch Henris Name genannt. Er hätte in dem Jahr (1986) Weltmeister werden sollen und wir dachten, es wäre gut, ihm unsere Veranstaltung zu widmen." Beim ersten Race of Champions in Paris vertrat Harri die Toivonen-Familie und überreichte die Trophäe mit der Aufschrift „Race of Champions – Souvenir Henri Toivonen".

Im Sommer 1989 war Harri hauptsächlich auf finnischen Rennstrecken unterwegs. Er fuhr einen von drei BMW M3 des örtlichen Importeurs. Mit dem Gruppe-A-Auto kam er gut zurecht und gewann den Titel in der größten Tourenwagenklasse, allerdings gleichauf mit Teamkollege Heikki Salmenautio. „Das ist blöd gelaufen", schnauft Harri. „Anfangs wurden mir Punkte vom letzten Lauf gestrichen, weil es nicht genug Starter gab. Dann habe ich die Hälfte davon zurückbekommen, weil die Zahl erst durch die Aufgaben nach dem Qualifying zu niedrig war. Damit wäre ich Meister gewesen, aber aus irgendeinem Grund wurde entschieden, dass der Titel zwischen uns aufgeteilt wird." Mit dem M3 gewann Harri auch das 500-Kilometer-Rennen von Kemora.

Der Wechsel auf die Rennstrecke war so einfach gewesen, dass sich Harri jetzt höhere Ziele setzte. Ein Sprung von der Gruppe A in die Gruppe C schien ungeheuerlich, aber damals gab es viele Fahrerplätze in den zahlreichen Porsche 962, die von den etablierten Sportwagengrößen fast schon übersehen wurden.

Im Frühjahr 1990 flog Harri Toivonen nach Monza, um sich ein Cockpit im 962 des schwedischen Convector-Teams zu sichern. Sein Eindruck bei den Tests war gut genug für einen Platz im Porsche Carrera 2, mit dem er den Porsche Cup bestreiten sollte. Seine Gruppe-C-Hoffnungen erlitten jedoch einen Rückschlag, als Anthony Reid das begehrte Cockpit bekam. Doch schon bald gab es eine Lösung: Franz Konrad nahm Harri in sein Team auf, die beiden teilten sich einen 962 in der Weltmeisterschaft.

Der Porsche Cup brachte Harri wenig Freude. „Der Porsche war schrecklich und es gab definitiv Unterschiede zwischen den Autos", erklärt Harri. Verständlicherweise lag seine Priorität bei der Gruppe C: „Ich habe am Nürburgring getestet und bin ab Silverstone in der WM mitgefahren. Konrads Team war fantastisch, um diese Art des Rennfahrens zu lernen."

Die Erwartungen hielten sich in Grenzen, denn gegen die Werkswagen von Mercedes, Jaguar, Nissan oder Toyota hatte das Privatteam keine Chance. Der Konrad-962 gehörte nicht einmal zu den schnelleren Porsche, da das Team noch den alten Dreilitermotor hatte, während einige Konkurrenten schon die neuere 3,2-Liter-Variante fuhren. In Silverstone erreichten Konrad und Toivonen Platz 14 mit neun Porsche vor ihnen und sechs dahinter. Beim nächsten Rennen in Spa waren sie eine Position besser, diesmal waren nur sechs Porsche vor ihnen und neun dahinter. „Ich denke, Harri ist gut, aber er braucht mehr Zeit im Auto", urteilte der Teamchef.

pedal, whereas Harri sometimes hesitated. He could lift, have a look, and then step on it again. Henri had that confidence, which Harri still had to build up." That might suggest Harri had a brighter future in racing where he knew which way the track went.

The memory of Henri Toivonen was still fresh for everyone closely related with rallying. In December 1988, a fitting tribute was established when Michèle Mouton organized the "Race of Champions", the first in a long line of invitation events that has carried on into the new millennium. "We wanted a race with all the World Champions in equal equipment. We started to make a list of champions and spontaneously the name of Henri came up. He should have been a champion, for sure, that year and we thought it was good to dedicate this event to him," explains Michèle. Harri represented the family at the inaugural event in Paris and presented a trophy inscribed "Race of Champions – Souvenir Henri Toivonen."

Harri's focus for the summer of 1989 lay on Finnish racing circuits, competing in a three-car BMW Dealer Team. He had no trouble getting to grips with a Group A BMW M3 and took the national title in the biggest touring car class, albeit ex-aequo with team-mate Heikki Salmenautio. "It was a bit silly", Harri snorts. "I first lost points from the last round, because there were not enough starters, but then got half of them back, because this had only been the case after a post-qualifying withdrawal. That would have made me champion, but for some reason they decided to split the title between the two of us." He also used the M3 to win the Kemora 500 km enduro.

The transition to racing had happened with such ease that it encouraged Harri to set his sights considerably higher. A jump from Group A to Group C may seem outrageous, but at this time there were plenty of drives available in the numerous Porsche 962s, which were about to be overlooked by the established stars of sports car racing.

In the spring of 1990, Harri Toivonen flew to Monza to test one of these, vying for a place in the Swedish Convector team. He made a good enough impression to land a deal to drive a Porsche Carrera 2 in the Porsche Cup, but the Group C aspirations seemed to take a knock when Anthony Reid was given that seat. Very soon a solution was found, however, where Harri was to join Franz Konrad in the Austrian's own team, sharing a 962 with him in World Championship races.

The Porsche Cup did not bring much joy. "It was a terrible car that year and there was definitely disparity between them", Harri insists. Understandably, Group C soon took priority: "I got to test at the Nürburgring and then joined the world series from Silverstone onwards. Konrad's team was a fantastic place to learn about that type of racing."

Certainly, the weight of expectation was not overwhelming because there was no hope of challenging works cars from Mercedes-Benz, Jaguar, Nissan or Toyota. In fact, Konrad's 962 was not even among the quicker Porsches as it still had an original 3-litre engine while some of the opposition were using newer 3.2-litre units. In Silverstone, Konrad and Toivonen finished fourteenth with nine Porsches ahead of them and six behind. At the following race in Spa they got one place higher, now with six Porsches ahead, nine behind. "I think he is good, but he needs more time in the car", opined the team boss.

Mit dem Lancia Delta 4WD verbuchte Harri 1988 einige Erfolge, danach war er nur noch beim „Race of Champions" als Fahrer am Start. Bis heute erinnert die Veranstaltung an seinen Bruder Henri Toivonen.

A Lancia Delta 4WD gave Harri some success in 1988. After that he only entered the "Race of Champions" which today still remembers his brother Henri Toivonen.

Die normale Reihenfolge war, dass Franz Konrad beim Start und Ziel im Auto saß, während Harri den Mittelstint übernahm. Die Ergebnisse waren nicht herausragend, aber immerhin konnte der Neuling viel Erfahrung sammeln. Der kanadische WM-Lauf in Montreal war ein Rennen, an das sich Harri noch lange erinnern würde, leider aus den falschen Gründen: Jesus Pareja traf mit seinem Brun-Porsche einen losen Gullydeckel und hatte einen fürchterlichen Unfall, bei dem sein Auto in Flammen aufging. Nur ein anderer Fahrer stoppte an der Unfallstelle: Harri Toivonen. „Es ist sicher nicht schwer zu erraten warum", sagt er trocken. „Ich habe einen offenen Helm getragen, habe mir die Sturmhaube übers Gesicht gezogen und wollte gerade ins Auto klettern, als Pareja es schaffte herauszukommen."

Harri hatte zwei finnische Sponsoren mitgebracht, die das Programm unterstützten. Der Schiffsmotorenbauer Wärtsilä Diesel sollte 1991 an Bord bleiben, wenn Konrad ein neues Auto mit einem Saugmotor einsetzt. Durch Regeländerungen und die weltweite Wirtschaftskrise ging die Sportwagenszene aber schweren Zeiten entgegen. Konrads geplante Kooperation mit Spice scheiterte, als die englische Firma Konkurs ging. Das Team war gerade dabei sein eigenes Auto zu bauen, doch bis es so weit war, sollte noch einige Zeit vergehen.

„Franz wendete sich trotzdem an Wärtsilä. Er tat so, als stünde ich bei ihm unter Vertrag, und überzeugte die Firma, mit ihm direkt einen Deal zu machen. So stand ich ohne Sponsor und ohne Auto da", beschreibt Harri, dem sein Landsmann Keke Rosberg zur Hilfe eilte. „Er managte Manuel Reuter und konnte mich als Partner bei Kremer Racing unterbringen. Ohne mein Wissen hatte Pauli auch Geld für die Fahrten garantiert."

Das Kremer-Auto war definitiv schneller als das von Konrad. Der Porsche 962 Kremer CK6 basierte auf einem 962, hatte aber ein umgebautes Chassis aus Karbon-Verbundmaterial, eine veränderte Karosserie und einen größeren 3,2-Liter-Turbomotor. Was die Leistung betrifft, hinkte der Wagen hinter den neuesten Saugmotorautos her, die per Reglement offensichtlich bevorzugt wurden. Aber innerhalb der Porsche-Fraktion gehörte das Auto zu den besten.

Es gab lange Zeit Zweifel um die FIA Sportwagen-Weltmeisterschaft, aber letztlich begann die Saison wie geplant in Japan. Dort kam Harri Toivonen anfangs gar nicht zurecht: „Im Training war ich vollkommen abgeschlagen. Ich habe den Kurs von Suzuka einfach nicht hinbekommen, aber Keke beruhigte mich und im Rennen machte es dann ‚Klick'."

Gegen die Werkswagen mit Saugmotor hatte Manuel Reuter keine Chance, aber wegen einiger Ausfälle übergab er den Kremer-Porsche auf Platz Drei liegend an Harri. Durch einen langen Stopp fielen sie schon an der Box hinter den Turbo-Mercedes von Jochen Mass zurück. Harri fuhr einen soliden Mittelstint und musste nur den Spice von Cor Euser passieren lassen, den Manuel Reuter allerdings in der Schlussrunde wieder überholte. Dieses Manöver brachte dem Kremer-Duo Rang Drei ein, nachdem auch der Peugeot von Rosberg/Dalmas durch einen Kupplungsschaden ausgefallen war. „Es war ein fantastisches Gefühl, auf dem Podium zu stehen", schwärmt Harri. „Unglaublich!"

Das war für Toivonen der Beginn einer sehr guten Saison, in der er sich einen Namen als zuverlässiger und aufstrebender Sportwagenfahrer machte. In Monza wurde er Fünfter, als Cor Euser das Spiel von Suzuka herumdrehte und Manuel Reuter kurz vor der Ziellinie überholte. Silverstone brachte Rang Acht ein. Da sie ohne den dritten Gang auskommen mussten, waren sie hier nur das zweitbeste Porsche-Team hinter dem Brun-Auto von Oscar Larrauri/Jesus

The routine was for Franz Konrad to start and finish the races with Harri doing the middle stint. Results were not spectacular but it was all good experience for the newcomer. The Canadian round of the series on Montreal's Circuit Gilles Villeneuve became a race to remember, but for all the wrong reasons. Spaniard Jesus Pareja suffered a terrifying accident when his Brun Motorsport Porsche became engulfed in flames after hitting a loose manhole cover. Only one fellow competitor stopped at the scene: Harri Toivonen. "It's probably not too difficult to guess why", he says dryly. "I was wearing an open-face helmet and was just about to go in, pulling the balaclava over my face, when Pareja managed to get out."

Harri had brought two Finnish sponsors to support the programme and the plan was to carry backing from Wärtsilä Diesel marine engines into 1991 when Konrad was going to run a normally aspirated engine in a new car. Rule changes and the looming worldwide recession left sports car racing in dire straits, however, and Konrad's intended co-operation with Spice was scuppered when the latter called in the receiver to his company. The team was in the process of building its own car, but it would not be ready for quite some time.

"Franz went to Wärtsilä anyhow and, pretending he had me under contract, persuaded them to do a deal directly with him. That left me without either a sponsor or a car", rues Harri, who credits Keke Rosberg with saving his season. "He was managing Manuel Reuter and got me in as his driving partner at Kremer Racing. Without my knowledge, Dad also guaranteed funding for the drive."

Kremer's car was definitely faster than Konrad's had been. Although it was still a Porsche 962, it had a proprietary chassis made of carbon composite, a bigger 3.2-litre turbo engine and modified bodywork, all of which justified defining it as a "CK6" rather than a works specification 962 C. In competitive terms, it fell behind the latest atmospheric cars, which were openly prioritized in the series, but was perhaps the best among the reduced Porsche ranks.

Lack of support had thrown the FIA World Sports Car Championship into doubt, but eventually the series kicked off in Japan where Harri Toivonen felt lost at first: "I was way off the pace in practice. I just could not get my head around the Suzuka circuit, but Keke reassured me and in the race it all started to click."

Manuel Reuter could not hope to run with the works atmo cars but, when a couple of them dropped out, he handed the Kremer Porsche over to Harri in third place. A longer pit stop immediately dropped them behind the turbo Mercedes of Jochen Mass, but then Harri drove a solid middle stint, and although Cor Euser in his delayed Spice managed to work through to fourth, Reuter redressed the balance by pipping him on the last lap. This move claimed third place for the Kremer pair because, of the remaining works cars, the Peugeot of Rosberg/Dalmas had succumbed to clutch failure. "It was a fantastic feeling standing on that podium", Harri marvels. "Unbelievable!"

That was the beginning of a very productive season for Harri Toivonen, one in which he established a reputation as a reliable and still improving sports car racer. He finished fifth in Monza where, in a reversal of Suzuka, Cor Euser came past Manuel Reuter just before the flag. Silverstone only yielded eighth place when the loss of third gear reduced the pair to second best Porsche behind the Brun car of Oscar Larrauri/Jesus Pareja. "In Silverstone we ran with big 'Team Toivonen' stickers on the car. It was a poke in the eye for Wärtsilä, who had brought a lot of guests to that race", Harri jokes.

1990 wagte Harri in Silverstone den Sprung ins kalte Wasser der Gruppe-C-Sportwagen. „Er braucht mehr Zeit im Auto", sagte Franz Konrad, Besitzer des Porsche 962.
Harri Toivonen jumped in at the deep end when he took the wheel of a Porsche 962 at Silverstone in 1990. "He needs more time in the car", said team boss Franz Konrad.

Harri Toivonen Der Unvollendete / Unfulfilled promise

Pareja. „In Silverstone haben wir groß ‚Team Toivonen' aufs Auto geschrieben", lacht Harri. „Das war die Rache für Wärtsilä, die zu dem Rennen viele Gäste eingeladen hatten."

Bei den 24 Stunden von Le Mans wurden Reuter und Toivonen von einem weiteren Rosberg-Schützling unterstützt: Jyski Järvilehto, besser bekannt als JJ Lehto. Die Porsche wurden an der Sarthe mit Zusatzgewicht beladen, dennoch lag das Trio in den ersten Stunden in den Top Ten – noch vor den Teams, die am Ende auf dem Podium gelandet sind. Doch dann brach am Kremer-Auto beim Anflug auf die Indianapolis-Kurve die Hinterradaufhängung. „Ich habe versucht, das Auto vom Gras wegzuhalten. Ich wusste: Wenn ich das Auto hier verliere, dann habe ich bald starke Kopfschmerzen, da hilft auch keine Aspirin mehr."

Harri gelang es, den Unfall zu vermeiden und das Auto an die Box zu schleppen. „JJ wartete auf mich und küsste meinen Helm. Er hatte den Zwischenfall auf dem Fernseher gesehen und konnte nicht glauben, dass ich das Auto von der Mauer ferngehalten hatte", schwärmt Toivonen von seinem Manöver. Das Trio verlor fast 40 Minuten an der Box. Ohne diesen Zeitverlust wäre ein Podestplatz möglich gewesen, so wurde es nur Platz Neun.

Das Rennen auf dem Nürburgring zeigte Harri erneut die Gefahren dieses Sports auf. Drei Wochen zuvor war Paul Warwick in einem F3000-Rennen in Oulton Park tödlich verunglückt. Am „Ring" traf Harri den Bruder von Paul. Derek Warwick bestritt in der Eifel sein

For the Le Mans 24h race, Reuter and Toivonen were joined by another Rosberg protégé, Jyski Järvilehto, aka JJ Lehto. The Porsches were laden with more ballast for the French endurance race but, for the first few hours of the race, this trio was running most promisingly and well within the top ten – and ahead of the eventual podium finishers. That is until Harri Toivonen had the rear suspension collapse on the fearsomely fast approach to Indianapolis. "I tried to keep it from the grass, because I knew Aspirin would not be much of medication for the headache I'd get if the car got away from me!"

He somehow collected the huge moment that followed and limped to the pits for repairs. "JJ was waiting for me and came to kiss my helmet! He'd seen the incident on TV and could not believe I kept the car from the walls", explains the man, still delighted by his feat. The crew lost nearly forty minutes in the pits and, without that delay, they could well have been challenging for a podium finish. As it was, they ended up ninth.

The Nürburgring in August provided Harri with another reminder of the perils of his chosen sport. Three weeks earlier, Paul Warwick had been killed in a F3000 race in Oulton Park and it was an emotional moment when he came face-to-face with Paul's brother Derek at what was going to be the Jaguar driver's first race since the tragedy. "I know how you feel" was all Harri managed to say. "Neither of us could think of the right words, we just looked at each other with tears in our eyes."

Bemerkenswert ist der Hauptsponsor: „Toivoset" war eine Retourkutsche der Toivonen-Familie gegen den eigentlichen Sponsor Wärtsilä, der jetzt ein anderes Team unterstützte.
Note the main sponsor is "Toivoset" – that refers to the Toivonen family after Wärtsilä took their money elsewhere.

In Le Mans wurden Manuel Reuter und Harri Toivonen durch JJ Lehto verstärkt. Das Kremer-Porsche-Trio erreichte Platz Neun trotz eines langen Boxenstopps zu Beginn.
At Le Mans, Manuel Reuter and Harri Toivonen were joined by JJ Lehto. They took the Kremer Porsche to ninth despite a lengthy delay early on.

Harri Toivonen Der Unvollendete / Unfulfilled promise

Bei den 24 Stunden von Le Mans 1991 saß Harri Toivonen mehr als sieben Stunden hinter dem Lenkrad des Kremer-Porsche.
Harri Toivonen spent over seven hours behind the wheel of the Kremer Porsche during the 1991 Le Mans 24-hour race.

Harri absolvierte zwei Stints im Dunkeln. Von 01:38 bis 03:17 Uhr und von 04:44 bis kurz nach Sechs in der Früh.
Harri did two stints in the dark, from 01:38 to 03:17 and again from 04:44 to just after six in the morning.

erstes Rennen nach der Tragödie. Der Moment, wo sich beide in die Augen sahen, war sehr emotional. „Ich weiß, wie du dich fühlst", mehr konnte Harri nicht sagen. „Keiner von uns fand die richtigen Worte. Wir haben uns nur mit Tränen in den Augen angeschaut." Das Rennen ließ die schlimmen Gedanken kurz vergessen. Derek Warwick und David Brabham führten den Jaguar-Doppelsieg an, Toivonen und Reuter belegten den exzellenten dritten Rang. Durch den zweiten Podestplatz in diesem Jahr wurde Harri der dritte finnische Rennfahrer mit FIA-Prioritätsstatus. Nur Leo Kinnunen und Keke Rosberg war das vorher gelungen, aber Fahrer wie JJ Lehto oder Mika Häkkinen sollten noch folgen.

Der Vorteil der Saugmotor-Autos wurde immer deutlicher. In Suzuka hatten Reuter/Toivonen nur zwei Runden auf den Sieger verloren, am Nürburgring waren es schon sechs. Vier Wochen später wurde das Kremer-Duo Sechster in Magny Cours – mit acht Runden Rückstand. Den nächsten Lauf in Mexiko ließ Harri aus, das Finale in Japan brachte den einzigen Ausfall des Jahres. Immerhin sorgte dieser Lauf für eine bleibende Erinnerung: „Beim Qualifying in Autopolis hatte mein Auto 1.170 PS."

In Autopolis traf Toivonen die Vertreter eines neuen Teams mit großen Ambitionen. Er einigte sich schnell mit ihnen und wurde im Dezember als erster Werksfahrer von BRM verkündet. Auf Initiative von John Mangoletsi und mit Unterstützung der BRM-Besitzer, der Owen Group, kehrte der große Name auf die Rennstrecken zurück. Bei der Präsentation wurde der erste Prototyp des BRM P351 gezeigt. Es wurden viele Kandidaten für den zweiten Fahrerplatz gehandelt, darunter auch Damon Hill. Wie so oft verzögerte sich das Projekt. Anfang April erlebte der BRM auf dem Flugplatz von Preston seinen ersten Rollout. Harri fuhr einige Runden, bevor der erfahrenere Wayne Taylor das Steuer übernahm, der kurz darauf als Teamkollege unterzeichnete. Die Fahrer äußerten sich anfangs sehr positiv über den V12-Motor, dessen Leistung mit 630 PS angegeben wurde.

BRM erschien beim zweiten Lauf zur Sportwagen-WM in Silverstone, doch Probleme mit der Ölabsaugpumpe stoppten das Auto im Training und beim Warmup. Vor dem Rennen zog sich BRM aus dem Wettbewerb zurück. Toivonen war dennoch begeistert vom Handling. Er genoss den deutlich verbesserten Abtrieb im Vergleich zu den älteren Porsche.

Das Team beschloss, sich komplett auf Le Mans zu konzentrieren und absolvierte vorher nur Testfahrten in Silverstone und Snetterton. Für das 24-Stunden-Rennen wurde Richard Jones als dritter Fahrer verpflichtet. Das Unheil kündigte sich schon am ersten Trainingstag an, wo der BRM nicht auf der Strecke gesichtet wurde. Es fehlten noch ein paar Getriebe-Innereien. Zum zweiten Tag trafen die Teile ein, aber Wayne Taylor absolvierte nur sechs Runden, ehe das Getriebe hinüber war. Er war daher als einziger Fahrer fürs Rennen qualifiziert. Einen großen Unterschied machte das aber ohnehin nicht, denn der BRM war nach 20 Runden auch der erste Ausfall.

Toivonen konnte den BRM nie bei einem Rennen bewegen, denn das Projekt verlief nach Le Mans im Sand. Harris Fazit: „Sie hatten nicht das Geld um das Auto zu entwickeln, besonders den Motor. So wie ich das verstanden habe, gab es Versprechungen seitens der Owen Group für die Finanzierung zu sorgen, aber das kam nicht zustande."

Das Ende des BRM-Projekts und die weltweite Wirtschaftskrise schienen Harris Motorsportkarriere zu besiegeln. Harri war jetzt Familienvater. 1989 hatte er Marja Kinnunen geheiratet und mit ihr zwei Töchter bekommen: Fia und Bea. Die Erstgeborene hieß eigentlich Anna Sofia, und ihr Spitzname sorgte manchmal für

The race went some way towards dispelling dark thoughts from both men's minds as Derek Warwick headed a Jaguar 1-2 with David Brabham while Harri Toivonen claimed an excellent third place with Manuel Reuter. This second podium of the season made Harri only the third Finn so far to be included in the list of FIA graded racing drivers. Leo Kinnunen and Keke Rosberg had preceded him, but others like JJ Lehto and Mika Häkkinen had yet to follow.

The advantage enjoyed by the atmospherically engined cars was becoming more pronounced. While Reuter/Toivonen had only lost two laps to the winners in Suzuka, the gap in Nürburgring was six laps. Four weeks later, it stretched to eight laps when the Kremer duo finished sixth at Magny-Cours. After that, Harri skipped the Mexican round while the finale in Japan brought the season's only retirement. It still left him with one lasting memory: "For qualifying in Autopolis, I was given 1,170 horsepower!"

In Autopolis, Harri Toivonen met representatives of a new team with great ambitions. He quickly reached agreement with them and in December he was announced as the first driver for BRM, the once great name resurrected by the initiative of John Mangoletsi and with the support of its proprietors, the Owen Group. A car – the BRM P351 – was shown, still without many ancillaries, while other names were bandied about as candidates to join Toivonen, among them Damon Hill.

Predictably, the project got delayed and it was early April before the car was rolled out for a shakedown on Preston airfield. Harri got to do some laps and his work was then carried on by the more experienced Wayne Taylor, who was soon signed as his teammate. The drivers were initially very complimentary about the V12 engine built for the car by Terry Hoyle. It was said to give 630 bhp.

BRM made it to the second round of the World Sports Car Championship in Silverstone, but oil scavenge pump failures first stopped the car in practice, then in the warm-up, and it was withdrawn from the race. Harri Toivonen was still excited about its handling, no doubt enjoying the vastly improved downforce after being used to the Porsche of an earlier generation.

The team decided to concentrate on preparations for Le Mans and managed some testing in Silverstone and Snetterton before heading to the Sarthe. For the 24-hour race, Richard Jones was recruited as a third driver. Ominously, the car was not seen on the track at all during the first day of practice as some of its gearbox internals were still lacking. When they did arrive for the second day, Wayne Taylor managed to put in only six laps before the box failed. He was therefore the only driver qualified for the race … Not that it made much difference, because he was also the first retirement after just twenty laps.

Harri Toivonen never got to race the BRM as the project withered on the vine after Le Mans. "They just did not have the funds to develop it, especially the engine", he sums up. "My understanding was that there had been promises from the Owen Group to supply finances, but they never materialized."

That and the global economic gloom seemed to spell the end of Harri's motor sport career. He was now a family man, having married Marja Kinnunen in 1989, and they now had two young daughters, Fia and Bea. The firstborn was actually christened Anna Sofia and the shorter version could sometimes cause confusion as, for instance, on the occasion of the 1991 German GP. "I was sitting in the Williams's hospitality unit, when Nigel Mansell came to reminisce about a party we'd once been to in the Isle of Man",

Das Rennen am Nürburgring 1991 war für Harri sehr emotional. Dort traf er auf Derek Warwick, dessen Bruder kurz zuvor verstorben war. Im Rennen wurde Harri überraschend Dritter.
Nürburgring in 1991 was an emotional scene for Harri Toivonen. He went to console Derek Warwick, who had just lost his brother, and then, in the race, finished third.

Harri Toivonen Der Unvollendete / Unfulfilled promise

Harri fühlte sich in der Gruppe C pudelwohl und ist sich sicher, dass auch Henri im Sportwagen erfolgreich gewesen wäre, wenn er die Gruppe-B-Zeit überlebt hätte. „Ich denke, er hätte die Gruppe A langweilig gefunden und vielleicht wäre er dann in den Rennsport gewechselt", so Harri.

Harri Toivonen found Group C a great environment, where Henri too might have thrived, if he had survived the Group B era in rallying. "I think Henri would have found Group A cars boring and maybe swapped to racing instead", Harri once said.

Verwirrung. Zum Beispiel bei GP von Deutschland 1991: „Ich saß im Hospitality-Bereich von Williams, als Nigel Mansell zu mir kam, um in Erinnerungen über eine Party auf der Isle of Man zu schwelgen", blickt Harri zurück. „Ich dachte, es wäre lustig, ihn ein Foto für meine Tochter unterschreiben zu lassen. Als er ihren Namen hörte, wurde er stutzig. ‚Ich unterschreibe nichts für die FIA', brummte Nigel. Also unterschrieb er für Anna."

Harri hatte das Rennfahren nicht komplett aufgegeben, aber es musste schon ein gutes Cockpit sein, um ihn von einer Rückkehr zu überzeugen. Im Herbst 1995 klingelte aus dem Nichts heraus das Telefon. Ian Dawson war einer der Antreiber des BRM-Projekts gewesen. Er war nach dem Scheitern zu Pacific Racing gegangen, als Leiter des F1-Teams. Er wollte wissen, ob Harri Interesse hätte, für das Team zu fahren.

Pacific kämpfte ums Überleben und war abhängig von Bezahlfahrern wie Jean-Denis Délétraz und Giovanni Lavaggi. Auch Harri musste Sponsoren mitbringen, aber das war nicht der Grund, warum er kein Grand-Prix-Pilot wurde. „Harri hatte einen Vertrag für einen Test", bestätigt Dawson. „Das hätte hoffentlich dazu geführt, dass er die letzten Grand Prix des Jahres 1995 für uns fährt. Aber wir hatten schon die maximale Anzahl an Fahrerwechseln vorgenommen, wir durften keinen weiteren Piloten fahren lassen. Und nach 1995 wurde das ganze F1-Team aufgelöst."

Dawson sollte die Harris Rennsportkarriere auch in den kommenden Jahren am Leben halten. Doch zunächst gab es einen Einzelstart im Porsche 962 K8 Spyder von Kremer Racing bei den 24 Stunden von Le Mans 1996, bei dem Harri zeigte, dass er das Fahren trotz der langen Pause nicht verlernt hatte. Zusammen mit Christophe Bouchut und Jürgen Lässig hatte er eine Chance auf eine gute Platzierung. In den Anfangsstunden lag Bouchut auf Rang Zwei, doch als Harri das Steuer übernahm, waren die Hoffnungen schon verflogen, denn das Auto war durch Probleme mit der Kraftübertragung gestrandet. Später verunfallte Lässig mit dem Porsche. Das Aus.

Bei den 24 Stunden von Le Mans 1997 kehrte Harri Toivonen in den BRM zurück. Pacific Racing hatte das Auto übernommen, in einen Spyder verwandelt und mit einem V6-Motor von Nissan bestückt. Das Fahrverhalten des Autos war problematisch. Eliseo Salazar und Jesus Pareja schafften es nicht, eine Rundenzeit von unter vier Minuten zu erzielen. „Salazar wollte aufgeben und fragte Harri, ob er versuchen könnte, das Auto zu qualifizieren", erinnert sich Teamchef Ian Dawson. „Harri hatte nur noch Zeit für fünf Runden, aber er fuhr raus und schaffte die Runde in 3.56 Minuten – fünf Sekunden schneller als unsere bisherige Bestzeit. Das war beeindruckend!" Die Belohnung für diese Leistung fiel aber mager aus. Harri war nach einem Motorschaden in Runde Sechs der erste Ausfall.

Trotz seiner fast 70 Jahre leitete Pauli Toivonen noch immer drei Autohäuser, bis er 1998 eine Hirnblutung hatte und kürzer treten musste. „Pauli hat sich vollständig davon erholt, aber natürlich wurde ich dadurch mehr in die Verantwortung gezogen", sagt Harri. Dennoch streifte sich der Juniorchef den Helm über, wenn sich die Gelegenheit bot. Bei den 24 Stunden von Daytona 2000 teilte er sich einen Lola-Ford B98/10 mit Scott Maxwell und John Graham. Das Auto ging jedoch früh in Flammen auf. Ein Jahr später rief Ian Dawson erneut an. Dawson arbeitete jetzt mit Klaas Zwart zusammen, einem Geschäftsmann aus den Niederlanden, der mit Öltechnologien viel Geld verdient hatte. Zwart gehörte die Sportwagenmarke Ascari und Dawson leitete sein Rennteam.

Der Ascari-Rennwagen von 2001 basierte auf einem Gruppe-C-Lola, der zu einem offenen Le-Mans-Prototypen umgebaut wurde. Das

recalls Harri. "I thought it would be fun to ask him to sign a photo for my daughter, but hearing her name made him baulk. 'No way am I going to sign anything for FIA', Nigel grumbled! So he signed it for Anna instead."

Harri had not exactly given up on the idea of competing, but it was very hard to find a drive that would induce him to start again. In the autumn of 1995 the phone rang, quite out of the blue. Ian Dawson had been a prime mover in the BRM project and after its demise proceeded to work for Pacific Racing as its F1 team manager. He now wanted to know whether Harri had any interest in joining the outfit!

Pacific was struggling to survive financially and needed paying drivers like Jean-Denis Délétraz and Giovanni Lavaggi. Harri too needed to find funding, but that was not what stopped him from becoming a Grand Prix driver. "Harri did have a contract to do a test, which would have taken him hopefully on to race in the last couple of GPs of 1995", confirms Ian Dawson. "It turned out however that as we'd already used our season allocation of driver changes we could not have yet another one in the car. And then the whole F1 team was disbanded after 1995."

Ian Dawson was to keep Harri Toivonen's racing aspirations alive for years to come, but first a one-off Le Mans drive in Kremer Racing's Porsche 962 K8 Spyder showed that his skills had not been blunted by the long lay-off. Teaming up with Christophe Bouchut and Jürgen Lässig, Harri seemed to have a chance of a decent result in the 1996 24-hour race, particularly when, in the early hours, the Frenchman got them up to second place. Those chances were effectively over prior to Harri getting behind the wheel, however, as transmission trouble grounded the car in the Esses. That fixed, Lässig later crashed it out of the race.

For Le Mans 1997, Harri found himself back in the BRM, which had been taken over by Pacific Racing and converted to a spyder with a turbocharged Nissan V6 engine. It proved a troublesome car that drivers like Eliseo Salazar and Jesus Pareja just could not take to a lap time of under four minutes. "Salazar was ready to give in and asked Harri to have a go and see if he could qualify the car", recalls team manager Ian Dawson. "Harri only had time left for about five laps, but he went out and did one in 3min 56sec – five seconds quicker than our best lap up to that point! That was quite amazing." Again it was all for little reward, as Harri became the race's first retirement when the engine blew just six laps in.

Approaching seventy years of age, Pauli Toivonen was still in charge of his car dealerships until he suffered a brain haemorrhage in 1998 and had to take a back seat. "Dad made a full recovery from that, but naturally it increased my responsibilities in the business", says Harri. It did not stop him from donning his helmet when opportunity knocked. In 2000, a first attempt at the Daytona 24-hours did not last long before the Lola-Ford B98/10 he shared with Scott Maxwell and John Graham caught fire. One year later, Ian Dawson was on the phone again. He had got involved with Klaas Zwart, a Dutch businessman who had made a huge fortune with oil technologies. Zwart was now manufacturing Ascari sports cars and Dawson ran a race team for him.

The Ascari race car in 2001 was basically an old Group C Lola converted to an open Le Mans Prototype. It could be surprisingly quick, even if its reliability remained a bit suspect. Nevertheless, Harri eagerly grabbed the offer to drive again: "We went testing at Silverstone and the car felt really good. It was raining a lot, which proved good practice for Le Mans."

Auto war überraschend schnell, aber die Haltbarkeit problematisch. Trotzdem nahm Harri das Angebot begeistert an: „Wir haben in Silverstone getestet und das Auto fühlte sich richtig gut an. Es regnete stark, das war ein gutes Training für Le Mans."

In Le Mans teilte sich Harri den Ascari-Judd A410 mit Werner Lupberger und Ben Collins. Lupberger war im Training gut zehn Sekunden langsamer als die Pole-Zeit, doch als es im Rennen zu regnen begann, kletterte der Ascari in die Top Ten. Die wohl größte Stunde erlebte das Team rund um Mitternacht, wo Harri bei starkem Regen am Steuer saß. „Irgendwann im Nassen war er vermutlich der schnellste Fahrer auf der Strecke – ich weiß noch, dass er schnellere Runden fuhr als der Bentley", schwärmt Dawson. Als Ben Collins übernahm, lag der Ascari auf Rang Fünf. Doch dann streikte der Motor und sie mussten aufgeben.

Der Ascari war bei den 24 Stunden von Daytona 2002 die große Überraschung, wo Lupberger der Pole-Zeit sehr nahe kam. Während der ersten Stints fuhr Lupberger im Windschatten des siegreichen Dallara-Judd des Doran-Teams. Seine Teamkollegen Harri Toivonen, Timothy Bell Jr. sowie Teambesitzer Zwart blieben die ersten zehn Stunden in Schlagdistanz zum Führenden, bis Bell den Ascari in den Reifenstapeln parkte. Eine gebrochene Ventilfeder beendete letztlich das Abenteuer.

Im Frühjahr machte Harri doch noch seine ersten Formel-1-Erfahrungen. Klaas Zwart veranstaltete die BOSS Grand Prix Series für alte Formel-1-Autos und hatte selbst ein paar dieser Boliden in der Garage stehen, darunter einige Benettons aus den 1990ern. Harri fuhr zwei dieser Rennwagen: „Mein erster Test war am 2. Mai in Pembrey. Also auf den Tag genau zwölf Jahre nach Henris Unfall. Es war auch das erste Mal, dass ich wieder in Wales war. Als es zu regnen begann, sind mir viele Gedanken durch den Kopf geschossen …"

„Der Benetton war ohne Zweifel das interessanteste Auto, das ich je gefahren habe", erzählt Harri. „Es ist merkwürdig, wie sehr dieses Auto von den Flügeln abhängig ist. Als ich das Gaspedal gelupft habe, hat das Auto so sehr verzögert, dass ich zuerst dachte, der Wagen wäre kaputt. So sehr hat er gebremst." Harri fuhr ein gutes Dutzend Rennen in den Benettons von 1996 und 1997. Sein bestes Ergebnis war der zweite Platz in Donington.

Ian Dawson war beeindruckt vom Speed des über 40-jährigen Harri, der im letzten Jahrzehnt nur wenige Kilometer zurückgelegt hatte. „Ich habe schon immer an Harri geglaubt. Er war sehr gut, aber er hatte oft das Pech, am falschen Ort zu sein. Er kam auch gut mit den anderen Fahrern aus, ein großartiger Teamplayer, aber er hatte eben selten Glück." Später gingen Dawson und Toivonen sogar eine Kooperation ein. Sie wollten mit alternativen Kraftstoffen an Sportwagenrennen teilnehmen. Zunächst nutzten sie ein altes Lola-Chassis, später wechselten sie zu Radical. Es war ein mutiges Projekt mit begrenzten Mitteln. Es hätte den Finnen in den Motorsport zurückbringen können, aber am Ende verlief es enttäuschend.

Pauli Toivonen wurde zusehends älter. Wegen seiner gesundheitlichen Probleme verkaufte er zwei Autohäuser, das dritte überließ er Harri. Dadurch konnte Pauli mehr Zeit daheim mit Ulla verbringen, der er häufig Blumen schenkte, die er auf dem Heimweg von der Arbeit gekauft hatte. Am 14. Februar 2005, am Valentinstag, war er wieder einmal im Büro gewesen um zu sehen, wie sein Sohn das Geschäft führte. Zu Hause angekommen war Pauli müde und setzte sich in einen Massagestuhl, der sein Herzleiden milderte. Als sich Ulla für ein Nickerchen zurückzog, winkte er ihr beruhigend zu, um zu deuten, dass alles in Ordnung ist. Als Ulla aus dem Schlafzimmer zurückkehrte, war Pauli friedlich eingeschlafen. Für immer.

In Le Mans, Werner Lupberger qualified the Ascari-Judd A410 he shared with Harri and Ben Collins some ten seconds slower than Audi's pole time but, when rain arrived in the race, it helped the crew climb up to inside the top ten. Perhaps their finest hour came just after midnight when the rain intensified while Harri was at the wheel. "At some point in the wet, he was probably the quickest driver on the circuit – I know we were lapping faster than the Bentley", says Ian Dawson with genuine admiration. When Ben Collins took over, the crew actually got as high as fifth before trouble struck and they were forced out with engine failure.

The Ascari really surprised everyone in the 2002 Daytona 24-hours, where Lupberger came close to putting the car on pole. He shadowed eventual winner, the Doran Dallara-Judd, for the first stints and the car, which was also driven by Harri Toivonen, Timothy Bell Jr. and team owner Zwart, ran near the lead for the opening ten hours until Bell put it in the tyre wall exiting the road course section. A broken valve spring finally brought their run to an end.

In the spring, Harri got to experience Formula 1 after all. Klaas Zwart was running the BOSS Grand Prix Series for old F1 cars and had a plethora of such missiles in his garage including several Benettons from the 1990s. Harri Toivonen got to race two of them, now equipped with Judd engines instead of the Renaults that had supplied the power originally. "The first time I tested one was on the second of May in Pembrey. It was twelve years to the day after Henri's accident and my first time back in Wales. When rain began to fall, all sorts of thoughts ran through my mind …"

"It was without doubt the most interesting car I had driven, though. It was strange to experience how such a car lives so totally on its wings. When I lifted from the throttle, the deceleration at first made me think the thing was broken", quips Harri. He did a dozen races in Benettons of 1996 and 1997 vintages in Britain, Holland, France and the Czech Republic with a best placing of second in Donington.

Ian Dawson was impressed with the pace of a driver who was now in his forties and had very limited mileage in the past decade. "I always had a great belief in Harri", he says. "I think he was very good, but was not in the luckiest places a lot of the time. He was also good with the other drivers, a great team player, but very unfortunate." It came as no surprise that Dawson and Toivonen later joined forces to develop the idea of using alternative fuels for sports car racing, first using an old Lola chassis and then swapping to a Radical. It was a brave effort with limited resources that several times promised to bring the Finn back to racing, but ultimately it proved frustrating.

Pauli Toivonen mellowed considerably in his later years and his health problems eventually led to him selling two of the three car dealerships and leaving the remaining one to Harri. This saw Pauli spending more time at home with Ulla, whom he habitually delighted with flowers bought on the way back from work. On February 14th, 2005, (Valentine's Day) he had been to the office again, mainly just overseeing the way Harri was handling the business. Getting back home he was tired and sat in a massaging chair, which eased his heart condition. When Ulla retired to have a rest, Pauli gave her a reassuring wave of his hand to say that he was all right. A while later, when Ulla got up again, he had peacefully passed away in the chair.

It was unfortunate Pauli never got to witness the celebration of Henri's career in Jyväskylä on the occasion of the 2006 Rally

Harri Toivonen Der Unvollendete / Unfulfilled promise

Leider konnte Pauli die große Gedenkfeier zu Henris Ehren bei der Rallye Finnland 2006 nicht mehr miterleben. Henris Kinder Arla und Markus waren dort und verblüfften viele Leute mit ihrer unheimlichen Ähnlichkeit zu ihren Eltern. Genau wie Erja ihre Tochter Arla Mitte der 80er-Jahre auf Rallyes mitgenommen hatte, so hielt Arla jetzt ihr Baby in den Händen: den kleinen Henri.

Natürlich war auch Harri vor Ort. Der Fitness-Fanatiker nimmt heutzutage gerne an historischen Rallyes teil. „Henri hat immer gesagt, dass ich mehr Talent habe als er. Aber ich war faul! Es war immer fantastisch, gute Autos zu fahren. Aber vielleicht war ich im Kopf nicht genug bei der Sache", gesteht Harri ein. Heute geht ihm die Idee von einem kleinen Programm in der Weltmeisterschaft mit einem richtigen World Rally Car nicht aus dem Kopf. Diesen Wettbewerbsgedanken bekommt man aus den Toivonens anscheinend einfach nicht heraus. „Die waren alle so", sagt Mutter Ulla. „Immer in Bewegung – wie der Vater so die Söhne."

Finland. Henri's children, Arla and Markus, attended and stunned several old-timers with their uncanny likeness to their parents. Just as Erja had brought young Arla to rallies in the mid 1980s, Arla was now tending to a baby son, Henri.

Naturally Harri was there too. Increasingly a fitness fanatic, he has still enjoyed outings in historic rally cars. "Henri used to say I had even more talent than he did, but I've been lazy! It's always been fantastic to drive a good car, but maybe I have just not been applying my mind to it enough", he concedes. The idea of a limited programme of World Championship events in a proper World Rally Car still lingers in his mind, proving that it is very difficult to extinguish the competitive flame in the Toivonen men. "They've all been like that", says mother Ulla. "Always on the move – like father, like sons."

Bei der Rallye Finnland 2006 wurde der Karriere von Henri Toivonen gedacht. Zu diesem Anlass waren neben Harri auch prominente Gesichter wie Juha Piironen, Malcolm Wilson, Markku Alén und Paul White in Jyväskylä. Henris Kinder Marcus und Arla (mit Sohnemann Henri jr. auf dem Arm) verfolgten die gesamte Feier sehr interessiert.

The career of Henri Toivonen was celebrated on the occasion of the 2006 Neste Oil Rally Finland in Jyväskylä. Among those attending were naturally Harri as well as notable figures like Juha Piironen, Malcolm Wilson, Markku Alén and Paul White. Henri's children Arla and Marcus found it all rather intriguing. Basking in a moment of attention was also Arla's son Henri Jr.

Speed up your life ...

Group 4
From Stratos to Quattro

Die wilden 70er sind vielen Rallyefans noch heute in bester Erinnerung. Die Autoren beschreiben den Werdegang der legendären Autos, blicken zurück auf die WM-Jahre 1973 bis 1982 und erzählen interessante Anekdoten aus einer wilden Ära.

Most fans still have fond memories of rallying in the 1970's. The authors describe the history of the legendary rally cars they review the first WRC years from 1973 to 1982 and tell some of the stories from that wild and tough era.

By John Davenport & Reinhard Klein
Format: 24.5 x 30 cm, 256 pages, English & German texts in separate books, more than 350 images
Deutsche ISBN: 978-3-927458-53-6
English ISBN: 978-3-927458-54-3
Price: 49.90 Euro*

Group B
The rise and fall of rallying's wildest cars

Die Neuauflage dieses Standardwerks präsentiert sich ab sofort im kleineren Format und mit nur noch einer Sprache pro Buch. So gewannen die Autoren Raum für weitere faszinierende Bilder. Dieses Buch beschreibt die Geschichte der in der Gruppe B entwickelten Rallyeautos von 1983 bis 1986, von den Quattros bis hin zu den Lancia und Peugeot.

The new edition of this standard work comes in a smaller format and with just one language per book, giving us the chance to include even more fascinating images. This book tells the story of all the rally cars developed within Group B between 1983 and 1986, from the Quattros to the outstanding Lancias and Peugeots.

By John Davenport & Reinhard Klein,
Format: 24.5 x 30 cm, 256 pages, English & German texts in separate books, more than 420 images
Deutsche ISBN: 978-3-927458-55-0
English ISBN: 978-3-927458-56-7
Price: 49.90 Euro*

Group B Owner's Edition

Auf über 1.000 Seiten mit unzähligen bekannten wie unveröffentlichten Fotos, bisher nie erzählten Geschichten, geheimen Originaldokumenten und umfangreichen Statistiken beschreibt „Group B - Owner's Edition" die Rallyejahre 1983 bis 1986 in einer nie dagewesenen Tiefe.

With 1,000 pages, wonderful pictures and extensive statistics, there is no doubt that the "Group B - Owner's Edition" will delight all real motor sport fans. The authors tell all the stories and secrets from 1983 until the Group B was banned from rallying in 1986.

By John Davenport & Reinhard Klein
Size: 35 x 33 cm in two volumes, 1,008 pages, texts in English and German, limited to 500 numbered copies worldwide, hand-signed by Hannu Mikkola, Stig Blomqvist, Timo Salonen, Juha Kankkunen, Walter Röhrl, Markku Alén and the authors.
Price: 999.00 Euro*
Available exclusively through **www.thegroupbbook.com**

*incl. VAT, plus shipping / inkl. MwSt., zzgl. Versandkosten

Rallywebshop - In der Rosenau 19 - 51143 Köln - Germany - Tel: +49-2203-9242570 - www.rallywebshop.com